PUNITIVE DAMAGES IN PRIVATE INTERNATIONAL LAW

PUNITIVE DAMAGES IN PRIVATE INTERNATIONAL LAW

Lessons for the European Union

Cedric Vanleenhove

intersentia
Cambridge – Antwerp – Portland

Intersentia Ltd
Sheraton House | Castle Park
Cambridge | CB3 0AX | United Kingdom
Tel.: +44 1223 370 170 | Fax: +44 1223 370 169
Email: mail@intersentia.co.uk
www.intersentia.com | www.intersentia.co.uk

Distribution for the UK and Ireland:
NBN International
Airport Business Centre, 10 Thornbury Road
Plymouth, PL6 7 PP
United Kingdom
Tel.: +44 1752 202 301 | Fax: +44 1752 202 331
Email: orders@nbninternational.com

Distribution for Europe and all other countries:
Intersentia Publishing nv
Groenstraat 31
2640 Mortsel
Belgium
Tel.: +32 3 680 15 50 | Fax: +32 3 658 71 21
Email: mail@intersentia.be

Distribution for the USA and Canada:
International Specialized Book Services
920 NE 58th Ave. Suite 300
Portland, OR 97213
USA
Tel.: +1 800 944 6190 (toll free) | Fax: +1 503 280 8832
Email: info@isbs.com

Punitive Damages in Private International Law: Lessons for the European Union

ISBN 978-1-78068-416-1
D/2016/7849/107
NUR 822

GPRC
Guaranteed
Peer Reviewed
Content

British Library Cataloguing in Publication Data. A catalogue record for this book is available from the British Library.

ACKNOWLEDGEMENTS

This book is an updated version of my Ph.D. dissertation submitted at the University of Ghent. After starting at the end of 2010, I received the title of Doctor in Law during a defence ceremony on 16 September 2015. This book, therefore, represents the end of a journey. A number of "*compagnons de route*" travelled the road (or parts of it) with me.

First of all, my promotor Prof. Dr. Maud Piers. Her encouraging words, continuous encouragement and gentle nature pulled me through even the toughest periods. She supported me in every single endeavour I undertook. I could not be more proud to be the first researcher to obtain a Ph.D. under her supervision.

I was fortunate enough to have enjoyed the input of two consecutive promotors. My first promotor Emeritus Prof. Dr. Johan Erauw taught me the importance of conciseness, a lesson which I relied on in this book.

The members of my guidance committee and my examination committee equally deserve my gratitude: Prof. Dr. Patrick Wautelet, Prof. Dr. Marta Pertegas, Prof. Dr. François-Xavier Licari, Prof. Dr. Vernon Palmer and Prof. Dr. Stefaan Voet. Their questions, remarks and comments helped me to write this book.

During my doctoral period I had the opportunity to conduct research at foreign institutions. I wish to thank Prof. Dr. Stefan Vogenauer, former Director of the Institute of European and Comparative Law of Oxford University, for allowing me to join the Institute as a Visiting Fellow and for providing his insight into my research. For my time as a Visiting Researcher at Harvard Law School I am grateful to Prof. Dr. John Goldberg as well as to Prof. Dr. Joseph Singer.

I enjoyed the presence of my colleagues of the Department of Interdisciplinary Study of Law, Private Law and Business Law and the Department of Procedural Law, Arbitration and Private International Law. They are too numerous to name but Charlotte Willemot, Jan De Bruyne, Michael de Potter de ten Broeck, Thijs Tanghe and Annette Van Thienen definitely spring to mind. The secretaries Conny Loyson, Lieve Fornier, Mia De Meyer and Karen Emsens helped me with various aspects of my work.

Further thanks goes to my parents and especially my grandmother Monique Schapdryver, to whom I dedicate this book in recognition of her eternal love and support.

Cedric Vanleenhove
Bruges, 12 June 2016

CONTENTS

LIST OF ABBREVIATIONS

BGB	*Bürgerliches Gesetzbuch* (German Civil Code)
BGH	*Bundesgerichtshof* (German Supreme Court)
ECJ	European Court of Justice
EGBGB	*Einführungsgesetzes zum Bürgerlichen Gesetzbuche* (Introductory Law to the German Civil Code)
EU	European Union
PTIA	the Protection of Trading Interests Act 1980
RICO	the Racketeer Influenced and Corrupt Organizations Act
UK	United Kingdom
U.S.	United States
USD	American dollar
ZPO	*Zivilprozessordnung* (German Code of Civil Procedure)

INTRODUCTION

RESEARCH SETTING

1. Punitive damages are a typical and settled feature of American law. Other Common Law countries such as Australia, New Zealand, Canada and South Africa also provide for this type of damages. The remedy can be described as an additional amount of money awarded to the victim of an unlawful act on top of the compensatory damages. As opposed to the latter, punitive damages do not (primarily) compensate for a harm suffered. Instead, they pursue the punishment of the injurer and the deterrence of potential wrongdoers.

2. In the European Union only a handful of countries acknowledge this type of damages in their legal systems.[1] The most prominent of these countries is England where exemplary damages – the term used in English law – are available in a few strict categories of cases.[2]

3. In continental Europe punitive damages are said to be non-existent. The concept of punitive damages is considered contrary to the fundamental separation of criminal and private law. Civil Law countries in the European Union are wary of punitive damages as they are administered in civil proceedings but pursue objectives which are traditionally the focus of criminal law. Punitive damages are also held to be anathema to the principle of strict compensation and are seen as resulting in an unjust enrichment of the plaintiff.

4. The world we live in today is one where the practical significance of national boundaries is slowly eroding. Due to improved modes of transportation, people are able to visit other continents with relative ease. Similarly, with the rise of global commerce, businesses are expanding into other jurisdictions. Distances are no longer a hindrance to global mobility. It could be said that the world is becoming a "global village", not only on the level of electric communication as once conceived by Marshall McLuhan[3], but also in terms of tourism and trade.

---

1 These countries are: England, Wales, Ireland, Northern Ireland and Cyprus.

2 *Rookes* v. *Barnard*, [1964] 1 *All E.R.* 367, 410–11 (H.L.).

3 M. McLuhan, *The Gutenberg Galaxy: The Making of Typographic Man*, Toronto, Toronto University Press, 1962, 31.

5. This increased globalisation arguably results in an augmented number of law suits between Common Law and Civil Law parties. The effects of punitive damages are thus increasingly being felt outside the jurisdictions where they are awarded.[4] As punitive damages are predicted to remain a significant feature of U.S. litigation[5], European countries cannot ignore this important institution within American law.[6]

6. The collision between (American[7]) Common Law and Civil Law traditions comes to the surface through the application of private international law. This area of the law deals with disputes containing at least one foreign element. The confrontation of Civil Law systems with the concept of punitive damages takes place in three different areas of private international law.[8]

7. First, in the service of process, when a plaintiff is requesting service of an American claim for punitive damages on a defendant in the European Union in order to commence litigation in the United States. Second, in the context of applicable law, when a European judge has to establish the law governing the dispute before him and this analysis leads him to a provision of substantive American law granting punitive damages. Third, in the enforcement of judgments, when the enforcement of an American punitive damages judgment in the European Union is requested by the prevailing party of a law suit in the United States.

8. The remedy of punitive damages is, alongside, for instance, contingency fees, discovery[9] and class actions, one of the characteristics of the American

---

4 G. Nater-Bass, "U.S.-Style Punitive Damages Awards and their Recognition and Enforcement in Switzerland and Other Civil-Law Countries", 28 *Deutsch-Amerikanische Juristen-Vereinigung Newsletter* 2003, 154.

5 K. Browne, "Punitive damages in the U.S.: a primer for insurance buyers and brokers", Armonk, Swiss Re, 2011, 5.

6 T. Rouhette, "The availability of punitive damages in Europe: growing trend or nonexistent concept?", 74 *Defense Counsel Journal* 2007, 321.

7 The choice for American punitive damages will be explained *infra* in the section dealing with the scope of the book: see no. 14.

8 M. Requejo Isidro, "Punitive Damages From a Private International Law Perspective" in H. Koziol & V. Wilcox (eds.), *Punitive Damages: Common Law and Civil Law Perspectives*, Vienna, Springer, 2009, 238.

9 Note in that regard the existence of a transantlantic judicial conflict (also known as *Justizkonflikt*) between the U.S. and Europe in the 1980s resulting from various American extraterritorial injunctions ordering the disclosure of documents located in Europe. See: P. Schlosser, *Der Justizkonflikt zwischen USA und Europa*, Berlin, de Gruyter, 1985; R. Stürner, "Der Justizkonflikt zwischen USA und Europa" in W.J. Habscheid (ed.), *Der Justizkonflikt mit den Vereinigten Staaten von Amerika*, Bielefeld, Gieseking, 1986, 3–63. See for a current perspective: V.G. Curran, "U.S. Discovery and Foreign Blocking Statutes", *Louisiana Law Review* 2016, forthcoming, available at <http://papers.ssrn.com/sol3/papers.cfm?abstract_id=2732802>.

legal system which exemplifies the contrast between Civil Law and Common Law. The stark divergence in approach, referred to as "the Atlantic divide"[10], between dualistic[11] Common Law and monistic[12] Civil Law jurisdictions makes punitive damages an interesting study subject from a private international law perspective. The field of private international law is where the Civil Law's level of tolerance for this *"(undesired) peculiarity of American law"*[13] is tested.

9. It should be noted that the book does not examine whether punitive damages should be adopted as a private law instrument in European Union law or in the national law of the Member States.[14] It focuses on the distinct question whether, in terms of private international law, a legal system is receptive to such damages. It is one thing for a legislator to dismiss a normative option because he does not believe it is appropriate for regulating domestic cases, and another for such a norm not to be adopted by the system under any circumstances, because it violates the constitutional parameters on which the system is based.[15]

RESEARCH QUESTIONS AND METHODOLOGY

10. This book examines the private international law treatment of American punitive damages in the European Union.[16] It poses the question whether U.S. punitive damages (should) penetrate the borders of the European Union through the backdoor of private international law. This general question can be broken down in three separate sub-questions.

11. First, the current private international attitude in the European Union towards U.S. punitive damages is investigated in each of the three areas of private international law identified, *i.e.* service of process, applicable law and enforcement of judgments. This part seeks to determine to what extent the

---

10 E. de Kezel, "The Protection and Enforcement of Private Interests by (the Recognition of US) Punitive Damages in Belgium" in L. Meurkens & E. Nordin (eds.), *The Power of Punitive Damages – Is Europe Missing Out?*, Cambridge – Antwerp – Portland, Intersentia, 2012, 214.

11 This notion characterises legal systems which provide for compensatory damages as well as punitive damages.

12 This term refers to legal systems where only compensatory damages are available.

13 E. de Kezel, "The Protection and Enforcement of Private Interests by (the Recognition of US) Punitive Damages in Belgium" in L. Meurkens & E. Nordin (eds.), *The Power of Punitive Damages – Is Europe Missing Out?*, Cambridge – Antwerp – Portland, Intersentia, 2012, 235.

14 See for this question for instance: R.C. Meurkens, *Punitive Damages – The Civil Remedy in American Law. Lessons and Caveats for Continental Europe*, Deventer, Kluwer, 2014.

15 M. Requejo Isidro, "Punitive Damages From a Private International Law Perspective" in H. Koziol & V. Wilcox (eds.), Punitive Damages: Common Law and Civil Law Perspectives, Vienna, Springer, 2009, 237–238.

16 As already mentioned, the choice for American punitive damages will be explained *supra* in the section dealing with the scope of the book: see no. 14.

EU and its Member States (1) reject requests for service of punitive damages claims (chapter 2), (2) decline the application of foreign laws that allow punitive damages (chapter 3) and (3) refuse to recognise and to enforce American punitive damages judgments (chapter 4). In doing so the objections upon which such a refusal is based are laid bare. The answer to this sub-question thus requires an analysis of the legal status quo.

This part of the research is descriptive as well as analytical in nature. It is descriptive in the sense that it investigates the attitudes found in the European Union with regard to punitive damages through the application of private international law. It also contains an analytical component in the sense that it forms a necessary step in our research aims to a better understanding of the nature and concept of punitive damages. The collection and organisation of the relevant legislation, case-law and scholarly writings requires a strong interpretative dimension and will allow for the identification of a number of issues and their underlying nature. International public policy is the central mechanism at work to prevent the imposition of punitive damages through foreign laws or foreign decisions. We aim to describe the arguments used to (dis) allow punitive damages under this international public policy clause by using a functional comparative legal method where possible.

12. Second, the book evaluates whether the current private international law outlook on punitive damages in these three areas of private international law is (still) defendable (chapter 5). It assesses whether the objections used to bar the acceptance of punitive damages through private international law are still valid in light of the evolving concepts of international public policy in European private law. To that end, we study the internal coherence of the remedial system in Europe, as well as the international public policy arguments that are traditionally employed to avert the legal import through private international law of American punitive damages. We conduct a thorough examination through literature review and an analysis of the laws and court decisions of the EU as well as of those of the selected Member States.

13. Third, if the current situation is found to be legally untenable, the book examines the criteria on the basis of which the EU and the Member States' legal systems *should* allow or disallow the acceptance of American punitive damages through the operation of private international law mechanisms, and this in light of the current notion of international public policy in Europe (chapter 6). In this last prescriptive part of the book the aim is to formulate a framework that guides European courts to apply the rules of private international law in a way that is consistent with the current private law stance in the law of the European Union as well as in the selected Member States. Such a comprehensive attempt has not yet been undertaken in any academic work. Those scholars in favour of eliminating the international public policy objection against the concept of punitive damages itself have restricted themselves to stating that an excessiveness test should subsequently intervene, without offering any real guidance as to how to construe such a test. Rather than focusing on what is, the book seeks for what should be in light of the present-day notion of international public policy. The research results of the previous parts will be processed in order to establish guidelines to discern acceptable extra-compensatory damages from inadmissible punitive damages.

SCOPE

14. In this book we work with the American definition of punitive damages. This choice is prompted by three important considerations. First, European national court decisions on private international law deal almost exclusively with *American* punitive damages. The United States produces the most punitive damages judgments and its awards[17] reach the highest amounts.[18] A second factor is the particular position of the United States in the field of private international law which gives rise to interesting issues. The United States (contrary to Canada, New Zealand and Australia) is presently not a party to any bilateral treaty or multilateral international convention governing reciprocal recognition and enforcement of foreign judgments in Europe. As a consequence, parties seeking recognition of an American judgment containing punitive damages are subject to a patchwork of national laws governing the recognition of judgments. Lastly, the European Union's commerce is to a large extent focused on the United States. The country leads the ranking of the European Union's most important trading partners.[19]

15. The book intends to offer the European Union a framework for adopting the correct private international law stance to American punitive damages. It is, however, unfeasible to study all Member States as well as the law of the European Union itself. It is, therefore, important to set out which countries will be the subject of the research.

16. In the area of service of process Germany will be studied as it is the only country with case law on the subject. To our knowledge the issues surrounding

---

17 In this book the term "award" will be not be used to refer to arbitral awards but rather to a portion of a court judgment. In particular, the terms "punitive award" and "award for punitive damages" refer to the head of punitive damages within a foreign judgment.

18 C.I. Nagy, "Recognition and enforcement of US judgments involving punitive damages in continental Europe", *Nederlands Internationaal Privaatrecht* 2012, 4.

19 European Commission, Directorate-General for Trade, European Union, Trade in Goods with USA, 16 April 2014, 2, available at <http://trade.ec.europa.eu/doclib/docs/2006/september/tradoc_113465.pdf>.

the service of claims for punitive damages have only arisen in that country. The results of that part of the research can be extrapolated to the other Member States as they are, except for Austria and Malta[20], all Members to the Hague Convention on service abroad of 15 November 1965 (the Hague Service Convention).

17. As far as applicable law is concerned, most attention will be given to the Rome II Regulation as this instrument provides for uniform private international law rules for non-contractual obligations. For the few torts[21] not covered by the Regulation, the national private international law rules come into play. In that regard Germany offers an interesting perspective as its legal system contains a provision specifically dealing with extra-compensatory damages. Again, the conclusions for Germany will be extrapolated to the other countries of the European Union.

18. The examination of the private international law arena of the enforcement of judgments will be the most extensive of the three. Due to the absence of any treaty between the United States and the European Union or its Member States, the domestic law of each Member State determines the acceptability of American punitive damages awards. Here, the book looks at five Member States in order to determine their current positions on the enforceability of punitive awards: Italy, Germany, England, France and Spain. The validity of the international public policy objections rejecting enforcement will subsequently be analysed by examining the same five Member States' private law. It is believed that the conclusions reached for these countries will have an impact for both the other Member States and the European Union as a whole.

19. The selection of these five Member States is inspired by two findings. First, over 60% of the European Union's population lives on the territory of any of these five nations.[22] Moreover, these five countries represent the five largest economies of the European Union.[23] Second, in an area where the available case law is sparse, Italy, Germany, France and Spain are particularly interesting

---

20 Austria and Malta have, however, expressed their willingess to become a party to the Convention. See in that regard Council Decision (EU) 2016/414 of 10 March 2016 authorising the Republic of Austria to sign and ratify, and Malta to accede to, the Hague Convention of 15 November 1965 on the Service Abroad of Judicial and Extrajudicial Documents in Civil or Commercial Matters, in the interest of the European Union, *OJ* L 75 of 22 March 2016, 1.

21 The Rome II Regulation uses the term "non-contractual obligations". The latter notion is broader than "torts" and covers unjust enrichment, *negotiorum gestio* and *culpa in contrahendo* as well. In this book the term "tort" will be given preference because in the legal system of the United States punitive damages predominantly arise in (pure) tort cases.

22 See: <http://europa.eu/about-eu/countries/member-countries/index_en.htm>. In our calculation the United Kingdom instead of England is used.

23 The figures of the year 2013 are available on the website of the International Monetary Fund: <www.imf.org/external/pubs/ft/weo/2013/02/weodata/index.aspx>.

because the Supreme Courts of those countries have decided on the issue of the enforceability of (American) punitive damages. England is also included because of its familiarity with punitive damages. As English law provides for punitive damages, it is important to get acquainted with its private international law position on foreign punitive damages.

ECONOMIC AND SOCIAL RELEVANCE

20. It should again be underlined that this book does not address the question whether punitive damages should become a remedy in the substantive law of the European Union or its Member States. Instead, the perspective of the book is exclusively private international law-oriented. This private international law analysis is crucial for Europe and its Member States. The outcome of the research will provide an essential building block in the discussion in which law-makers in Europe and in its Member States are currently involved regarding compensation systems. The level of tolerance in private international law is an indicator of a legal system's openness for a full introduction of the remedy of punitive damages.

21. In addition, the book has economic importance and practical relevance given the ever-increasing rate of direct exports by entities lacking corporate presence in the target market.[24] In the international marketplace the tortfeasor's assets may not be situated in the country where the judgment was rendered and, therefore, more and more creditors may come to rely on the international enforcement of their judgments.[25] The book will tangibly contribute to legal certainty for European private persons and businesses that engage in legal action outside the European borders as it will describe the current situation with regard to punitive damages as well as define best practices for the courts. The focus on the United States will prove valuable for European businesses engaging in transcontinental trade.

STRUCTURE

22. The main body of this book is divided in 7 chapters. Each chapter describes in more detail its contents and objectives. The following serves as a general overview.

---

[24] J. Zekoll, "The Enforceability of American Money Judgments Abroad: A Landmark Decision by the German Federal Court of Justice", 30 *Columbia Journal of Transnational Law* 1992, 641–642.

[25] J. Berch, "The Need for Enforcement of U.S. Punitive Damages Awards by the European Union", 19 *Minnesota Journal of International Law* 2010, 59.

Chapter 1 explains the various aspects of punitive damages in the United States. In Europe American punitive damages are often surrounded by misunderstandings and viewed with a continental temperament of distrust.[26] It is, therefore, crucial to set the record straight, eliminate these misconceptions and start the private international law study with the right frame of mind.

Chapters 2, 3 and 4 then elaborate on the position of U.S. punitive damages within service of process, applicable law and enforcement of judgments respectively. They identify the arguments used to avert the legal import of punitive damages through private international law.

Chapter 5 focuses on applicable law and enforcement of judgments in particular and evaluates which position is consistent with the legal reality in European Union law as well as the laws of the Member States.

Chapter 6 formulates concrete guidelines on which European judges can rely when faced with U.S. punitive damages in their applicable law analysis or when requested to declare an American punitive damages judgment enforceable.

Chapter 7 is reserved for the formal answering of the research questions and some further concluding remarks.

23. The book states the law and state of play in the case law as at 1 April 2016.

[26] H. Brooke, "A Brief Introduction: The Origins of Punitive Damages" in H. Koziol & V. Wilcox (eds.), *Punitive Damages: Common Law and Civil Law Perspectives*, Vienna, Springer, 2009, 3.

CHAPTER 1
THE CONCEPT OF PUNITIVE DAMAGES IN AMERICAN LAW

24. This first chapter introduces the concept of punitive damages from an American perspective. First, an attempt is made at defining the remedy of punitive damages as it exists in the United States. The chapter then provides insight into the historical origins of this type of damages and into their development within American law. It sets out the requirements commonly put forward for the granting of punitive damages. Subsequently, the objectives behind the awarding of punitive damages are explored. It is further demonstrated that punitive awards do not occur in the amount and the frequency public opinion seems to believe they do. Lastly, the clear trend to limit both the number as well as the amount of punitive damages awards is described. Particular attention is dedicated to the U.S. Supreme Court's line of cases putting constraints on punitive damages by relying on the Due Process Clause of the Fourteenth Amendment to the American Constitution. The chapter lays the foundation and provides the background needed to address the position and treatment of U.S. punitive damages within private international law.

1.1. DEFINITION

25. The victim of a tort committed by another person, a legal entity or the government is entitled to be placed in the situation he or she would have been in had the tort not taken place.[27] This is a fundamental principle of tort law in the United States[28] as well as in the European Union.[29] The tortfeasor must pay damages to compensate for the harm suffered by the plaintiff as a result of the tort. These compensatory damages (also referred to as actual damages) are

---

27 D.G. Owen, *Philosophical Foundations of Tort Law*, New York, Oxford University Press, 1997, 21; W. Van Gerven, J. Lever & P. Larouche, *Tort Law*, Oxford, Hart Publishing, 2000, 770.

28 See for a general discussion of the principles of American tort law: M.S. Shapo, *Principles of tort law*, St. Paul, Minnesota, Thomson/West, 2010; D. Dobbs, P. Hayden & E. Bublick, *The Law of Torts, Practitioner Treatise Series*, Minneapolis, West, 2011.

29 See for a general discussion of the principles of tort law in Europe: C. Van Dam, *European Tort Law*, Oxford, Oxford University Press, 2006.

further categorised into patrimonial (or pecuniary) and non-patrimonial (non-pecuniary or extra-patrimonial) damages. The former serve to reimburse the plaintiff's quantifiable monetary losses, such as property damage and medical expenses. The latter compensate for non-monetary forms of damage, with physical or emotional pain and suffering and loss of reputation as most common examples.[30]

26. Punitive damages[31] on the other hand provide plaintiffs in civil procedures with additional monetary relief beyond the value of the harm incurred.[32] The remedy transcends the corrective objective of re-establishing an arithmetical equilibrium of gains and losses between the injurer and the injured.[33] Punitive damages are awarded in excess of any compensatory or nominal damages.[34] Punitive damages are not (primarily) intended to compensate the plaintiff for harm done. Where the law of damages is monistic (restricted to compensation) in Civil Law jurisdictions, it is dualistic (aimed at both compensation and punishment) in countries which make punitive damages available.[35]

27. Punitive damages exist in various countries around the world. The United States, Canada, Australia, South Africa and New Zealand are the main examples of third state jurisdictions[36] which allow for this type of damages. Within the European Union only England, Wales, Ireland, Northern Ireland and Cyprus provide for this kind of damages in their respective legal systems. In contrast to their acceptance within Common Law jurisdictions, they are said to be relatively

30 M. Tolani, "U.S. Punitive Damages Before German Courts: A Comparative Analysis with Respect to the Ordre Public", 17 *Annual Survey of International & Comparative Law* 2011, 187; T. Rouhette, "The availability of punitive damages in Europe: growing trend or nonexistent concept?", 74 *Defense Counsel Journal* 2007, 325.

31 Also called: exemplary damages, added damages, imaginary damages, vindictive damages, punitory damages, presumptive damages, aggravated damages, speculative damages, punies, "smart money".

32 B.A. Garner (ed.), *Black's Law Dictionary*, St. Paul, Minnesota, West, 3rd pocket edition, 2006, 175.

33 F. Quarta, "Foreign Punitive Damages Decisions and Class Actions in Italy" in D. Fairgrieve and E. Lein (eds.), *Extraterritoriality and Collective Redress*, Oxford, Oxford University Press, 2012, 280; R.A. Posner, "The Concept of Corrective Justice in Recent Theories of Tort Law", 10 *Journal of Legal Studies* 1981, 187.

34 G. Nater-Bass, "U.S.-Style Punitive Damages Awards and their Recognition and Enforcement in Switzerland and Other Civil-Law Countries", 28 *Deutsch-Amerikanische Juristen-Vereinigung Newsletter* 2003, 154.

35 V. Behr, "Punitive Damages in American and German Law – Tendencies Towards Approximation of Apparently Irreconcilable Concepts", 78 *Chicago – Kent Law Review* 2003, 105–106.

36 Third state jurisdictions are those located outside the European Union.

non-existent in Civil Law countries. As mentioned before[37] this book only deals with American punitive damages because the United States produces the largest number of judgments containing such damages. The American punitive awards, moreover, reach the highest amounts.[38] Additionally, of all countries which allow for punitive damages, the European Union has the most extensive (trade) relations with the United States. The United States is actually the European Union's largest trading partner.[39]

28. In the United States the Second Restatement of Torts and Black's Law Dictionary define punitive damages as: "*damages, other than compensatory or nominal damages, awarded against a person to punish him for his outrageous conduct and to deter him and others like him from similar conduct in the future*".[40] The United States Supreme Court views punitive damages as: "*private fines levied by civil juries to punish reprehensible conduct and to deter its future occurrence*".[41] The most common definitions thus focus on the socio-legal significance of the wrongdoing and on the importance of discouraging its repetition.[42]

29. Both these definitions mention the two main objectives of punitive damages: punishment and deterrence.[43] The functions of punishing and deterring are traditionally attached to criminal law sanctions. It is, therefore, often argued that punitive damages pursue criminal law objectives rather than private law objectives.[44] As a quasi-criminal institution they are halfway between civil and criminal law and they put the boundaries between both areas of the law into question.[45] Their hybrid character, *i.e.* neither completely

37 See *supra* no. 14.

38 C.I. Nagy, "Recognition and enforcement of US judgments involving punitive damages in continental Europe", *Nederlands Internationaal Privaatrecht* 2012, 4.

39 European Commission, Directorate-General for Trade, European Union, Trade in Goods with USA, 16 April 2014, 2, available at <http://trade.ec.europa.eu/doclib/docs/2006/september/tradoc_113465.pdf>.

40 Second Restatement of Torts §908 (1979); B.A. Garner (ed.), *Black's Law Dictionary*, St. Paul, Minnesota, West, 2006, 3rd pocket edition, 175.

41 *Gertz v. Robert Welch, Inc.*, 418 U.S. 323 (1974), 350.

42 F. Quarta, "Foreign Punitive Damages Decisions and Class Actions in Italy" in D. Fairgrieve and E. Lein (eds.), *Extraterritoriality and Collective Redress*, Oxford, Oxford University Press, 2012, 280.

43 For a more extensive overview of the purposes of punitive damages, see *infra* no. 58 *et seq.*

44 L. Meurkens, "The punitive damages debate in Continental Europe: food for thought" in L. Meurkens & E. Nordin (eds.), *The Power of Punitive Damages – Is Europe Missing Out?*, Cambridge – Antwerp – Portland, Intersentia, 2012, 4.

45 22 Am. Jur. 2d Damages §541; T. Rouhette, "The availability of punitive damages in Europe: growing trend or nonexistent concept?", 74 *Defense Counsel Journal* 2007, 320; Y. Adar, "Touring the Punitive Damages Forest: A Proposed Roadmap", *Osservatorio del diritto civile e commerciale* 2012, 302.

civil nor criminal, causes the controversy that has always surrounded this remedy.[46]

30. Punitive damages have always been the subject of political and academic debate.[47] In the United States they are a much discussed matter, similar to issues as gun control or abortion.[48] They are a controversial feature of U.S. law which adds to defendants' perception of the American tort system as capricious, hostile and an avenue for "jackpot justice".[49] Opponents of punitive damages have suggested that punishment should remain the responsibility of the state and that a defendant who is facing punitive damages should be entitled to the criminal law safeguards.[50] In *Fay v. Parker*, the New Hampshire Supreme Court ordered exemplary damages, but nevertheless held (through Justice William Foster) that: "*The idea [of punitive damages] is wrong. It is a monstrous heresy. It is an unsightly and unhealthy excrescence, deforming the symmetry of the body of law [...]*".[51] However, despite being considered an anomaly in the law of torts[52], punitive damages are an accepted form of penal remedy in American civil law.[53] In *Luther v. Shaw*, for example, the Wisconsin Supreme Court stated that: "*The law giving exemplary damages is an outgrowth of the English love of liberty regulated by law (...) [that] (...) restrains the strong, influential, and unscrupulous, vindicates the right of the weak, and encourages recourse to and confidence in the courts of law by those wronged or oppressed by acts or practices not cognizable in or not sufficiently punished by the criminal law*".[54]

---

46 L.L Schlueter, *Punitive Damages – Volume I*, Newark, New Jersey, LexisNexis, 2005, 82; D.G. Owen, *Products Liability Law*, St. Paul, Minnesota, Thomson/West, 2005, 1122; B.C. Zipursky, "A Theory of Punitive Damages", 84 *Texas Law Review* 2005, 107.

47 L. Meurkens, "The punitive damages debate in Continental Europe: food for thought" in L. Meurkens & E. Nordin (eds.), *The Power of Punitive Damages – Is Europe Missing Out?*, Cambridge – Antwerp – Portland, Intersentia, 2012, 22; Y. Adar, "Touring the Punitive Damages Forest: A Proposed Roadmap", *Osservatorio del diritto civile e commerciale* 2012, 301 and 347.

48 M. Galanter, "Shadow Play: The Fabled Menace of Punitive Damages", *Wisconsin Law Review* 1998, 14.

49 V.E. Schwartz, M.A. Behrens & J.P. Mastrosimone, "Reining in Punitive Damages "Run Wild": Proposals for Reform by Courts and Legislatures", 65 *Brooklyn Law Review* 1999, 1004.

50 22 Am. Jur. 2d Damages §541; L. Meurkens, "The punitive damages debate in Continental Europe: food for thought" in L. Meurkens & E. Nordin (eds.), *The Power of Punitive Damages – Is Europe Missing Out?*, Cambridge – Antwerp – Portland, Intersentia, 2012, 5.

51 New Hampshire Supreme Court, *Fay v. Parker*, 53 New Hampshire Reports (N.H.) 342 (1872), 382.

52 C. Morris, "Punitive Damages in Tort Cases", 44 *Harvard Law Review* 1931, 1176; L.L. Schlueter, *Punitive Damages – Volume 1*, Newark, New Jersey, LexisNexis 2005, 79.

53 R.L. Blatt, R.W. Hammesfahr & L.S. Nugent, *Punitive Damages: A State-by-State Guide to Law and Practice*, Eagan, Minnesota, Thomson Reuters/West, 2008, 40; D.G. Owen, *Products Liability Law*, St. Paul, Minnesota, Thomson/West, 2005, 1122.

54 Wisconsin Supreme Court, *Luther v. Shaw*, 147 N.W. 18 (1914), 20.

1.2. THE HISTORY OF (U.S.) PUNITIVE DAMAGES

1.2.1. EARLY SOURCES

31. Punitive damages are by no means a recently invented legal instrument. It could be argued that already in the Code of Hammurabi (18th century BC) one can find references to multiple damages, a form of punitive damages calculated according to a predetermined scale.[55] Section 107, for instance, reads: "*If the merchant cheat the agent, in that as the latter has returned to him all that had been given him, but the merchant denies the receipt of what had been returned to him, then shall this agent convict the merchant before God and the judges, and if he still deny receiving what the agent had given him shall pay six times the sum to the agent*". Similar provisions can be found in sections 5[56] and 8.[57]

32. The Bible also contains traces of punitive damages. Verse 37 of chapter 21 as well as verses 1, 4, 7 and 9 of chapter 22 provide for an early form of punitive damages. The first verse of chapter 22, for instance, lays down the rule that: "*If a man shall steal an ox, or a sheep, and kill it, or sell it; he shall restore five oxen for an ox, and four sheep for a sheep*".

33. In Roman law the idea of punishment within private law was not unusual.[58] Punitive damages were used to express society's distaste for the offence rather than to compensate the victim.[59] Under Roman law it was sometimes possible to bring three different actions against an offender: (1) a criminal one, (2) a delictual (private law) one and (3) a claim *in rem* (for restitution of the item) or *in personam* (for the value of the item). The delictual claim led to a monetary penalty to be paid to the victim.[60] An action *in personam* and delict combined together resulted in the plaintiff receiving more than his loss, up to four times the original damages.[61]

---

55 D.G. Owen, "Punitive Damages Overview Functions, Problems and Reform", 39 *Villanova Law Review* 1994, 368.

56 "*If a judge try a case, reach a decision, and present his judgment in writing; if later error shall appear in his decision, and it be through his own fault, then he shall pay twelve times the fine set by him in the case, and he shall be publicly removed from the judge's bench, and never again shall he sit there to render judgement.*"

57 "*If any one steal cattle or sheep, or an ass, or a pig or a goat, if it belong to a god or to the court, the thief shall pay thirtyfold therefor; if they belonged to a freed man of the king he shall pay tenfold; if the thief has nothing with which to pay he shall be put to death.*"

58 M. Tolani, "U.S. Punitive Damages Before German Courts: A Comparative Analysis with Respect to the Ordre Public", 17 *Annual Survey of International & Comparative Law* 2011, 186.

59 S.P. Calandrillo, "Penalizing Punitive Damages: Why the Supreme Court Needs a Lesson in Law and Economics", 78 *George Washington Law Review* 2010, 780.

60 B. Nicholas, *An Introduction to Roman Law*, Oxford, Oxford University Press, 1969, 208.

61 B. Nicholas, *An Introduction to Roman Law*, Oxford, Oxford University Press, 1969, 210; R. Fowler, "Why Punitive Damages Should Be a Jury's Decision in Kansas: A Historical

1.2.2. ENGLISH ROOTS

34. The roots of modern punitive damages can be found in England. The first statutory recognition of multiple damages took place in 1275. The relevant provision in the Statute of Westminster read: "*Trespassers against religious persons shall yield double damages*".[62] Between 1275 and 1763 Parliament enacted at least 64 other provisions for double, treble and quadruple damages.[63] In 1763 in the case of *Huckle v. Money* exemplary damages[64] were first expressly recognised in England.[65] The early case-law used punitive damages to punish the defendant for the insulting and humiliating nature of his act. The English judiciary awarded such damages in two types of cases: (1) oppressive conduct by public officers and (2) misuse of social power to – usually publicly – abuse the victim.[66]

35. *Huckle v. Money* is a prime example of the first category. The printer of a newspaper that was allegedly libellous against King George III sued the Crown for false imprisonment. The judge instructed the jury that they were not bound to a certain amount of damages. The jury returned with a verdict for 300 pounds even though actual damages were only 20 pounds. The Crown requested the verdict to be set aside as it found the damages to be excessive. It argued that the printer was only confined for a few hours and treated "*very civilly [...] with beef-steaks and beer*". The Court, however, refused to interfere with the jury's determination and left the award intact.[67]

36. A similar and related case of abuse of official authority is *Wilkes v. Wood*. Decided in the same year as *Huckle*, the case involved a law enforcement officer

---

Perspective", 52 *Kansas Law Review* 2004, 636; W.W. Buckland, *A Text-Book of Roman Law from Augustus to Justinian*, Cambridge, Cambridge University Press, 3rd edition (revised by D. Stein), 1963, 581–584; D.G. Owen, "Punitive Damages Overview Functions, Problems and Reform", 39 *Villanova Law Review* 1994, 368; K. Browne, "Punitive damages in the U.S.: a primer for insurance buyers and brokers", Armonk, Swiss Re, 2011, 4.

62 Synopsis of Statute of Westminster I, 3 Edw., c. 1 (Eng.), quoted in D.G. Owen, "Punitive Damages Overview Functions, Problems and Reform", 39 *Villanova Law Review* 1994, 368.

63 R. Fowler, "Why Punitive Damages Should Be a Jury's Decision in Kansas: A Historical Perspective", 52 *Kansas Law Review* 2004, 636.

64 The case can also be seen as the beginning of the English courts' use of the term "exemplary damages" for damages awarded above the level of compensation with the purpose of deterring and punishing the defendant: J.B. Sales & K.B. Cole, Jr., "Punitive Damages, A Relic That Has Outlived Its Origins", 37 *Vanderbilt Law Review* 1984, 1119–1120.

65 *Huckle v. Money*, 95 English Reports, King's Bench (Eng. Rep.) 768 (K.B. 1763).

66 A.J. Sebok, "Punitive Damages in the United States" in H. Koziol & V. Wilcox (eds.), *Punitive Damages: Common Law and Civil Law Perspectives*, Vienna, Springer, 2009, 159.

67 *Huckle v Money*, 95 English Reports, King's Bench (Eng. Rep.) 768 (K.B. 1763); A.J. Sebok, "Punitive Damages in the United States" in H. Koziol & V. Wilcox (eds.), *Punitive Damages: Common Law and Civil Law Perspectives*, Vienna, Springer, 2009, 159; D.G. Owen, "Punitive Damages Overview: Functions, Problems and Reform", 39 *Villanova Law Review* 1994, 369, footnote 25.

called Wood. The latter had used the same general warrant as in *Huckle* to gain entry to the plaintiff's home where he seized property belonging to the victim. The cause for this illegal action was again the publication by the plaintiff, John Wilkes (Huckle's employer), of a pamphlet criticising the king. The Court of King's Bench ruled that the conduct of the king's agent Wood amounted to an abuse of power that jeopardised the constitutional rights of ordinary people and that, therefore, punitive damages were warranted. The Court held that: "*Damages are designed not only as a satisfaction to the injured person, but likewise as a punishment to the guilty, to deter from any such proceeding for the future, and as a proof of the detestation of the jury to the action itself*".[68]

37. In addition to these cases of abuse of official authority, there was a second line of cases in which punitive damages were awarded. These judgments granted punitive damages to the plaintiff because the defendant had made use of his public power to abuse the plaintiff. An example of this second group of these early cases is *Benson v. Frederick*. A colonel whipped a common soldier and was ordered to pay punitive damages because the victim was "*scandalized and disgraced*".[69]

1.2.3. RECEPTION IN AMERICAN LAW

38. United States punitive damages grew out of English common law but developed further independently from other Commonwealth countries.[70] Like the early English case law, the first American punitive damages cases (18th and 19th century) emphasised the insulting and humiliating nature of the defendant's action.[71]

39. In the first case in which punitive damages were granted, *Genay v. Norris*, a doctor had slipped poison in the victim's wine glass. The man collapsed in public, suffered extreme and excruciating pain and had to forfeit his planned duel with the offender.[72] In another case of the same period, *Coryell v. Collbaugh*,

---

68 *Wilkes v. Wood*, 98 Eng. Rep. 498–499 (C.P. 1763).

69 *Benson v. Frederick*, 97 Eng. Rep. 1130 (K.B. 1766); E. Baldoni, *Punitive damages: a comparative analysis*, Universita degli studi di Macerata, unpublished Ph.D thesis, 2012, 10–11.

70 A.J. Sebok, "Punitive Damages in the United States" in H. Koziol & V. Wilcox (eds.), *Punitive Damages: Common Law and Civil Law Perspectives*, Vienna, Springer, 2009, 156.

71 A.J. Sebok, "Punitive Damages in the United States" in H. Koziol & V. Wilcox (eds.), *Punitive Damages: Common Law and Civil Law Perspectives*, Vienna, Springer, 2009, 160.

72 *Genay v. Norris*, 1 South Carolina Law Reports (S.C.L.) (1 Bay) 6 (1784); A.J. Sebok, "Punitive Damages in the United States" in H. Koziol & V. Wilcox (eds.), *Punitive Damages: Common Law and Civil Law Perspectives*, Vienna, Springer, 2009, 160; K. Browne, "Punitive damages in the U.S.: a primer for insurance buyers and brokers", Armonk, Swiss Re, 2011, 4.

a father sued the defendant for breach of promise to marry his daughter. The judge instructed the jury to "*give damages for example's sake, to prevent such offences in future,*" and that they "*might give such a sum as would mark their disapprobation*".[73]

40. In 1851 the United States Supreme Court for the first time expressly recognised punitive damages in the *Day v. Woodworth* judgment. Elaborating on the damages available to the victim in a trespass action, the Court asserted that: "*It is a well established principle of the common law that in actions of trespass and all actions on the case for torts, a jury may inflict what are called exemplary, punitive, or vindictive damages upon a defendant, having in view the enormity of his offense, rather than the measure of compensation to the plaintiff...[I]f repeated judicial decisions for more than a century are to be received as the best exposition of what the law is, the question will not admit of argument*".[74]

41. Punitive damages entered a new phase at the turn of the 20th century when their availability was widened to cases where commercial actors engaged in anti-social behaviour through an abuse of power or position. There were, for example, railroad cases in which victims were harmed by the defendant's employees' behaviour[75] and the corporate defendant knew of, ratified or tolerated the acts of their employees.[76] The core of the abuse of power lay in the defendant's unequal or unfair treatment of the plaintiff.[77] The corporation felt that it was in a position, given its market position or size, to ignore the plaintiff's complaint with impunity.[78]

42. Another, relatively less important, group of cases falling under the abuse of power label were fraud cases in which the defendant's greed led him to take advantage of the defendant's weaker position. The courts required more than simple greed for the awarding of punitive damages. There had to be some specific desire by the tortfeasor to use the power (mostly knowledge about the true state of things) he had over the victim. This additional exercise of power was usually

---

73 *Coryell v. Collbaugh*, 1 New Jersey Law Reports (N.J.L.) 77 (1791); A.J. Sebok, "Punitive Damages in the United States" in H. Koziol & V. Wilcox (eds.), *Punitive Damages: Common Law and Civil Law Perspectives*, Vienna, Springer, 2009, 160; K. Browne, "Punitive damages in the U.S.: a primer for insurance buyers and brokers", Armonk, Swiss Re, 2011, 4.

74 *Day v. Woodworth*, 54 U.S. (13 How.) 371 (1851).

75 Conduct such as: wrongfully ejecting passengers, refusing to carry the blind, carrying passengers past their stations: A.G. Nichols, Jr., "Comment, Punitive Damages in Mississippi – A Brief Survey", 37 *Mississippi Law Journal* 1965, 138.

76 T. Sedgwick, *A Treatise on the Measure of Damages vol. 1*, (9th ed. 1913) revised by A.G. Sedgwick & J.H. Beale, New York, Baker, Voorhis & Co. Law Publishers, 9th ed., 1913, 742.

77 A.J. Sebok, "Punitive Damages in the United States" in H. Koziol & V. Wilcox (eds.), *Punitive Damages: Common Law and Civil Law Perspectives*, Vienna, Springer, 2009, 163 and 169.

78 A.J. Sebok, "Punitive Damages in the United States" in H. Koziol & V. Wilcox (eds.), *Punitive Damages: Common Law and Civil Law Perspectives*, Vienna, Springer, 2009, 164.

referred to by the courts as "oppression".[79] In *C.C. Williams v. Detroit Oil & Cotton Company*, for example, an employer took money from his employee with the promise to take out accident insurance but kept the money instead.[80] By the middle of the 20th century, the popularity of punitive damages appeared to be on the rise in the United States courts, and on the decline in English and Canadian courts.[81]

43. In the last three decades, the applicability of United States punitive damages extended to product liability and business torts involving insurance, employment, real property, contract and commercial and consumer sales in order to promote social efficiency.[82] Punitive damages are frequently requested in product liability because every claim under product liability law can be framed as – at least alleging – a "wilful and reckless disregard" of the plaintiff's rights. The "wilful and reckless disregard" standard was introduced in the late 1970s as the threshold for punitive damages in product liability cases. It paved the way for a high number of claims for punitive damages as plaintiffs assert that a producer almost always makes conscious design choices inspired by a cost-benefit analysis.[83]

44. An example of such product liability litigation and probably one of the most (in)famous punitive damages cases in the United States is the one of *Stella Liebeck v. McDonald's*.[84] The plaintiff had been burned by hot coffee which she had purchased at the fast food restaurant. She suffered third- and fourth-degree burns (some all the way to the bone) in her pelvic region when she spilled the hot coffee on her lap. She initially spent eight days in hospital and her burns were so severe that she almost died. The victim showed that McDonald's had settled claims of victims with similar injuries from hot coffee and that the company had never changed its policy of selling coffee at that temperature. The jury awarded the plaintiff USD 2.7 million in punitive damages (in addition to USD 160.000 in

79 A.J. Sebok, "Punitive Damages in the United States" in H. Koziol & V. Wilcox (eds.), *Punitive Damages: Common Law and Civil Law Perspectives*, Vienna, Springer, 2009, 164.

80 *C.C. Williams v. Detroit Oil & Cotton Company*, 52 Texas Civil Appeals Reports (Tex. Civ. App.) 243, 249 (1908).

81 In England and Canada the applicability of punitive damages was restricted to a much greater extent than in the United States. See, *e.g.*, *Rookes* v. *Barnard*, [1964] 1 *All E.R.* 367, 410–11 (H.L.) (punitive damages can only be awarded in three scenarios: abuses of power by government officials, torts committed for profit, or express statutory authorisation); *Thompson* v. *Commissioner of Police of Metropolis*, [1998] *Q.B.* 498, 518 (Canadian case establishing that the ratio of punitive damages to compensatory damages should seldom exceed 3:1, and suggesting limits for the monetary sum of punitive damages awards).

82 A.J. Sebok, "Punitive Damages in the United States" in H. Koziol & V. Wilcox (eds.), *Punitive Damages: Common Law and Civil Law Perspectives*, Vienna, Springer, 2009, 165 and 168.

83 A.J. Sebok, "Punitive Damages in the United States" in H. Koziol & V. Wilcox (eds.), *Punitive Damages: Common Law and Civil Law Perspectives*, Vienna, Springer, 2009, 165–166.

84 *Liebeck v. McDonald's Restaurants, P.T.S., Inc.*, 1995 WL 360309 (N.M. Dist. 1994).

compensation). However, the amount of punitive damages was later reduced to USD 480.000 (3 times the compensatory damages) by the trial judge. Before an appeal was decided, parties settled for a confidential amount.[85]

1.3. PUNITIVE DAMAGES AWARDS IN THE U.S.

1.3.1. OCCURRENCE

45. Punitive damages most often arise under state tort law.[86] Each state of the U.S. has a wide discretion in imposing punitive damages. The federal system of the U.S. has created considerable diversity among the 50 states as to the form and content of punitive damages.[87] The U.S. Constitution, however, can and has put significant limitations on the divergences between states.[88, 89] In addition to the various state laws, the federal level also provides for punitive damages in certain statutes. Under the Clayton Antitrust Act, the Racketeer Influenced and Corrupt Organizations Act (RICO) and the Comprehensive Environmental Response, Compensation, and Liability Act (CERCLA), for instance, treble damages[90] can be awarded.

46. Punitive damages are generally accepted in 45 states of the United States.[91] Five states have different levels of admission, varying from non-existence to conditional acceptance. New Hampshire has refused the remedy

85 For a collection of blog posts offering different unique insights into the case, see <http://abnormaluse.com/?s=liebeck>. There is also a 2011 documentary film entitled Hot Coffee (directed by Susan Saladoff) which discusses the case.

86 A.J. Sebok, "The U.S. Supreme Court's Theory of Common Law Punitive Damages" in L. Meurkens & E. Nordin (eds.), *The Power of Punitive Damages – Is Europe Missing Out?*, Cambridge – Antwerp – Portland, Intersentia, 2012, 133.

87 W. Schubert, "Simplifying Punitive Damages: Due Process and the Pursuit of Manageable Awards and Procedures in U.S. Courts", *European Journal of Consumer Law* 2011, 832; A.J. Sebok, "Punitive Damages in the United States" in H. Koziol & V. Wilcox (eds.), *Punitive Damages: Common Law and Civil Law Perspectives*, Vienna, Springer, 2009, 156.

88 A.J. Sebok, "Punitive Damages in the United States" in H. Koziol & V. Wilcox (eds.), *Punitive Damages: Common Law and Civil Law Perspectives*, Vienna, Springer, 2009, 156.

89 The U.S. Supreme Court jurisprudence on the permissibility of punitive damages will be discussed *infra* in no. 72 *et seq.*

90 Treble damages are a form of multiple damages achieved by trebling the compensatory award. The punitive portion of the award will thus amount to twice the compensatory damages.

91 A.J. Sebok, "Punitive Damages in the United States" in H. Koziol & V. Wilcox (eds.), *Punitive Damages: Common Law and Civil Law Perspectives*, Vienna, Springer, 2009, 155; A.J. Sebok, "The U.S. Supreme Court's Theory of Common Law Punitive Damages" in L. Meurkens & E. Nordin (eds.), *The Power of Punitive Damages – Is Europe Missing Out?*, Cambridge – Antwerp – Portland, Intersentia, 2012, 134, footnote 5.

by statute.[92] The Constitution of Nebraska bars punitive damages awards.[93] In the states of Louisiana (a Civil Law system with some Common Law influences), Massachusetts and Washington a plaintiff cannot obtain punitive damages unless there is specific statutory authorisation.[94] In Connecticut punitive damages are permitted but only to compensate the plaintiff for his legal expenses, less taxable costs.[95]

47. The availability of punitive damages is in principle restricted to tort actions.[96] In practice, however, American courts award punitive damages in a wide array of cases.[97] The plaintiff in a contractual dispute may receive punitive damages if the defendant's breach of contract constitutes an intentional tort as well.[98] The Second Restatement of Contracts states in that regard that "*Punitive damages are not recoverable for a breach of contract unless the conduct constituting the breach is also a tort for which punitive damages are recoverable*".[99] Insurance bad faith cases, for instance, can lead to an award of punitive damages if the insurer's breach of contract is so outrageous that it amounts to a breach of the duty of good faith and fair dealing which is implied in every insurance policy.[100]

48. Even though compensation of the victim is not a primary objective of punitive damages, the plaintiff will receive all or some portion of the punitive award.[101] In some American states part of the award needs to be paid to the state.[102] In Oregon, for instance, a statute allocates 70% of the punitive damages awarded to the state.[103] California law provides that 75% of the award flows to

92 N.H. Rev. Stat. Ann. §507:16 (1997).

93 *Distinctive Printing and Packaging Co. v. Cox*, 232 Neb. 846, 857, 443 N. W. 2d 566, 574 (1989).

94 See for example *Int'l Harvester Credit Corp. v. Seale*, 518 So.2d 1039, 1041 (La. 1988); *Dailey v. North Coast Life Ins. Co.*, 919 P.2d 589, 590–91 (Wash. 1996); *Fleshner v. Technical Communications Corp.*, 575 N.E.2d 1107, 1112 (Mass. 1991).

95 *Venturi v. Savit, Inc.*, 191 Conn. 588, 592, 468 Atlantic Reporter, Second Series (A. 2d) 933, 935 (1983) (citing *Collens v. New Canaan Water Co.*, 155 Conn. 477, 489, 234 A.2d 825, 832 (1967)); *Kelsey v. Connecticut State Emp. Ass'n*, 179 Conn. 606, 427 A.2d 420 (1980).

96 22 Am. Jur. 2d Damages §568, 569, 570; 25 C.J.S. Damages §198, 199, 200.

97 L.L. Schlueter, *Punitive Damages – Volume I*, Newark, New Jersey, LexisNexis 2005, 399; 25 C.J.S. Damages §199.

98 W. Burnham, *Introduction to the law and Legal system of the United States*, St. Paul, Minnesota, Thomson/West, 4th edition, 2006, 241.

99 Second Restatement of Contracts, §355 (1981).

100 H.R. Levine, "Demonstrating and Preserving the Deterrent Effect of Punitive Damages in Insurance Bad Faith Actions", 13 *University of San Francisco Law Review* 1979, 618; J.M. Barrett, "Contort: Tortious Breach of the Implied Covenant of Good Faith and Fair Dealing in Noninsurance Commercial Contracts – Its Existence and Desirability", 60 *Notre Dame Law Review* 1985, 510 and footnote 2 with the references therein.

101 P.S. Ryan, "Revisiting the United States application of punitive damages: separating myth from reality", 10 *ILSA Journal of International & Comparative Law* 2003, 76 and 92.

102 A.J. Sebok, "Punitive Damages in the United States" in H. Koziol & V. Wilcox (eds.), *Punitive Damages: Common Law and Civil Law Perspectives*, Vienna, Springer, 2009, 176.

103 Or. Rev. Stat. §31.735 (2003).

a Public Benefit Trust Fund.[104] These split-recovery schemes can have various purposes: reducing the number of frivolous law suits, preventing a windfall for the plaintiff or generating income for the state.[105]

1.3.2. JURY DISCRETION

49. The decision whether to grant the plaintiff punitive damages and the determination of the amount lies with the jury or, in cases without a jury, the judge acting as finder of fact.[106] The judge acts as gatekeeper and must determine whether there is sufficient evidence to support an award for punitive damages. If the judge is satisfied that that is the case, the question of punitive damages can be submitted to the jury.[107] There is no obligation to award punitive damages even if the evidence would justify them.[108] The amount awarded by the jury is subjected to review by the trial judge who can reduce the award or remove it from the final judgment.[109]

1.3.3. REQUIREMENTS

50. The foundational requirement for punitive damages is the infringement of a legally protected interest.[110] In order to be able to obtain punitive damages, the plaintiff must have suffered actual damage and must provide sufficient evidence thereof. There is thus no separate cause of action for punitive damages.[111]

51. Despite the varying applications of punitive damages in the different states of the U.S., each state's approach to punitive damages can be analysed from three different angles: (1) the requisite culpability, (2) the standard of proof and (3) the relevant factors used in the determination of the amount.[112]

---

104 Cal. Civ. Code §3294.5.

105 A.J. Sebok, "Punitive Damages in the United States" in H. Koziol & V. Wilcox (eds.), *Punitive Damages: Common Law and Civil Law Perspectives*, Vienna, Springer, 2009, 177.

106 25 C.J.S. Damages §196; A.J. Sebok, "Punitive Damages in the United States" in H. Koziol & V. Wilcox (eds.), *Punitive Damages: Common Law and Civil Law Perspectives*, Vienna, Springer, 2009, 180.

107 22 Am. Jur. 2d Damages §550; L. Meurkens, "The punitive damages debate in Continental Europe: food for thought" in L. Meurkens & E. Nordin (eds.), *The Power of Punitive Damages – Is Europe Missing Out?*, Cambridge – Antwerp – Portland, Intersentia, 2012, 10.

108 22 Am. Jur. 2d Damages §550.

109 22 Am. Jur. 2d Damages §605; W. Burnham, *Introduction to the law and Legal system of the United States*, St. Paul, Minnesota, Thomson/West, 4th edition, 2006, 453.

110 22 Am. Jur. 2d Damages §551.

111 25 C.J.S. Damages §197; 22 Am. Jur. 2d Damages §551, 553.

112 A.J. Sebok, "Punitive Damages in the United States" in H. Koziol & V. Wilcox (eds.), *Punitive Damages: Common Law and Civil Law Perspectives*, Vienna, Springer, 2009, 180–181.

a. Requisite culpability

52. The fact that the defendant has acted in an unlawful manner does not suffice for punitive damages to be awarded. The conduct in question must involve a degree of aggravation.[113] The Restatement of Torts emphasises that "*punitive damages may be awarded for conduct that is outrageous, because of the defendant's evil motive or his reckless indifference to the rights of others*".[114] Across the different American states a varying terminology is employed to express the required high standard of misconduct: "egregious", "reprehensible", "bad faith", "fraud", "malice", "oppression", "outrageous", "violent", "wanton", "wicked" and "reckless".[115] Mere negligence can never form the basis for a punitive damages award.[116] Some states allow punitive damages in cases where the tortfeasor's behaviour amounts to gross negligence, but then the negligence must be so gross that there was a conscious indifference to the rights and safety of the plaintiff.[117]

b. Standard of proof

53. In private law cases in the United States the plaintiff must most often prove by "a preponderance of the evidence" that the facts that he puts forward are actually true. This means that more than 50% of the evidence needs to be in the plaintiff's favour, making it more likely than not that the plaintiff's claim is true.

54. In criminal law a higher standard of proof needs to be satisfied in order to secure a conviction. The prosecution is required to show that the defendant is guilty "beyond a reasonable doubt". Even though this does not equate to absolute certainty (but rather to virtual certainty[118]), the trier of fact must be convinced that there is no other reasonable alternative than the defendant's commission of the crime.[119]

---

113 22 Am. Jur. 2d Damages §569; L. Meurkens, "The punitive damages debate in Continental Europe: food for thought" in L. Meurkens & E. Nordin (eds.), *The Power of Punitive Damages – Is Europe Missing Out?*, Cambridge – Antwerp – Portland, Intersentia, 2012, 10.

114 Restatement of Torts, §908.

115 22 Am. Jur. 2d Damages §558; A.J. Sebok, "Punitive Damages in the United States" in H. Koziol & V. Wilcox (eds.), *Punitive Damages: Common Law and Civil Law Perspectives*, Vienna, Springer, 2009, 181; K. Browne, "Punitive damages in the U.S.: a primer for insurance buyers and brokers", Armonk, Swiss Re, 2011, 4.

116 25 C.J.S. Damages §205; L.L. Schlueter, *Punitive Damages – Volume I*, Newark, New Jersey, LexisNexis 2005, 162.

117 L.L. Schlueter, *Punitive Damages – Volume I*, Newark, New Jersey, LexisNexis 2005, 161; A.J. Sebok, "Punitive Damages in the United States" in H. Koziol & V. Wilcox (eds.), *Punitive Damages: Common Law and Civil Law Perspectives*, Vienna, Springer, 2009, 155.

118 K.M. Clermont & E. Sherwin, "A Comparative View of Standards of Proof", 50 *American Journal of Comparative Law* 2002, 251.

119 A.J. Sebok, "Punitive Damages in the United States" in H. Koziol & V. Wilcox (eds.), *Punitive Damages: Common Law and Civil Law Perspectives*, Vienna, Springer, 2009, 184.

55. In a large number[120] of states, punitive damages are subjected to an intermediate standard, *i.e.* "clear and convincing evidence" instead of the normal "preponderance of the evidence" requirement for civil claims.[121] This standard of proof entails that the claim presented by a party is substantially more likely to be true than not. The Hawaiian Supreme Court in *Masaki v. General Motors Corp.* explained that: "*It is that degree of proof which will produce in the mind of the trier of fact a firm belief or conviction as to the allegations sought to be established, and requires the existence of a fact be highly probable*".[122, 123]

c. *Relevant factors used in the determination of the amount*

56. There is no rigid standard for the calculation of the amount of punitive damages.[124] Therefore the size of the punitive award varies greatly among the states.[125] The jury (or in some cases the judge) decides on the amount to be awarded using its discretion.[126] The factors for determining appropriate punitive damages generally include: the nature of the wrong, the reprehensibility of the wrongdoing, the enormity of the wrong, the duration of the wrong, the wrongdoer's intent or motivation, his awareness of any hazard the conduct has caused, and other circumstances relating to the wrongdoer's actions.[127] Most states also allow the defendant's financial condition to be taken into account.[128] These factors confirm that the trier of fact must focus on the defendant's conduct rather than on the plaintiff's harm as punitive damages are not primarily aimed at compensating the victim but at punishing and deterring the wrongdoer.[129]

---

120 Thirty-five states have adopted the "clear and convincing evidence" standard: L.L Schlueter, *Punitive Damages – Volume I*, Newark, New Jersey, LexisNexis, 2005, 313–315. In Colorado claims for punitive damages need to overcome the "beyond a reasonable doubt" standard: Colo. Rev. Stat. §13–25–127(2) (2001).

121 22 Am. Jur. 2d Damages §706; A.J. Sebok, "Punitive Damages in the United States" in H. Koziol & V. Wilcox (eds.), *Punitive Damages: Common Law and Civil Law Perspectives*, Vienna, Springer, 2009, 184.

122 *Masaki v. General Motors Corp.*, 71 Hawaii Reports (Haw.), 14 (1989).

123 A.J. Sebok, "Punitive Damages in the United States" in H. Koziol & V. Wilcox (eds.), *Punitive Damages: Common Law and Civil Law Perspectives*, Vienna, Springer, 2009, 184.

124 22 Am. Jur. 2d Damages §604.

125 A.J. Sebok, "Punitive Damages in the United States" in H. Koziol & V. Wilcox (eds.), *Punitive Damages: Common Law and Civil Law Perspectives*, Vienna, Springer, 2009, 184.

126 22 Am. Jur. 2d Damages §604.

127 22 Am. Jur. 2d Damages §606.

128 22 Am. Jur. 2d Damages §606; Restatement of Torts, §908; A.J. Sebok, "Punitive Damages in the United States" in H. Koziol & V. Wilcox (eds.), *Punitive Damages: Common Law and Civil Law Perspectives*, Vienna, Springer, 2009, 186; L. Meurkens, "The punitive damages debate in Continental Europe: food for thought" in L. Meurkens & E. Nordin (eds.), *The Power of Punitive Damages – Is Europe Missing Out?*, Cambridge – Antwerp – Portland, Intersentia, 2012, 10.

129 J.J. Kircher & C.M. Wiseman, *Punitive Damages Law and Practice*, part 1, Eagan, Minnesota, Thomson/West, 2000, §5:18; 25 C.J.S. Damages §213.

57. The jury's discretion is by no means unbridled. The amount of the punitive award should be reasonable in relation to the harm suffered by the victim and to the tortfeasor's ability to pay.[130] In order to punish effectively and deter the wrongdoer the award should be sufficiently large but should not go beyond that.[131] Its purpose should never be to bring the defendant to financial ruin or bankruptcy.[132] The amount of the punitive award can be tested by the trail judge and/or the appellate court using the same factors mentioned above.[133, 134]

1.3.4. OBJECTIVES

58. In its pursuit of an efficient legal system the United States, compared to other nations, relies more heavily on private litigation than on administrative oversight and enforcement.[135] In the United States the judiciary is, therefore, left to regulate whereas in Europe the legislative and executive branch perform that task.[136] In order to stimulate the use of private civil litigation the U.S. has an array of tools available. Class actions, contingent attorney fees, and punitive damages are probably the most important examples in that regard. Punitive damages are a form of private fines which contribute to society's endeavour to obtain the desired level of law enforcement. By awarding them in a large number of situations the U.S. has reduced the need for governmental intervention in law enforcement.[137]

59. The specific objectives pursued by punitive damages were enumerated by the German Supreme Court (*Bundesgerichtshof*) in *John Doe v. Eckhard Schmitz*, dealing with the enforcement of a U.S. punitive damages judgment[138]: (1) to punish the offender for its improper conduct; (2) to deter the offender and others from similar conduct in the future; (3) to reward the plaintiff for enforcing the

---

130 22 Am. Jur. 2d Damages §604.

131 22 Am. Jur. 2d Damages §604.

132 22 Am. Jur. 2d Damages §607 and §542.

133 See *supra* no. 56.

134 22 Am. Jur. 2d Damages §605.

135 W. Schubert, "Simplifying Punitive Damages: Due Process and the Pursuit of Manageable Awards and Procedures in U.S. Courts", *European Journal of Consumer Law* 2011, 861.

136 M. Tolani, "U.S. Punitive Damages Before German Courts: A Comparative Analysis with Respect to the Ordre Public", 17 *Annual Survey of International & Comparative Law* 2011, 205.

137 W. Schubert, "Simplifying Punitive Damages: Due Process and the Pursuit of Manageable Awards and Procedures in U.S. Courts", *European Journal of Consumer Law* 2011, 861.

138 BGH 4 June 1992, *BGHZ* 118, 312, English translation in 32 *International Legal Materials* 1993, 1320. See *infra* no. 234 for an extensive commentary.

law and (4) to supplement otherwise inadequate compensatory damages.[139] The remedy serves the individual interests of the victim as well as larger societal interests.[140] Although punishment and deterrence can be classified as the two main purposes of punitive awards[141], they are not the only aims pursued. The various objectives of punitive damages will now be discussed.

a. Punishment

60. More than two thirds of the American states refer in their legislation and/or case law to punishment for wrongful acts as one of the motivations behind the institution of punitive damages. The idea of punishment is based on a broader notion of public morality which condemns unlawful violations of another person's rights. The victim of wrongful behaviour is entitled to be avenged and the tortfeasor ought to be punished.[142] Through the punitive award the victim is able to actively address the defendant and recover his or her honour.[143] The function of retribution that lies within the punishment of the culprit not only protects the private rights of the victim but serves society as a whole.[144] Indeed, in addition to personal vindication, punitive damages seek to offer vindication for the insult suffered by the state as a result of the tortfeasor's conduct.[145] By punishing the defendant on behalf of the public, punitive damages enter the realm of criminal law. The imposition of the "quasi-criminal" remedy of punitive damages, however, does not require adherence to the procedural safeguards that are applicable in criminal law cases.[146]

---

139 BGH 4 June 1992, 32 *International Legal Materials* 1993, 1337; R. Brand, "Punitive Damages Revisited: Taking the Rationale for Non-Recognition of Foreign Judgments Too Far", 24 *Journal of Law and Commerce* 2005, 185; C. Vanleenhove, "Punitive Damages and European Law: Quo Vademus?" in L. Meurkens & E. Nordin (eds.), *The Power of Punitive Damages – Is Europe Missing Out?*, Cambridge – Antwerp – Portland, Intersentia, 2012, 337.

140 L. Meurkens, "The punitive damages debate in Continental Europe: food for thought" in L. Meurkens & E. Nordin (eds.), *The Power of Punitive Damages – Is Europe Missing Out?*, Cambridge – Antwerp – Portland, Intersentia, 2012, 4.

141 L.L Schlueter, *Punitive Damages – Volume I*, Newark, New Jersey, LexisNexis, 2005, 16; S.C. Yeazell, *Civil Procedure*, New York, Aspen Law & Business, 2008, 273; D.G. Owen, *Products Liability Law*, St. Paul, Minnesota, Thomson/West, 2005, 1132; 22 Am. Jur. 2d Damages §542.

142 D.D. Ellis, "Fairness and Efficiency in the Law of Punitive Damages", 56 *Southern California Law Review* 1982, 5.

143 A.J. Sebok, "Punitive Damages in the United States" in H. Koziol & V. Wilcox (eds.), *Punitive Damages: Common Law and Civil Law Perspectives*, Vienna, Springer, 2009, 174.

144 25 C.J.S. Damages §195; 22 Am. Jur. 2d Damages §544; A.P. Harris, "Rereading Punitive Damages: Beyond the Public/Private Distinction", 40 *Alabama Law Review* 1989, 1102.

145 A.J. Sebok, "Punitive Damages in the United States" in H. Koziol & V. Wilcox (eds.), *Punitive Damages: Common Law and Civil Law Perspectives*, Vienna, Springer, 2009, 175.

146 T.B. Colby, "Beyond the Multiple Punishment Problem: Punitive Damages as Punishment for Individual, Private Wrongs", 87 *Minnesota Law Review* 2003, 606; A.J. Sebok, "Punitive Damages in the United States" in H. Koziol & V. Wilcox (eds.), *Punitive Damages: Common Law and Civil Law Perspectives*, Vienna, Springer, 2009, 175–176.

b. *Deterrence/prevention*

61. The second main rationale behind punitive damages is the desire to prevent the occurrence of the same or similar wrongful behaviour in the future. Punitive damages awards are instrumental in that regard as they send the message that committing a tort does not pay since the price of getting caught is higher than the benefit that may come out of committing the wrongful act.[147]

62. The goal of improving societal safety is achieved by deterrence on two levels.[148] First, the punitive award attempts to dissuade the tortfeasor from repeating his unlawful conduct in the future. This type of deterrence is called specific deterrence and is aimed at the defendant individually.[149] The prospect of punitive damages might encourage the defendant to abstain from continuing or duplicating the reprehensible act. Second, punitive damages produce a general deterring effect in that they set an example for other potential wrongdoers. They serve as a warning for society at large that the behaviour exhibited by the defendant will not be tolerated. Hence the term "exemplary damages" sometimes used by United States courts and to a larger extent by English courts.[150]

63. Closely related to both the punishment and deterrence functions of punitive damages is the educational objective. Punitive damages reflect the desire of society to educate individuals and affirm societal standards of conduct.[151]

c. *Compensation*

64. Punitive damages are focused on punishing and deterring the defendant's reprehensible behaviour for the benefit of society and not on providing reparation for the individual victim's loss.[152] Compensation of the plaintiff is, therefore, not a primary objective of punitive awards. In the majority of American states the imposition and amount of damages in addition to compensatory damages

---

147 L. Meurkens, "The punitive damages debate in Continental Europe: food for thought" in L. Meurkens & E. Nordin (eds.), *The Power of Punitive Damages – Is Europe Missing Out?*, Cambridge – Antwerp – Portland, Intersentia, 2012, 6.

148 D.D. Ellis, "Fairness and Efficiency in the Law of Punitive Damages", 56 *Southern California Law Review* 1982, 8.

149 A.J. Sebok, "Punitive Damages in the United States" in H. Koziol & V. Wilcox (eds.), *Punitive Damages: Common Law and Civil Law Perspectives*, Vienna, Springer, 2009, 178.

150 A.J. Sebok, "Punitive Damages in the United States" in H. Koziol & V. Wilcox (eds.), *Punitive Damages: Common Law and Civil Law Perspectives*, Vienna, Springer, 2009, 179–180.

151 V. Behr, "Punitive Damages in American and German Law – Tendencies Towards Approximation of Apparently Irreconcilable Concepts", 78 *Chicago – Kent Law Review* 2003, 121; D.G. Owen, "A Punitive Damages Overview: Functions, Problems and Reform", 39 *Villanova Law Review* 1994, 374–380.

152 25 C.J.S. Damages §195; 22 Am. Jur. 2d Damages §544.

need not and cannot be limited by the desire to redress the plaintiff's injury.[153] Punitive damages, however, remain linked to private redress in the sense that almost all states require a finding of actual (or at least nominal) damage before a punitive award can be issued.[154]

65. The idea that punitive damages offer compensation for injuries that were not fully redressed by compensatory damages already existed in the 19th century. Some American courts referred to compensation for insult as the basis for punitive damages awards.[155] In recent years scholars have rediscovered the value of punitive damages in forcing wrongdoers to reimburse the victim for all losses suffered.[156] It is possible that material and/or legal obstacles prevent the recovery of full compensation. The impossibility to prove the extent of the loss sustained can, for instance, be classified as a material obstacle. The American rule on distribution of costs forms perhaps the most important legal impediment to full recovery of the plaintiff.

66. Under the United States system each party is responsible for its own attorney's fees[157], except if specific authority granted by contract or statute allows the recovery of these costs.[158] Whereas the winning party in a litigation in almost every Western democratic country can recover the attorneys' fees from the losing side, the American rules do not allow such transfer of costs. Punitive damages can be used to – whether openly or covertly – circumvent this prohibition.[159] As mentioned before[160], in Connecticut punitive damages are recoverable in an amount equal to the plaintiff's "expenses of litigation".[161] In the

153 A.J. Sebok, "Punitive Damages in the United States" in H. Koziol & V. Wilcox (eds.), *Punitive Damages: Common Law and Civil Law Perspectives*, Vienna, Springer, 2009, 173.

154 A.J. Sebok, "Punitive Damages in the United States" in H. Koziol & V. Wilcox (eds.), *Punitive Damages: Common Law and Civil Law Perspectives*, Vienna, Springer, 2009, 171.

155 See *e.g. Detroit Dailey Post v. McArthur*, 16 Mich., 447 (1868); *Chiles v. Drake*, 59 Ky. (2 Met.), 151 (1859); *Wardrobe v. Cal. Stage Co.*, 7 Cal. 118 (1857); *Hendrickson.v Kingsbury*, 21 Iowa 379 (1866).

156 D.G. Owen, "Punitive Damages as Restitution" in L. Meurkens & E. Nordin (eds.), *The Power of Punitive Damages – Is Europe Missing Out?*, Cambridge – Antwerp – Portland, Intersentia, 2012, 120–121; S.P. Calandrillo, "Penalizing Punitive Damages: Why the Supreme Court Needs a Lesson in Law and Economics", 78 *George Washington Law Review* 2010, 802; L. Meurkens, "The punitive damages debate in Continental Europe: food for thought" in L. Meurkens & E. Nordin (eds.), *The Power of Punitive Damages – Is Europe Missing Out?*, Cambridge – Antwerp – Portland, Intersentia, 2012, 9.

157 T.J. Centner, *America's Blame Culture. Pointing Fingers and Shunning Restitution*, Durham, North Carolina, Carolina Academic Press, 2008, 34–35.

158 The Federal Magnuson-Moss Warranty Act forms one of the many exceptions to the default rule. It allows the prevailing consumer to obtain reimbursement of the reasonable legal costs.

159 F.X. Licari, "Prendre les punitive damages au sérieux: propos critiques sur un refus d'accorder l'exequatur à une décision californienne ayant alloué des dommages intérêts punitifs", *Journal du droit international (Clunet)* October/November/December 2010/4, 1255.

160 See *supra* no. 46.

161 See *Collens v. New Canaan Water Co.*, 234 A.2d 825, 831–832 (Conn. 1967).

situations where compensatory damages fall short punitive damages can thus contribute to the full redress of the plaintiff.

d. Reward the plaintiff for enforcing the law

67. As the American legal system relies to a large extent on private enforcement of rights, there must be incentives for potential plaintiffs to initiate litigation. In the United States, punitive damages are one of the procedural mechanisms which encourage recourse to the courts.[162] They, furthermore, add to the trust citizens put in the court system and they help preserve the peace in the community.[163]

1.3.5. FREQUENCY AND SIZE

68. It is an intractable myth that punitive damages awards are all very large. This misconception is created by the media who only pay attention to extreme awards.[164] Newspapers and television shows focus on billion dollar jury awards and "runaway" juries[165] have often been the inspiration for popular films and books.[166] In the abovementioned *Liebeck v McDonald's* case, for instance, the jury's USD 2.7 million punitive award received world-wide coverage.[167] The later reduction of the punitive damages to USD 480.000 by the trial judge, however, was for the most part left unreported.[168] The lack of reliable databases collecting punitive damages awards and the impossibility to determine the number of settlements in punitive damages cases before the appeal stage, add to the mystique that surrounds the remedy. There are, however, a few studies

162 M.H. Redish & A.L. Mathews, "Why Punitive Damages are Unconstitutional", 53 *Emory Law Journal* 2004, 2; F.X. Licari, "Prendre les punitive damages au sérieux: propos critiques sur un refus d'accorder l'exequatur à une décision californienne ayant alloué des dommages intérêts punitifs", *Journal du droit international (Clunet)* October/November/December 2010/4, 1254–1255.

163 Conversely, there is the *in terrorem* effect of punitive damages: the threat of punitive damages may be abused as a "wild card" to force higher settlements: G.L. Priest, "Punitive Damages Reform: The Case of Alabama", 56 *Louisiana Law Review* 1996, 829.

164 J.K. Robbennolt, "Determining Punitive Damages: Empirical Insights and Implications for Reform", 50 *Buffalo Law Review* 2002, 159; A.J. Sebok, "Punitive Damages: From Myth to Theory", 92 *Iowa Law Review* 2007, 962.

165 A "runaway" jury can be described as a jury which is out of control in the sense that they award a very high amount of (punitive) damages.

166 K. Browne, "Punitive damages in the U.S.: a primer for insurance buyers and brokers", Armonk, Swiss Re, 2011, 5.

167 See *supra* no. 44.

168 L. Meurkens, "The punitive damages debate in Continental Europe: food for thought" in L. Meurkens & E. Nordin (eds.), *The Power of Punitive Damages – Is Europe Missing Out?*, Cambridge – Antwerp – Portland, Intersentia, 2012, 8.

which contain data regarding the frequency and size of punitive awards.[169] The figures they provide seem to indicate that plaintiffs do not receive high amounts of punitive damages as often as the general public might believe.[170]

69. It is first of all important to note that in the United States only a small portion of litigation reaches the verdict stage. Many conflicts are resolved by settlements, either before or after a law suit has been served. A survey of trials in state courts in the United States' seventy-five most populous counties indicates that in 2005 only around 3% of the cases filed went to verdict.[171] In over half of these 26.948 cases the plaintiff prevailed. Punitive damages were requested by 13% of the plaintiff winners but only granted in 5% (*i.e.* 700) of the verdicts.[172] This percentage has remained stable over the years. In 1992 and 2001 punitive damages were awarded in respectively 5.9% and 5.5% of the jury cases with a plaintiff winner.[173]

70. Of the 700 cases that led to punitive damages in 2005, 27% involved an award in favour of the plaintiff of more than USD 250.000. 13% of the time the award equalled or exceeded USD 1 million.[174] The 1992 survey produced similar results: approximately 24% of plaintiffs' punitive awards went above USD 250.000 and almost 12% made the USD 1 million mark.[175] The median[176] punitive amount awarded to plaintiffs in 2005 was USD 64.000.[177] Again, this figure does not differ remarkably from previous years as both the 1992 and the 2001 survey reveal that the median in those years was USD 50.000.[178] The

169 K. Browne, "Punitive damages in the U.S.: a primer for insurance buyers and brokers", Armonk, Swiss Re, 2011, 5.

170 L. Meurkens, "The punitive damages debate in Continental Europe: food for thought" in L. Meurkens & E. Nordin (eds.), *The Power of Punitive Damages – Is Europe Missing Out?*, Cambridge – Antwerp – Portland, Intersentia, 2012, 8.

171 T.H. Cohen & L. Langton, Civil Bench and Jury Trials in State Courts, 2005, Bureau of Justice Statistics, 28 October 2008, 9.

172 T.H. Cohen & L. Langton, Civil Bench and Jury Trials in State Courts, 2005, Bureau of Justice Statistics, 28 October 2008, 6.

173 C.J. DeFrances et al., Civil Jury Cases and Verdicts in Large Counties, 1992, U.S. Department of Justice, Doc. No. NCJ-154346, 8, table 8; T.H. Cohen, Punitive Damages Awards in Large Counties, 2001, U.S. Department of Justice, Doc. No. NCJ-208445, 3, table 1.

174 T.H. Cohen & L. Langton, Civil Bench and Jury Trials in State Courts, 2005, Bureau of Justice Statistics, 28 October 2008, 6.

175 C.J. DeFrances et al., Civil Jury Cases and Verdicts in Large Counties, 1992, U.S. Department of Justice, Doc. No. NCJ-154346, 6.

176 The median is the numerical value separating the higher half of a data sample from the lower half. It can be found by arranging all the values in descending order and locating the middle one.

177 T.H. Cohen & L. Langton, Civil Bench and Jury Trials in State Courts, 2005, Bureau of Justice Statistics, 28 October 2008, 6, table 7.

178 C.J. DeFrances et al., Civil Jury Cases and Verdicts in Large Counties, 1992, U.S. Department of Justice, Doc. No. NCJ-154346, 8, table 8; T.H. Cohen, Punitive Damages Awards in Large Counties, 2001, U.S. Department of Justice, Doc. No. NCJ-208445, 4, table 2.

mean[179] awards, however, are obviously much higher (USD 735.000 in 1992 for instance[180]) and this creates the impression of rare multi-million dollar awards.[181] In fact, between 1985 and 2008 only 100 punitive awards exceeding USD 100 million have been issued.[182] Moreover, the rise in the amount of mean punitive awards has been less than the growth in damages overall.[183] Punitive damages representing astronomical amounts thus do exist but the chances of obtaining such an award are relatively small.

1.4. MULTI-LEVEL TREND TO REDUCE THE AMOUNTS OF PUNITIVE DAMAGES IN THE U.S.

71. The existence of these excessive punitive awards has, however, spurred on a movement to impose limits on punitive damages awards. The U.S. Supreme Court, lower federal courts, state courts, Congress and state legislatures have all contributed to this nationwide effort to moderate both the number of awards as well as their amounts.[184]

1.4.1. THE UNITED STATES SUPREME COURT

72. Towards the end of the 1980s the highest federal court started to set out boundaries for states' punitive damages by reviewing the constitutionality of such awards.[185] The primary source of these constitutional constraints on punitive damages was the Due Process Clause of the Fourteenth Amendment.[186]

---

179 The mathematical term for 'average'.

180 C.J. DeFrances et al., Civil Jury Cases and Verdicts in Large Counties, 1992, U.S. Department of Justice, Doc. No. NCJ-154346, 8, table 8.

181 A.J. Sebok, "Punitive Damages in the United States" in H. Koziol & V. Wilcox (eds.), *Punitive Damages: Common Law and Civil Law Perspectives*, Vienna, Springer, 2009, 157.

182 A.F. Del Rossi & W. Kip Viscusi, "The Changing Landscape of Blockbuster Punitive Damage Awards", Vanderbilt Law & Economics Research Paper No. 09-33, 2009.

183 T. Eisenberg, "Engle v. R.J. Reynolds Tobacco Co.: Lessons In State Class Actions, Punitive Damages, and Jury Decision-Making Damage Awards in Perspective: Behind the Headline-Grabbing Awards in Exxon Valdez and Engle", 36 *Wake Forest Law Review* 2001, 1138–1139.

184 J. Berch, "The Need for Enforcement of U.S. Punitive Damages Awards by the European Union", 19 *Minnesota Journal of International Law* 2010, 62.

185 A.J. Sebok, "The U.S. Supreme Court's Theory of Common Law Punitive Damages" in L. Meurkens & E. Nordin (eds.), *The Power of Punitive Damages – Is Europe Missing Out?*, Cambridge – Antwerp – Portland, Intersentia, 2012, 132.

186 R.L. Blatt, R.W. Hammesfahr & L.S. Nugent, *Punitive Damages: A State-by-State Guide to Law and Practice*, Eagan, Minnesota, Thomson Reuters/West, 2008, 37; W. Schubert, "Simplifying Punitive Damages: Due Process and the Pursuit of Manageable Awards and Procedures in U.S. Courts", *European Journal of Consumer Law* 2011, 832.

The relevant part of section 1 reads: "[...] *nor shall any State deprive any person of life, liberty, or property, without due process of law* [...]". Constitutional due process requires that fundamental fairness, notions of fair play and substantial justice, together with the basic rules of law, are applied in legal proceedings.[187] The Due Process Clause contains two distinct guarantees: substantive due process and procedural due process.[188] The former protects the civil defendants from grossly excessive awards by limiting the permissible size of the punitive award. The latter restricts the array of permissible methods for awarding punitive damages and ensures that reasonable factors are used in the calculation of the award.[189] In its case law the Supreme Court has shown preference for procedural due process as the basis for limitations on punitive damages. Rather than laying down restrictions on the size of the award, the Court has regulated the permissible ways of calculating the award.[190]

a. Browning-Ferris v. Kelco

73. In *Browning-Ferris v. Kelco* petitioners had been held liable for antitrust violations and tortuous interference with Kelco's contractual relations.[191] The compensatory damages amounted to USD 51.146 but the jury also awarded USD 6 million in punitive damages. Before the United States Supreme Court the petitioners argued that the award rendered by the jury infringed the Excessive Fines Clause of the Eight Amendment of the U.S. Constitution.[192] The United States Supreme Court, however, disagreed and ruled that the Clause does not apply in private law cases between private litigants. It can only come into play when a party is subjected to criminal fines by the government or when the government is seeking to obtain money from a private actor. The Excessive Fines Clause thus does not impose limits on punitive damages awarded to private parties in civil litigation.[193] The United States Supreme Court left open

187 M.Y. Yelenick & M. Pulaski-Kelly, "Court Discusses Guidelines for Review of Punitive Damages", 18 January 2001, no page numbers, available at < www.internationallawoffice.com>.

188 *Philip Morris II*, 549 U.S., 353; W. Schubert, "Simplifying Punitive Damages: Due Process and the Pursuit of Manageable Awards and Procedures in U.S. Courts", *European Journal of Consumer Law* 2011, 844.

189 W. Schubert, "Simplifying Punitive Damages: Due Process and the Pursuit of Manageable Awards and Procedures in U.S. Courts", *European Journal of Consumer Law* 2011, 844–845.

190 W. Schubert, "Simplifying Punitive Damages: Due Process and the Pursuit of Manageable Awards and Procedures in U.S. Courts", *European Journal of Consumer Law* 2011, 830 and 844.

191 *Browning-Ferris Industries of Vermont, Inc., et al.* v. *Kelco Disposal, Inc., et al.*, 492 U.S. 257 (1989).

192 The eighth Amendment reads: "*Excessive bail shall not be required, nor excessive fines imposed, nor cruel and unusual punishments inflicted.*"

193 *Browning-Ferris Industries of Vermont, Inc., et al.* v. *Kelco Disposal, Inc., et al.*, 492 U.S. 263–264 and 275–276 (1989).

the possibility that punitive damages awards could be challenged on other constitutional grounds. In an *obiter dictum* it held that the Due Process Clause of the Fourteenth Amendment could be used to demarcate the acceptable boundaries of punitive damages awards. The United States Supreme Court, nevertheless, did not embark upon an analysis of this line of thinking as the petitioners had failed to raise the due process argument, either before the District Court, the Court of Appeals or in the petition for certiorari.[194]

b. Pacific Mutual Life Insurance Co. v. Haslip

74. In *Pacific Mutual Life Insurance Co. v. Haslip* the United States Supreme Court examined the compatibility of a punitive award with the Due Process Clause for the first time.[195] An agent of the petitioner had misappropriated health insurance premiums issued by the respondents' employer. The agent's actions left the respondents uncovered and they consequently suffered financial losses. The insurance company was held liable for the fraud of the agent and ordered to pay USD 200.000 in compensatory damages and USD 840.000 in punitive damages. The petitioner was of the opinion that the punitive damages award violated its due process right.

75. This argument did not convince the United States Supreme Court as it decided that the method of determining punitive damages in this case did not lack "objective criteria" and was surrounded by a whole range of procedural protections.[196] The United States Supreme Court did, however, establish that defendants have a due process right. The majority opinion did not elaborate on the content of this right. With regard to the constitutionally tolerable size of a punitive award, the United States Supreme Court explained that: "*We need not, and indeed we cannot, draw a mathematical bright line between the constitutionally acceptable and the constitutionally unacceptable that would fit every case. We can say, however, that general concerns of reasonableness and adequate guidance from the court when the case is tried to a jury properly enter into the constitutional calculus*".[197]

---

194 *Browning-Ferris Industries of Vermont, Inc., et al.* v. *Kelco Disposal, Inc., et al.*, 492 U.S. 276–277 (1989); W. Schubert, "Simplifying Punitive Damages: Due Process and the Pursuit of Manageable Awards and Procedures in U.S. Courts", *European Journal of Consumer Law* 2011, 845–846; A.J. Sebok, "The U.S. Supreme Court's Theory of Common Law Punitive Damages" in L. Meurkens & E. Nordin (eds.), *The Power of Punitive Damages – Is Europe Missing Out?*, Cambridge – Antwerp – Portland, Intersentia, 2012, 136; A.J. Sebok, "Punitive Damages in the United States" in H. Koziol & V. Wilcox (eds.), *Punitive Damages: Common Law and Civil Law Perspectives*, Vienna, Springer, 2009, 189.

195 *Pacific Mutual Life Insurance Co. v. Haslip et al*, 499 U.S. 1 (1991).

196 *Pacific Mutual Life Insurance Co. v. Haslip et al*, 499 U.S. 17–18 (1991).

197 *Pacific Mutual Life Insurance Co. v. Haslip et al*, 499 U.S. 18 (1991); W. Schubert, "Simplifying Punitive Damages: Due Process and the Pursuit of Manageable Awards and Procedures in U.S. Courts", *European Journal of Consumer Law* 2011, 846.

c. TXO Production Corp. v. Alliance Resources Corp.

76. The *Haslip* approach was again applied in the case of *TXO Production Corp. v. Alliance Resources Corp.*[198] The plaintiff had brought a bad faith law suit against the defendant based on certain oil and gas development rights which it knew belonged to the defendant. The objective of this claim was connected with an effort to renegotiate its royalty arrangement with the latter. Alliance filed a counterclaim for slander of title and received USD 19.000 in actual damages and USD 10 million in punitive damages. TXO had proposed the "objective criteria" to be used for the review of the award: it suggested that the United States Supreme Court look at punitive damages awards against other defendants in the same jurisdiction, awards upheld for similar conduct in other jurisdictions, legislative penalty decisions for similar conduct, and the ratio between previous punitive damages amounts and the compensatory damages connected with them.[199] The United States Supreme Court rejected the proposal and concluded that the *Haslip* test was satisfied because the state's process of determining the punitive award offered the necessary "objective criteria".[200] It did not find a violation of the due process rights of TXO and upheld the award.[201] The United States Supreme Court noted that only "grossly excessive" awards pose constitutional problems under the substantive prong of the Due Process Clause but reaffirmed its unwillingness to define "grossly excessive" through a bright numerical line.[202]

d. Honda Motor Co. v. Oberg

77. The United States Supreme Court continued on the same path in *Honda Motor Co. v. Oberg.*[203] Respondent Oberg had sustained significant and permanent injuries while driving an all-terrain vehicle manufactured and sold by Honda. His claim that the design of the vehicle was inherently and unreasonably dangerous was successful and resulted in a USD 5 million punitive award, in addition to over USD 700.000 in compensation. Both the Oregon Court of Appeals and the Oregon Supreme Court affirmed the award. The Supreme Court of the United States observed that Oregon was the only state where punitive awards could not be subjected to judicial review. The United States Supreme Court stated that Oregon's failure to allow for judicial review of the size of punitive damages awards violated due process as well as the ruling

---

198 *TXO Production Corp. v Alliance Resources Corp.*, 509 U.S. 443 (1993).

199 *TXO Production Corp. v Alliance Resources Corp.*, 509 U.S. 455–456 (1993).

200 A.J. Sebok, "The U.S. Supreme Court's Theory of Common Law Punitive Damages" in L. Meurkens & E. Nordin (eds.), *The Power of Punitive Damages – Is Europe Missing Out?*, Cambridge – Antwerp – Portland, Intersentia, 2012, 137.

201 *TXO Production Corp. v Alliance Resources Corp.*, 509 U.S. 446, 453 and 457 (1993).

202 *TXO Production Corp. v Alliance Resources Corp.*, 509 U.S. 458 (1993).

203 *Honda Motor Co., Ltd., et al. v. Oberg*, 512 U.S. 415 (1994).

in *Haslip*.[204] It once again noted that only punitive damages awards that are "grossly excessive" in size violate the Constitution.[205] On remand the Oregon Supreme Court did not alter the award as it found that the amount was neither unreasonable nor "grossly excessive" given the circumstances of the case.[206] The case demonstrates the minimalistic constitutional interference with the states' common law rules: any mechanism for awarding punitive damages is allowed as long as it provides "objective criteria" and the state allows review of the award afterwards.[207]

e. *BMW of North America, Inc. v. Gore*

78. *BMW of North America, Inc. v. Gore* marked the next step in the United States Supreme Court's jurisprudence.[208] Dr. Gore had purchased a new BMW 535i for USD 40.750 from an authorised Alabama dealer in 1990. He later learned that the car had been repainted due to exposure to acid rain during transit from the BMW factory in Germany. Under BMW's company policy pre-sale repairs costing less than 3% of the price of the car were not disclosed to the customer. In total BMW had sold 983 of these repainted cars, 14 of which in Alabama, without informing the buyers. The plaintiff received USD 4.000 in compensatory damages and USD 4 million in punitive damages. The jury arrived at this number by multiplying Dr. Gore's compensatory amount by the number of customers the company had defrauded (approximately 1000).[209]

79. Despite the award being cut in half on appeal, the United States Supreme Court declared the award to be "grossly excessive" under the Constitution's Due Process Clause. *BMW v. Gore* remains the only case in which the United States Supreme Court rejected a state court's punitive award on substantive due process grounds.[210]

---

204 A.J. Sebok, "The U.S. Supreme Court's Theory of Common Law Punitive Damages" in L. Meurkens & E. Nordin (eds.), *The Power of Punitive Damages – Is Europe Missing Out?*, Cambridge – Antwerp – Portland, Intersentia, 2012, 137.

205 G. Cavalier, "Punitive Damages and French International Public Policy", in R. Stürner and M. Kawono (eds.), *Comparative Studies on Business Tort Litigation*, Tübingen, Mohr Siebeck, 2011, 220.

206 *Oberg v. Honda Motor Co.*, No. SC S38436,1995 Ore. LEXIS 2 (Or. 1995); M.Y. Yelenick & M. Pulaski-Kelly, "Court Discusses Guidelines for Review of Punitive Damages", 18 January 2001, no page numbers, available at < www.internationallawoffice.com>.

207 A.J. Sebok, "The U.S. Supreme Court's Theory of Common Law Punitive Damages" in L. Meurkens & E. Nordin (eds.), *The Power of Punitive Damages – Is Europe Missing Out?*, Cambridge – Antwerp – Portland, Intersentia, 2012, 137.

208 *BMW of North America, Inc. v. Gore*, 517 U.S. 559 (1995).

209 J. Berch, "The Need for Enforcement of U.S. Punitive Damages Awards by the European Union", 19 *Minnesota Journal of International Law* 2010, 64, footnote 38.

210 W. Schubert, "Simplifying Punitive Damages: Due Process and the Pursuit of Manageable Awards and Procedures in U.S. Courts", *European Journal of Consumer Law* 2011, 847.

80. The United States Supreme Court set out three guideposts to be used when determining whether a punitive damages award is "grossly excessive": (1) the reprehensibility of the defendant's conduct, (2) the ratio between the punitive and compensatory damages awarded and (3) a comparison of the punitive damages to the criminal penalties that could be imposed for similar misconduct.[211] The guideposts developed by the United States Supreme Court resemble the test suggested by petitioner TXO in *TXO Production Corp. v. Alliance Resources Corp.*[212] When reviewing whether the punitive award produced by the fact finder is constitutionally excessive, these three factors need to be taken into account. Consequently, even though the United States Supreme Court did not require the state of Alabama to inform its juries of certain criteria to determine an acceptable amount of punitive damages in light of the United States Constitution, the trial judge should include these standards in his instructions to the jury in order to avoid a constitutionally excessive jury award.[213]

81. The United States Supreme Court then emphasised the importance of the first guidepost, the reprehensibility of the wrongdoer's conduct, describing it as "*the most important indicium of the reasonableness of a punitive damages award*".[214] It provided guidance on how to assess the reprehensible nature of the behaviour by formulating five probative questions: courts and juries should consider whether (1) the harm caused was physical or rather merely economic, (2) the tortious conduct evinced an indifference to or a reckless disregard of the health or safety of others, (3) the victim was financially vulnerable, (4) the conduct involved repeated actions or was an isolated incident and (5) the harm was the result of intentional malice, trickery, or deceit, or mere accident.[215] In the eyes of the United States Supreme Court BMW's conduct had not been sufficiently reprehensible to justify a USD 2 million punitive award as none of the aggravating circumstances were present. It also found the 500:1 ratio between punitive and compensatory damages "breath-taking" and unreasonable. Lastly, it observed that the maximum civil penalty for a violation

---

211 *BMW of North America, Inc. v. Gore*, 517 U.S. 574–575 (1995).

212 See *supra* no. 76.

213 J. Berch, "The Need for Enforcement of U.S. Punitive Damages Awards by the European Union", 19 *Minnesota Journal of International Law* 2010, 65, footnote 41; A.J. Sebok, "Punitive Damages in the United States" in H. Koziol & V. Wilcox (eds.), *Punitive Damages: Common Law and Civil Law Perspectives*, Vienna, Springer, 2009, 191; A.J. Sebok, "The U.S. Supreme Court's Theory of Common Law Punitive Damages" in L. Meurkens & E. Nordin (eds.), *The Power of Punitive Damages – Is Europe Missing Out?*, Cambridge – Antwerp – Portland, Intersentia, 2012, 138.

214 *BMW of North America, Inc. v. Gore*, 517 U.S. 575, (1995).

215 *BMW of North America, Inc. v. Gore*, 517 U.S. 576, (1995); W. Schubert, "Simplifying Punitive Damages: Due Process and the Pursuit of Manageable Awards and Procedures in U.S. Courts", *European Journal of Consumer Law* 2011, 847.

of the Alabama Deceptive Trade Practices Act was USD 2.000, an amount substantially lower than the punitive award.[216]

82. On remand, the Alabama Supreme Court, in line with the United States Supreme Court's clarification that punitive damages cannot be assessed for out-of-state conduct, reduced the punitive award to USD 50.000 on the basis that only a few repainted vehicles were sold in the state of Alabama.

f. Cooper Industries, Inc. v. Leatherman Tool Group Inc.

83. In *Cooper Industries, Inc. v. Leatherman Tool Group Inc.* the United States Supreme Court added to the *BMW v. Gore* ruling.[217] It clarified that a review of punitive damages must encompass all three *Gore* factors and must be done "de novo". This standard of review is more permissive than the more deferential "abuse of discretion" standard and therefore contributes to the further narrowing of the scope of tolerable state common law theories of punitive damages.[218]

g. State Farm Mutual Automobile Insurance Co. v. Campbell

84. A reversal of a punitive damages award on procedural due process grounds was the end result in *State Farm Mutual Automobile Insurance Co. v. Campbell.*[219] Respondent Campbell had caused a car accident in which one person was killed and another permanently disabled. Campbell was insured for this liability with State Farm. Instead of settling for the USD 50.000 policy limit the insurer decided to take the case to trial. The judgment exceeded the policy limit by more than three times. Campbell then brought suit against State Farm for bad faith failure to settle, fraud and intentional infliction of emotional distress. The jury awarded USD 2.6 million in compensatory and USD 125 million in punitive damages, reduced by the trial court to USD 1 and 25 million respectively. The Supreme Court of the state of Utah, however, reinstated the USD 125 million punitive award.

85. The United States Supreme Court rejected the punitive damages award under due process, condemning the lower courts' acceptance of evidence of State Farm's nationwide policy to defraud their customers.[220] Campbell

216 *BMW of North America, Inc. v. Gore*, 517 U.S. 575–585, (1995).

217 *Cooper Industries, Inc. v. Leatherman Tool Group Inc.*, 532 U.S. 424 (2001).

218 A.J. Sebok, "The U.S. Supreme Court's Theory of Common Law Punitive Damages" in L. Meurkens & E. Nordin (eds.), *The Power of Punitive Damages – Is Europe Missing Out?*, Cambridge – Antwerp – Portland, Intersentia, 2012, 138; J. Berch, "The Need for Enforcement of U.S. Punitive Damages Awards by the European Union", 19 *Minnesota Journal of International Law* 2010, 65.

219 *State Farm Mutual Automobile Insurance Co. v. Campbell et al.*, 538 U.S. 408, (2003).

220 *State Farm Mutual Automobile Insurance Co. v. Campbell et al.*, 538 U.S. 415 and 418, (2003).

had introduced this evidence in an attempt to prove the reprehensibility of the insurer's conduct.[221] A state court may not allow the jury to punish the defendant for out-of-state conduct with no "*nexus to the specific harm suffered by the plaintiff*".[222] Only evidence that bears a "relation" with the victim's harm may serve as the basis for punitive damages.[223]

86. In the *dicta* the United States Supreme Court explored the second *BMW* guidepost in more detail. The court asserted that "*in practice, few awards exceeding a single-digit ratio between punitive and compensatory damages, to a significant degree, will satisfy due-process*".[224] This statement is not binding but does create a presumption against double-digit punitive-to-compensatory damages ratios.[225] The United States Supreme Court's *obiter dictum* seemed to end its reluctance to establish a mathematical threshold.[226, 227]

87. The United States Supreme Court envisaged this single-digit rule (9:1) to be flexible in certain circumstances. It first reiterated its opinion previously explained in *BMW v. Gore* where it was held that the maximum may be exceeded in an egregious case where there are only small economic damages.[228] But the United States Supreme Court also stated that the converse is true: "*when compensatory damages are substantial, then a lesser ratio perhaps only equal to compensatory damages, can reach the outermost limit of the due process guarantee*".[229]

h. Philip Morris USA v. Williams (Philip Morris II)

88. In *Philip Morris USA v. Williams (Philip Morris II)* the United States Supreme Court was confronted with a law suit in Oregon state court brought by the estate of Jesse Williams, a long-time smoker who had died from lung

---

221 A.J. Sebok, "Punitive Damages in the United States" in H. Koziol & V. Wilcox (eds.), *Punitive Damages: Common Law and Civil Law Perspectives*, Vienna, Springer, 2009, 191.

222 *State Farm Mutual Automobile Insurance Co. v. Campbell et al.*, 538 U.S. 422, (2003); W. Schubert, "Simplifying Punitive Damages: Due Process and the Pursuit of Manageable Awards and Procedures in U.S. Courts", *European Journal of Consumer Law* 2011, 848.

223 *State Farm Mutual Automobile Insurance Co. v. Campbell et al.*, 538 U.S. 422, (2003).

224 *State Farm Mutual Automobile Insurance Co. v. Campbell et al.*, 538 U.S. 425, (2003).

225 W. Schubert, "Simplifying Punitive Damages: Due Process and the Pursuit of Manageable Awards and Procedures in U.S. Courts", *European Journal of Consumer Law* 2011, 848; M.A. Geistfeld, "Due Process and the Deterrence Rationale for Punitive Damages" in L. Meurkens & E. Nordin (eds.), *The Power of Punitive Damages – Is Europe Missing Out?*, Cambridge – Antwerp – Portland, Intersentia, 2012, 115.

226 J. Berch, "The Need for Enforcement of U.S. Punitive Damages Awards by the European Union", 19 *Minnesota Journal of International Law* 2010, 66.

227 Admittedly, as the Court itself notes before establishing the single-digit rule and in support thereof, in both *Haslip* and *BMW* it had already referenced to a 4:1 ratio.

228 *BMW of North America, Inc. v. Gore*, 517 U.S. 582 (1995).

229 *State Farm Mutual Automobile Insurance Co. v. Campbell et al.*, 538 U.S. 425 (2003).

cancer.[230] His wife as representative of the estate alleged that tobacco company Philip Morris had fraudulently convinced her husband by advertisements that smoking did not pose any health risks. The company maintained its publicity strategy in order to dupe the public into smoking cigarettes, despite having knowledge of the cigarettes' negative impact on the smoker's health.[231] Plaintiff's counsel requested the jury to punish the defendant for fraud and negligence but also for the effects of its behaviour on the (smoking) public at large.[232] This strategy refers back to the *BMW v. Gore* case where the jury awarded Dr. Gore punitive damages on the basis of harms to other victims.[233] The jury found in favour of the plaintiff, awarding over USD 800.000 in compensation and USD 79.5 million as punitive damages.[234]

89. The trial court reduced both awards but the Oregon Court of Appeals reinstated the original amounts. In its view the punitive award was not constitutionally excessive.[235] After the Oregon Supreme Court denied Philip Morris' petition for review, the case reached the United States Supreme Court for the first time.[236] The United States Supreme Court decided to vacate the punitive award. It did not issue a written opinion but instructed the Oregon Court of Appeals to reconsider its judgment taking the United States Supreme Court's ruling in *State Farm Mutual Automobile Insurance Co. v. Campbell* into account.[237] The Court of Appeals, nevertheless, reinstated the punitive damages award, arguing that the unique facts of the case called for an exception to the single-digit rule.[238] The Oregon Court opined that juries are allowed to include harm to others than the plaintiff when calculating the amount of punitive damages.[239] Philip Morris' attempt to get this decision overturned proved unsuccessful as the Oregon Supreme Court sided with the lower court.[240] It concluded that a jury instruction allowing for non-party harm in the

---

230 *Philip Morris USA v. Williams*, 549 U.S. 346 (2007).

231 M.A. Geistfeld, "Due Process and the Deterrence Rationale for Punitive Damages" in L. Meurkens & E. Nordin (eds.), *The Power of Punitive Damages – Is Europe Missing Out?*, Cambridge – Antwerp – Portland, Intersentia, 2012, 107.

232 W. Schubert, "Simplifying Punitive Damages: Due Process and the Pursuit of Manageable Awards and Procedures in U.S. Courts", *European Journal of Consumer Law* 2011, 849.

233 J. Berch, "The Need for Enforcement of U.S. Punitive Damages Awards by the European Union", 19 *Minnesota Journal of International Law* 2010, 68, footnote 64.

234 *Philip Morris USA v. Williams*, 48 P.3d, 828 (Oregon Court of Appeals 2002).

235 *Philip Morris USA v. Williams*, 48 P.3d, 840–843 (Oregon Court of Appeals 2002).

236 *Philip Morris USA v. Williams* (*Philip Morris I*), 540 U.S. 801 (2003).

237 *Philip Morris USA v. Williams* (*Philip Morris I*), 540 U.S. 801 (2003); W. Schubert, "Simplifying Punitive Damages: Due Process and the Pursuit of Manageable Awards and Procedures in U.S. Courts", *European Journal of Consumer Law* 2011, 850.

238 *Williams* v. *Philip Morris USA*, 92 P.3d 126, 145 (Oregon Court of Appeals 2004).

239 W. Schubert, "Simplifying Punitive Damages: Due Process and the Pursuit of Manageable Awards and Procedures in U.S. Courts", *European Journal of Consumer Law* 2011, 850.

240 *Williams v. Philip Morris USA*, 127 P. 3d., 1168 (Oregon Supreme Court 2006).

determination of the punitive amount was not in violation of the Due Process Clause.[241]

90. The case's second visit to the United States Supreme Court resulted in the establishment of the non-party harm rule. The highest federal court disagreed with the state courts on the permissibility of the trial judge's instruction. It laid down the prohibition to punish a defendant for injury inflicted on non-parties.[242] When determining the appropriate size of the punitive award, the jury should only consider the future harm the defendant might cause to the plaintiff but not to non-parties. In essence, the judgment thus blocks the possibility of achieving general deterrence through a punitive damages judgment.[243] By introducing the non-party harm rule the United States Supreme Court tried to counter the so-called 'multiple punishments problem'.[244] This issue arises when a civil defendant (who cannot rely on the *non bis in idem*-exception applicable in criminal law) has caused injury to multiple plaintiffs by a single act, faces multiple punitive damages awards for that conduct.[245] The jury can, however, consider the harm to others when evaluating the reprehensibility of the tortfeasor's actions (the first aspect of the *BMW* test) but the trial judge should clarify to the jury that punishment specifically for this harm will be unacceptable.[246]

91. After the United States Supreme Court's ruling, the case travelled back to Oregon. The Oregon Supreme Court yet again reinstated the whole award despite the U.S. Supreme Court's endorsement of the tobacco company's argument on the unconstitutionality of the jury instructions.[247] It argued that there

---

241 *Williams v. Philip Morris USA*, 127 P. 3d., 1181–1182 (Oregon Supreme Court 2006); M.A. Geistfeld, "Due Process and the Deterrence Rationale for Punitive Damages" in L. Meurkens & E. Nordin (eds.), *The Power of Punitive Damages – Is Europe Missing Out?*, Cambridge – Antwerp – Portland, Intersentia, 2012, 107.

242 *Philip Morris II*, 549 U.S., 353 (2007); A.J. Sebok, "Punitive Damages in the United States" in H. Koziol & V. Wilcox (eds.), *Punitive Damages: Common Law and Civil Law Perspectives*, Vienna, Springer, 2009, 192.

243 M.A. Geistfeld, "Due Process and the Deterrence Rationale for Punitive Damages" in L. Meurkens & E. Nordin (eds.), *The Power of Punitive Damages – Is Europe Missing Out?*, Cambridge – Antwerp – Portland, Intersentia, 2012, 108.

244 J. Gash, "Understanding and Solving the Multiple Punishments Problem" in L. Meurkens & E. Nordin (eds.), *The Power of Punitive Damages – Is Europe Missing Out?*, Cambridge – Antwerp – Portland, Intersentia, 2012, 94.

245 J. Gash, "Understanding and Solving the Multiple Punishments Problem" in L. Meurkens & E. Nordin (eds.), *The Power of Punitive Damages – Is Europe Missing Out?*, Cambridge – Antwerp – Portland, Intersentia, 2012, 65.

246 *Philip Morris II*, 549 U.S., 354–355 (2007); A.J. Sebok, "The U.S. Supreme Court's Theory of Common Law Punitive Damages" in L. Meurkens & E. Nordin (eds.), *The Power of Punitive Damages – Is Europe Missing Out?*, Cambridge – Antwerp – Portland, Intersentia, 2012, 137.

247 *Philip Morris v. Williams*, 176 P.3d 1255 (Oregon Supreme Court 2008); A.J. Sebok, "Punitive Damages in the United States" in H. Koziol & V. Wilcox (eds.), *Punitive Damages: Common Law and Civil Law Perspectives*, Vienna, Springer, 2009, 194.

was an independent state law ground to refuse the proposed jury instruction.[248] The U.S. Supreme Court eventually declined to address the matter for a third time.[249]

i. Exxon Shipping Co. v. Baker

92. Even when deciding non-constitutional issues, the United States Supreme Court is prepared to impose substantive limitations on punitive damages.[250] In *Exxon Shipping Co.* v. *Baker* it laid down a maximum punitive-to-compensatory damages ratio of 1:1 for federal maritime tort cases.[251] After the oil tanker Exxon Valdez ran aground in the Gulf of Alaska and spilled hundreds of thousands of barrels, a large group of fishermen, property owners and other victims brought suit against Exxon. As the spill took place in navigable waters, U.S. federal maritime law was applicable.[252] The jury decided to entitle the plaintiffs to USD 507,5 million in compensatory damages and USD 5 billion in punitive damages (later reduced by the trial court to USD 2.5 billion).

93. The United States Supreme Court rendered judgment under federal common law and not under the Due Process Clause. In light of the need to protect against unpredictable awards, it decided to restrict the ratio between punitive and compensatory damages to a maximum of 1:1 absent extraordinary circumstances. Even though the judgment did not concern a constitutional holding, by introducing a hard cap rule in federal maritime law it arguably sends a strong message capable of resonating throughout the whole of common law.[253]

---

248 J. Berch, "The Need for Enforcement of U.S. Punitive Damages Awards by the European Union" 19 *Minnesota Journal of International Law* 2010, 68, footnote 66.

249 *Philip Morris USA Inc.* v. *Williams*, 129 S.Ct. 1436 (2009) (No. 07–1216).

250 J. Berch, "The Need for Enforcement of U.S. Punitive Damages Awards by the European Union", 19 *Minnesota Journal of International Law* 2010, 69; W. Schubert, "Simplifying Punitive Damages: Due Process and the Pursuit of Manageable Awards and Procedures in U.S. Courts", *European Journal of Consumer Law* 2011, 844.

251 *Exxon Shipping* Co. *v. Baker*, 554 U.S. 471 (2008).

252 A.J. Sebok, "The U.S. Supreme Court's Theory of Common Law Punitive Damages" in L. Meurkens & E. Nordin (eds.), *The Power of Punitive Damages – Is Europe Missing Out?*, Cambridge – Antwerp – Portland, Intersentia, 2012, 139.

253 W. Schubert, "Simplifying Punitive Damages: Due Process and the Pursuit of Manageable Awards and Procedures in U.S. Courts", *European Journal of Consumer Law* 2011, 857; A.J. Sebok, "The U.S. Supreme Court's Theory of Common Law Punitive Damages" in L. Meurkens & E. Nordin (eds.), *The Power of Punitive Damages – Is Europe Missing Out?*, Cambridge – Antwerp – Portland, Intersentia, 2012, 141.

1.4.2. LOWER FEDERAL COURTS AND STATE COURTS

94. Aside from the United States Supreme Court, other courts have also been active in imposing boundaries on punitive damages. State courts rely on their states' Constitutions to restrict punitive amounts in an effort to achieve a reasonable relationship between the compensatory and punitive award.[254] However, these constitutional limitations are not the only restrictions that federal and state courts have created. BERCH gives three examples of methods states have employed to – directly or indirectly – control the level of punitive damages awarded.

95. First, some states only allow punitive damages if statutorily authorised.[255] Second, as mentioned before, punitive damages need to satisfy a heightened burden of proof. Instead of the usual civil law standard of the "preponderance of the evidence", the establishment of punitive damages requires "clear and convincing evidence".[256] These mechanisms lower the frequency and amount of punitive awards. Lastly, a number of states require or allow the plaintiff to present evidence of the defendant's financial condition.[257] An insight into the wrongdoer's financial situation enables juries and courts to modulate the appropriate level of monetary punishment.[258]

96. Additionally, the defendant may challenge the excessive nature of the punitive damages award and appeal it before a higher court. The review of the appeal court will examine the reasonableness of the amount and whether the award complies with the standards the state has laid down. It has to be noted that courts are reluctant to overturn the punitive award out of respect for the jury's role as a representative of society.[259]

1.4.3. CONGRESS AND STATE LEGISLATURES

97. On the federal as well as the state level elected lawmakers have enacted statutes that introduce limitations on punitive damages, either through absolute

---

254 J. Berch, "The Need for Enforcement of U.S. Punitive Damages Awards by the European Union", 19 *Minnesota Journal of International Law* 2010, 70.

255 Massachusetts is an example of such a state. See *supra* no. 46.

256 See *supra* no. 55.

257 This is, for instance, the case in California.

258 J. Berch, "The Need for Enforcement of U.S. Punitive Damages Awards by the European Union", 19 *Minnesota Journal of International Law* 2010, 70–72.

259 A.J. Sebok, "Punitive Damages in the United States" in H. Koziol & V. Wilcox (eds.), *Punitive Damages: Common Law and Civil Law Perspectives*, Vienna, Springer, 2009, 188.

dollar caps or maximum ratios between punitive and compensatory damages (*i.e.* so-called multiplier statutes).[260]

98. In 2009 cap statutes were in force in a total of 18 states.[261] Virginia does not allow punitive damages over USD 350.000.[262] Under Alabama law an award of punitive damages shall in most cases not exceed three times the compensatory damages awarded or USD 500.000, whichever is greater.[263] This type of rule seems to combine an absolute cap with a ratio cap. In Kansas the statutory ceiling is attached to the defendant's net worth, in line with the objective to punish but not to destroy the offender. The punitive award should not exceed USD 10 million or 3% of the defendant's net worth, whichever is less.[264] Federal statutes contain similar provisions. In the Civil Rights Act of 1991, for example, punitive damages in cases of intentional discrimination in employment are subjected to a sliding scale cap depending on the number of employees of the defendant.[265]

99. Multiplier statutes allow or require the compensatory award to be multiplied by a factor to calculate the punitive award.[266] The end result is often referred to as multiple damages. These damages are subject to restrictions in the sense that the punitive award cannot be more than the provided statutory multiple (as deemed appropriate by elected officials) of the compensatory damages.[267] Multiplier statutes essentially strike the balance between avoiding unlimited jury discretion and the need to deter heinous conduct.[268] In Ohio, for instance, in most tort cases the acceptable punitive-to-compensatory ratio is two since state law provides that a court shall not enter judgment for punitive damages in excess of two times the amount of the compensatory damages.[269] Section 4 of federal Clayton Antitrust Act equally makes treble damages (*i.e.* punitive damages amounting to twice the compensatory damages[270]) available to parties injured by violations of the Act.

---

260 J. Berch, "The Need for Enforcement of U.S. Punitive Damages Awards by the European Union", 19 *Minnesota Journal of International Law* 2010, 62.

261 A.J. Sebok, "Punitive Damages in the United States" in H. Koziol & V. Wilcox (eds.), *Punitive Damages: Common Law and Civil Law Perspectives*, Vienna, Springer, 2009, 188.

262 Va. Code Ann. §8.01–38.1 (2008).

263 Ala. Code §6–11–21 (a).

264 Mont. Code Ann. §27–1–220(3) (2003).

265 Civil Rights Act of 1991, 42 U.S.C. §1981a(b)(3)(A)-(D) (2006).

266 J. Berch, "The Need for Enforcement of U.S. Punitive Damages Awards by the European Union", 19 *Minnesota Journal of International Law* 2010, 74, footnote 94.

267 J. Berch, "The Need for Enforcement of U.S. Punitive Damages Awards by the European Union", 19 *Minnesota Journal of International Law* 2010, 74–75.

268 J. Perczek, "On Efficiency, Deterrence, and Fairness: A Survey of Punitive Damages Law and a Proposed Jury Instruction", 27 *Suffolk University Law Review* 1993, 866–867; J. Berch, "The Need for Enforcement of U.S. Punitive Damages Awards by the European Union", 19 *Minnesota Journal of International Law* 2010, 74–75.

269 Ohio Revised Code Annotated §2315.21(D)(2)(a).

270 See *supra* footnote no. 90.

100. Both multiplier and cap statutes limit the amount of punitive damages awarded, and these statutes demonstrate the United States' judicial and political commitment to restricting punitive damages awards.[271] These statutes are complemented by the aforementioned judicial trend (on a federal and state level) in limiting those punitive damages that escape any statutory limitations.[272]

1.5. CONCLUSION

101. This chapter discussed the institution of American punitive damages. These damages do not pursue compensation as their main objective but instead focus on punishing and deterring the wrongdoer. They can be traced back to English law where they blossomed from the thirteenth century onwards. In the eighteenth century they found their way to the United States where they have been developed as one of the instruments of private enforcement. Punitive damages are accepted in all but a handful of states as well as on the federal level and are mainly used as a tort law remedy.

102. The chapter further pointed to studies which debunk the myth that the American legal system produces a large number of excessive punitive awards. Furthermore, both at the federal and at the state level legislative and judicial efforts have been undertaken to curb punitive damages awards and the amounts in which they are granted. Especially the United States Supreme Court has established constitutional restraints under the Due Process Clause of the Fourteenth Amendment.

103. The Supreme Court first hinted at the existence of a due process boundary on punitive damages in *Browning-Ferris v. Kelco*. In *Pacific Mutual Life Insurance Co. v. Haslip* it then established a due process right for defendants. The Supreme Court's preference for the procedural prong of the due process right when setting limits in punitive damages cases became clear in the early judgments of *Pacific Mutual Life Insurance Co. v. Haslip, TXO Production Corp. v. Alliance Resources Corp.* and *Honda Motor Co. v. Oberg.*

104. In those decisions the Supreme Court refused to impose a clear substantive due process limit on punitive damages awards, other than the "grossly excessive" standard. In *BMW of North America, Inc. v. Gore*, however,

---

271 J. Berch, "The Need for Enforcement of U.S. Punitive Damages Awards by the European Union", 19 *Minnesota Journal of International Law* 2010, 77; A.J. Sebok, "Punitive Damages in the United States" in H. Koziol & V. Wilcox (eds.), *Punitive Damages: Common Law and Civil Law Perspectives*, Vienna, Springer, 2009, 188.

272 J. Berch, "The Need for Enforcement of U.S. Punitive Damages Awards by the European Union", 19 *Minnesota Journal of International Law* 2010, 73–74.

it clarified this standard and set out three guideposts: (1) the reprehensibility of the defendant's conduct, (2) the ratio between the punitive and compensatory damages awarded and (3) a comparison of the punitive damages to the criminal penalties that could be imposed for similar misconduct. The Supreme Court shed light on the examination of the reprehensible nature of the behaviour by formulating five probative questions: courts and juries should consider whether (1) the harm caused was physical or rather merely economic, (2) the tortious conduct evinced an indifference to or a reckless disregard of the health or safety of others, (3) the victim was financially vulnerable, (4) the conduct involved repeated actions or was an isolated incident and (5) the harm was the result of intentional malice, trickery, or deceit, or mere accident. The application of the Supreme Court's newfound guiding rules led to the rejection of the punitive award on substantive due process grounds.

105. The Supreme Court subsequently returned to its procedural due process approach. The prohibition to consider out-of-state conduct in the assessment of the reprehensibility of the defendant's behaviour in *State Farm Mutual Automobile Insurance Co. v. Campbell* and the non-party harm rule of *Philip Morris USA v. Williams (Philip Morris II)* clearly demonstrate this. However, the Court still showed a willingness to curtail the size of punitive awards. In the *dicta* of *State Farm Mutual Automobile Insurance Co. v. Campbell* it introduced the single-digit rule (9:1), prohibiting punitive-to-compensatory damages ratios exceeding this limit. The Court's 1:1 ceiling in federal maritime law in *Exxon Shipping Co.* v. *Baker* provides further evidence in that regard, even though the case did not involve constitutional issues.

CHAPTER 2

PUNITIVE DAMAGES AND SERVICE OF PROCESS

Serving U.S. Punitive Damages Claims on Defendants in the EU

106. The field of service of process is the first area of private international law in which the Common Law concept of punitive damages comes into contact with continental Europe. The commencement of a law suit in the U.S. requires the service of the claim on the defendant. When the defendant is not domiciled or not present in the U.S., service will have to take place abroad.

107. The United States and all European Union Member States (except – at least for now[273] – Austria and Malta) are Members of the Hague Convention on service abroad of 15 November 1965 (the Hague Service Convention).[274] This instrument provides a mechanism for allowing the formal transmission of judicial or extrajudicial documents in civil and commercial matters from one Contracting State to another, for service in the latter State. Each Contracting State designates a Central Authority which arranges for the document to be served or serves it itself. The Convention facilitates service because it replaces time-consuming means of service (such as service through diplomatic channels). By expediting and simplifying cross-border transmission of documents, the Convention improves legal certainty of service.

108. This chapter looks at issues that have arisen when serving U.S. punitive damages claims in the EU. In Germany there have been instances where service of such a claim has been denied. This part of the book examines the grounds in the Hague Service Convention on which these refusals of service have been based. First, it analyses the cases in which punitive damages have been classified as falling under criminal/public law. As article 1 of the Hague Service Convention provides that the Convention only applies to civil

---

273 See *supra* footnote no. 20.

274 For an overview of the current Members: see <www.hcch.net/index_en.php?act=conventions.status&cid=17>.

and commercial matters, this reasoning allows a refusal to serve punitive damages claims under the Convention. Second, the chapter discusses the cases regarding the exception clause of the Convention. Article 13.1 allows states to refuse service if it would violate the requested state's sovereignty or security. There is German case law denying the service of punitive damages on the basis of this provision.

109. We argue that service of U.S. punitive damages should not be refused. Claims for punitive damages do fall under the scope of the Hague Service Convention as defined in article 1. The requested state also cannot rely on the escape mechanism of article 13.1 to deny service because punitive damages claims do not violate the requested state's sovereignty or security. The requested state should not draw premature conclusions based on the anticipated outcome of the law suit. Any objections against the American proceedings should be brought and scrutinised at the enforcement stage. Refusal would, moreover, be useless as possible objections against service of the claim can be circumvented by simply avoiding service in the EU altogether or by initially limiting the suit to compensatory damages. The methods thereto will be elaborated on.

2.1. ARTICLE 1 OF THE HAGUE SERVICE CONVENTION: THE CIVIL NATURE OF PUNITIVE DAMAGES

110. The ambit of the Hague Service Convention is defined in article 1. The relevant part reads: "*The present Convention shall apply in all cases, in civil or commercial matters, where there is occasion to transmit a judicial or extrajudicial document for service abroad*". Only documents that need to be transmitted in civil and commercial matters can, therefore, be served through the mechanism introduced by the Convention. Although not explicitly excluded by the text of Convention, it follows that actions belonging to the realm of public law do not fall under the material scope of the Convention. Consequently, if punitive damages were to be labelled as public in nature, they would not be covered by the Convention and service of a claim for such damages could be denied under the Convention.

111. The distinction between public and private law actions triggers the question of the characterisation of a claim. Characterisation can be described as the placing of the specific action into its correct legal category. In purely national cases domestic law will govern the issue of characterisation. In private international law, however, multiple legal orders are involved and it is conceivable that they all offer differ solutions, creating a conflict of characterisation.[275] It is, therefore, essential to establish which legal system will determine the public or private nature of the action for which service is required.

112. As VON HEIN points out, several options are available to resolve the question of characterisation. One could look at the law of the requesting state to determine whether the claim is a civil matter. Another method would be to give precedence to the law of the requested state. Further possibilities are an alternative approach, where the matter will be regarded as civil if at least one of the laws considers it to be so, or a cumulative approach, where both legal systems need to qualify the claim as civil. All these methods are flawed. The use of national rules for the interpretation of the notions in the Convention leads to divergent results. Furthermore, cumulative characterisation would restrict the applicability of the Convention to a large extent, whereas an alternative characterisation would be overstretching its ambit.[276] We are, therefore, of the opinion that an autonomous interpretation of article 1 of the Hague Service Convention should prevail.[277] Such an approach brings consistency and uniformity and has, for instance, been followed for the Brussels I, Rome I and Rome II Regulations as well.

113. The Convention itself does not define the term "civil or commercial" and its negotiating history is also not helpful as to the intended meaning of the phrase. Likewise, neither the earlier conventions using the term (*i.e.* the 1905 and 1954 Hague Civil Procedure Conventions) nor their drafting histories offer a clear definition.[278]

114. The Vienna Convention on the Law of Treaties[279], which the United States has never ratified, sets out the international rules on treaty interpretation.[280] It lays down that a treaty should be interpreted in good faith in accordance with the

---

275 V. Allarousse, "A Comparative Approach to the Conflict of Characterisation in Private International Law", 23 *Case Western Reserve Journal of International Law* 1991, 479.

276 J. von Hein, "Recent German Jurisprudence on Cooperation with the United States" in E. Gottschalk, R. Michaels, G. Rühl & J. von Hein (eds.), *Conflict of Laws in a Globalized World*, Cambridge, Cambridge University Press, 2007, 118–119.

277 M. Requejo Isidro, "Punitive Damages From a Private International Law Perspective" in H. Koziol & V. Wilcox (eds.), *Punitive Damages: Common Law and Civil Law Perspectives*, Vienna, Springer, 2009, 239; Oberlandesgericht Koblenz 27 June 2005, *Praxis des Internationalen Privat- und Verfahrensrechts* 2006, 31–34.

278 G. Born, *International Civil Litigation in United States Courts: Commentary and Materials*, The Hague, Kluwer Law International, 1996, 800.

279 Articles 31–33 of the Vienna Convention on the Law of Treaties of 23 May 1969, 1155 United Nations Treaty Series 331.

280 The Vienna Convention does not apply to the United States. However, it has been accepted that articles 31 and 32 reflect customary international law: L.F. Damrosch et al., *International Law*, St. Paul, Minnesota, West Group, 2001, 453–454.

ordinary meaning to be given to the terms of the treaty in their context and in light of its object and purpose (article 31). This basic rule has only limited added value in the interpretation of the phrase "civil and commercial". Furthermore, article 32 of the Vienna Convention allows a deviation from the adherence to the text. The preparatory materials may be taken into account if the meaning under article 31 is ambiguous or leads to an absurd or unreasonable result. As stated before, these preparatory documents exhibit a clear lack of guidance on this point.

2.1.1. THE MINORITY VIEW: DENYING THE CIVIL CHARACTER

115. As mentioned, Germany is the only European country where there is case law on the refusal of service of punitive damages. The commentaries dealing with these cases are, therefore, mainly found in the German doctrine. A very small part of the German scholarship defended the position that punitive damages are not "civil" (or "commercial") for the purposes of the Hague Service Convention.[281] The foundation of this opinion lies in the objectives pursued by punitive damages. Punishment and deterrence are for the most part public goals and the action to obtain such damages, therefore, does not constitute a civil or commercial matter.

116. This point of view has always lacked widespread support. It has, nevertheless, been followed in a relatively recent case before the *Oberlandesgericht* (Higher Regional Court) Koblenz.[282] A group of consumers had brought a class action suit in the U.S. District Court for the District of Minnesota against a number of pharmaceutical companies. One of the defendants was the German corporation Boehringer-Ingelheim. In their claim the plaintiffs asserted multiple antitrust violations and sought treble damages. Many consumers in the United States had noticed the lower prices of prescription drugs on the Canadian market. For that reason, they ordered their drugs online with pharmacies in Canada or through internet retailers. In order to safeguard their profits American and European pharmaceutical companies pressured the clients of their Canadian subsidiaries into not selling to U.S. residents.

---

281 See for instance: H.H. Hollmann, "Auslandszustellung in U.S.-amerikanischen Zivil- undVerwaltungssachen", *Recht der internationalen Wirtschaft* 1982, 786; C. Wölki, "Das Haager Zustellungsabkommen und die U.S.A.", *Recht der internationalen Wirtschaft* 1985, 533.

282 Oberlandesgericht Koblenz 27 June 2005, *Praxis des Internationalen Privat- und Verfahrensrechts* 2006, 25.

117. Service of the claim in Germany was necessary to bring Boehringer-Ingelheim into the proceedings before the federal court in Minnesota. In Germany the Ministry of Justice of each *Bundesland* (state) or the president of a court within a *Bundesland* acts as Central Authority.[283] The serving of the claim form needs to take place in the state where the defendant has its principal place of business. When a dispute arose as to whether service could be performed on Boehringer-Ingelheim, the *Oberlandesgericht* Koblenz had to rule on the matter. In such proceedings the plaintiff challenges the decision of the Central Authority directly before the *Oberlandesgericht*.[284] The Central Authority acts as defendant and no appeal is allowed.[285]

118. The Koblenz court had to decide whether the serving of the claim for treble damages constituted a "civil or commercial" matter under article 1 of the Hague Service Convention. Using the autonomous method of interpreting the notion of a "civil or commercial" matter, it noted that the classification of the damages depended on the weight of the interests (public or private) considered.[286] The court argued that, at least in antitrust cases, collective actions for treble damages are aimed at upholding free competition, an objective that takes precedence over the interests of private parties seeking compensatory damages.[287] The public goal thus trumps the private interests. This brought the court to the conclusion that the claim belonged to the public realm and, therefore, fell outside of the scope of article 1 of the Convention. Service on the German defendant was subsequently denied.[288]

119. This decision of the *Oberlandesgericht* Koblenz is open to criticism.[289] First, the joining of several private law claims in one single class action procedure

---

[283] See for the list of German Central Authorities: <www.hcch.net/upload/auth14_de.pdf>.

[284] §23 *Einführungsgesetz zum Gerichtsverfassungsgesetz* (Introductory Act to the Judicature Act).

[285] G. Wegen & J. Sherer, "Recognition and Enforcement of US Punitive Damages Judgments in Germany – A Recent Decision of the German Federal Court of Justice", 21 *International Business Lawyer* 1993, 487.

[286] Oberlandesgericht Koblenz 27 June 2005, *Praxis des Internationalen Privat- und Verfahrensrechts* 2006, 25; M. Requejo Isidro, "Punitive Damages From a Private International Law Perspective" in H. Koziol & V. Wilcox (eds.), *Punitive Damages: Common Law and Civil Law Perspectives*, Vienna, Springer, 2009, 241, footnote 17.

[287] Oberlandesgericht Koblenz 27 June 2005, *Praxis des Internationalen Privat- und Verfahrensrechts* 2006, 31–4; J. von Hein, "Recent German Jurisprudence on Cooperation with the United States" in E. Gottschalk, R. Michaels, G. Rühl & J. von Hein (eds.), *Conflict of Laws in a Globalized World*, Cambridge, Cambridge University Press, 2007, 119.

[288] Oberlandesgericht Koblenz 27 June 2005, *Praxis des Internationalen Privat- und Verfahrensrechts* 2006, 33–34.

[289] See for instance: A. Piekenbrock, "Zur Zustellung kartellrechtlicher trebledamages-Klagen in Deutschland", *Praxis des Internationalen Privat- und Verfahrensrechts* 2006, 6.

does not alter the civil character of each individual claim.[290] The fact that the treble damages requested contribute to the enforcement of antitrust rules and have a deterrent effect on potential wrongdoers does not change their legal nature.[291] Treble damages remain a private law instrument available to private plaintiffs, despite partially pursuing more public goals such as punishment and deterrence of those who breach antitrust laws. All forms of punitive damages are intended to fulfil such public law objectives. In the case of treble damages this private enforcement element is simply more apparent than with regard to "normal" punitive damages. It is thus understandable that the facts of the case confused the court.

120. The Koblenz court did not solely rely on the classification of the claim under article 1 of the Convention to deny service but also argued an infringement of Germany's sovereignty and security (as provided for in article 13.1[292]). This in itself could indicate the court's uncertainty about the validity of its reasoning with regard to the Convention's scope.[293]

2.1.2. THE OVERWHELMING MAJORITY VIEW: CLASSIFICATION AS CIVIL CLAIM

121. In disputes about the service of punitive damages, a number of courts have taken the – in our view correct – position that claims for such damages are to be categorised as civil. Reference can be made to a decision of the *Oberlandesgericht* Munich of 9 May 1989.[294] The *Oberlandesgericht* had to rule on the Bavarian Ministry of Justice's (the competent Central Authority) refusal to serve a complaint (filed in an American court) on a company in Munich. The law suit in the United States was brought by an insurance company domiciled there and directed against an insurance company doing business in Munich. The American insurance company had placed a reinsurance contract with the German company. The latter did not honour the former's claim for

---

290 J. von Hein, "Recent German Jurisprudence on Cooperation with the United States" in E. Gottschalk, R. Michaels, G. Rühl & J. von Hein (eds.), *Conflict of Laws in a Globalized World*, Cambridge, Cambridge University Press, 2007, 119.

291 J. von Hein, "Recent German Jurisprudence on Cooperation with the United States" in E. Gottschalk, R. Michaels, G. Rühl & J. von Hein (eds.), *Conflict of Laws in a Globalized World*, Cambridge, Cambridge University Press, 2007, 119–120.

292 For an extensive discussion of the exception ground of article 13.1: see *infra* no. 129 *et seq.*

293 Oberlandesgericht Koblenz 27 June 2005, *Praxis des Internationalen Privat- und Verfahrensrechts* 2006, 34–8; J. von Hein, "Recent German Jurisprudence on Cooperation with the United States" in E. Gottschalk, R. Michaels, G. Rühl & J. von Hein (eds.), *Conflict of Laws in a Globalized World*, Cambridge, Cambridge University Press, 2007, 120.

294 Oberlandesgericht München 9 May 1989, *Recht der Internationalen Wirtschaft* 1993, 70, translation by B.A. Ristau, *International Legal Materials* 1989, 1570.

reimbursement. The plaintiff sought restitution and damages but also requested punitive damages for malicious and intentional delay in paying the restitution amounts. The Bavarian Ministry of Justice declined to serve the documents. The plaintiff requested the *Oberlandesgericht* to order the Ministry of Justice to serve the claim.

122. Before the court, the Bavarian Ministry of Justice submitted *inter alia* that the request related to a criminal and not to a civil matter. It advanced the argument that the damages had a penal character. As a consequence the request would fall outside of the ambit of the Convention.

123. The *Oberlandesgericht* of Munich, however, disagreed with this line of thought. It ruled that punitive damages do not form part of criminal law. Although their primary objectives are punishment and deterrence, they are civil in nature. The court identified three characteristics of punitive damages which are decisive in that regard. First, punitive damages arise out of individual claims by private parties against other private parties. The assertion of such claims is a discretionary decision of these private actors. Second, the damages benefit only the injured party.[295] Third, the court enumerated a number of formal criteria to distinguish punitive damages from criminal sanctions.[296] It noted that the defendant who is ordered to pay punitive damages is not regarded as having been convicted of a crime. The judgment is not added to the defendant's criminal record. The purpose of criminal law, on the other hand, is the prosecution of wrongdoers by the sovereign, leading to the criminal conviction of the offender. The court, therefore, held that the Bavarian Ministry of Justice was compelled to give effect to the request for service, despite the claim for punitive damages.[297]

124. The criteria set out by the court bear some similarities to those put forward by the Special Commission of the Hague Conference on Private International Law. One month before the ruling of the *Oberlandesgericht* Munich a Special Commission of the Hague Conference on Private International Law already reflected on the Bavarian Central Authority's refusal to perform service of punitive damages claims. The experts supported a liberal interpretation of the scope of the Hague Service Convention. They argued that, to the extent they are to be paid to the plaintiff[298], punitive damages are an element of a civil

---

295 This is not always the case as split-recovery schemes exist in the United States: see *supra* no. 48.

296 M. Requejo Isidro, "Punitive Damages From a Private International Law Perspective" in H. Koziol & V. Wilcox (eds.), *Punitive Damages: Common Law and Civil Law Perspectives*, Vienna, Springer, 2009, 240.

297 Oberlandesgericht München 9 May 1989, *Recht der Internationalen Wirtschaft* 1993, 483.

298 Doubts as to the classification of the action could, therefore, still arise when punitive damages are sought by a public organism acting in its official capacity or when part of a punitive award is allocated to the treasury as is the case with split-recovery statutes: M. Requejo Isidro,

or commercial action. Furthermore, the amount claimed is irrelevant in the assessment of the civil nature of the action because the amount sought has no impact on the classification of the claim.[299]

125. The reasoning of the *Oberlandesgericht* Munich was later followed by a decision of the *Oberlandesgericht* Düsseldorf[300] and by another decision of the *Oberlandesgericht* Munich of the same year.[301] Together with most legal scholars we approve of this position.[302] Further support can be found in the *Napster* judgment of the German Constitutional Court (*Bundesverfassungsgericht*). In that decision the Constitutional Court implicitly accepted the civil nature of a class action suit for excessive damages as it focused on other grounds instead of elaborating on the scope of the Convention.[303] More recently, at least five appellate judgments have reaffirmed this traditional point of view.[304]

126. The Munich court in its 1989 judgment did not find it necessary to decide on the issue of characterisation as it believed each method to lead to the same result: punitive damages are a civil institution.[305] As indicated, we believe an autonomous interpretation of the provisions of the Hague Service Convention should prevail.[306] Even if we would employ the laws of the requesting state or the requested state, the outcome would indeed be identical. This can serve as guidance when interpreting the notion of "civil or commercial" in the Convention.

"Punitive Damages From a Private International Law Perspective" in H. Koziol & V. Wilcox (eds.), *Punitive Damages: Common Law and Civil Law Perspectives*, Vienna, Springer, 2009, 241.

299 Paragraphs 8.b to 8.d of the Special Commission Report on the Operation of the Hague Service Convention and the Hague Evidence Convention, 17–20 April 1989, *International Legal Materials* 1989, 1559.

300 Oberlandesgericht Düsseldorf 19 February 1992, *Neue Juristische Wochenschrift* 1992, 3110.

301 Oberlandesgericht München 15 July 1992, *Recht der Internationalen Wirtschaft* 1993, 70.

302 See for instance: H. Morisse, "Die Zustellung U.S.-amerikanischer Punitive-damages-Klagen in Deutschland", *Recht der Internationalen Wirtschaft* 1995, 371; H. Koch, "Zur Praxis der Rechtshilfe im amerikanisch-deutschen Prozessrecht – Ergebnis seeiner Umfragezu den Haager Zustellungs- und Beweisübereinkommen", *Praxis des Internationalen Privat- und Verfahrensrechts* 1985, 246.

303 Bundesverfassungsgericht 25 July 2003, *BverfGE* 108, 238.

304 Oberlandesgericht Naumburg 9 February 2006, *Wirtschaft und Wettbewerb* 2006, 932; Oberlandesgericht Celle 20 July 2006, *Niedersächsische Rechtspflege* 2006, 275; Oberlandesgericht Düsseldorf 21 April 2006, *Recht der Internationalen Wirtschaft* 2006, 629; Oberlandesgericht München 7 June 2006, 9 VA 3/04, *unpublished*; Oberlandesgericht Düsseldorf 22 September 2008, I-3 VA 6/08, available at <http://openjur.de/u/133301.html>; J. von Hein, "Recent German Jurisprudence on Cooperation with the United States" in E. Gottschalk, R. Michaels, G. Rühl & J. von Hein (eds.), *Conflict of Laws in a Globalized World*, Cambridge, Cambridge University Press, 2007, 120.

305 Oberlandesgericht München 9 May 1989, *Recht der Internationalen Wirtschaft* 1989, 483.

306 See *supra* no. 112.

127. We find further support for our view in American and German case law outside the field of service of process. In *Browning-Ferris Industries of Vermont, Inc. v. Kelco Disposal, Inc.* the U.S. Supreme Court clearly built up its reasoning from the premise that U.S. law views punitive damages actions as civil in nature.[307] In the landmark case of *John Doe v. Eckhard Schmitz* concerning the enforcement of an American judgment containing punitive damages the German Supreme Court (*Bundesgerichtshof*) confirmed the civil character of punitive damages as well. The *Bundesgerichtshof* viewed them as private remedies and not as criminal sanctions. It defined civil cases as matters which relate to the existence or non-existence of private rights and the legal relationships between parties of equal standing. In the case before it the punitive damages had to be paid to the victim. The *Bundesgerichtshof* did not decide whether a different stance would be appropriate when the award is to be paid to the state.[308]

128. In sum, we endorse the argument that punitive damages are "civil" for the purposes of the Hague Service Convention. An action seeking punitive damages falls under the scope of the Convention as defined in its article 1. A Central Authority should, therefore, not refuse to serve documents concerning such a suit on the basis of the ambit of the Convention. There is, however, another ground for refusal of which the validity could be scrutinised.

2.2. ARTICLE 13.1 OF HAGUE SERVICE CONVENTION: AN INFRINGEMENT OF THE SOVEREIGNTY OR SECURITY OF THE REQUESTED STATE

129. A further ground used against allowing service of a foreign claim for punitive damages is the provision found in article 13 of the Hague Service Convention. This article provides, in its first paragraph, that: "*Where a request for service complies with the terms of the present Convention, the State addressed may refuse to comply therewith only if it deems that compliance would infringe its sovereignty or security.*" Again, Germany is the country in which punitive damages claims have been refused service due to an infringement of article 13.1.[309]

307 *Browning-Ferris Industries of Vermont, Inc., et al.* v. *Kelco Disposal, Inc., et al.*, 492 U.S. 257 (1989).

308 BGH, 4 June 1992, *BGHZ* 118, 312, English translation in 32 *International Legal Materials* 1993, 1320. See *infra* no. 234 for an extensive commentary.

309 M. Requejo Isidro, "Punitive Damages From a Private International Law Perspective" in H. Koziol & V. Wilcox (eds.), *Punitive Damages: Common Law and Civil Law Perspectives*, Vienna, Springer, 2009, 243.

2.2.1. THE FIRST CASES: REJECTION OF THE CENTRAL AUTHORITIES' REFUSALS

130. Towards the end of the 1980s, Central Authorities in various *Länder* took a more hostile position with regard to requests for service of U.S. actions seeking punitive damages.[310] Germany, however, found no support among other European countries for this increasingly unsympathetic stance.[311] The case law at that time also did not follow the Central Authorities' unreceptive attitude.[312] Judges reasoned that they should not rule on the merits of the American cases at such an early stage of the proceedings. Instead, the question of the compatibility of punitive damages with German law should be dealt with at the enforcement stage.

131. The above-mentioned[313] judgment of the *Oberlandesgericht* Munich of 9 May 1989 exemplifies the stance taken in the early cases. In addition to the argument based on article 1 of the Convention, the Bavarian Ministry of Justice invoked article 13.1 to refuse the request for service of a claim for punitive damages. The *Oberlandesgericht* first made clear that it did not want to rule on the nature of the escape clause in article 13.1. It did not find it necessary to decide whether the infringement of national public policy or an international public policy standard is required to justify the application of the refusal ground in article 13.1. The Munich court then explained that in the case at hand the service of punitive damages does not violate either domestic public policy or international public policy. Service can only be refused under very limited circumstances and in exceptionally weighty cases. Therefore, a Central Authority can only refuse service if transmittance of the claim would cause grave injury to the legal order of the requested state. In the case before it, the Court did not find such situation. It, therefore, quashed the Central Authority's decision and allowed service against the German defendant.[314]

---

310 C. Böhmer, "Spannungen im deutsch-amerikanischen Rechtsverkehr in Zivilsachen", *Neue Juristische Wochenschrift* 1990, 3050.

311 C. Böhmer, "Spannungen im deutsch-amerikanischen Rechtsverkehr in Zivilsachen", *Neue Juristische Wochenschrift* 1990, 3051; J. von Hein, "Recent German Jurisprudence on Cooperation with the United States" in E. Gottschalk, R. Michaels, G. Rühl & J. von Hein (eds.), *Conflict of Laws in a Globalized World*, Cambridge, Cambridge University Press, 2007, 109.

312 See for instance: Oberlandesgericht München 9 May 1989, *Recht der Internationalen Wirtschaft* 1989, 483; Oberlandesgericht Frankfurt am Main 21 March 1991, *Praxis des Internationalen Privat- und Verfahrensrechts* 1992, 166; Oberlandesgericht Düsseldorf 19 February 1992, *Neue Juristische Wochenschrift* 1992, 3110; Oberlandesgericht München 15 July 1992, *Recht der Internationalen Wirtschaft* 1993, 70.

313 See *supra* no. 121.

314 Oberlandesgericht München 9 May 1989, *Recht der Internationalen Wirtschaft* 1989, 484, *International Legal Materials* 1989, 1574–1575; K.J. Beucher & J.B. Sandage, "United States Punitive Damage Awards in German Courts: The Evolving German position on Service and Enforcement", 23 *Vanderbilt Journal of Transnational Law* 1990–1991, 979.

132. The fact that the Higher Regional Courts all adopted the same position made it impossible to obtain a judgment from the *Bundesgerichtshof* on the matter. German law provides that the highest federal court can only intervene in cases of international judicial assistance if an *Oberlandesgericht* intends to depart from earlier decisions by other Higher Regional Courts.[315] The only way of obtaining a ruling on the federal level was, therefore, to file a constitutional complaint with the *Bundesverfassungsgericht* (German Constitutional Court).[316]

2.2.2. *BUNDESVERFASSUNGSGERICHT* 1994: THE FIRST SENATE

133. In 1994 the *Bundesverfassungsgericht* decided on such a constitutional complaint. The complaint challenged an order by the Berlin *Kammergericht* (the *Oberlandesgericht*/Higher Regional Court for the state of Berlin) allowing service. In that case an American company had concluded a distribution agreement for pharmaceutical products with the American subsidiary of a German company. When differences arose out of the relationship, the American firm brought proceedings in Pittsburgh against its counterparty and the German mother company (with seat in Berlin). The American plaintiff sought compensatory damages (at least USD 2 million) and punitive damages in an unspecified amount. Service on the American subsidiary took place without any problems. However, service on the German company in the United States was unsuccessful. The plaintiff subsequently requested the Central Authority in Berlin to serve the claim under the Hague Service Convention. The dissatisfied German mother company decided to challenge the Central Authority's approval before the Berlin *Kammergericht*. The Berlin court rejected the application to lift the Central Authority's decision in a judgment of 5 July 1994. The German company then resorted to the Constitutional Court for a constitutional review of the judgment. It alleged a violation of its civil rights under article 2.1 (free development of personality)[317, 318] of the German Grundgesetz (Constitution) in connection with the principle of the rule of law.

---

315 *Einführungsgesetz zum Gerichtsverfassungsgesetz* (Introductory Law to the Code Organizational Statute) 27 January 1877, RGB l. I, 77, last amended by Gesetz 19 April 2006 BGBl. I, 866, article 14, §29 (1); J. von Hein, "Recent German Jurisprudence on Cooperation with the United States" in E. Gottschalk, R. Michaels, G. Rühl & J. von Hein (eds.), *Conflict of Laws in a Globalized World*, Cambridge, Cambridge University Press, 2007, 109.

316 J. von Hein, "Recent German Jurisprudence on Cooperation with the United States" in E. Gottschalk, R. Michaels, G. Rühl & J. von Hein (eds.), *Conflict of Laws in a Globalized World*, Cambridge, Cambridge University Press, 2007, 109.

317 Article 2.1: "*Every person shall have the right to free development of his personality insofar as he does not violate the rights of others or offend against the constitutional order or the moral law.*"

318 Article 2.1 forms the basis of a general right of personality in Germany. See also *infra* no. 422 *et seq*.

a. The injunction of 3 August 1994 prohibiting service

134. The *Bundesverfassungsgericht* rendered two decisions in this case. In the first, of 3 August 1994, it issued a temporary[319] order forbidding service.[320] In the judgment the Constitutional Court gave an overview of the main findings of the Berlin *Kammergericht*.

135. The Berlin court's reasoning seemed to reflect the position that is typical for German case law. The *Kammergericht* did not find a ground for refusal under article 13.1 of the Hague Service Convention. It had referred to the important judgment of the *Bundesgerichtshof* in *John Doe v. Eckhard Schmitz* concerning the enforcement of U.S. punitive damages.[321] The *Bundesgerichtshof* had declared that a foreign judgment awarding lump sum punitive damages of a not inconsiderable amount in addition to the damages for material and immaterial losses generally cannot be enforced in Germany.[322, 323] The Berlin court ruled that the unenforceability of punitive damages in Germany does not prevent the German authorities from cooperating in the service of such actions in Germany. In that regard it underlined the possibility that the enforcement of the American judgment (resulting from a claim for which service in Germany was requested) takes place in the United States (instead of Germany). It noted that enterprises active in international business must accept the risk of having their foreign assets seized by a foreign jurisdiction. According to the Berlin court any objections against the enforcement of a foreign ruling in Germany can be raised at the enforcement stage, when the legal basis and the amount of the damages is known. The purposes of the Hague Service Convention would not be served by a comprehensive and lengthy study of the claim at the time of service. Mere speculations about the future decision of a foreign court should not prevent the service of the claim.[324]

136. The *Bundesverfassungsgericht* then examined the petitioner's application for a temporary order. The latter had argued that service of the action would irreparably disadvantage it. Under U.S. law it would be considered part of the U.S. proceedings. This would remain so even if the *Bundesverfassungsgericht* would decide in a later judgment on the merits that judicial assistance should not have been granted.

---

319 For a period of six months or until a decision on the merits was rendered, whichever came first.

320 Bundesverfassungsgericht 3 August 1994, *Neue Juristische Wochenschrift* 1994, 3281, translation by G. Wegen & C. Kuner, *International Legal Materials* 1995, 978.

321 BGH 4 June 1992, *Neue Juristische Wochenschrift* 1992, 3096–3106.

322 BGH 4 June 1992, *Neue Juristische Wochenschrift* 1992, 3100–3102.

323 For a detailed analysis of this case, see *infra* no. 234 *et seq.*

324 Bundesverfassungsgericht 3 August 1994, *International Legal Materials* 1995, 982–983.

137. The Constitutional Court applied its usual two-step test to determine the necessity of the temporary order. It first established whether the constitutional complaint proved to be inadmissible or clearly unfounded. Such a finding would lead to an immediate rejection of the request. Since this was not the case, the *Bundesverfassungsgericht* moved to the second prong of the test. It compared the consequences of the granting of the temporary order with the consequences of not granting such an order. It argued that if the order was issued and the complaint was later found to lack merit, the U.S. proceedings would merely have been delayed. The U.S. plaintiff would thereby suffer no irrevocable legal disadvantage. It further asserted that the relations between Germany and the U.S. would also not have been seriously harmed. If, however, the order was not granted and the *Bundesverfassungsgericht* would later hold the judicial assistance to be unconstitutional, the Constitutional Court stated that one is to assume that the petitioner has become part of the U.S. proceedings. The petitioner would thus be exposed to a judgment which does not meet German constitutional standards. In the eyes of the *Bundesverfassungsgericht* the possibility of unenforceability of the foreign judgment (in accordance with the *Bundesgerichtshof*'s decision in *John Doe v. Eckhard Schmitz*) in Germany does not fully protect the petitioner because its assets in the United States could be seized to execute the U.S. judgment.[325]

b. The decision on the merits: 7 December 1994

138. In its decision of 7 December 1994 on the merits of the constitutional complaint the *Bundesverfassungsgericht* ruled that service of the U.S. claim for *inter alia* punitive damages would not violate the German Constitution.[326] The German company's civil right under article 2.1 of the German Constitution in connection with the principle of the rule of law is not infringed by the Berlin *Kammergericht*'s decision to allow service.[327]

139. Article 2.1 guarantees freedom of action to any person. However, this right is subjected to certain limits as specified in the last part of the provision ("*insofar as he does not violate the rights of others or offend against the constitutional order or the moral law*"). Any rule of law that meets the procedural and substantive requirements of the Constitution is considered part of the constitutional order and can, therefore, impose a restriction on article 2.1.[328] The Hague Service Convention can thus be considered as a source of law capable of limiting the

---

325 Bundesverfassungsgericht 3 August 1994, *International Legal Materials* 1995, 984–985.

326 Bundesverfassungsgericht 7 December 1994, *Neue Juristische Wochenschrift* 1995, 649, translation by G. Wegen & C. Kuner, *International Legal Materials* 1995, 986.

327 Bundesverfassungsgericht 7 December 1994, *International Legal Materials* 1995, 989.

328 Bundesverfassungsgericht 23 May 1980, *BVerfGE* 54, 143, *Neue Juristische Wochenschrift* 1980, 2572.

right of freedom of development of personality. The *Bundesverfassungsgericht* can review each restriction of the rights guaranteed by article 2.1 for their justification and their adherence to the principle of proportionality.[329] In other words, the restriction on the constitutional right of the German defendant needs to be justified and proportional.

140. The Constitutional Court did not see the need to decide whether service of process constitutes an intrusion on the right guaranteed by article 2.1 of the Constitution. It found that, even if there was an intrusion, this invasion of rights was compatible with article 2.1. The service under the Hague Service Conventions meets the constitutional requirements for a justified intrusion on the right protected by article 2.1. The Hague Service Convention pursues important interests of the common good which justify intrusion into the right of freedom of action. The Constitutional Court referred to the aims of timely service of foreign judicial and extrajudicial documents and to the improved judicial assistance through the simplification of the service procedure.[330]

141. As to proportionality, the *Bundesverfassungsgericht* equally did not see any problems with the Hague Service Convention. Signatory states are not allowed to refuse service when they are of the opinion that the plaintiff's claim conflicts with their internal public policy. Service can only be denied when it endangers the sovereignty or security of the requested state (article 13.1).[331] With this statement, classified by Rasmussen-Bonne as an *obiter dictum*[332], the Court shed light on the nature of the escape mechanism of article 13.1 of the Hague Service Convention. The Court did not attempt to formulate an exhaustive definition of this narrow concept[333] but did correctly distinguish the exception in article 13.1 from domestic public policy.[334] If domestic public policy would be the yardstick, the objectives of the Convention would be significantly hindered. An examination of the complaint's compatibility with internal public policy creates long delays in service which jeopardise the aim of smooth international

329 I.L. Lenhardt, "Service of U.S. Punitive Damages Complaint Passes Constitutional Muster in Germany", 29 *Vanderbilt Journal of Transnational Law* 1996, 296.

330 Bundesverfassungsgericht 7 December 1994, *International Legal Materials* 1995, 990.

331 Bundesverfassungsgericht 7 December 1994, *International Legal Materials* 1995, 990.

332 H.E. Rasmussen-Bonne, "The Pendulum Swings Back: The Cooperative Approach of German Courts to International Service of Process" in P. Hay, L. Vekas, Y. Elkana & N. Dimitrijevic (eds.), *Resolving International Conflicts – Liber Amicorum Tibor Varady*, Budapest – New York, Central European University Press, 2009, 248.

333 P. Huber, "Playing the same old song – German courts, the "Napster"-case and the international law of service of process" in H.P. Mansel, T. Pfeiffer, H. Kronke, C. Kohler & R. Hausmann (eds.), *Festschrift für Erik Jayme*, Munich, Sellier European Law Publishers, 2004, 363.

334 J. von Hein, "Recent German Jurisprudence on Cooperation with the United States" in E. Gottschalk, R. Michaels, G. Rühl & J. von Hein (eds.), *Conflict of Laws in a Globalized World*, Cambridge, Cambridge University Press, 2007, 111.

judicial assistance. Moreover, extending national legal concepts to other countries forms an obstacle to the goal of facilitating proceedings abroad by a foreign plaintiff against a domestic defendant.[335]

142. The Constitutional Court further pointed out that the Convention improves the legal position of German parties. Persons or companies domiciled or registered in Germany cannot become involved in foreign proceedings of which they have no knowledge. Moreover, the Convention provides for safeguards to ensure that German defendants can defend themselves effectively. Signatory countries were expected to do away with forms of domestic service on foreigners. To the extent that service abroad on foreigners under national law is necessary, the Convention guarantees service of the claim in such a way that the recipient is given a fair hearing before the foreign court.[336]

143. The *Bundesverfassungsgericht* found the service of an action for *inter alia* punitive damages not unreasonable. It did not answer the question whether the *Bundesgerichtshof*'s ruling in *John Doe v. Eckhard Schmitz* (that punitive damages are a sanction falling within the State's monopoly on punishment) should be binding as a matter of constitutional law. Similarly, it did not rule whether service of a claim would be in accordance with article 2.1 of the Constitution if the aim of the action clearly violates non-derogable principles of a free, democratic State under the rule of law, as incorporated in international human right conventions. This criterion is called the "obvious violation test".[337] The Constitutional Court did, however, state that non-derogable principles of the free State under the rule of law are, in any case, not violated by the mere possibility that punitive damages may be awarded against the defendant. Article 13.1 could, therefore, not be employed to refuse the request for service in the case before the Court.[338]

2.2.3. *BUNDESVERFASSUNGSGERICHT* 2003: THE SECOND SENATE IN THE *NAPSTER* CASE

144. A decade later the German Constitutional Court again ruled on the issue of refusal of service under article 13.1 of the Hague Service Convention.[339] The litigation before the *Bundesverfassungsgericht* found its roots in the legal battle

[335] Bundesverfassungsgericht 7 December 1994, *International Legal Materials* 1995, 990–991.

[336] Bundesverfassungsgericht 7 December 1994, *International Legal Materials* 1995, 991.

[337] P. Huber, "Playing the same old song – German courts, the "Napster"-case and the international law of service of process" in H.P. Mansel, T. Pfeiffer, H. Kronke, C. Kohler & R. Hausmann (eds.), *Festschrift für Erik Jayme*, Munich, Sellier European Law Publishers, 2004, 366.

[338] Bundesverfassungsgericht 7 December 1994, *International Legal Materials* 1995, 993–994.

[339] Bundesverfassungsgericht 25 July 2003, *BVerfGE* 108, 238.

surrounding Napster, the now-defunct peer-to-peer file sharing service. The company filed for bankruptcy in 2002 after U.S. District Court Judge Marilyn PATEL had issued an injunction ordering Napster to remove all copyrighted material from its service.[340] A group of U.S. music authors and publishers subsequently initiated a class action against the German publishing house Bertelsmann AG before the District Court for the Southern District of New York. The latter had given loans to Napster in exchange for the option to buy a controlling interest in the company (a so-called leveraged buy-out). It never exercised this option. However, the plaintiffs claimed the loans had prolonged the existence of the file sharing service. Bertelsmann had, therefore, aided and abetted to the infringement of the plaintiff's copyrights. The plaintiffs sued for an amount of USD 17 billion. They arrived at this number by multiplying over 100.000 counts of copyright infringement with the statutory damages provided. Although no punitive damages were requested, commentators attach importance to the case due to the enormity of the amount claimed.[341]

145. The plaintiffs served the claim on two subsidiaries of Bertelsmann in the United States. They, nevertheless, also attempted to serve process at the company's headquarters in Gütersloh (Germany). When Bertelsmann's employees refused to accept the service, the *Oberlandesgericht* Düsseldorf had to intervene in the matter and had to rule on the legality of the service. The *Oberlandesgericht* confirmed that service could take place.[342] Bertelsmann then sought constitutional review of the decision before the *Bundesverfassungsgericht*. It asserted that service should be refused under article 13.1 of the Hague Service Convention because it might lead to a violation of its constitutional rights. The German company referred to the extremely large amount requested and to the class action nature of the U.S. proceedings.

146. On 25 July 2003 the Second Senate of the *Bundesverfassungsgericht* issued a temporary order prohibiting service of the claim for six months or until the date of the decision on the merits of the constitutional complaint. It renewed this order every six months. It applied its two-step approach to reach the conclusion that such an order was warranted.

147. The Constitutional Court first established that the complaint was not inadmissible as well as not plainly unfounded. The Court did not rule whether an

---

340 United States District Court for the Northern District of California, order of 5 March 2001, available at <www.techlawjournal.com/courts/napster/20010305inj.asp>.

341 One could develop the argument that the *Napster* case is interesting for the discussion surrounding punitive damages because the large claim for compensatory damages harboured an extra-compensatory element.

342 Oberlandesgericht Düsseldorf 11 July 2003, *Wertpapier-Mitteilungen für Wirtschafts- und Bankrecht* 2003, 1587.

actual violation of the Constitution existed but found that such a violation could not entirely be excluded. It reiterated the First Senate's ruling that service could not be refused merely due to the fact that the claim seeks punitive damages. The Second Senate, however, used the opening created by the First Senate in the decision of 7 December 1994. Under the obvious violation test service can be refused pursuant to article 13.1 of the Hague Service Convention if the aim of the claim manifestly violates indispensable principles of a free, democratic state under the rule of law. In the eyes of the Second Senate there might be a violation of the fundamental principles of the constitutional state when proceedings abroad are being brought in an obviously abusive manner. This could be the case when the claim has no substantive basis and media pressure and the risk of an unfavourable judgment are exerted to push the defendant into complying with the plaintiffs' will.[343] What the *Bundesverfassungsgericht* seems to suggest is that punitive damages can be part of a pressure campaign to force a defendant to settle. In such an instance the obvious violation test would be satisfied and refusal to serve the claim justified.

148. When addressing the second part of the test to determine whether an interim order should be granted, the Constitutional Court argued that the advantage was on the side of the defendant. The balancing of the outcomes revealed that the damage for Bertelsmann of wrongfully refusing the suspension of the service of the claim outweighed the damage for the plaintiffs as a result of an unjustified injunction.[344] The reasoning seems to be identical to the First Senate's analysis of the second step in its decision of 7 December 1994. The *Bundesverfassungsgericht*, therefore, decided to grant an injunction.

149. The decision has triggered a great deal of controversy in the legal world. The ruling has been criticised in several ways. Sebok asserts that the Court viewed class actions for billions of dollars as an inherent abuse of the American legal system. Back in 1994 the First Senate had not used the procedural differences between both nations as a reason to block service.[345] We would not go as far as to suggest that the decision was a political one, inspired by a hostile scepticism of the civil litigation system in the United States and a desire

[343] Bundesverfassungsgericht 25 July 2003, *BVerfGE* 108, 238; P. Huber, "Playing the same old song – German courts, the "Napster"-case and the international law of service of process" in H.P. Mansel, T. Pfeiffer, H. Kronke, C. Kohler & R. Hausmann (eds.), *Festschrift für Erik Jayme*, Munich, Sellier European Law Publishers, 2004, 364.

[344] Bundesverfassungsgericht 25 July 2003, *BVerfGE* 108, 238; P. Huber, "Playing the same old song – German courts, the "Napster"-case and the international law of service of process" in H.P. Mansel, T. Pfeiffer, H. Kronke, C. Kohler & R. Hausmann (eds.), *Festschrift für Erik Jayme*, Munich, Sellier European Law Publishers, 2004, 365.

[345] A.J. Sebok, "Why the Latest Chapter in the Napster Saga Raises Issues About U.S./European Judicial Cooperation", 2003, no page numbers, available at <http://writ.news.findlaw.com/sebok/20031117.html>.

to protect a German company against American interests.[346] It does, however, seem that the Constitutional Court's Second Senate overstretched the opening created by the First Senate. One cannot sustain that the sovereignty or security of the German state was threatened by the U.S. proceedings. Only the existence of a single German company, albeit a large one, was in jeopardy (at least theoretically because American money claims should always be taken with a pinch of salt[347]).

150. Besides, the First Senate had explicitly referred to the violation of international human rights as the benchmark for the obvious violation test. In its 2003 decision, the Second Senate only invoked German constitutional rights. Furthermore, the Second Senate mentioned the public policy exception in article 40.3 of the *Einführungsgesetz zum Bürgerlichen Gesetzbuche* (Introductory Act to the German Civil Code).[348] The First Senate, on the other hand, rightly did not equate article 13.1 of the Hague Service Convention to national public policy because such an interpretation would obstruct the goals pursued by the Convention.[349] The Second Senate did not efficaciously address the issue of delay in service caused by an investigation of the claim under domestic public policy. Instead it attempted to win time by disallowing a hearing for the American plaintiffs and thus founding its decision on the (inherently one-sided) evidence brought forward by Bertelsmann. Ironically, despite classifying the case as urgent, the Constitutional Court kept prolonging the order without reaching a decision on the merits.[350] These arguments lead us to the opinion that the ruling's application of the obvious violation test should be disregarded. The test should receive a much narrower interpretation, to which we come back below.[351]

151. The issues arising from this case were never subjected to an analysis on the merits.[352] In November 2005 Bertelsmann withdrew the complaint it had lodged before the *Bundesverfassungsgericht* as it had come to realise that the U.S. proceedings could continue even if the Constitutional Court would forbid

---

346 *Contra* A.J. Sebok, "Why the Latest Chapter in the Napster Saga Raises Issues About U.S./European Judicial Cooperation", 2003, no page numbers, available at <http://writ.news.findlaw.com/sebok/20031117.html>.

347 A. J. Sebok, "Why the Latest Chapter in the Napster Saga Raises Issues About U.S./European Judicial Cooperation", 2003, no page numbers, available at <http://writ.news.findlaw.com/sebok/20031117.html>.

348 See *infra* no. 200 for a discussion of this provision.

349 J. von Hein, "Recent German Jurisprudence on Cooperation with the United States" in E. Gottschalk, R. Michaels, G. Rühl & J. von Hein (eds.), *Conflict of Laws in a Globalized World*, Cambridge, Cambridge University Press, 2007, 114.

350 J. von Hein, "Recent German Jurisprudence on Cooperation with the United States" in E. Gottschalk, R. Michaels, G. Rühl & J. von Hein (eds.), *Conflict of Laws in a Globalized World*, Cambridge, Cambridge University Press, 2007, 114–115.

351 See *infra* no. 160 *et seq* and 164.

352 W. Wurmnest, "Recognition and Enforcement of U.S. Money Judgments in Germany", 23 *Berkeley Journal of International Law* 2005, 193.

service of the claim in its final judgment. A board member of the Bertelsmann company had been served the claim while present in the United States. Under Rule 4(h)(1) of the Federal Rules of Civil Procedure this constitutes valid service and involved Bertelsmann in the U.S. proceedings. In 2006 a deal was subsequently reached between French Vivendi, the owner of one of the plaintiffs, and Bertelsmann to purchase BMG (Bertelsmann's corporation) for the sum of USD 2.1 billion. This was followed by a settlement between Universal Music (owned by French Vivendi) and Bertelsmann entailing the payment of USD 60 million by the German company.[353]

2.2.4. *OBERLANDESGERICHT* CELLE 1 JUNE 2007: RELIANCE ON THE *NAPSTER* RULING

152. According to Rasmussen-Bonne there is one decision which has relied on the *Napster* ruling in order to prohibit service. The *Oberlandesgericht* Celle was confronted with a claim brought in a federal court in New York. The dispute arose after the plaintiff had inherited a house from his business partner. The plaintiff had lived with him at the latter's address in Göttingen. The house burnt down after the death of the business partner. The defendant was the property manager of the house but seemed to have no other relation to the damage. The plaintiff sued for around USD 25 million in damages. The *Oberlandesgericht* decided to suspend the order for service. It found that the particular circumstances of the case supported the application of the article 13.1 exception. The American claim violated fundamental constitutional principles as the amount sought was obviously frivolous and only intended to threaten the existence of the defendant. There was no link between the damages requested and the damage suffered. The plaintiff had randomly sued other parties and had also already filed claims in the United States against other defendants. All of those were dismissed as abusive by American courts. The Court further took account of the defendant's outcry that defending himself in the U.S. proceedings would be very expensive and that he would not be able to recover any of these expenses due to the American rule of costs (*i.e.* each side pays their own legal costs, even if victorious).[354]

---

353 J. von Hein, "Recent German Jurisprudence on Cooperation with the United States" in E. Gottschalk, R. Michaels, G. Rühl & J. von Hein (eds.), *Conflict of Laws in a Globalized World*, Cambridge, Cambridge University Press, 2007, 115–116; H.E. Rasmussen-Bonne, "The Pendulum Swings Back: The Cooperative Approach of German Courts to International Service of Process" in P. Hay, L. Vekas, Y. Elkana & N. Dimitrijevic (eds.), *Resolving International Conflicts – Liber Amicorum Tibor Varady*, Budapest – New York, Central European University Press, 2009, 233.

354 Oberlandesgericht Celle 1 June 2007, 16 VA 1/07, *Niedersächsische Rechtspflege* 2007, 331; H.E. Rasmussen-Bonne, "The Pendulum Swings Back: The Cooperative Approach of German Courts to International Service of Process" in P. Hay, L. Vekas, Y. Elkana & N. Dimitrijevic

153. Although these allegations might be true, we argue that they should not be addressed when deciding whether or not to serve a foreign claim. The reason for this view is that unfounded claims or abusive procedures should be dealt with by the court ruling on the merits of the dispute. The service phase is not the appropriate time to opine on the potential outcome of the case. By following the Second Senate's ruling in *Napster*, the *Oberlandesgericht* Celle overstepped its authority and gave too wide an interpretation to the article 13.1 exception.

2.2.5. THE SECOND SENATE'S OPENING FOR A CLEAR ABUSE OF PROCESS FROM THE OUTSET

a. Abuse of process as exception to the obligation to effectuate service

154. In three decisions rendered after the *Napster* case, the Second Senate leaned more towards the position taken by the First Senate in its final ruling of 1994.

155. In the first decision, the *Bundesverfassungsgericht* had to rule with regard to the request for service made by an employee of a German company's Puerto Rican[355] subsidiary. The former senior executive had sued both the subsidiary and the parent company for unfair dismissal before the American courts. In the claim the plaintiff asked over USD 11 million in punitive damages. The Constitutional Court did not block service and held that a claim for punitive damages does not violate the essential principles of a free state governed by the rule of law. The Central Authority cannot refuse a request to serve a U.S. claim unless there is a clear abuse of rights from the outset. The Court decided that such a situation did not present itself in this case.[356]

156. The second case involved several class action suits for treble damages. The defendant was an automobile manufacturer, registered in Germany. It was alleged that the company had made agreements to prevent motor vehicles being imported from Canada into the United States. This anti-competitive strategy kept the prices in the United States at a high level. The German defendant objected to service in Germany and eventually brought the matter before the Constitutional

(eds.), *Resolving International Conflicts – Liber Amicorum Tibor Varady*, Budapest – New York, Central European University Press, 2009, 249–251.

355 Puerto Rico is considered U.S. territory.

356 Bundesverfassungsgericht 24 January 2007, *BVerfGK* 10, 203; H.E. Rasmussen-Bonne, "The Pendulum Swings Back: The Cooperative Approach of German Courts to International Service of Process" in P. Hay, L. Vekas, Y. Elkana & N. Dimitrijevic (eds.), *Resolving International Conflicts – Liber Amicorum Tibor Varady*, Budapest – New York, Central European University Press, 2009, 235.

Court. The *Bundesverfassungsgericht* again favoured a narrow interpretation of article 13.1 of the Hague Service Convention. It stated that service may be denied if the objective pursued obviously violates essential principles of a free state governed by the rule of law. The Constitutional Court argued, however, that the class actions in this case did not satisfy this requirement. It is only when damages claims appear from the outset to violate the abuse of law principle that service may be incompatible with the essential principles of a free state governed by the rule of law.[357]

157. In the third case the *Bundesverfassungsgericht* repeated that the article 13.1 exception can only be triggered by circumstances which amount to an obvious abuse of process from the outset. In those situations service would conflict with fundamental constitutional principles. The Court gave a few examples of such circumstances: the alleged claim has no substantive basis, the defendant has obviously nothing to do with the harmful conduct or significant media pressure has been created to push the defendant into an unfair settlement.[358] These refer back to the *Napster* case. On this point the judgment should in our view not receive approval because it construes the exception clause in article 13.1 too broadly. The circumstances mentioned cannot affect the sovereignty or security of the (German) state.

158. In summary, these cases seem to indicate that a difference in legal institutions (class actions or punitive damages being prime examples) between nations is not a reason to block service under the Hague Service Convention. Service of the document cannot be stopped on the ground that the U.S. claim seeks punitive damages. The escape mechanism in article 13.1 of the Hague Service Convention must be more narrowly construed than domestic public policy. Only when the claim constitutes a clear abuse of process from the outset, refusal to serve the documents is allowed.

159. In a ruling of 2013 the *Bundesverfassungsgericht* consolidated its existing case law on the service of punitive damages claims. It refused to entertain the

---

357 Bundesverfassungsgericht 14 June 2007, *Neue Juristische Wochenschrift* 2007, 3709, available in English at <www.bundesverfassungsgericht.de/entscheidungen/rk20070614_2bvr224706en.html>; H.E. Rasmussen-Bonne, "The Pendulum Swings Back: The Cooperative Approach of German Courts to International Service of Process" in P. Hay, L. Vekas, Y. Elkana & N. Dimitrijevic (eds.), *Resolving International Conflicts - Liber Amicorum Tibor Varady*, Budapest - New York, Central European University Press, 2009, 235–236.

358 Bundesverfassungsgericht 4 September 2008, 2 BvR 1739/06, 2 BvR 1811/06, available at <https://www.bundesverfassungsgericht.de/entscheidungen/rk20080904_2bvr173906.html>; H.E. Rasmussen-Bonne, "The Pendulum Swings Back: The Cooperative Approach of German Courts to International Service of Process" in P. Hay, L. Vekas, Y. Elkana & N. Dimitrijevic (eds.), *Resolving International Conflicts - Liber Amicorum Tibor Varady*, Budapest - New York, Central European University Press, 2009, 236–237.

constitutional complaint made against the service of an American punitive damages action. A German corporation had been in conflict with an American company over intellectual property rights. When the American company initiated proceedings in the Northern District Court of California, service in Germany was needed to notify the defendant of the suit. The German defendant tried to resist service on the basis of article 13.1 of the Hague Service Convention but its efforts led to nothing. Finally, it filed a complaint with the German Constitutional Court. As to the punitive damages requested by the plaintiff, the Court repeated that they do not *per se* violate fundamental principles of a free constitutional state. Moreover, at the time of service the Court is not able to assess the (dis)proportionate nature of the damages claimed. The Court also did not label the factual situation as one that would meet the *Napster* requirements. The media campaign that was triggered by the U.S. claim was not sufficient to amount to an obvious abuse of rights. The article 13.1 exception could, therefore, not apply to the case.[359]

b. *"An abuse of process from the outset": quid?*

160. The case law discussed makes it clear that a mere claim for punitive damages should never be refused service under article 13.1 of the Hague Service Convention as such an action does not infringe the sovereignty or security of the requested state. This is even acknowledged in the dissident and anomalous[360] *Napster* decision of the Second Senate.

161. The question then becomes which circumstances do meet the narrow concept of "an abuse of process from the outset". It is not the purpose of this book to come up with an extensive list of circumstances which would justify the application of the exception mechanism in the Hague Service Convention. The core message here is that an American claim for punitive damages should not be blocked at the service level by another signatory state on the ground that such a claim forms an infringement to the requested state's sovereignty or security.

162. However, in order to demonstrate the exceptional nature and limited scope of the article 13.1 provision, two examples of situations which we believe would qualify are given. First, the refusal of service would be legally acceptable when the document to be served incites others to commit illegal acts.[361] A second situation comes from a case before the *Landgericht* (Regional Court)

---

359 Bundesverfassungsgericht 9 January 2013, *Neue Juristische Wochenschrift* 2013, 990.

360 H.E. Rasmussen-Bonne, "The Pendulum Swings Back: The Cooperative Approach of German Courts to International Service of Process" in P. Hay, L. Vekas, Y. Elkana & N. Dimitrijevic (eds.), *Resolving International Conflicts – Liber Amicorum Tibor Varady*, Budapest – New York, Central European University Press, 2009, 252.

361 P. Schlosser, *EU-Zivilprozessrecht*, Munich, Beck, 2003, 498.

Stuttgart.[362] Although the case is a purely domestic one, the facts would be able to trigger non-compliance if the document had to be served under the Hague Service Convention. A political party (assumed to be right-wing) sued one of its former members for payment of annual party contributions. The plaintiff's claim was printed on the party's letterhead and contained the phrase "*Germany is larger than the Federal Republic*". It also featured a map of Germany prior to 1945 (Germany included parts of Russia, Poland and the Czech Republic in those days). As this violated the constitutional principles of the German state, the *Landgericht* required the plaintiff to file his claim on neutral paper. The plaintiff, however, disregarded multiple requests. The *Landgericht*, therefore, ruled that the plaintiff had abused the process by using the claim as a means to disseminate its propaganda. Service was subsequently denied.[363] This case is representative for a category of situations in which documents are to be served which – on their face – contain information that would insult or embarrass the requested state politically or legally. By refusing service the requested state does not criticise foreign legal concepts but merely protects its own reputation.[364, 365]

2.3. CONCLUSION

2.3.1. DEFERRAL TO THE ENFORCEMENT STAGE

163. In this chapter we first supported the view that actions for punitive damages are to be considered a civil matter. The ambit of the Hague Service Convention, therefore, covers American claims for punitive damages. A refusal to serve such claims on the basis of the argument that they go beyond the scope of the Convention is thus not justified.

164. We then turned to the escape mechanism of the Hague Service Convention. The exception in article 13.1 is reminiscent of an international public policy clause, which we encounter as the yardstick for the enforcement of judgments under national law.[366] As it is an exception which finds its origin in a convention, its application must be in accordance with the goals pursued by that convention. The Hague Service Convention aims to facilitate cross-

362 Landgericht Stuttgart 5 October 1993, *Neue Juristische Wochenschrift* 1994, 1077.

363 Landgericht Stuttgart 5 October 1993, *Neue Juristische Wochenschrift* 1994, 1077.

364 P. Huber, "Playing the same old song – German courts, the "Napster"-case and the international law of service of process" in H.P. Mansel, T. Pfeiffer, H. Kronke, C. Kohler & R. Hausmann (eds.), *Festschrift für Erik Jayme*, Munich, Sellier European Law Publishers, 2004, 369.

365 J. von Hein, "Recent German Jurisprudence on Cooperation with the United States" in E. Gottschalk, R. Michaels, G. Rühl & J. von Hein (eds.), *Conflict of Laws in a Globalized World*, Cambridge, Cambridge University Press, 2007, 111.

366 See *infra* no. 208.

border service of documents. The fluent and speedy (transatlantic) delivery of judicial paperwork would be hindered if the requested state were to perform a fully-fledged public policy review of the claim submitted by the plaintiff. The provision in article 13.1 leaves no room for an analysis under domestic public policy but should instead be interpreted restrictively.[367] As demonstrated, a ground for refusal of service will only be present in extremely rare cases.[368]

165. The service stage of the proceedings is not the appropriate time for a detailed public policy review of a claim. Central Authorities in Europe (and the national courts ruling in these matters) cannot and should not speculate on the outcome of the case by conducting a pre-trial on the merits. Whether punitive damages will be awarded and, if so, in which amount, is unknown at that point and should not influence the decision to effectuate service of the claim form. The Hague Service Convention was introduced to avoid time-consuming means of service and does not provide an instrument for requested states to impose their own legal views on other nations or to protect their own nationals from foreign litigation. Besides, one must remember that Central Authorities have an administrative and not a judicial function (even if a court or a judge is fulfilling the role of Central Authority).[369] Any objections surrounding the legality or fairness of the American proceedings should be brought before the American court which decides on the merits of the dispute. The requested state is only allowed to intervene when its sovereignty or security is under threat. This will only very seldom be the case. The possibility that punitive damages will be awarded against the defendant never meets this exceptional standard.[370] European courts should thus assist the parties in going forward with the American litigation, even though the punitive damages portion of the final U.S. judgment might be refused recognition and enforcement.[371]

---

367 M. Requejo Isidro, "Punitive Damages From a Private International Law Perspective" in H. Koziol & V. Wilcox (eds.), *Punitive Damages: Common Law and Civil Law Perspectives*, Vienna, Springer, 2009, 243.

368 P. Huber, "Playing the same old song – German courts, the "Napster"-case and the international law of service of process" in H.P. Mansel, T. Pfeiffer, H. Kronke, C. Kohler & R. Hausmann (eds.), *Festschrift für Erik Jayme*, Munich, Sellier European Law Publishers, 2004, 369.

369 H.E. Rasmussen-Bonne, "The Pendulum Swings Back: The Cooperative Approach of German Courts to International Service of Process" in P. Hay, L. Vekas, Y. Elkana & N. Dimitrijevic (eds.), *Resolving International Conflicts – Liber Amicorum Tibor Varady*, Budapest – New York, Central European University Press, 2009, 252.

370 P. Huber, "Playing the same old song – German courts, the "Napster"-case and the international law of service of process" in H.P. Mansel, T. Pfeiffer, H. Kronke, C. Kohler & R. Hausmann (eds.), *Festschrift für Erik Jayme*, Munich, Sellier European Law Publishers, 2004, 367.

371 P. Hay, "The Recognition and Enforcement of American Money-Judgments in Germany – The 1992 Decision of the German Supreme Court", 40 *The American Journal of Comparative Law* 1992, 746, footnote 70; P. Huber, "Playing the same old song – German courts, the "Napster"-case and the international law of service of process" in H.P. Mansel, T. Pfeiffer, H. Kronke,

166. Once a decision has been rendered in the American court and the plaintiff seeks enforcement of the (punitive damages) judgment in the country where service took place, the requested state can indeed perform a full-scale international public policy analysis of the foreign award. Any outrageous characteristics of the U.S. system can then be dealt with. In chapter 4 we discuss how the courts in Italy, Germany, England, France and Spain have treated U.S. punitive damages awards when asked to enforce them in their territory. Chapter 5 is dedicated to supporting the argument that U.S. punitive damages as a concept do not violate international public policy. Instead, punitive damages should be subjected to an excessiveness/proportionality test. In chapter 6 we then propose guidelines which can help European judges with this international public policy analysis. More in particular, we discuss how they should approach the excessiveness review.

2.3.2. FUTILITY OF A REFUSAL TO SERVE

167. Furthermore, it should be noted that it would be futile to attempt to resist service of punitive damages claims. Plaintiffs have at least two methods available which allow them to avoid problems related to the service of punitive damages claims under the Hague Service Convention. This observation has been made by several courts and runs as a common theme through various judgments mentioned in this chapter. In its decision of 7 December 1994 the *Bundesverfassungsgericht*, for instance, highlights that blocking service is ultimately pointless. The Constitutional Court refers to two techniques that can be employed to circumvent any issues raised by unwilling Central Authorities.[372] The Second Senate in *Napster* did not go into the futility argument raised by the First Senate.[373]

a. The Schlunk doctrine

168. First, the plaintiff can rely on the *Schlunk* judgment of the U.S. Supreme Court. In that case Herwig Schlunk started a law suit against Volkswagen of America in the Circuit Court of Cook County (Illinois) after the death of his parents. He alleged that the car they were driving had defects which had caused or contributed to their deaths. The plaintiff later amended his wrongful death claim by adding a second defendant to the proceedings: Volkswagen

C. Kohler & R. Hausmann (eds.), *Festschrift für Erik Jayme*, Munich, Sellier European Law Publishers, 2004, 366.

372 Bundesverfassungsgericht 7 December 1994, *International Legal Materials* 1995, 994.

373 J. von Hein, "Recent German Jurisprudence on Cooperation with the United States" in E. Gottschalk, R. Michaels, G. Rühl & J. von Hein (eds.), *Conflict of Laws in a Globalized World*, Cambridge, Cambridge University Press, 2007, 115.

Aktiengesellschaft, the German owner of Volkswagen of America. Schlunk tried to serve the claim on the German company by serving Volkswagen of America as the German company's agent. The German defendant attempted to evade service by arguing that service should be effected in accordance with the Hague Service Convention and that the plaintiff had failed to follow the provisions of that convention.[374]

169. The Supreme Court of the United States ruled that the Hague Service Convention is the exclusive means of service when service has to take place in another signatory state. However, when service abroad is not necessary because American law allows for service within the United States, this domestic way of service can be used instead.[375] In other words, the Hague Service Convention is not the compulsory route to serve documents on a foreign counterparty. If alternative ways of (domestic) service are available (such as service on an American subsidiary of the defendant), service outside the United States and the application of the Hague Service Convention can be avoided.

170. On a side note: in cases where domestic service is not possible and service needs to take place in accordance with the Hague Service Convention, a Central Authority's efforts to interpret the scope of the Convention narrowly in order to be able to refuse service would be counterproductive. Rule 4(f)(3) of the Federal Rules of Civil Procedure grants U.S. courts discretion to effect service through other means when the Convention does not apply. The U.S. proceedings would in that regard thus not be obstructed by one of the Central Authorities in Europe.[376]

b. Extension of the claim after service has been performed

171. Second, the U.S. plaintiff can elect to limit his claim to compensatory damages until service abroad has been effected. When an American lawyer appears to defend against the action, the additional claim for punitive damages can then be served on this representative of the defendant.[377] It has been held in the past that the danger of an extension of the claim to punitive damages may not lead to a refusal of service.[378]

---

374 *Volkswagen Aktiengesellschaft v. Schlunk*, 486 U.S. 696–697 (1988).

375 *Volkswagen Aktiengesellschaft v. Schlunk*, 486 U.S. 698–706(1988).

376 J. von Hein, "Recent German Jurisprudence on Cooperation with the United States" in E. Gottschalk, R. Michaels, G. Rühl & J. von Hein (eds.), *Conflict of Laws in a Globalized World*, Cambridge, Cambridge University Press, 2007, 121.

377 Bundesverfassungsgericht 7 December 1994, *International Legal Materials* 1995, 994.

378 Oberlandesgericht Frankfurt am Main 21 March 1991, *Praxis des Internationalen Privat- und Verfahrensrechts* 1992, 166.

172. By using any of these two methods, the plaintiff ensures that the U.S. law suit for punitive damages does not run into service issues abroad.

2.3.3. STRATEGY CONSIDERATIONS

173. Even in cases where service abroad is inevitable, attempting to block service might not be the best strategic option for the defendant.[379] Its German assets would be shielded from the plaintiff because invalid service is a reason to refuse enforcement in Germany (pursuant to article 328, (1), 2) of the Code of Civil Procedure (*Zivilprozessordnung* – ZPO). Reliance on the non-enforcement of the judgment is, however, only possible if the defendant has not participated in the U.S. proceedings. If the defendant has assets in the United States, these are not protected by the service block and can thus be seized to satisfy the American judgment.[380]

174. This leaves the German defendant holding assets in both jurisdictions with a dilemma. The American court could ignore the foreign service block and be satisfied with another form of service. The defendant's absence in the U.S. court can then lead to a default judgment being rendered, exposing its American assets to seizure. By participating in the U.S. proceedings, on the other hand, the defendant's German assets become available to the plaintiff but the defendant can at least influence the court's decision as to the merits of the case and endeavour to protect its assets located in the U.S. as well as in its home country.[381] Furthermore, the effect of blocking service in Europe as a bargaining tool seems minimal. As the plaintiffs are rarely allowed a hearing before the courts dealing with the service issue, they incur few costs related to those proceedings. The avoidance of service, therefore, does not help a defendant in its pursuit of a settlement.[382]

---

379 B. Friedrich, "Federal Constitutional Court Grants Interim Legal Protection Against Service of a Writ of Punitive Damages Suit", *German Law Journal* 2003, 1239.

380 The risk of having one's foreign assets seised is inherently connected to doing business in foreign markets. See: Oberlandesgericht München 9 May 1989, *Recht der Internationalen Wirtschaft* 1989, 484, *International Legal Materials* 1989, 1574 and 1576.

381 J. von Hein, "Recent German Jurisprudence on Cooperation with the United States" in E. Gottschalk, R. Michaels, G. Rühl & J. von Hein (eds.), *Conflict of Laws in a Globalized World*, Cambridge, Cambridge University Press, 2007, 122.

382 J. von Hein, "Recent German Jurisprudence on Cooperation with the United States" in E. Gottschalk, R. Michaels, G. Rühl & J. von Hein (eds.), *Conflict of Laws in a Globalized World*, Cambridge, Cambridge University Press, 2007, 123.

CHAPTER 3
PUNITIVE DAMAGES AND APPLICABLE LAW

3.1. INTRODUCTION

175. The second area in which U.S. punitive damages come into conflict with the European legal systems is the field of applicable law. When a dispute containing cross-border elements is brought before a court of an EU Member State, the court will first establish whether it has jurisdiction to adjudicate the matter. If the answer is positive, the court then needs to determine what jurisdiction's law will apply to the case. The judge will look at the forum's private international law rules to select which country's laws will apply to the lawsuit. This is, mostly in the United States, referred to as the choice-of-law analysis.

176. When the private international law rules point to the application of American law (*i.e.* federal law or the laws of one of the states), it is possible that the designated law provides for punitive damages. At that point the penetration of foreign punitive damages into Civil Law is imminent. The question to be answered is whether the court will apply that foreign rule or will dismiss it for contrariety to public policy.[383] This issue will be addressed in this chapter.

3.2. THE CONCEPT OF PUBLIC POLICY

177. Both public policy and its cognate notion of international public policy were briefly mentioned in chapter 2. It was explained how the escape provision in article 13.1 of the Hague Service Convention is to be construed very restrictively and is, therefore, closely related to the narrow notion of international public policy. The escape clause allowing for refusal of service can certainly not be equated to the broader domestic public policy.[384]

---

383 T. Rouhette, "The availability of punitive damages in Europe: growing trend or nonexistent concept?", 74 *Defense Counsel Journal* 2007, 329.

384 See *supra* no. 164.

178. As the public policy mechanism plays a prime role in the private international law arenas of applicable law and enforcement of judgments, it deserves further elaboration. The notion of public policy or *ordre public* refers to the common core of principles that are vital for the effective operation and social acceptance of a legal system. It reflects the fundamental socio-economic and moral values of a society.[385] It has both a procedural and a substantive dimension.[386] For punitive damages the latter is usually the most relevant of the two.[387]

179. Private international law cases, however, deal with a more restricted form of public policy, namely international public policy.[388] The latter is, despite the name, a purely national concept.[389] Only international public policy can act as a barrier to the application of a foreign law or the enforcement of a foreign judgment. It contains those fundamental rules of domestic or internal public policy which a legal system wants respected in international cases as well.[390, 391] In enforcement cases as well as in cases of applicable law comity requires a legal system to be more tolerant than it would be in purely domestic affairs.[392] Moreover, it is not the foreign law or the foreign decision that must be scrutinised but the concrete effect its application or enforcement generates in the forum.[393] In practice, courts and scholars are sometimes not aware of the

---

385 H. Auf'mkolk, "U.S. punitive damages awards before German courts – Time for a new approach", *Freiburg Law Students Journal* 2007, 4.

386 H. Gaudemet-Tallon, *Compétence et exécution des jugements en Europe*, Paris, LGDJ, 2010, no. 402 *et seq.*

387 J. Dollinger, "World Public Policy: Real International Public Policy in the Conflict of Laws", 17 *Texas International Law Journal* 1982, 170; M. Requejo Isidro, "Punitive Damages: How Do They Look Like When Seen From Abroad?" in L. Meurkens & E. Nordin (eds.), *The Power of Punitive Damages – Is Europe Missing Out?*, Cambridge – Antwerp – Portland, Intersentia, 2012, 323.

388 P. Mayer & V. Heuzé, *Droit international privé*, Paris, Montchrestien, 2004, 149, no. 205; A. Mills, *The Confluence of Public and Private International Law – Justice, Pluralism and Subsidiarity in the International Constitutional Ordering of Private Law*, Cambridge, Cambridge University Press, 2009, 275–277; A. Mills, "The Dimensions of Public Policy in Private International Law", *Journal of Private International Law* 2008, 213; P. Bernard & H. Salem, "Further developments for qualification of foreign judgments for recognition and enforcement in France: the test for punitive damage awards", *International Bar Association* 2011, 18.

389 J. Dollinger, "World Public Policy: Real International Public Policy in the Conflict of Laws", 17 *Texas International Law Journal* 1982, 170.

390 A.S. Sibon, "Enforcing Punitive Damages Awards in France: Facing Proportionality within International Public Policy", no page numbers, available at <http://ssrn.com/abstract=2382817>.

391 Both concepts can be visualised as two concentric circles, with domestic public policy being the larger of the two. All principles belonging to international public policy also have domestic public policy status but not vice versa.

392 B. Janke & F.-X. Licari, "Enforcing Punitive Damage Awards in France after Fountaine Pajot", 60 *The American Journal of Comparative Law* 2012, 792.

393 V. Behr, "Punitive Damages in American and German Law – Tendencies Towards Approximation of Apparently Irreconcilable Concepts", 78 *Chicago-Kent Law Review* 2003,

difference between the two notions of public policy. Similarly, they use the term 'public policy' for both concepts instead of reserving it for the domestic variant.

180. International public policy works in a negative way[394], in the sense that it acts as a gatekeeper to keep away foreign law or foreign judgments that are absolutely unacceptable when measured against domestic legal standards.[395] For the activation of international public policy it is not sufficient that the solution offered by the foreign nation is different[396], it has to be shocking for the forum.[397] International public policy thus protects the whole of fundamental societal values from phenomena that are at odds with it, through negation.[398]

181. As is the case for chapter 4 as well, when referring to public policy in the context of applicable law, one should understand this as international public policy, unless indicated otherwise.

3.3. THE ROME II REGULATION'S APPROACH TO FOREIGN PUNITIVE DAMAGES

182. In the European Union the private international law rules determining the law applicable to torts have been harmonised by the Rome II Regulation.[399] The Regulation indicates which law has to be applied to non-contractual obligations. As of 11 January 2009 it replaced the national choice-of-law rules in non-contractual obligations which fall within its scope.[400] The Regulation

153; P. Klötgen, "L'appréhension des punitive damages par le droit allemande", *Revue Lamy Droit des Affaires* 2013, 126; BGH 26 September 1979, *BGHZ* 1980, 171; B. Janke & F.-X. Licari, "Enforcing Punitive Damage Awards in France after Fountaine Pajot", 60 *The American Journal of Comparative Law* 2012, 792.

394 A. Dickinson, *The Rome II Regulation – The Law Applicable to Non-Contractual Obligations*, Oxford-New York, Oxford University Press, 2008, 631, no. 15.13; A.J. Belohlavek, "Public Policy and Public Interest in International Law and EU Law", *Czech Yearbook of International Law* 2012, 144.

395 H. Auf'mkolk, "U.S. punitive damages awards before German courts – Time for a new approach", *Freiburg Law Students Journal* 2007, 5.

396 A. Dickinson, *The Rome II Regulation – The Law Applicable to Non-Contractual Obligations*, Oxford-New York, Oxford University Press, 2008, 626, no. 15.04.

397 G. Cuniberti, "The Liberization of the French Law of Foreign Judgments", 56 *International Comparative Law Quarterly* 2007, 933.

398 A.J. Belohlavek, "Public Policy and Public Interest in International Law and EU Law", *Czech Yearbook of International Law* 2012, 142.

399 Regulation No. 864/2007 of the European Parliament and of the Council of 11 July 2007 on the law applicable to non-contractual obligations, *OJ* L 199 of 31 July 2007, 40. The Regulation applies to all EU Member States except Denmark.

400 Article 32 of the Rome II Regulation; P. Beaumont & Z. Tang, "Classification of Delictual Damages: *Harding v Wealands* and the Rome II Regulation", *Edinburgh Law Review* 2008, 135.

has universal application, which means that the law specified by the Regulation shall apply, whether or not it is the law of an EU Member State (article 3). It is therefore conceivable that the Rome II Regulation requires a judge of an EU Member State to apply the law of a country where punitive damages are awarded (such as the United States).

3.3.1. SCOPE OF THE REGULATION

183. Article 15 c) of the Regulation provides that: "*The law applicable to non-contractual obligations under this Regulation shall govern in particular: [...] c) the existence, the nature and the assessment of damage or the remedy claimed.*" This provision seems to suggest that the Regulation does not view damage as the basis for repair. It leaves room for damages based on principles other than full compensation (such as punitive damages).[401]

184. The Rome II Regulation indicates in its article 1.3 that it does not apply to procedural and evidentiary matters. These are governed by the law indicated by the domestic private international law rules which may, for instance, lead to the application of the law of the forum (*lex fori*).[402] The formulation of article 15 c), however, is wide enough to support the view that the Rome II Regulation classifies all matters relating to damages as substantive.[403] A matter falling within article 15 c) can, therefore, not be held to be a matter of evidence or procedure for the purposes of the Rome II Regulation (instead it falls under the *lex causae*, *i.e.* the law applicable to the tort as designated by the Regulation).[404] Article 15 c) thus allows for an award of punitive damages if such damages are permitted under the applicable law.[405]

---

401 A. Dickinson, *The Rome II Regulation – The Law Applicable to Non-Contractual Obligations*, Oxford-New York, Oxford University Press, 2008, 576, no. 14.20 and 301, no. 4.09–4.10; O. Boskovic, "Le domaine de la loi applicable" in S. Corneloup & N. Joubert (eds.), *Le Règlement Communautaire Rome II sur la loi applicable aux obligations non contractuelles*, Paris, Litec, 2008, 189; M. Requejo Isidro, "Punitive Damages: How Do They Look Like When Seen From Abroad?" in L. Meurkens & E. Nordin (eds.), *The Power of Punitive Damages – Is Europe Missing Out?*, Cambridge – Antwerp – Portland, Intersentia, 2012, 315.

402 A. Dickinson, *The Rome II Regulation – The Law Applicable to Non-Contractual Obligations*, Oxford-New York, Oxford University Press, 2008, 593, no. 14.57.

403 P. Beaumont & Z. Tang, "Classification of Delictual Damages: *Harding v Wealands* and the Rome II Regulation", *Edinburgh Law Review* 2008, 135; A. Rushworth, "Remedies and the Rome II Regulation" in J. Ahern & W. Binchy (eds.), *The Rome II Regulation on the Law Applicable to Non-Contractual Obligations*, Leiden – Boston, Martinus Nijhoff Publishers, 2009, 201.

404 R. Morse, "Substance and Procedure: Aspects of Damages in Torts in the Conflict of Laws" in The Permanent Bureau of the Hague Conference, *A Commitment to Private International Law. Essays in honour of Hans van Loon*, Cambridge-Antwerp-Portland, Intersentia, 2013, 391.

405 R. Morse, "Substance and Procedure: Aspects of Damages in Torts in the Conflict of Laws" in The Permanent Bureau of the Hague Conference, *A Commitment to Private International*

3.3.2. *LEX LOCI DAMNI* AS BASIC PRINCIPLE

185. The cornerstone of the Rome II Regulation can be found in article 4.1.[406] The law applicable to a non-contractual obligation arising out of a tort shall be the law of the country in which the damage occurs (*lex loci damni*) irrespective of the country in which the event giving rise to the damage occurred. If the damage occurred in the United States, it is possible that punitive damages become available. If both the tortfeasor and the victim have their habitual residence in the same country at the time the damages occurs, the law of that country will apply (article 4.2). Again, this law might provide for punitive damages.[407]

3.3.3. PUBLIC POLICY EXCEPTION

186. The application of foreign law by an EU Member State court is, however, subjected to certain limitations. Article 26 of the Regulation, entitled 'Public policy of the forum', states that: "*The application of a provision of the law of any country specified by this Regulation may be refused only if such application is manifestly incompatible with the public policy* (ordre public) *of the forum*". Whenever the application of foreign law violates the public policy of the forum, the court is allowed to disregard the rules of the foreign law.[408] It should be noted that it is the application of a rule, and not its content in the abstract, that must offend the public policy of the forum.[409] Whether the court will replace the foreign law with the *lex fori* or whether it will dismiss the claim depends on the national law, as the Rome II Regulation is silent on this issue.[410]

187. In addition to this general public policy clause, recital 32 addresses punitive damages in particular. The recital reads, in its relevant part: "*In particular, the application of a provision of the law designated by this Regulation which would have the effect of causing non-compensatory exemplary or punitive*

Law. Essays in honour of Hans van Loon, Cambridge-Antwerp-Portland, Intersentia, 2013, 395.

406 A. Dickinson, *The Rome II Regulation – The Law Applicable to Non-Contractual Obligations*, Oxford-New York, Oxford University Press, 2008, 307, no. 4.22.

407 The Rome II Regulation has a series of conflict of laws rules for specific situations such as product liability (article 5), unfair competition (article 6), environmental damage (article 7). Given the universal application of the Regulation, each of these rules may point to a legal system which contains provisions for punitive damages.

408 A. Dickinson, *The Rome II Regulation – The Law Applicable to Non-Contractual Obligations*, Oxford-New York, Oxford University Press, 2008, 576, no. 14.21.

409 A. Dickinson, *The Rome II Regulation – The Law Applicable to Non-Contractual Obligations*, Oxford-New York, Oxford University Press, 2008, 631, no. 15.13.

410 A. Fuchs, "Article 26" in P. Huber (ed.), *Rome II Regulation – Pocket Commentary*, Munich, Sellier, 2011, 430, no. 18.

damages of an excessive nature to be awarded may, depending on the circumstances of the case and the legal order of the Member State of the court seized, be regarded as being contrary to the public policy (ordre public) *of the forum*". The current text of the Rome II Regulation is obviously the most important tool in determining whether the awarding of U.S. punitive damages is allowed in the European Union through the applicable law. It is, nevertheless, interesting to look at the drafting history of the provisions. The turbulent legislative history reflects the difficulties the EU institutions encountered when attempting to formulate a clear and unambiguous position on the application of punitive damages through the applicable law.

a. Drafting history

188. The original proposal from 2003 combined a general rule on public policy (*ordre public*) in its article 22 with a more specific rule on non-compensatory damages in its Article 24. Article 24 read as follows:

> "*The application of a provision of the law designated by this regulation which has the effect of causing non-compensatory damages, such as exemplary or punitive damages, to be awarded shall be contrary to Community public policy*".[411]

189. The insertion of a separate article was inspired by a predominately German call for a rule corresponding to article 40, paragraph 3, (1) of the *Einführungsgesetz zum Bürgerlichen Gesetzbuche* (EGBGB) (Introductory Act to the Civil Code). That German provision, although not explicitly mentioning punitive damages, rejects the application of any claims that "*substantially go beyond what is necessary for an adequate compensation of the injured party*".[412] During the consultation phase, the German Federal Bar, along with other contributors, had expressed the concern that the absence of provisions limiting liability would be problematic. It found the mechanism of a general *ordre public* exception (as later set out in article 22) insufficient to avoid exorbitant damages such as punitive damages.[413] The idea of applying the law of a third country providing for damages not calculated to compensate for damage sustained worried many contributors to the written consultation.[414]

---

411 Proposal for a Regulation of the European Parliament and the Council on the law applicable to non-contractual obligations ("Rome II"), 22 July 2003, COM/2003/0427 final.

412 See *infra* no. 200.

413 Position of the Bundesrechtsanwaltskammer (The German Federal Bar) on the Preliminary Draft Proposal for a Council Regulation on the Law Applicable to Non-Contractual Obligations, par. 8, available at <http://ec.europa.eu/justice/news/consulting_public/rome_ii/contributions/bundesrechtsanwaltskammer_en.pdf>).

414 Explanatory Memorandum to the Proposal for a Regulation of the European Parliament and the Council on the law applicable to non-contractual obligations ("Rome II"), COM/2003/0427 final, 29.

190. The inclusion of the express rule of article 24 suggested that punitive damages violate some kind of Community public policy.[415] This expression has rarely been used by the Community courts and seems to have no settled meaning.[416] The Commission, however, seemed to have forgotten how the legal systems of the European countries that provide for punitive damages, such as England and Ireland, actually operate.[417] The original draft would have had illogical consequences for those Member States since an English court, for instance, would have had to refuse the application of a foreign law granting punitive damages and (possibly) replace it by its own domestic law (*lex fori*) which awards such damages itself.[418] Article 24 would also have covered other non-compensatory damages such as restitutionary damages[419] which have an important function and are fundamentally different from punitive damages. This was caused by the lack of specificity as to the types of non-compensatory damages article 24 aims to exclude. In our view the Commission did not intend to forbid such remedies.[420]

191. The Report on the proposal (also known as the WALLIS report) dropped the reference to the Community public policy. Rapporteur Diana WALLIS thought it beyond the scope of the Regulation[421] to introduce this new concept and to remove the possibility of awarding punitive damages as the Commission proposed in article 24.[422] Even though she felt sympathetic towards the proposed provision, she preferred to have article 22 amended and made the suggestion to return to the mere possibility for the forum to refuse the application of a foreign law allowing for punitive damages.[423]

---

415 B.A. Koch, "Punitive Damages in European Law" in H. Koziol & V. Wilcox (eds.), *Punitive Damages: Common Law and Civil Law Perspectives*, Vienna, Springer, 2009, 198.

416 A. Dickinson, *The Rome II Regulation - The Law Applicable to Non-Contractual Obligations*, Oxford-New York, Oxford University Press, 2008, 577, footnote 55.

417 H.D. Tebbens, "Punitive damages: towards a rule of reason for U.S. awards and their recognition elsewhere" in G. Venturini & S. Bariatti (eds.), *Liber Fausto Pocar, Volume II - Nuovi strumenti del diritto internazionale private*, Milan, Giuffre, 2009, 286.

418 B.A. Koch, "Punitive Damages in European Law" in H. Koziol & V. Wilcox (eds.), *Punitive Damages: Common Law and Civil Law Perspectives*, Vienna, Springer, 2009, 199.

419 A. Dickinson, *The Rome II Regulation - The Law Applicable to Non-Contractual Obligations*, Oxford-New York, Oxford University Press, 2008, 42, no. 1.70.

420 European Union Committee of the House of Lords, The Rome II Regulation, 8th Report of Session 2003–2004, no. 169–170.

421 We interpret this as meaning that, although there would be competence under the Treaty on the Functioning of the European Union for this inclusion, it would be an undesirable legislative choice. Unfortunately, the reasoning behind this statement was not elaborated upon.

422 Draft Report on the proposal for a regulation of the European Parliament and of the Council on the law applicable to non-contractual obligations ("Rome II"), COD/2003/0168, 31.

423 Draft Report on the proposal for a regulation of the European Parliament and of the Council on the law applicable to non-contractual obligations ("Rome II"), COD/2003/0168, 33.

192. The Commission subsequently amended its proposal by deleting article 24 and merging it with article 23. In article 23 it was stated that:

> "*The application of a rule of the law of any country specified by this Regulation may be refused only if such application is manifestly incompatible with the public policy* ('ordre public') *of the forum. In particular, the application under this Regulation of a law that would have the effect of causing non-compensatory damages to be awarded that would be excessive may be considered incompatible with the public policy of the forum.*"[424]

193. Instead of automatically ruling out punitive damages as violating the public policy of the European Community, this new article left the national judges free to decide whether punitive damages are acceptable in light of their own countries' public policy. Furthermore, only "excessive" punitive damages were deemed to fall under the umbrella of the public policy exception.

194. However, this softened approach was not followed by the Council which in its Common Position deleted the rule due to difficulties in establishing a definition of public policy.[425] In the final version of the Rome II Regulation only the first sentence of article 23 of the proposal was retained in current article 26 which deals with the public policy of the forum. The Commission and Parliament managed to sneak a reminder of the discussion on punitive damages into the Regulation's preamble.[426] As mentioned before, the relevant part of recital 32 reads:

> "*In particular, the application of a provision of the law designated by this Regulation which would have the effect of causing non-compensatory exemplary or punitive damages of an excessive nature to be awarded may, depending on the circumstances of the case and the legal order of the Member State of the court seized, be regarded as being contrary to the public policy* (ordre public) *of the forum.*"

b. *The effect of recital 32*

195. The wording of recital 32 is similar to the second sentence of article 23 of the proposal. With this formula the European Union implicitly acknowledges that civil liability can have functions other than compensatory ones.[427] The

---

424 Amended proposal for a European Parliament and Council Regulation on the law applicable to non-contractual obligations ("Rome II"), 21 February 2006, COD/2003/0168.

425 Common Position adopted by the Council on 25 September 2006 with a view to the adoption of a Regulation of the European Parliament and of the Council on the law applicable to non-contractual obligations ("Rome II") No. 22/2006, *OJ* C 289/3, 68.

426 B.A. Koch, "Punitive Damages in European Law" in H. Koziol & V. Wilcox (eds.), *Punitive Damages: Common Law and Civil Law Perspectives*, Vienna, Springer, 2009, 199.

427 G. Cavalier, "Punitive Damages and French International Public Policy", in R. Stürner and M. Kawono (eds.), *Comparative Studies on Business Tort Litigation*, Tübingen, Mohr Siebeck, 2011, 230; M. Requejo Isidro, "Punitive Damages: How Do They Look Like When Seen From

transfer of the reference to punitive damages from the main text to the preamble makes little difference. A Member State court can still find punitive damages in violation of the public policy of the forum even though article 26 does not mention this *expressis verbis*.[428] Although recital 32 has no binding effect, it still provides a hint to Member States that the incompatibility of punitive damages with public policy requires more than the mere non-compensatory nature of the remedy. Punitive damages are as such not automatically contrary to public policy[429] but need to be of an excessive nature for the public policy mechanism to be able to intervene.[430] That is exactly the message chapter 5 of this book wants to convey. The concept of punitive damages is, as such, not contrary to public policy. Rather, the damages should be analysed from a proportionality/ excessiveness point of view. The inclusion of the recital in the Regulation is meaningful because it enables the European Court of Justice to draw the line as to what amounts to an excessive non-compensatory award, thereby defining and policing the boundaries of public policy.[431, 432]

c. *Application of the public policy exception in case law*

196. The doctrine has noted the absence of any (reported) case in which the problem of the application of foreign punitive damages has been considered.[433] We have, nevertheless, been able to find one case of 2012 in which the issue of the applicability of American punitive damages was raised and decided upon.

Abroad?" in L. Meurkens & E. Nordin (eds.), *The Power of Punitive Damages – Is Europe Missing Out?*, Cambridge – Antwerp – Portland, Intersentia, 2012, 319.

428 B.A. Koch, "Punitive Damages in European Law" in H. Koziol & V. Wilcox (eds.), *Punitive Damages: Common Law and Civil Law Perspectives*, Vienna, Springer, 2009, 199. In the same sense: R. Plender & M. Wilderspin, *The European Private International Law of Obligations*, London, Sweet & Maxwell, 2009, 751.

429 C.I. Nagy, "Recognition and enforcement of US judgments involving punitive damages in continental Europe", *Nederlands Internationaal Privaatrecht* 2012, 10.

430 M. Requejo Isidro, "Punitive Damages: How Do They Look Like When Seen From Abroad?" in L. Meurkens & E. Nordin (eds.), *The Power of Punitive Damages – Is Europe Missing Out?*, Cambridge – Antwerp – Portland, Intersentia, 2012, 319.

431 R. Plender & M. Wilderspin, *The European Private International Law of Obligations*, London, Sweet & Maxwell, 2009, 752; *contra* P. Klötgen, "L'appréhension des punitive damages par le droit allemande", *Revue Lamy Droit des Affaires* 2013, 128.

432 C. Vanleenhove, "Punitive Damages and European Law: Quo Vademus?" in L. Meurkens & E. Nordin (eds.), *The Power of Punitive Damages – Is Europe Missing Out?*, Cambridge – Antwerp – Portland, Intersentia, 2012, 338–340.

433 M. Requejo Isidro, "Punitive Damages From a Private International Law Perspective" in H. Koziol & V. Wilcox (eds.), *Punitive Damages: Common Law and Civil Law Perspectives*, Vienna, Springer, 2009, 238, footnote 4 and 255.; M. Requejo Isidro, "Punitive Damages: How Do They Look Like When Seen From Abroad?" in L. Meurkens & E. Nordin (eds.), *The Power of Punitive Damages – Is Europe Missing Out?*, Cambridge – Antwerp – Portland, Intersentia, 2012, 315, footnote 20; T. Rouhette, "The availability of punitive damages in Europe: growing trend or nonexistent concept?", 74 *Defense Counsel Journal* 2007, 330.

197. In a case before the district court of Amsterdam the court applied the Rome II Regulation and determined that American law was applicable on the acts of stalking and threatening via the internet. The court based its decision on article 4.1 of the Regulation (which refers to the *lex loci damni*) and found that the damaging effect of the internet publications was felt in the United States (California to be precise), where the plaintiffs lived and worked.[434] It, subsequently, ruled that both plaintiffs were entitled to punitive damages under California law. The fact that these damages are unknown in the Netherlands did not form an obstacle for awarding them under American law. Although the court did not explicitly mention the public policy clause of article 26 of the Rome II Regulation, it did rule that Dutch public policy is not violated if the punitive damages are awarded to the plaintiffs. In the relation between the plaintiffs and the defendant the damages also do not violate the principles of reasonableness and fairness.[435] The court's use of the yardstick of reasonableness could perhaps be interpreted as a reference to the requirement of *manifest* incompatibility of article 26 as well as to the excessiveness criterion in recital 32. Both plaintiffs were awarded EUR 5000 in punitive damages.[436]

3.4. NATIONAL RULES ON THE APPLICATION OF FOREIGN PUNITIVE DAMAGES

198. In the vast majority of cases in the European Union the Rome II Regulation will be the legal source that determines which law applies to a non-contractual matter. However, not all cases are covered by this European instrument. Article 1.2 enumerates a number of non-contractual obligations that fall outside of the Regulation's ambit. Article 1.2 g), for instance, provides that non-contractual obligations arising out of violations of privacy and rights relating to personality, including defamation, are excluded from the scope of the Rome II Regulation. For such tort cases the national conflict of laws rules will lay down the applicable law.

199. The approach taken by the Rome II Regulation does not align with the stances adopted at the national level. In Germany, for instance, the *Einführungsgesetzes zum Bürgerlichen Gesetzbuche* (EGBGB) (Introductory Law to the Civil Code) regulates the German private international law rules on

434 Rechtbank Amsterdam 15 June 2012, no. 4.2, available at: <http://uitspraken.rechtspraak.nl/inziendocument?id=ECLI:NL:RBAMS:2012:BW9838>.

435 Rechtbank Amsterdam 15 June 2012, no. 4.14, available at: <http://uitspraken.rechtspraak.nl/inziendocument?id=ECLI:NL:RBAMS:2012:BW9838>.

436 Rechtbank Amsterdam 15 June 2012, no. 5.5 and 5.6, available at <http://uitspraken.rechtspraak.nl/inziendocument?id=ECLI:NL:RBAMS:2012:BW9838>.

applicable law. It contains a general public policy clause in article 6 as well as a specific provision for torts in article 40, paragraph 3.

Article 6 reads: "*A provision of the law of another country shall not be applied where its application would lead to a result which is manifestly incompatible with the fundamental principles of German law. In particular, inapplicability ensues, if its application would be incompatible with civil rights*". This is just a generic public policy exception, similar to the one found in article 26 of the Rome II Regulation. The specific public policy exception found in article 40, paragraph 3, however, prohibits recourse to this general public policy provision.[437]

200. In article 40 of the EGBGB the first two paragraphs lay down the law applicable to torts. The basic rule holds that tort claims are governed by the law of the country in which the liable party has acted (paragraph 1). If, however, both the liable party and the injured party have their habitual residence in the same country at the time of the damaging event, the law of that country will apply (paragraph 2).

The third paragraph consists of important provisions regarding the treatment of foreign tort laws awarding non-compensatory damages. Paragraph 3 reads, in its relevant part:

Claims governed by the law of another country cannot be raised insofar as they

1. *go substantially beyond what is necessary for an adequate compensation of the injured party,*
2. *obviously serve purposes other than an adequate compensation of the injured party or*
3. *[...]*

201. This special public policy clause saw the light in 1999. Before that time, old article 38 EGBGB protected German defendants against tort actions going beyond the sums available under German law.[438] German citizens could not be subjected to greater liability under the applicable foreign law than they would incur under German law. In the current article 40, on the other hand, protection against punitive damages is no longer restricted to German defendants.[439]

437 V. Behr, "Myth and Reality of Punitive Damages in Germany", 24 *Journal of Law and Commerce* 2004–2005, 201.

438 V. Behr, "Myth and Reality of Punitive Damages in Germany", 24 *Journal of Law and Commerce* 2004–2005, 200.

439 V. Behr, "Myth and Reality of Punitive Damages in Germany", 24 *Journal of Law and Commerce* 2004–2005, 201; P. Hay, "Contemporary Approaches to Non-Contractual Obligations in Private International Law (Conflict of Laws) and the European Community's "Rome II" Regulation", *The European Legal Forum* 2007, 148.

202. Article 40, paragraph 3 consists of two subsections which are relevant to the awarding of punitive damages. The first subsection indicates that foreign damages which go *substantially* beyond what is necessary to compensate the victim should be refused. It protects the tortfeasor against excessive damages, both compensatory and punitive.[440] The word 'substantially' seems to leave some room for punitive damages. Foreign punitive damages may be awarded by the German court, at least to the extent that they are not *substantially* exceeding the compensation required. In that sense the first subsection somewhat resembles the excessiveness test found in recital 32 of the Rome II Regulation.

203. The second subsection, however, removes any possibility of punitive damages being granted to a plaintiff under American law. The provision bars foreign damages which obviously serve purposes other than an adequate compensation of the injured party. Here, contrary to the notion 'substantially' in subsection 1, we believe the word 'obviously' does not leave any room to manoeuvre. As the core objectives of U.S. punitive damages are punishment and deterrence,[441] these damages will always 'obviously' pursue other aims than compensation.[442] The punitive and deterrent objective within punitive damages forms the very essence of their existence. What the addition of 'obviously' does seem to achieve is that it leaves the inherent side-effects of compensatory damages, namely punishment and deterrence,[443] intact.

3.5. CONCLUSION

204. Considering article 40, paragraph 3, (2) EGBGB, one has to draw the conclusion that a German court cannot award punitive damages under U.S. law.[444] This rule, however, does not reflect the legal status quo. As will be demonstrated in chapter 5, in the European Union there exists a number of private law instruments which resemble punitive damages or which pursue the

---

440 V. Behr, "Myth and Reality of Punitive Damages in Germany", 24 *Journal of Law and Commerce* 2004–2005, 201.

441 See *supra* no. 60 *et seq.*

442 P. Klötgen, "L'appréhension des punitive damages par le droit allemande", *Revue Lamy Droit des Affaires* 2013, 128.

443 See *infra* no. 351.

444 M. Requejo Isidro, "Punitive Damages From a Private International Law Perspective" in H. Koziol & V. Wilcox (eds.), *Punitive Damages: Common Law and Civil Law Perspectives*, Vienna, Springer, 2009, 252; T. Rouhette, "The availability of punitive damages in Europe: growing trend or nonexistent concept?", 74 *Defense Counsel Journal* 2007, 329; V. Behr, "Myth and Reality of Punitive Damages in Germany", 24 *Journal of Law and Commerce* 2004–2005, 201.

same goals. The presence of these punitive-like remedies in continental private law refutes the idea that punitive damages violate international public policy. Instead, national rules should follow the rule proclaimed by (non-binding) recital 32 of the Rome II Regulation. U.S. punitive damages may be applied by European courts but may be curtailed to the extent that they are excessive. In chapter 6 the issue of the excessiveness test will be elaborated upon further.

CHAPTER 4
THE ENFORCEMENT OF AMERICAN PUNITIVE DAMAGES IN THE EUROPEAN UNION

205. The enforcement of judgments is the third area of private international law in which the study of punitive damages is relevant. When an American court orders punitive damages against the defendant, he or she must pay the amount due to the plaintiff. If a debtor is unwilling to pay, the judgment needs to be enforced against his assets. When the debtor has no or insufficient assets in the jurisdiction where the judgment was rendered, enforcement needs to take place in a country where the judgment-debtor has assets. This chapter looks at the enforcement of United States punitive damages judgments in the European Union.

206. In this regard the book addresses five European Union countries: Italy, Germany, England, France and Spain. The reason for choosing these five Member States is twofold. First, these countries play an important role in the EU as over 60% of the European Union's population lives in those five nations.[445] Moreover, these five countries represent the five largest economies of the European Union.[446] Second, in Italy, Germany, France and Spain the Supreme Court has decided on the enforceability of (American) punitive damages. England is also included because it is one of the only Common Law countries in the European Union. As England is familiar with punitive damages, it is important to get acquainted with their position on foreign punitive damages.

207. The aim of the chapter is to describe these countries' current attitude towards foreign punitive damages. The order in which we discuss these countries has been carefully considered. It ranks the countries' stance from conservative (Italy and Germany), over mixed (England) to progressive (France

---

[445] See: <http://europa.eu/about-eu/countries/member-countries/index_en.htm>. In our calculation the United Kingdom instead of England is used.

[446] The figures of the year 2013 are available on the website of the International Monetary Fund: <www.imf.org/external/pubs/ft/weo/2013/02/weodata/index.aspx>.

and Spain). In all these countries the enforceability of American punitive damages awards depends (at least in part) on the interpretation of the public policy exception.

208. It is once again underlined that international cases trigger the more narrow concept of international public policy. This is the appropriate yardstick when dealing with cases which are not purely domestic.[447] In cases with a cross-border element a legal system is supposed to be more tolerant and cannot impose its rules of domestic public policy on the matter.[448] Especially in the field of enforcement of judgments, legislators, courts and scholars sometimes fail to make the appropriate distinction between public policy and the narrower concept of international public policy. More often, they realise the existence of a division but, nevertheless, muddy the waters by also employing the term public policy when referring to international public policy. The use of the notion of public policy for both domestic public and international public policy creates confusion as it is sometimes unclear which of the two is meant. The difference between the two is, however, of paramount importance. In chapter 5 we will demonstrate that objections against the enforcement of punitive damages do not belong to international public policy, although they might still be principles that merit domestic public policy protection.

209. To stay in line with the original legal sources, we did not systematically add the word 'international' to every mention of public policy. Whenever the notion public policy is used in this chapter, it should thus be understood as meaning 'international public policy'. If domestic public policy is meant, this will be explicitly indicated as such.

210. After giving an overview of the different positions in the five selected Member States, we will in chapter 5 defend the position that the progressive approach is the correct one, given the existence of punitive mechanisms in the private law of the five Member States. We will argue that punitive damages as a concept can no longer be held contrary to international public policy, the standard (that should be) used to reject this type of damages. Punitive damages awards should only be refused enforcement if their amount is excessive. In Chapter 6 we subsequently formulate guidelines on how to construe this progressive approach, especially with regard to the excessiveness test.

---

[447] See *supra* no. 179 for the same remark in the context of applicable law and an explanation of the difference between domestic and international public policy.

[448] B. Janke & F.-X. Licari, "Enforcing Punitive Damage Awards in France after Fountaine Pajot", 60 *The American Journal of Comparative Law* 2012, 792.

4.1. ITALY

4.1.1. CONDITIONS FOR ENFORCEMENT

211. Neither the EU nor Italy itself has a treaty with the United States arranging for the mutual recognition and enforcement of judgments. The Brussels *Ibis* Regulation does not apply because that instrument only deals with intra-EU judgments. The recognition and enforcement of foreign decisions in Italy is, therefore, governed by articles 64 to 71 of the Law Number 218 of 31 May 1995[449] which replaced articles 796 to 805 of the Italian Code of Civil Procedure as of 1 October 1996.

212. Pursuant to article 64 of Law Number 218 recognition of the foreign judgment will take place if the conditions set out in the article are fulfilled, without a need for any kind of proceedings. These requirements include *inter alia* the regularity of the foreign trial, the competence of the foreign judge and the rights of the defence. For the purposes of this book article 64, g) is of particular interest because this provision demands the foreign judgment's compliance with Italian (international) public policy.[450]

213. Although *recognition* is automatic, when the recognition of the judgment is in dispute, any party concerned may request the competent Court of Appeal to rule on the compliance with the conditions.[451] As far as *enforcement* is concerned, the intervention of the competent Court of Appeal is always necessary. A request for enforcement should be presented to the Court of Appeal. As enforcement presupposes the preceding recognition of the judgment by the Italian Court of Appeal, enforcement can only be granted after such a formal recognition has occurred. The 26 Court of Appeals have jurisdiction in first instance.[452]

4.1.2. THE *FIMEZ* RULING OF THE ITALIAN SUPREME COURT

a. *District Court of Jefferson County*

214. The Italian debate about the enforcement of foreign punitive damages is centred around the – up until recently – only known case addressing the issue.

449 Legge italiana 31 maggio 1995, n. 218, Riforma del sistema italiano di diritto internazionale private, *Gazzetta Ufficiale* 3 June 1995, n. 128, S.O. n. 68.

450 S.A.L. Corongiu, *Punitive Damages Awards in the US Judicial Experience and Their Recognition in Italy*, Universita degli studi di Urbino, 2004–2005, unpublished PhD thesis, 76.

451 Article 67 of Law Number 218 of 31 May 1995.

452 L. Ostoni, "Italian Rejection of Punitive Damages in a U.S. Judgment", 24 *Journal of Law and Commerce* 2004–2005, 246, footnote 4.

The matter originated in the U.S. state of Alabama. In September 1985 fifteen year old Kurt Parrott got involved in a traffic accident in the city of Opelika, Alabama. A car did not give way and hit the boy's motorcycle, causing him to be thrown off his bike. The buckle of his helmet failed and his unprotected head hit the pavement, resulting in instant death. His mother, Judy Glebosky, sued the driver, the American distributor of the helmet as well as some additional defendants for the amount of USD 3 million before the District Court of Jefferson County in Alabama. Fimez SpA, the Italian manufacturer of the helmet, was later also brought into the proceedings. At trial all parties agreed to a settlement, the amount of which remains undisclosed. Fimez SpA, however, had abandoned the case before this settlement agreement. In a judgment of 14 September 1994 the District Court of Jefferson County in Alabama held the defendant liable for the negligent design of the defective crash helmet.[453] The District Court awarded the victim's mother USD 1 million in damages, without further specification.[454]

b. *Venice Court of Appeal*

215. The plaintiff then tried to enforce the judgment in Italy against Fimez SpA's assets. On 15 October 2001 the Venice Court of Appeal ruled on the request for enforcement of the American decision of 14 September 1994.[455, 456] The Court applied article 796 *et seq.* of the Civil Procedure Code because Law Number 218 of 31 May 1995 had not yet entered into force at the time the plaintiff filed for recognition and enforcement of the U.S. judgment.[457] Fimez SpA raised a large number of objections to the recognition of the judgment. In one of its arguments it asserted that the Alabama Court did not provide any reasons for the damages awarded and that the damages were of a punitive nature. This would violate Italian public policy and lead to the unenforceability of the award.

---

453 The District Court had already rendered the USD 1 million award in a non-final decision of 1 April 1991 or 1 January 1991 (the Venice Court of Appeal's judgment mentions both dates throughout its text). The judgment of 14 September 1994 confirmed the previous order, declared it final and added reasons for it.

454 L. Ostoni, "Italian Rejection of Punitive Damages in a U.S. Judgment", 24 *Journal of Law and Commerce* 2004–2005, 246.

455 The Venice Court of Appeal explained that under the foreign procedural law the District Court's judgments were to be viewed as one single decision even if rendered public in two separate steps.

456 Court of Appeal Venice 15 October 2001, *Rep Foro it* 2003, *Delibazione* no. 29; *Giur. It.* II 2002, 1021; the decision was translated by L. Ostoni, "Italian Rejection of Punitive Damages in a U.S. Judgment", 24 *Journal of Law and Commerce* 2004–2005, 251–262.

457 This made no difference as to the material conditions for recognition and enforcement because these remained the same anyway.

216. In the section responding to this particular point, the Venice Court first discussed the character of the USD 1 million damages awarded. The Court found that the foreign judgment lacked a rationale, making it impossible to understand the grounds on which the amount was awarded, the nature of the damages recovered and the basis for the recovery of damages. It was, therefore, unable to establish and assess the criteria used by the Alabama Court to qualify the nature of the damages awarded and to quantify those damages. This led the Venice Court to the conclusion that the damages awarded were punitive in nature, even though the U.S. Court did not expressly qualify them as such.[458]

217. The Venice Court of Appeal must have been unaware of the exact meaning of the Alabama wrongful death statute[459] which applied in this case.[460] Under this unique rule the descendants or heirs are only allowed to recover punitive damages for wrongful death. Compensatory damages are not available. The Alabama Supreme Court, however, explained that the remedy serves multiple functions.[461] It provides a "*mere solatium to the wounded feelings of surviving relations, [or] compensation for the [lost] earnings of the slain*"[462] but it also aims "*to prevent homicides*"[463] by making the amount of damages dependent on "*the gravity of the wrong done*".[464, 465] It was, therefore, clear that the award rendered against Fimez SpA pursued a compensatory objective, in addition to the sanctioning and deterring purposes.[466] The Venice Court did not consider this and instead seems to have based the penal classification of the judgment on the amount awarded.[467] This judicial mistake, nevertheless, does not affect the

---

458 Court of Appeal Venice 15 October 2001, *Rep Foro it* 2003, *Delibazione* no. 29; *Giur. It.* II 2002, 1021; L. Ostoni, "Italian Rejection of Punitive Damages in a U.S. Judgment", 24 *Journal of Law and Commerce* 2004–2005, 249.

459 Alabama Code §6–5–410 (1975).

460 F. Quarta, "Foreign Punitive Damages Decisions and Class Actions in Italy", in D. Fairgrieve and E. Lein (eds.), *Extraterritoriality and Collective Redress*, Oxford, Oxford University Press, 2012, 276.

461 F. Quarta, "Class Actions, Extra-Compensatory Damages, and Judicial Recognition in Europe", Conference paper – "Extraterritoriality and Collective Redress", London 15 November 2010, Draft 19 November 2010, 7.

462 *Savannah & Memphis Railroad v. Shearer*, 58 Ala. (1877), 680.

463 *South & North Alabama Railroad v. Sullivan*, 59 Ala. (1877), 278.

464 *Estes Health Care Ctrs Inc v. Bannerman*, 411 So2d (1982), 113.

465 F. Quarta, "Class Actions, Extra-Compensatory Damages, and Judicial Recognition in Europe", Conference paper – "Extraterritoriality and Collective Redress", London 15 November 2010, Draft 19 November 2010, 6–7.

466 F. Quarta, "Foreign Punitive Damages Decisions and Class Actions in Italy", in D. Fairgrieve and E. Lein (eds.), *Extraterritoriality and Collective Redress*, Oxford, Oxford University Press, 2012, 276; F. Quarta, "Class Actions, Extra-Compensatory Damages, and Judicial Recognition in Europe", Conference paper – "Extraterritoriality and Collective Redress", London 15 November 2010, Draft 19 November 2010, 7.

467 M. Requejo Isidro, "Punitive Damages From a Private International Law Perspective" in H. Koziol & V. Wilcox (eds.), *Punitive Damages: Common Law and Civil Law Perspectives*, Vienna, Springer, 2009, 248; C.I. Nagy, "Recognition and enforcement of US judgments

Venice Court's message as to the unacceptability of punitive damages. Besides, in light of the Alabama wrongful death statute, the American court would have probably classified the damages as punitive if it had decided to label the damages it awarded.

218. The Italian Court categorically denied the recognition and enforcement of the punitive damages awarded as the concept of punitive damages violates Italian public policy, *i.e.* the fundamental principles of Italy's legal system.[468] A number of arguments were put forward to support this holding.

First, the Venice Court noted that the plaintiff is the one benefitting from the punitive damages, not the community in general or in part. Sanctioning the wrongdoer in combination with awarding the plaintiff compensation for the injury suffered, therefore, leads to the plaintiff enjoying an unjust enrichment, which is inconsistent with the Italian legal system.

Second, the court noted that punitive damages have features in common with criminal law because a private party exercises the function of the public authority. The private party brings the suit in lieu of the public authorities for the protection of a public interest (for instance the prevention of future harmful conduct).

Third, punitive damages conflict with public policy since in tort (and contract) cases a private law principle dictates that compensation for the victim must be based on the damages actually suffered by that party.[469] According to the Venice Court public policy requires punitive remedies to stay in the criminal law arena and compensation to remain the only function served by civil judgments.[470]

219. The Italian Court did acknowledge that remedies relatively similar to punitive damages exist in Italian law. Article 1382 of the Civil Code allows contracting parties to insert penalty clauses in their contract. However, these are different from punitive damages because the penalty clause is based on the contractual autonomy of the parties. Moreover, these penalties are pre-defined

---

involving punitive damages in continental Europe", *Nederlands Internationaal Privaatrecht* 2012, 7.

468 G. Nater-Bass, "U.S.-Style Punitive Damages Awards and their Recognition and Enforcement in Switzerland and Other Civil-Law Countries", 28 *Deutsch-Amerikanische Juristen-Vereinigung Newsletter* 2003, 156; Traverso & Associati, "Foreign Punitive Damages Awards Conflict With Italian Public Order", International Law Office – Legal Newsletter, 27 May 2003, no page numbers, available at <www.intemationallawoffice.com>.

469 Court of Appeal Venice 15 October 2001, *Rep Foro it* 2003, *Delibazione* no. 29; *Giur. It.* II 2002, 1021; L. Ostoni, "Italian Rejection of Punitive Damages in a U.S. Judgment", 24 *Journal of Law and Commerce* 2004–2005, 249–250.

470 F. Quarta, "Foreign Punitive Damages Decisions and Class Actions in Italy", in D. Fairgrieve and E. Lein (eds.), *Extraterritoriality and Collective Redress*, Oxford, Oxford University Press, 2012, 275.

(making them predictable[471]) and do not depend on proof of damages.[472] The Court of Appeal further admitted that non-economic damages (such as moral damages) may pursue punitive and deterrent purposes.[473] The Court's reasoning on this point is very difficult to comprehend due to the confusing language it employed. It stated that a remedy pursuing goals of public interest in a civil suit is inconsistent with the Italian legal system and its general principles.[474] This would imply that non-economic damages would be inconsistent with public policy. According to Ostoni, Italian case law only grants non-economic damages on an equitable basis. Punitive damages cannot be assimilated to the common recovery of moral damages.[475] In the eyes of the Court the existence of these various remedies does not distort the fundamental principle that damages can only compensate for damage actually suffered.[476]

220. On the basis of these arguments the Court concluded that the award against Fimez SpA constituted a sanction. While summarising the points leading to this finding, it added two more reasons: the remarkable amount of the compensation and the fact that the defendant was a manufacturer.[477] One may thus assume that the Venice Court attached weight to the professional capacity of the defendant. The Court of Appeal found the punitive and deterrent purposes which the sanction pursued to be outside the Italian legal system and refused the plaintiff's request.[478]

c. *Italian Supreme Court*

221. Judy Glebosky did not accept the decision and brought the case before the Italian Supreme Court (*Corte di Cassazione*). With regard to punitive damages her arguments can be summarised in two points. First, the Court of Appeal had erred in finding the Alabama award to be punitive and excessive. Second,

---

471 L. Ostoni, "Italian Rejection of Punitive Damages in a U.S. Judgment", 24 *Journal of Law and Commerce* 2004–2005, 250.

472 Even though the actual damages might ultimately influence the amount of the contractual penalty. Article 1384 of the Civil Code allows the judge to reduce the penalty if the party in breach partly performed or if the penalty is excessive.

473 Court of Appeal Venice 15 October 2001, *Rep Foro it* 2003, *Delibazione* no. 29; *Giur. It.* II 2002, 1021.

474 Court of Appeal Venice 15 October 2001, *Rep Foro it* 2003, *Delibazione* no. 29; *Giur. It.* II 2002, 1021.

475 L. Ostoni, "Italian Rejection of Punitive Damages in a U.S. Judgment", 24 *Journal of Law and Commerce* 2004–2005, 250.

476 Court of Appeal Venice 15 October 2001, *Rep Foro it* 2003, *Delibazione* no. 29; *Giur. It.* II 2002, 1021.

477 Court of Appeal Venice 15 October 2001, *Rep Foro it* 2003, *Delibazione* no. 29; *Giur. It.* II 2002, 1021.

478 Court of Appeal Venice 15 October 2001, *Rep Foro it* 2003, *Delibazione* no. 29; *Giur. It.* II 2002, 1021.

punitive damages are compatible with Italian public policy as the Italian legal system contains and permits instruments of a comparable punitive nature.[479]

222. The Italian Supreme Court first ruled that a lack of rationale does not prevent a foreign judgment from being enforced. However, the same lack of rationale can serve as an argument for the punitive character of the damages awarded. The *Corte di Cassazione* further explained that the finding of excessiveness of the damages and their classification as punitive depend on the facts of the individual situation. This analysis is left to the Court of Appeal whose factual finding cannot be reserved. Moreover, although it could not have intervened even if it wanted to, the Supreme Court indicated that the Venice Court of Appeal's finding seemed justified in this case. The Supreme Court is only entitled to reverse matters of law, such as a different definition of public policy. However, the Supreme Court did not find fault with the interpretation of public policy rendered by the Venice Court.[480]

223. The Supreme Court indeed disagreed with the appellant's contention that the U.S. decision did not violate public policy because the Italian liability system contains several legal institutions, such as penalty clauses and moral damages, which pursue punitive objectives.

224. It found that penalty clauses are not punitive in nature and do not have a retributive aim. They serve to strengthen a contractual relationship and quantify damages in advance. The Supreme Court noted that the amount of the contractual penalty can be reduced if the judge finds an abuse of the parties' freedom of contract contrary to the principle of proportionality. It concluded that penalty clauses cannot be compared to punitive damages, despite the penalty being due regardless of proof of the damage suffered and a strong correlation with the extent of the damage. Punitive damages are an institution that is not only connected to the tortfeasor's conduct and not to the damage suffered but is also unjustifiably disproportional to the harm actually incurred.[481]

225. The Court rejected the suggested equivalence between punitive damages and moral damages as well. Moral damages reflect a loss suffered by the victim

---

479 Cass. Civ. 19 January 2007, no. 1183, *Rep Foro it* 2007 *v Delibazione* no. 13 and *v Danni Civili* no. 316; *Corr. Giur.*, 2007, 4, 497; translated by F. Quarta, "Recognition and Enforcement of U.S. Punitive Damages Awards in Continental Europe: The Italian Supreme Court's Veto", 31 *Hastings International & Comparative Law Review* 2008, Appendix A, 780–782.

480 Cass. Civ. 19 January 2007, no. 1183, *Rep Foro it* 2007 *v Delibazione* no. 13 and *v Danni Civili* no. 316; *Corr. Giur.*, 2007, 4, 497; F. Quarta, "Recognition and Enforcement of U.S. Punitive Damages Awards in Continental Europe: The Italian Supreme Court's Veto", 31 *Hastings International & Comparative Law Review* 2008, 757.

481 Cass. Civ. 19 January 2007, no. 1183, *Rep Foro it* 2007 *v Delibazione* no. 13 and *v Danni Civili* no. 316; *Corr. Giur.*, 2007, 4, 497.

and recovery is based on that loss. The focus of moral damages lies on the injured party, not on the wrongdoer. Compensation is the primary objective of moral damages whereas in the case of punitive damages there is no relation between the damages awarded and the harm incurred.[482]

226. According to the Italian Supreme Court, damages in private law are unrelated to the idea of punishment or to the wrongdoer's misconduct. These damages are intended to restore damage incurred by the injured party by eliminating the consequences of the inflicted harm through the award of a sum of money. This is true for every type of civil damages, moral damages included, which are not influenced by the victim's conditions and the wrongdoer's wealth but require concrete and factual evidence of the loss suffered.[483] In other words, Italy's highest court made a clear distinction between compensatory and punitive damages, with absolutely no room for overlap whatsoever. Compensatory damages, such as moral damages, focus on the victim, relate to his or her loss and intend to make him or her whole. Punitive damages, on the other hand, centre around the wrongdoer's behaviour, are not connected to the damage suffered, and pursue the punishment of the tortfeasor.

227. Consequently, the Supreme Court rejected the analogy (between penalty clauses and moral damages on the one hand and punitive damages on the other) put forward by plaintiff Judy Glebosky. It confirmed the Venice Court of Appeal's view that punitive damages are in violation of public policy and declined to enforce the Alabama USD 1 million award.[484] As a result, the plaintiff was left without any compensation. It has been argued that such an outcome is inconsistent with articles 24 and 25[485] of the Italian Constitution and contrary to public policy.[486] Furthermore, given the Court's reasoning, there should be no doubt about the enforcement of compensatory damages. As long as

---

482 Cass. Civ. 19 January 2007, no. 1183, *Rep Foro it* 2007 v *Delibazione* no. 13 and v *Danni Civili* no. 316; *Corr. Giur.*, 2007, 4, 497.

483 Cass. Civ. 19 January 2007, no. 1183, *Rep Foro it* 2007 v *Delibazione* no. 13 and v *Danni Civili* no. 316; *Corr. Giur.*, 2007, 4, 497.

484 Cass. Civ. 19 January 2007, no. 1183, *Rep Foro it* 2007 v *Delibazione* no. 13 and v *Danni Civili* no. 316; *Corr. Giur.*, 2007, 4, 497.

485 Article 24 provides: "*Anyone may bring cases before a court of law in order to protect their rights under civil and administrative law. Defense is an inviolable right at every stage and instance of legal proceedings. The poor are entitled by law to proper means for action or defense in all courts. The law shall define the conditions and forms of reparation in case of judicial errors.*" Article 25 reads: "*No case may be removed from the court seized with it as established by law. No punishment may be inflicted except by virtue of a law in force at the time tehe offence was committed. No restriction may be placed on a person's liberty save for as provided by law.*" English translation available at <https://www.senato.it/documenti/repository/istituzione/costituzione_inglese.pdf>.

486 C.I. Nagy, "Recognition and enforcement of US judgments involving punitive damages in continental Europe", *Nederlands Internationaal Privaatrecht* 2012, 7; F. Quarta, "Class Actions, Extra-Compensatory Damages, and Judicial Recognition in Europe", Conference

the compensatory damages are clearly distinguished from the punitive damages, the enforcement should not pose any public policy concerns.[487]

d. Post-Fimez case law

228. In the years after the *Fimez* case the Italian judicial stance remained the same. In a judgment of 16 August 2008 the Court of Appeal of Trento rejected the enforcement of the punitive portion of a judgment from Florida. In that case a number of American citizens were awarded compensatory damages as well as twice the amount of the compensatory damages as punitive damages.[488] The Trento Court of Appeal emphasised the retributive function of the civil liability system: *i.e.* the compensation of victims of wrongful conduct. It attached constitutional protection (under article 3 of the Italian Constitution) to this retributive justice principle.[489] Criminal justice on the other hand focuses on the punishment of the wrongdoer and envisages dissuasion. The Court noted that U.S. punitive damages pursue the same objectives of punishment and deterrence. In Italian law, however, these objectives are not assigned to civil courts but to public prosecutors and administered by criminal courts. The Trento Court noted that the recognition of the judgment would lead to double punishment as a civil court would be allowed to lay down penalties analogous to those ordered by criminal courts. Besides, such a course of action would also infringe the *non bis in idem* principle. In addition, the Court of Appeal ruled that recognising the American judgment would produce an (constitutionally problematic) inequality between foreign and domestic creditors. The former would be able to access the assets of the defendant to a larger extent than the latter, even if the latter suffered more harm.[490] We find the latter reasoning also in the *John Doe v. Eckhard Schmitz* judgment of the German *Bundesgerichtshof* of 1992.[491]

229. The Italian Supreme Court itself affirmed its own position in a judgment of 8 February 2012.[492] The Middlesex Superior Court in Massachusetts had ordered an Italian company to pay USD 8 million to an employee who had

---

paper – "Extraterritoriality and Collective Redress", London 15 November 2010, Draft 19 November 2010, 8.

487 C.I. Nagy, "Recognition and enforcement of US judgments involving punitive damages in continental Europe", *Nederlands Internationaal Privaatrecht* 2012, 7.

488 Court of Appeal Trento 16 August 2008, *Danno resp.* 2009, 22, *Riv. Dir. Priv. e Proc.* 2009, 448.

489 E. Baldoni, *Punitive damages: a comparative analysis*, unpublished Ph.D thesis, 2012, 117.

490 Court of Appeal Trento 16 August 2008, *Danno resp.* 2009, 22, *Riv. Dir. Priv. e Proc.* 2009, 448; Traverso & Associati, "Foreign Punitive Damages Awards Conflict With Italian Public Order", International Law Office – Legal Newsletter, 27 May 2003, available at <www.intemationallawoffice.com>.

491 See *infra* no. 243–244 and 361–362 for the *Bundesgerichtshof*'s ruling on this point and the criticism developed against this argument.

492 Supreme Court 8 February 2012, Soc Ruffinatti v Oyola-Rosado, no. 1781/2012, *Danno resp* 2012, 609.

suffered injuries in an accident at the Italian corporation's U.S. subsidiary. The judgment did not mention punitive damages nor the criteria used to quantify the award. As was the case in *Fimez*, the Italian courts were confronted with a global award without further specification or demarcation. The Court of Appeal of Turin declared the whole award enforceable because the judgment did not refer to punitive damages and the amount was reasonable and fair in light of the seriousness of the employee's injuries. The Supreme Court, however, overturned the Court of Appeal's decision. It yet again labelled the damages as punitive in nature despite the fact that the U.S. judgment never discussed punitive damages. The Court reiterated that the Italian civil liability system is strictly compensatory and not punitive. The USD 8 million in damages awarded was thus unenforceable on the basis of the public policy exception.[493]

4.2. GERMANY

4.2.1. CONDITIONS FOR ENFORCEMENT

230. In the absence of a treaty between Germany and the U.S. the enforcement of U.S. civil judgments in Germany is governed by article 722 *et seq.* of the Code of Civil Procedure (*Zivilprozessordnung* – ZPO). According to article 722 (1) a German judgment needs to declare the foreign judgment admissible for enforcement before such enforcement can take place. The German court competent for issuing a judgment of enforceability shall only do so when it is satisfied that the foreign judgment has *res judicata* effect in its country of origin (article 723 (2), first sentence). Furthermore, article 723 (1) forbids a review of the legality of the foreign decision (*i.e.* a prohibition on *révision au fond*).[494, 495]

231. For the conditions of enforcement article 723 (2), second sentence refers back to article 328 which sets out the requirements for recognition of judgments. The German court receiving the request for enforcement will, therefore, assess

---

493 LS Lexjus Sinacta, "Italian Supreme Court Confirms Stance On Punitive Damages", International Law Office – Legal Newsletter, 21 December 2012, no page numbers, available at <www.intemationallawoffice.com>; X, "Italian Supreme Court Affirms Position Against Punitive Damage Awards", 31 January 2013, no page numbers, available at <www.goldbergsegalla.com/resources/news-and-updates/italian-supreme-court-affirms-position-against-punitive-damage-awards>; F. Quarta, "Foreign Punitive Damages Decisions and Class Actions in Italy", in D. Fairgrieve and E. Lein (eds.), *Extraterritoriality and Collective Redress*, Oxford, Oxford University Press, 2012, 275, footnote 32.

494 P. Klötgen, "L'appréhension des punitive damages par le droit allemande", *Revue Lamy Droit des Affaires* 2013, 126.

495 M. Tolani, "U.S. Punitive Damages Before German Courts: A Comparative Analysis with Respect to the Ordre Public", 17 *Annual Survey of International & Comparative Law* 2011, 200.

whether the requirements for recognition are fulfilled.[496] The article enumerates five circumstances under which recognition shall not be granted.[497] When deciding whether or not to allow enforcement the judge verifies the foreign judgment's compliance with these requirements.[498]

232. For U.S. judgments containing punitive damages awards the prerequisite demanding the most attention is article 328 (1), 4). Under this substantive public policy clause recognition of the judgment should not lead to a result that is manifestly incompatible with essential principles of German law and with fundamental rights in particular. Public policy embodies legal norms which are considered to be indispensable in a free and democratic society. The basic rights guaranteed in the German Constitution are part of these norms.[499] The concept of public policy is a fluid notion that reflects changes in the underlying principles of the German system.[500]

The public policy test is only concerned with the result of the recognition of the foreign judgment. The theoretical foundations of the foreign system or the divergence between the foreign system and the German system cannot form the basis of a public policy objection. The German court must judge whether the concrete result the foreign decision produces is compatible with the fundamental principles of German law.[501] The public policy defence is only to be invoked in extreme cases where the fundamental values of the German state are in jeopardy.[502] As the task of determining the borderlines of the public policy

---

496 W. Wurmnest, "Recognition and Enforcement of U.S. Money Judgments in Germany", 23 *Berkeley Journal of International Law* 2005, 181.

497 M. Tolani, "U.S. Punitive Damages Before German Courts: A Comparative Analysis with Respect to the Ordre Public", 17 *Annual Survey of International & Comparative Law* 2011, 201; P. Klötgen, "L'appréhension des punitive damages par le droit allemande", *Revue Lamy Droit des Affaires* 2013, 126.

498 G. Wegen & J. Sherer, "Germany: Federal Court of Justice decision concerning the recognition and enforcement of U.S. judgments awarding punitive damages", 32 *International Legal Materials* 1993, 1321.

499 D. Martiny, "Recognition and Enforcement of Foreign Money Judgments in the Federal Republic of Germany", 35 *American Journal of Comparative Law* 1987, 745; P.J. Nettesheim & H. Stahl, "Bundesgerichtshof Rejects Enforcement of United States Punitive Damages Award", 28 *Texas International Law Journal* 1993, 417, footnote 8.

500 V. Behr, "Punitive Damages in American and German Law – Tendencies Towards Approximation of Apparently Irreconcilable Concepts", 78 *Chicago-Kent Law Review* 2003, 153.

501 V. Behr, "Punitive Damages in American and German Law – Tendencies Towards Approximation of Apparently Irreconcilable Concepts", 78 *Chicago-Kent Law Review* 2003, 153; P. Klötgen, "L'appréhension des punitive damages par le droit allemande", *Revue Lamy Droit des Affaires* 2013, 126; BGH 26 September 1979, *BGHZ* 1980, 171.

502 J. Zekoll, "The Enforceability of American Money Judgments Abroad: A Landmark Decision by the German Federal Court of Justice", 30 *Columbia Journal of Transnational Law* 1992, 646; V. Behr, "Myth and Reality of Punitive Damages in Germany", 24 *Journal of Law and Commerce* 2004–2005, 204; M. Tolani, "U.S. Punitive Damages Before German Courts: A Comparative Analysis with Respect to the Ordre Public", 17 *Annual Survey of International*

exception lies with the courts, the German judges have to decide whether such an extreme case presents itself before them.[503]

233. In the context of U.S. punitive damages, the question thus becomes whether, and if so to what extent, an American judgment containing punitive damages can be classified as an exceptional case capable of triggering the public policy clause of article 328 (1), 4 of the German Code of Civil Procedure. The first and pivotal decision of the *Bundesgerichtshof* (the German Supreme Court) denied recognition and enforcement of the punitive damages portion of a California judgment on this ground.

4.2.2. THE *BUNDESGERICHTSHOF*'S CASE OF *JOHN DOE v. ECKHARD SCHMITZ*

a. *California Superior Court*

234. The case involved a fourteen year old boy, a California resident, who had been the victim of sexual abuse. The defendant, also living in Stockton, California, had been sentenced in California to a lengthy prison term for the sexual misconduct. The victim sought to recover damages from the culprit. Before the case was tried before the civil courts, the perpetrator, who had dual (American and German) citizenship, fled to Germany where he owned property. He did not appear in the civil case and left no property in California. The California Superior Court (County of San Joaquin) awarded the victim USD 150.260 for past and future medical expenses. For anxiety, pain and suffering the Court held an amount of USD 200.000 to be appropriate. In addition to these compensatory damages, the culprit had to pay USD 400.000 in punitive and exemplary damages. The California Court ruled that 40% of the entire award represented the plaintiff's lawyer's fees.[504] The lack of any assets in the

& Comparative Law 2011, 201; H. Bungert, "Enforcing U.S. Excessive and Punitive Damages Awards in Germany", 27 *International Lawyer* 1993, 1079.

503 V. Behr, "Myth and Reality of Punitive Damages in Germany", 24 *Journal of Law and Commerce* 2004–2005, 204.

504 California Superior Court (County of San Joaquin) 24 April 1985, John Doe v. Eckhard Schmitz, No. 168–588, *unpublished*. The facts are to be found in the judgment of the *Bundesgerichtshof*: BGH 4 June 1992, *BGHZ* 118, 312, *Neue Juristische Wochenschrift* 1992, 3096, *Recht der Internationalen Wirtschaft* 1993, 132, *ZIP* 1992, 1256 (English translation of the relevant parts of the judgment by G. Wegen & J. Sherer, "Germany: Federal Court of Justice decision concerning the recognition and enforcement of U.S. judgments awarding punitive damages", 32 *International Legal Materials* 1993, 1329); J. Zekoll, "The Enforceability of American Money Judgments Abroad: A Landmark Decision by the German Federal Court of Justice", 30 *Columbia Journal of Transnational Law* 1992, 644; S. Baumgartner, "How well do U.S. judgments fare in Europe?", 40 *George Washington International Law Review* 2008–2009, 203.

U.S. forced the victim to enforce the judgment against the perpetrator's assets in Germany. During these enforcement proceedings the question arose as to whether a decision containing a punitive award could be enforced on German territory.[505] This issue had never been addressed before as previous awards against German parties did not need to be enforced in Germany because the defendants had sufficient assets in the U.S.[506]

b. *Lower German courts*

235. At the first instance level, the judgment was allowed complete enforceability in Germany by the *Landgericht* Düsseldorf.[507] On appeal, the *Oberlandesgericht* (Court of Appeal) Düsseldorf confirmed this decision with regard to the medical expenses but rejected the USD 200.000 for pain and suffering on the basis that it was excessive in light of German public policy. It reduced the award to USD 70.000. The Court also limited the punitive damages award to USD 55.065, an amount the Court believed represented acceptable lawyer's fees awarded in the guise of punitive damages.[508]

c. *The Bundesgerichtshof's ruling*

i. Unenforceability of punitive damages

236. The *Bundesgerichtshof* upheld the lower courts' ruling on the medical expenses. However, it reversed the appellate court's decision regarding the damages for pain and suffering and the punitive damages. The Court accepted the full USD 200.000 for pain and suffering but rejected the punitive award in its entirety on the basis of the public policy clause.[509] The judgment was thus declared enforceable for an amount of USD 350.260.

237. With respect to the compensatory portion (*i.e.* the medical expenses and the damages for pain and suffering) of the U.S. judgment, the *Bundesgerichtshof*

---

505 M. Tolani, "U.S. Punitive Damages Before German Courts: A Comparative Analysis with Respect to the Ordre Public", 17 *Annual Survey of International & Comparative Law* 2011, 186.

506 J. Zekoll, "The Enforceability of American Money Judgments Abroad: A Landmark Decision by the German Federal Court of Justice", 30 *Columbia Journal of Transnational Law* 1992, 656.

507 Landgericht Düsseldorf 12 April 1990, 13 O 456/89, *unpublished.*

508 Oberlandesgericht Düsseldorf 28 May 1991, *Recht der Internationalen Wirtschaft* 1991, 594; J. Zekoll, "The Enforceability of American Money Judgments Abroad: A Landmark Decision by the German Federal Court of Justice", 30 *Columbia Journal of Transnational Law* 1992, 644.

509 BGH 4 June 1992, *Neue Juristische Wochenschrift* 1992, 3096–3106; J. Zekoll, "The Enforceability of American Money Judgments Abroad: A Landmark Decision by the German Federal Court of Justice", 30 *Columbia Journal of Transnational Law* 1992, 644–645.

noted the difference between California law and German law. Whereas California law allowed the victim to claim damages for medical expenses without intending to undergo medical treatment, German law did not permit such fictitious damages. However, this difference in the assessment of damages did not lead to an intolerable result. The *Bundesgerichtshof* therefore did not find a violation of public policy under article 328 (1), 4) ZPO (Code of Civil Procedure) on this point. Similarly, the fact that the award for pain and suffering was very high to German standards did not preclude its enforcement.[510]

238. The punitive damages award, on the other hand, did not survive the public policy analysis. In addressing the fate of the punitive award, the German Supreme Court stated that a foreign judgment awarding lump sum punitive damages of a not inconsiderable amount in addition to the damages for material and immaterial losses generally cannot be enforced in Germany.[511]

239. The *Bundesgerichtshof* first confirmed the civil nature of the judgment. This determination is of crucial importance as penal judgments are unenforceable in Germany. The American judgment thus fell under the scope of the Code of Civil Procedure (ZPO) and was therefore in principle enforceable.[512, 513] The Court did not clarify whether characterisation of the judgment should be determined according to the law of the requesting state, the requested state or both. The Court felt it could leave the issue unanswered since both countries accepted punitive damages as a civil matter.[514] It has been argued that the law of the requested state will determine the nature of the judgment.[515]

---

510 BGH 4 June 1992, *Neue Juristische Wochenschrift* 1992, 3100–3102; G. Wegen & J. Sherer, "Germany: Federal Court of Justice decision concerning the recognition and enforcement of U.S. judgments awarding punitive damages", 32 *International Legal Materials* 1993, 1323 and 1325; A.R. Fiebig, "The Recognition and Enforcement of Punitive Damage Awards in Germany: Recent Developments", 22 *Georgia Journal of International & Comparative Law* 1992, 648.

511 BGH 4 June 1992, *Neue Juristische Wochenschrift* 1992, 3102 and 3104; V. Behr, "Punitive Damages in American and German Law – Tendencies Towards Approximation of Apparently Irreconcilable Concepts", 78 *Chicago-Kent Law Review* 2003, 158.

512 A.R. Fiebig, "The Recognition and Enforcement of Punitive Damage Awards in Germany: Recent Developments", 22 *Georgia Journal of International & Comparative Law* 1992, 648.

513 Nettesheim and Stahl even argue that the Court had to accept the civil character of the case to be able to address the real issue, namely whether or not the award could be granted enforcement: P.J. Nettesheim & H. Stahl, "Recent Development – Bundesgerichtshof Rejects Enforcement of United States Punitive Damages Award", 28 *Texas International Law Journal* 1993, 420.

514 BGH 4 June 1992, *Neue Juristische Wochenschrift* 1992, 3102; P.J. Nettesheim & H. Stahl, "Recent Development – Bundesgerichtshof Rejects Enforcement of United States Punitive Damages Award", 28 *Texas International Law Journal* 1993, 419; H. Bungert, "Enforcing U.S. Excessive and Punitive Damages Awards in Germany", 27 *International Lawyer* 1993, 1079.

515 H. Bungert, "Enforcing U.S. Excessive and Punitive Damages Awards in Germany", 27 *International Lawyer* 1993, 1078.

In the Court's opinion, civil cases in German law concern the existence or non-existence of private rights and the legal relationships between parties of equal standing. Punitive damages can be classified as a special form of damages between private individuals, notwithstanding the purposes behind the award of such damages. The *Bundesgerichtshof* did not doubt the civil nature of the punitive damages in the case before it because the damages had to be paid to the victim. The Court left open the question whether a different view should be adopted if the punitive award is to be paid to the state or another institution.[516]

240. The Court then elaborated on the reasons why the punitive damages awarded to the American plaintiff violated the public policy standard. The German private law system provides compensation for damage suffered but does not intend an enrichment of the victim.[517] The Court held the legal principle of awarding the victim damages with the sole purpose of reimbursing what he has lost to be a fundamental principle of German law.[518] Punishment and deterrence, the main objectives pursued by punitive damages, are aims of criminal law rather than of civil law. Punitive damages allow a plaintiff to act as a private public prosecutor. This interferes with the state's monopoly on penalisation. Besides, the defendant cannot rely on the special procedural guarantees provided for in criminal law.[519]

241. The *Bundesgerichtshof* noted the existence of a penal institution within German civil law. Contractual penalties provide for punishment in civil law.[520] This finding could have dismantled the civil-criminal division that the Court embraced and could have created an opening for punitive damages. However, contractual penalties originate from a legal agreement between parties and are, therefore, irrelevant in the eyes of the German Supreme Court. Fifteen years before *Fimez* the German Supreme Court thus already rejected the suggested analogy between punitive damages and contractual penalties.[521]

---

516 BGH 4 June 1992, *Neue Juristische Wochenschrift* 1992, 3102–3103.

517 W. Kühn, "Rico Claims in International Arbitration and their Recognition in Germany", 11 *Journal of International Arbitration* 1994, 44.

518 V. Behr, "Myth and Reality of Punitive Damages in Germany", 24 *Journal of Law and Commerce* 2004–2005, 205.

519 BGH 4 June 1992, *Neue Juristische Wochenschrift* 1992, 3103; M. Tolani, "U.S. Punitive Damages Before German Courts: A Comparative Analysis with Respect to the Ordre Public", 17 *Annual Survey of International & Comparative Law* 2011, 202; P.J. Nettesheim & H. Stahl, "Recent Development – Bundesgerichtshof Rejects Enforcement of United States Punitive Damages Award", 28 *Texas International Law Journal* 1993, 419; N. Jansen & L. Rademacher, "Punitive Damages in Germany" in H. Koziol & V. Wilcox (eds.), *Punitive Damages: Common Law and Civil Law Perspectives*, Vienna, Springer, 2009, 76.

520 Article 340–341 BGB (German Civil Code).

521 BGH 4 June 1992, *Neue Juristische Wochenschrift* 1992, 3103; P.J. Nettesheim & H. Stahl, "Recent Development – Bundesgerichtshof Rejects Enforcement of United States Punitive Damages Award", 28 *Texas International Law Journal* 1993, 420.

242. It was further held that the core aims of punitive damages, punishment and deterrence, cannot be compared with the function of satisfaction or gratification ("*Genugtuungsfunktion*"). The latter function is a component in the assessment of damages for pain and suffering in cases of bodily harm.[522] Damages for pain and suffering are meant to compensate the plaintiff but also to satisfy his feelings.[523] The *Genugtuungsfunktion* addresses the victim's need for (legal) redress after having been violated.[524] The *Bundesgerichtshof* denounced the idea that the punitive award could be enforced because it could be viewed as comparable to the *Genugtuungsfunktion*.[525] It stated that the primary factor in the assessment of damages is not the function of satisfaction but rather the degree and duration of the pain and suffering. Furthermore, because the function of satisfaction is inextricably linked with the function of compensation, the *Genugtuungsfunktion* does not give the damages for pain and suffering an immediate penal effect.[526] The German Supreme Court specified that punitive damages would be enforceable if they are intended to compensate for immaterial damage. The general amount awarded on top of the tangible and intangible damages, however, does not correspond to the *Genugtuungsfunktion*. The latter had already been served by the separate award for pain and suffering.[527] We agree with the reasoning of the *Bundesgerichtshof* on this point. The *Genugtuungsfunktion* should be viewed as a representation of the plaintiff's interest in the preservation of his

---

522 Article 253 BGB; BGH 29 November 1994, *BGHZ* 128, 117; P.J. Nettesheim & H. Stahl, "Recent Development - Bundesgerichtshof Rejects Enforcement of United States Punitive Damages Award", 28 *Texas International Law Journal* 1993, 421.

523 U. Magnus, "Punitive Damages and German Law" in L. Meurkens & E. Nordin (eds.), *The Power of Punitive Damages - Is Europe Missing Out?*, Cambridge - Antwerp - Portland, Intersentia, 2012, 252; E. C. Stiefel, R. Stürner & A. Stadler, "The Enforceability Of Excessive U.S. Punitive Damage Awards In Germany", 39 *American Journal of Comparative Law* 1991, 794.

524 E.C. Stiefel, R. Stürner & A. Stadler, "The Enforceability Of Excessive U.S. Punitive Damage Awards In Germany", 39 *American Journal of Comparative Law* 1991, 794; P.J. Nettesheim & H. Stahl, "Recent Development - Bundesgerichtshof Rejects Enforcement of United States Punitive Damages Award", 28 *Texas International Law Journal* 1993, 421.

525 P.J. Nettesheim & H. Stahl, "Recent Development - Bundesgerichtshof Rejects Enforcement of United States Punitive Damages Award", 28 *Texas International Law Journal* 1993, 421.

526 BGH 4 June 1992, *Neue Juristische Wochenschrift* 1992, 3103; V. Behr, "Punitive Damages in American and German Law - Tendencies Towards Approximation of Apparently Irreconcilable Concepts", 78 *Chicago-Kent Law Review* 2003, 158 and 159; M. Tolani, "U.S. Punitive Damages Before German Courts: A Comparative Analysis with Respect to the Ordre Public", 17 *Annual Survey of International & Comparative Law* 2011, 202; A.R. Fiebig, "The Recognition and Enforcement of Punitive Damage Awards in Germany: Recent Developments", 22 *Georgia Journal of International & Comparative Law* 1992, 654–655.

527 BGH 4 June 1992, *Neue Juristische Wochenschrift* 1992, 3103; P.J. Nettesheim & H. Stahl, "Recent Development - Bundesgerichtshof Rejects Enforcement of United States Punitive Damages Award", 28 *Texas International Law Journal* 1993, 421.

subjective rights. A violation of that interest leads to an autonomous injury which requires compensation.[528]

243. Finally, the *Bundesgerichtshof* developed the argument that enforcement of the punitive damages award should be rejected because their availability in the U.S. and subsequent enforcement in Germany would put foreign creditors in a better position than domestic creditors. The former would be able to gain access to the assets of German debtors to a considerably greater extent than the latter would be able to, even if the latter had suffered more damage. The fact that foreign creditors can obtain punitive damages leads, according to the Court, to a lack of equal treatment.[529, 530] It thus seems that the *Bundesgerichtshof* tried to protect the German industry from U.S. litigation.[531] The Court also pointed to the significant economic consequences on the insurance industry resulting from excessive punitive damages.[532]

244. Hay turns the reasoning of the *Bundesgerichtshof* around and looks at the policy-oriented argument from the point of view of an American competitor of the German judgment debtor. He wonders why the German debtor (who is active on the American territory) should receive immunity from liability for punitive damages incurred in the United States whereas an American market participant cannot escape this liability. Furthermore, the enforcement of American pain and suffering awards seems to be unproblematic in Germany, even if they are substantially larger than the amounts German courts would grant. This would make the foreign creditor better off than the domestic one but the Court does not make mention of this scenario.[533]

245. The *Bundesgerichtshof* also noted that the application of the public policy clause requires a strong link between the facts of the case and the forum where enforcement is sought.[534] For the public policy exception to apply a connection

528 N. Jansen & L. Rademacher, "Punitive Damages in Germany" in H. Koziol & V. Wilcox (eds.), *Punitive Damages: Common Law and Civil Law Perspectives*, Vienna, Springer, 2009, 79–80.

529 BGH 4 June 1992, *Neue Juristische Wochenschrift* 1992, 3104.

530 M. Requejo Isidro, "Punitive Damages From a Private International Law Perspective" in H. Koziol & V. Wilcox (eds.), *Punitive Damages: Common Law and Civil Law Perspectives*, Vienna, Springer, 2009, 246.

531 S. Baumgartner, "Understanding the Obstacles to the Recognition and Enforcement of U.S. Judgments Abroad", 45 *New York University Journal of International Law and Politics* 2013, 998.

532 BGH 4 June 1992, *Neue Juristische Wochenschrift* 1992, 3104; P.J. Nettesheim & H. Stahl, "Recent Development – Bundesgerichtshof Rejects Enforcement of United States Punitive Damages Award", 28 *Texas International Law Journal* 1993, 424.

533 P. Hay, "The Recognition and Enforcement of American Money-Judgments in Germany – The 1992 Decision of the German Supreme Court", 40 *The American Journal of Comparative Law* 1992, 746–747, footnote 72.

534 BGH 4 June 1992, *BGHZ* 118, 348.

between the case and the requested state is needed. This connection is referred to as *Inlandsbeziehung* or *Inlandsbezug*. The weaker the connection, the less likely the exception will apply and the more likely enforcement will be granted.[535] If the connection to the forum country is low, that country has less interest in a close policing of its public policy.[536] In *John Doe v. Eckhard Schmitz* there was no close connection to Germany. The crime was committed in the U.S. The young victim was a U.S. citizen. The perpetrator had dual citizenship but had only moved to Germany after having being convicted of the crime. Under these circumstances one would expect the public policy exception to be more restrained. The rejection of punitive damages despite the slight connection of the case to the forum indicates a strong German antipathy towards this type of damages.[537]

246. These arguments led the *Bundesgerichtshof* to the conclusion that the punitive damages were unenforceable because they violated essential fundamental principles of German law.

ii. Proportionality test

247. Although this finding of incompatibility with public policy was reason enough to reject the punitive award, the Supreme Court, nevertheless, continued its analysis. It looked at the punitive damages to determine whether they would pass the proportionality test.[538] This principle gives German courts the responsibility to ensure that a damage award does not exceed the amount needed for the compensation of the injured party.[539] The Court did emphasise the compensation of the victim as the sole appropriate aim of a civil action. It expressed its disapproval of sums of money imposed on top of the compensation for damages. Such an approach would leave no room for any amount of punitive damages. However, the Court found that enforcement of the punitive damages award in the case before it would be excessive because the punitive damages awarded are higher in amount than the sum of all the compensatory damages.[540] This statement leads us to believe that the *Bundesgerichtshof* views

535 M. Requejo Isidro, "Punitive Damages From a Private International Law Perspective" in H. Koziol & V. Wilcox (eds.), *Punitive Damages: Common Law and Civil Law Perspectives*, Vienna, Springer, 2009, 245–246.

536 S. Baumgartner, "How well do U.S. judgments fare in Europe?", 40 *George Washington International Law Review* 2008–2009, 205, footnote 189.

537 C.I. Nagy, "Recognition and enforcement of US judgments involving punitive damages in continental Europe", *Nederlands Internationaal Privaatrecht* 2012, 8.

538 BGH 4 June 1992, *Neue Juristische Wochenschrift* 1992, 3104.

539 P.J. Nettesheim & H. Stahl, "Recent Development – Bundesgerichtshof Rejects Enforcement of United States Punitive Damages Award", 28 *Texas International Law Journal* 1993, 423–424.

540 BGH 4 June 1992, *Neue Juristische Wochenschrift* 1992, 3104.

a 1:1 ratio between compensatory and punitive damages as the maximum allowed.[541] This opinion was merely academic for the *John Doe v. Eckhard Schmitz* case. However, the *Bundesgerichtshof*'s opinion on proportionality will prove to be crucial if the compatibility of punitive damages with (German) international public policy can be demonstrated.[542] Indeed, if the compatibility of the concept of punitive damages with international public policy can be demonstrated, the excessiveness check is the only obstacle remaining before the judgment can be enforced.[543] The *Bundesgerichtshof*'s judgment gave no explicit indication as to the consequences of a finding of excessiveness for the enforcement of the non-excessive part of the punitive damages award, although it did mention that a court should not cut up the punitive award at its own free discretion.[544]

iii. The exception for the compensatory part of the punitive award

248. The *Bundesgerichtshof* carved out an exception to the unenforceability of punitive damages. It ruled that it would allow the enforcement of punitive damages if and to the extent that the punitive award serves a compensatory function.[545] Punitive damages may occasionally serve as compensation for losses that are difficult to prove, for losses that are not covered by other types of damages or as a means to deprive the defendant of the gains he or she acquired through his or her wrongful behaviour.[546] The Court had already mentioned that the punitive award did not compensate for immaterial injury as

---

541 In our opinion the French Cour de Cassation adopted the same 1:1 ceiling 18 years later in *Fountaine Pajot*. See *infra* no. 307.

542 Chapter 5 will provide evidence for the position that punitive damages do not violate the international public policy of Germany.

543 Interestingly, in its decision the *Bundesgerichtshof* rejected punitive damages of "*a not inconsiderable amount*". This is surprising because the amount should have been irrelevant to the German Supreme Court, given that the non-compensatory nature of the remedy alone was enough to refuse enforcement: V. Behr, "Punitive Damages in American and German Law – Tendencies Towards Approximation of Apparently Irreconcilable Concepts", 78 *Chicago-Kent Law Review* 2003, 159. It might indicate an opening for punitive damages after all.

544 BGH 4 June 1992, *Neue Juristische Wochenschrift* 1992, 3104. Likewise, the French Supreme Court in *Fountaine Pajot* seems to have decided that the exceeding of the maximum ratio leads to the rejection of the whole punitive award. See *infra* no. 307.

545 BGH 4 June 1992, *Neue Juristische Wochenschrift* 1992, 3103.

546 W. Wurmnest, "Recognition and Enforcement of U.S. Money Judgments in Germany", 23 *Berkeley Journal of International Law* 2005, 196–197; G. Nater-Bass, "U.S.-Style Punitive Damages Awards and their Recognition and Enforcement in Switzerland and Other Civil-Law Countries", 28 *Deutsch-Amerikanische Juristen-Vereinigung Newsletter* 2003, 156; G. Wegen & J. Sherer, "Recognition and Enforcement of U.S. Punitive Damages in Germany – A Recent Decision of the German Federal Court of Justice", 21 *International Business Lawyer* 1993, 486; A.R. Fiebig, "The Recognition and Enforcement of Punitive Damage Awards in Germany: Recent Developments", 22 *Georgia Journal of International & Comparative Law* 1992, 649.

the award for pain and suffering addresses this damage.[547] More importantly, the Court referred to legal costs which, under the U.S. system, the prevailing party in principle cannot recoup from the losing party.[548] It, however, refused to accept that one of the reasons for awarding punitive damages is invariably the shifting of the victorious party's legal costs onto the losing party.[549, 550] The *Oberlandesgericht* Düsseldorf had adopted the latter reasoning.

249. Rather than acknowledging an automatic fee shifting intention in every punitive award, the German Supreme Court required that the foreign judgment clearly indicates the (partly) compensatory purpose of the punitive award.[551] Unless the foreign court provides clear and comprehensible information itself, the German enforcing court cannot ascertain the motives behind the award, as doing so would run counter to the prohibition of *révision au fond* laid down in article 723, (1) ZPO. The *Bundesgerichtshof* did not find any reliable information in the California judgment or in the transcript to support the finding that the punitive damages were intended to cover the legal costs incurred by the plaintiff. Although the American court had awarded 40% of the judgment to the plaintiff's lawyer, the German Supreme Court argued that, since the 40% related to the *entire* judgment, it could not exclude the possibility that the sums paid as compensatory damages - which the *Bundesgerichtshof* appeared to find generous - already included an element addressing those costs.[552, 553] The *Bundesgerichtshof* therefore could not deviate from the conclusion that the punitive award in its entirety should be rejected.[554]

250. In practice the possibility of enforcing the portion of the punitive award corresponding to the prevailing party's legal costs will be of limited use as it is rare for U.S. courts to plainly state that compensatory objective in their judgments.[555] The opening created by the *Bundesgerichtshof* will

547 P. Klötgen, "L'appréhension des punitive damages par le droit allemande", *Revue Lamy Droit des Affaires* 2013, 127; See *supra* no. 242.

548 See *supra* no. 66.

549 P. Hay, "The Recognition and Enforcement of American Money-Judgments in Germany - The 1992 Decision of the German Supreme Court", 40 *The American Journal of Comparative Law* 1992, 747.

550 BGH 4 June 1992, *Neue Juristische Wochenschrift* 1992, 3103.

551 J. Zekoll, "The Enforceability of American Money Judgments Abroad: A Landmark Decision by the German Federal Court of Justice", 30 *Columbia Journal of Transnational Law* 1992, 657.

552 C.I. Nagy, "Recognition and enforcement of US judgments involving punitive damages in continental Europe", *Nederlands Internationaal Privaatrecht* 2012, 8.

553 BGH 4 June 1992, *Neue Juristische Wochenschrift* 1992, 3103.

554 BGH 4 June 1992, *Neue Juristische Wochenschrift* 1992, 3104.

555 W. Wurmnest, "Recognition and Enforcement of U.S. Money Judgments in Germany", 23 *Berkeley Journal of International Law* 2005, 197; J. Zekoll, "The Enforceability of American Money Judgments Abroad: A Landmark Decision by the German Federal Court of Justice", 30 *Columbia Journal of Transnational Law* 1992, 657; A.R. Fiebig, "The Recognition and

only be relevant for judgments originating in the few states which view compensation as a legitimate objective of punitive damages. The judgment will have to identify explicitly the compensatory motive for the punitive award.[556] The *Bundesgerichtshof* thus adopted a very formalistic approach. As a result, judgments awarding a general lump-sum; judgments referring to statutes explicitly spelling out non-penal functions of punitive damages; or judgments based on jury instructions which referred to compensation as one of the purposes of a punitive award, do not fulfil the strict requirements of the *Bundesgerichtshof*. The punitive damages in these judgments will not fall under the exception created by the German Supreme Court and will thus be unenforceable.[557]

251. Although the *Bundesgerichtshof* mentioned that a German exequatur court should not be entitled to cut up the punitive damages award at its own free discretion[558], Hay is of the opinion that a complete rejection of the punitive damages award was not the only possible approach. Note that the U.S. court in *John Doe v. Eckhard Schmitz* reserved 40% of the *total* amount awarded for the lawyer costs incurred by the plaintiff. In other words, the California court allocated USD 300.104 to the winning party's legal team. The *Bundesgerichtshof* could have allowed the enforcement of the (unproblematic) compensatory damages plus 40% on that amount, charging the 40% against the punitive damages, as the recovery of compensatory damages in addition to litigation expenses is compatible with German international public policy. This way the purely punitive damages (including the 40% of the lawyer's fee attributable to them) could have been removed from the judgment, while granting the compensatory fragments only. This method would have allowed to take

Enforcement of Punitive Damage Awards in Germany: Recent Developments", 22 *Georgia Journal of International & Comparative Law* 1992, 649; P. Klötgen, "L'appréhension des punitive damages par le droit allemande", *Revue Lamy Droit des Affaires* 2013, 127.

556 G. Wegen & J. Sherer, "Recognition and Enforcement of U.S. Punitive Damages in Germany – A Recent Decision of the German Federal Court of Justice", 21 *International Business Lawyer* 1993, 487; P. Klötgen, "L'appréhension des punitive damages par le droit allemande", *Revue Lamy Droit des Affaires* 2013, 127; H. Bungert, "Enforcing U.S. Excessive and Punitive Damages Awards in Germany", 27 *International Lawyer* 1993, 1083.

557 J. Zekoll, "The Enforceability of American Money Judgments Abroad: A Landmark Decision by the German Federal Court of Justice", 30 *Columbia Journal of Transnational Law* 1992, 657; P.J. Nettesheim & H. Stahl, "Recent Development – Bundesgerichtshof Rejects Enforcement of United States Punitive Damages Award", 28 *Texas International Law Journal* 1993, 425; H. Bungert, "Enforcing U.S. Excessive and Punitive Damages Awards in Germany", 27 *International Lawyer* 1993, 1083–1084.

558 BGH 4 June 1992, *Neue Juristische Wochenschrift* 1992, 3104; P. Klötgen, "L'appréhension des punitive damages par le droit allemande", *Revue Lamy Droit des Affaires* 2013, 127; P.J. Nettesheim & H. Stahl, "Recent Development – Bundesgerichtshof Rejects Enforcement of United States Punitive Damages Award", 28 *Texas International Law Journal* 1993, 423; C.I. Nagy, "Recognition and enforcement of US judgments involving punitive damages in continental Europe", *Nederlands Internationaal Privaatrecht* 2012, 8.

the California court's judgment at face value instead of second-guessing its meaning.[559] The plaintiff would have been USD 140.104 better off.

252. In a case before the German Supreme Court in 1999 the plaintiff, a U.S. company, had been awarded over USD 2 million in damages, including USD 1 million in punitive damages, by a Wisconsin court. When the plaintiff sought enforcement of the judgment in Germany, it did not even request enforcement of the punitive portion but instead focused all its efforts on the compensatory damages. The lawyers in this case thus seem to have accepted the *Bundesgerichtshof*'s decision in *John Doe v. Eckhard Schmitz*.[560]

4.3. ENGLAND

4.3.1. CONDITIONS FOR ENFORCEMENT

253. As is the case in all EU Member States, the enforcement of U.S. punitive damages awards in England is not regulated by supranational legislation. The U.S. and the UK are not parties to a bilateral or multilateral treaty on the recognition and enforcement of judgments. In 1976 the U.S. and the UK tried to conclude a bilateral agreement on the reciprocal recognition and enforcement of judgments in civil matters but failed.[561] The English private international law rules therefore apply to American judgments seeking recognition and enforcement in England and Wales.

254. Under English common law the institution of a fresh legal action is required for the enforcement of a foreign judgment. The foreign decision imposes an obligation on the defendant. This obligation then becomes the subject matter of the new action for the amount of the debt in England. However, the plaintiff may apply for summary judgment under Part 24 of the Civil Procedure Rules on the basis that the judgment-debtor has no defence to the claim. In any event, the English court will verify whether the foreign court had jurisdiction to adjudicate the claim against the defendant. Only when, in the view of English

---

559 P. Hay, "The Recognition and Enforcement of American Money-Judgments in Germany – The 1992 Decision of the German Supreme Court", 40 *The American Journal of Comparative Law* 1992, 747–748.

560 BGH 29 April 1999, *BGHZ* 141, 286; V. Behr, "Myth and Reality of Punitive Damages in Germany", 24 *Journal of Law and Commerce* 2004–2005, 205 and footnote 39.

561 Convention on the Reciprocal Recognition and Enforcement of Judgments in Civil Matters, 26 October 1976, 16 *International Legal Materials* 1977, 71. See H. Smit, "The Proposed United States-United Kingdom Convention on Recognition and Enforcement of Judgments: A Prototype for the Future?", 17 *Virginia Journal of International Law* 1977, 443–468; P. Hay & R. Walker, "The Proposed U.S.-UK Recognition-of-Judgments Convention: Another Perspective", 18 *Virginia Journal of International Law* 1978, 753–770.

law, the foreign court was entitled to summon the defendant and subject him to judgment, enforcement in England will be possible.[562]

255. A defendant can rely on nine grounds to challenge the enforcement of the unfavourable judgment.[563] Three are particularly relevant in the context of a punitive damages award. First, the Protection of Trading Interests Act of 1980 (PTIA) bars the enforcement of multiple damages in England. Second, English courts will not enforce foreign penal judgments. Lastly, the defendant may invoke the public policy exception to exclude the possibility of enforcement of a punitive award.[564]

256. In what follows we will study whether, and if so how, the English courts have applied these three grounds in the context of a foreign punitive damages judgment. A distinction is made between multiple damages (for which specific legislation, namely PTIA, exists) and punitive damages other than multiple damages (for which no such legislation exists).

4.3.2. MULTIPLE DAMAGES

a. *Ratio legis of the Protection of Trading Interests Act 1980*

257. The Protection of Trading Interest Act is a statute from 1980 which prohibits the enforcement of multiple damages in England. As stated above, multiple damages are a form of punitive damages arrived at by multiplying the amount of compensatory damages.[565] PTIA attempts to thwart the exercise of U.S. extraterritorial jurisdiction over foreign citizens.[566] The *Westinghouse* litigation formed the direct impetus to the legislation. In that case a number of defendants, including British nationals, were subjected to antitrust suits in the U.S. for an alleged uranium cartel.[567] Similarly, another litigation also sparked

---

562 J. Fawcett & J.M. Carruthers, *Cheshire, North & Fawcett: Private International Law*, Oxford, Oxford University Press, 14th edition, 2008, 516–517; M. Polonsky, "Particular Issues Affecting the Recognition and Enforcement of U.S. Judgments", 19 *International Law Practicum* 2006, 156.

563 J. Fawcett & J.M. Carruthers, *Cheshire, North & Fawcett: Private International Law*, Oxford, Oxford University Press, 14th edition, 2008, 551.

564 R. Merkin, "Enforceability of Awards of Punitive Damages in the United Kingdom", *International Journal of Insurance Law* 1994, 19.

565 See *supra* no. 31.

566 T.J. Kahn, "The Protection of Trading Interests Act of 1980: Britain's Response to U.S. Extraterritorial Antitrust Enforcement", 2 *Northwestern Journal of International Law & Business* 1980, 479.

567 T.J. Kahn, "The Protection of Trading Interests Act of 1980: Britain's Response to U.S. Extraterritorial Antitrust Enforcement", 2 *Northwestern Journal of International Law & Business* 1980, 483, 484 and 488.

the enactment of the Protection of Trading Interests Act. The U.S. Department of Justice prosecuted European shipping lines for antitrust violations. A grand jury investigation revealed a conspiracy to fix freight rates in the North Atlantic liner trades. In 1979 a Washington grand jury indicted among others three European shipping companies for price fixing violations under section 1 of the Sherman Act. The British government reacted hostile to this unilateral attempt by the United States to impose their domestic legislation outside their own territory with regard to behaviour which is not be illegal in the UK.[568]

258. The United States has always emphasised the need for and legality of enforcing its antitrust laws against parties that lack a connection to the U.S. territory but whose actions nevertheless have an effect on the U.S. The British government on the other hand believed that these antitrust laws should only apply to the promulgating nation's own territory or citizens.[569] This disagreement could not be solved by diplomatic means and legal warfare ensued.[570]

b. Section 5 of PTIA: unenforceability of multiple damages

259. The British government enacted PTIA which provides in its section 5 that a judgment of an overseas country cannot be registered and no court in the UK may entertain proceedings at common law for the recovery of any sum payable under such a judgment, where that judgment grants multiple damages.[571] Analogous statutes are in force in Australia[572] and in Canada.[573, 574] The rule represents the British belief that the treble damages which are recoverable under U.S. antitrust law are penal in nature and should not be available to private plaintiffs acting as private attorneys general.[575] Section 5 aims to neutralise the treble damages incentive for private parties in U.S. legislation in that it forces

568 T.J. Kahn, "The Protection of Trading Interests Act of 1980: Britain's Response to U.S. Extraterritorial Antitrust Enforcement", 2 *Northwestern Journal of International Law & Business* 1980, 491–492.

569 T.J. Kahn, "The Protection of Trading Interests Act of 1980: Britain's Response to U.S. Extraterritorial Antitrust Enforcement", 2 *Northwestern Journal of International Law & Business* 1980, 514.

570 J. Fawcett & J.M. Carruthers, *Cheshire, North & Fawcett: Private International Law*, Oxford, Oxford University Press, 14th edition, 2008, 561.

571 Sections 5.1 and 5.2. A judgment for multiple damages is defined in section 5(3) as "*a judgment for an amount arrived at by doubling, trebling or otherwise multiplying a sum assessed as compensation for the loss or damage sustained by the person in whose favour the judgment was given.*"

572 The Foreign Anti-Trust Judgments (Restriction of Enforcement) Act 1979.

573 The Foreign Extraterritorial Measures Act 1985.

574 J. Fawcett & J.M. Carruthers, *Cheshire, North & Fawcett: Private International Law*, Oxford, Oxford University Press, 14th edition, 2008, 561, footnote 370.

575 T.J. Kahn, "The Protection of Trading Interests Act of 1980: Britain's Response to U.S. Extraterritorial Antitrust Enforcement", 2 *Northwestern Journal of International Law & Business* 1980, 489.

private litigants to weigh the benefits and costs of such an action given the unenforceability in the UK.[576] Although intended to apply to multiple damages (treble damages) arising out of antitrust litigation, a literal reading of the Act prohibits the enforcement of any type of multiple damages irrespective of the underlying cause of action.[577] The Act only applies to multiple damages and does not cover other punitive damages.[578]

260. It has to be noted that section 5 of PTIA renders the compensatory element of a multiple damages award unenforceable as well. This follows from a textual interpretation of the Act and is supported by DICEY and MORRIS who state that: "*Judgments caught by section 5 are wholly unenforceable, and not merely as regards that part of the judgment which exceeds the damages actually suffered by the judgment creditor*".[579] Judge PARKER (and Lord DIPLOCK later agreed on that point[580]) remarked in *British Airways v. Laker Airways* that section 5 of PTIA is aimed at judgments in antitrust matters and affects the whole award, not just the multiple damages part of it.[581, 582] The fact that Lewis did not raise this issue on appeal in *Lewis v. Eliades* also confirms this view.[583]

c. *Court of Appeal in Lewis v. Eliades*

261. In *Lewis v. Eliades* a part of a U.S. judgment provided for treble damages for violations under the United States federal Racketeer Influenced and Corrupt Organisations Act (RICO).[584] RICO permits litigants to recover civil damages based on a number of criminal violations and provides the opportunity for a claimant to obtain treble damages in addition to the costs of the law suit.[585] The English courts were faced with the question whether the presence of these treble damages would make the whole judgment unenforceable in England under PTIA.

576 T.J. Kahn, "The Protection of Trading Interests Act of 1980: Britain's Response to U.S. Extraterritorial Antitrust Enforcement", 2 *Northwestern Journal of International Law & Business* 1980, 510, 513 and 515.

577 T.J. Kahn, "The Protection of Trading Interests Act of 1980: Britain's Response to U.S. Extraterritorial Antitrust Enforcement", 2 *Northwestern Journal of International Law & Business* 1980, 510.

578 For the enforceability of these other punitive damages, see *infra* no. 273 *et seq.*

579 L. Collins (ed.), *Dicey & Morris on the conflict of laws*, London, Sweet and Maxwell, 13th edition, 2000, 566.

580 *British Airways v. Lakers Airways* [1985] AC 58, 89.

581 *British Airways v. Laker Airways* [1984] QB 142, 161.

582 E. Kellman, "Enforcement of Judgments and Blocking Statutes: Lewis v Eliades", 53 *International & Comparative Law Quarterly* 2004, 1028.

583 E. Malcolm, "Winning the fight for the enforcement of US damages", 15 *Entertainment Law Review* 2004, 133.

584 *Lewis v. Eliades* [2004] 1 WLR 692.

585 18 USC 1964(c); E. Kellman, "Enforcement of Judgments and Blocking Statutes: Lewis v Eliades", 53 *International & Comparative Law Quarterly* 2004, 1028.

i. Procedural history

262. The proceedings in this case started in the United States District Court for the Southern District of New York. Former managers and promoters of the famous English boxer Lennox Lewis brought a suit in federal court against him after the breakdown of their relationship. Lewis counterclaimed on the basis of *inter alia* breach of contract, fraud and racketeering contrary to RICO. In its judgment of 15 March 2002 the U.S. District Court held each of the defendants on the counterclaim liable for an amount of USD 7.273.641. The District Court awarded USD 6.821.159 for breach of fiduciary duty, USD 56.400 for fraud and USD 369.082 as damages under RICO. The latter sum, however, was the compensatory amount without the treble multiplication.[586]

263. Lennox Lewis then sought to enforce the judgment in England. The defendants in the enforcement proceedings argued that the judgment could not be enforced because of section 5 of PTIA. They asserted that Lewis was entitled to an automatic trebling of the compensatory damages under RICO and that this blocked the enforcement of the New York judgment in its entirety. On 1 August 2002 Master WHITAKER declined to follow the defendants' argument and granted summary judgment for an amount of USD 6.273.641, *i.e.* the original amount awarded minus USD 1 million as agreed set-off between parties.

264. In the High Court proceedings Judge NELSON also rejected this argument. In a decision of 28 February 2003 he noted that the trebling of the basic compensatory award was clearly not automatic. The claimant can decide to waive his right to recover these damages, can withdraw his application for treble damages or can decide not to enforce the multiple portion of the award.[587] In the case at hand Judge NELSON made his decision to enforce the American judgment conditional on (1) Lewis withdrawing two motions he had filed in the U.S. District Court for the Southern District of New York or (2) on his undertaking not to enforce the multiple damages against the defendants. Lewis had requested the U.S. District Court to treble the amount of the compensatory damages under RICO and to issue these treble damages in a separate judgment (in order to prevent any problems under PTIA). Judge NELSON, however, made it clear that the latter technique would not hinder the application of section 5 of PTIA.[588, 589] The High Court's ruling thus depended on the factual

586 E. Kellman, "Enforcement of Judgments and Blocking Statutes: Lewis v Eliades", 53 *International & Comparative Law Quarterly* 2004, 1025.

587 *Lewis v. Eliades* [2003] 1 All ER (Comm) 850, 862; E. Kellman, "Enforcement of Judgments and Blocking Statutes: Lewis v Eliades", 53 *International & Comparative Law Quarterly* 2004, 1026, footnote 4.

588 *Lewis v. Eliades* [2003] 1 All ER (Comm) 850, 863.

589 E. Kellman, "Enforcement of Judgments and Blocking Statutes: Lewis v Eliades", 53 *International & Comparative Law Quarterly* 2004, 1026.

circumstances surrounding the case. It can arguably be derived from the decision that an unmultiplied award is enforceable in England if the judgment creditor agrees not to request multiplication in the rendering court, withdraws a pending application for multiplication or undertakes not to enforce the award beyond its compensatory element.[590]

265. Lennox Lewis complied with the condition laid down by Judge Nelson. For an unknown reason the clerk in the United States District Court, nevertheless, ordered the issuance of a separate judgment for treble RICO damages. Judge Baer of the United States District Court subsequently set this order aside and ordered a single judgment (bearing the date of the original judgment) to replace the original judgment for an amount of USD 8.065.805. The new amount reflected the – unwanted as a result of Lewis' withdrawal – trebling of the RICO damages of USD 396.082 to USD 1.188.246 plus an additional USD 40 for an earlier miscalculation.[591]

ii. Court of Appeal

266. On appeal before the Court of Appeal in England the situation had thus significantly changed. With the RICO damages having been trebled, the question to be answered became how section 5 of PTIA had to be interpreted. One interpretation was that the treble damages tainted the other heads of damages, resulting in the total rejection of the judgment for enforcement purposes. Another understanding of section 5 of PTIA meant that the other heads of damages could be enforced despite the statutory rejection of a judgment for treble damages. It should be remarked that Lewis did not try to enforce the RICO damages themselves which indicates that his lawyers probably believed that this would not stand a chance given the clear language of the Act.[592]

267. On 9 October 2003 the Court of Appeal ruled that the presence of treble damages does not mean that other damages are not recoverable.[593] It found that the non-RICO damages could be severed and distinguished from the

590 E. Kellman, "Enforcement of Judgments and Blocking Statutes: Lewis v Eliades", 53 *International & Comparative Law Quarterly* 2004, 1029–1030.

591 E. Kellman, "Enforcement of Judgments and Blocking Statutes: Lewis v Eliades", 53 *International & Comparative Law Quarterly* 2004, 1026.

592 E. Malcolm, "Winning the fight for the enforcement of US damages", 15 *Entertainment Law Review* 2004, 133; E. Kellman, "Enforcement of Judgments and Blocking Statutes: Lewis v Eliades", 53 *International & Comparative Law Quarterly* 2004, 1026.

593 *Lewis v. Eliades* [2004] 1 WLR 692; M. Polonsky, "Particular Issues Affecting the Recognition and Enforcement of U.S. Judgments", 19 *International Law Practicum* 2006, 158; T. Rouhette, "The availability of punitive damages in Europe: growing trend or nonexistent concept?", 74 *Defense Counsel Journal* 2007, 335.

unenforceable treble damages.[594] The Court of Appeal dismissed arguments based on Judge Parker's observation in *British Airways v. Laker Airways* and the opinion of Dicey and Morris[595] as these relate to the compensatory part of a treble damages award and not the legal fate of the other heads of damages in a mixed judgment.[596] It, therefore, held that the whole judgment was enforceable, save the treble RICO damages in the amount of USD 1.188.246 and the sum of USD 1 million as set-off between the parties.[597]

268. Ironically, the American judge's action of awarding Lewis more money by trebling the damages under RICO resulted in a lower amount to be recovered from the defendants in England due to section 5 of PTIA. Judgment creditors seeking to enforce RICO claims or other claims for multiple damages against the English assets of the defendant should thus make certain that these multiple damages are clearly separated from other heads of damage. Moreover, in order to ensure maximum return in the UK, the plaintiff should consider not requesting the multiplication of the basic compensatory award provided for by the applicable statute.[598]

d. Section 6 of PTIA: claw-back provision

269. Enforcement in the UK is not necessary when the defendant possesses sufficient assets in the U.S. Through a freezing order the plaintiff prevents the defendant from dissipating these assets from beyond the jurisdiction of the American courts. In such a scenario enforcement in the UK will not be sought and section 5 will consequently not deter plaintiffs from pursuing a claim for multiple damages.[599]

270. Section 6 of PTIA, however, gives certain qualifying defendants (namely United Kingdom citizens, companies incorporated in the United Kingdom and persons carrying on business there) who have paid multiple damages in a foreign suit a right of action in a court of the United Kingdom to recover against a person to whom such multiple damages were paid (whether this person is within

594 M. Polonsky, "Particular Issues Affecting the Recognition and Enforcement of U.S. Judgments", 19 *International Law Practicum* 2006, 158.

595 Both referred to *supra* in no. 260.

596 E. Kellman, "Enforcement of Judgments and Blocking Statutes: Lewis v Eliades", 53 *International & Comparative Law Quarterly* 2004, 1027–1028.

597 *Lewis v. Eliades* [2004] 1 WLR 692, 705.

598 M. Polonsky, "Particular Issues Affecting the Recognition and Enforcement of U.S. Judgments", 19 *International Law Practicum* 2006, 159.

599 T.J. Kahn, "The Protection of Trading Interests Act of 1980: Britain's Response to U.S. Extraterritorial Antitrust Enforcement", 2 *Northwestern Journal of International Law & Business* 1980, 512.

the jurisdiction of the High Court or not) the part of the multiple damages that exceeds the portion attributable to compensation.[600] The qualifying defendant may not invoke the Act for activities exclusively carried on within the United States.[601] The English legislator's aversion to foreign multiple damages thus does not only manifest itself with regard to the enforcement of such damages in England. It could even affect multiple damages awards rendered abroad that will never reach the English borders.

271. For U.S. treble damages, for instance, this means that if a U.S. plaintiff obtains an award for such damages in the U.S. and finds adequate assets there to fulfil the judgment, the UK defendant (*i.e.* a UK citizen, a corporation incorporated in the UK, or a person who carries on business in the UK) can recover two-thirds of that amount in proceedings in the UK. As mentioned, it is not required that the U.S. plaintiff is within the jurisdiction of the English courts for the UK defendant to bring an action but the Act effectively only applies if the U.S. plaintiff has attachable assets in Great Britain.[602] From the U.S. point of view the provision undermines the integrity of the treble damages award, an important instrument of American antitrust enforcement.[603]

272. In case of partial payment in the U.S., the original U.S. plaintiff may end up with less than the amount of compensation because the 'claw-back' proceedings entitle the defendant to recoup two-thirds of the amount paid. An example makes this clear. An American court awards treble damages in the amount of USD 300.000 against a British company but the latter's assets in the U.S. only generate USD 150.000. The pro-rate recovery in the UK (provided the U.S. plaintiff has assets in the UK) would then enable the UK party to recuperate USD 100.000, leaving the original plaintiff with USD 50.000 or half of the full compensation.[604]

---

600 P.F. Ndikum & S.-D. Ndikum, *Encyclopaedia of International Aviation Law: Liability Rules Developed by European Union, Australian, United Kingdom and United States of America Courts According to European Community Treaty – Warsaw 1929 – Montreal 1999*, Volume 3, 2013, 871.

601 Section 6(4) PTIA.

602 X., "Enjoining the Application of the British Protection of Trading Interests Act in Private American Antitrust Litigation", 79 *Michigan Law Review* 1981, 1576; M. Polonsky, "Particular Issues Affecting the Recognition and Enforcement of U.S. Judgments", 19 *International Law Practicum* 2006, 159.

603 X., "Enjoining the Application of the British Protection of Trading Interests Act in Private American Antitrust Litigation", 79 *Michigan Law Review* 1981, 1575.

604 T.J. Kahn, "The Protection of Trading Interests Act of 1980: Britain's Response to U.S. Extraterritorial Antitrust Enforcement", 2 *Northwestern Journal of International Law & Business* 1980, 511, footnote 238.

4.3.3. PUNITIVE DAMAGES

273. Forms of punitive damages which do not involve the multiplication of the compensatory damages are outside the ambit of PTIA and, therefore, follow a different regime. It is well settled in England that an English court will not lend its aid to the enforcement of a foreign penal law.[605] By imposing a penalty a state exercises its sovereign power. Such an act of sovereignty cannot have any effect in the territory of another nation.[606] English courts will, therefore, not enforce a foreign judgment when it is given in respect of a fine or penalty. However, a sum payable to a private individual is not a fine or penalty.[607]

274. In the early 20th century case of *Raulin v. Fisher* this principle was applied.[608] The matter involved an American lady who injured a French officer in the Bois de Boulogne (France) while riding her horse recklessly. She was prosecuted for criminal negligence and fined 100 francs. Under French law a criminal court can rule on the civil claim for damages as well if the victim decides to intervene in the criminal proceedings. The victim opted to do so and was awarded 15.917 francs for damages and costs in the same judgment. When the victim tried to enforce the judgment in England, Judge Hamilton made a distinction between the fine and the compensation. He ruled that the civil damages were recoverable because they were payable to an individual and not to the state. These damages could be severed from the fine which was unenforceable due to its penal character.[609] The crucial criterion to determine whether a foreign measure is a penalty therefore appears to be the receiver of the sums. If the money goes to the foreign state, the sum has to be classified as penal.

275. This formalistic approach was confirmed in *S.A Consortium General Textiles v. Sun and Sand Agencies Ltd.*[610] This is the only case touching upon the issue of the enforceability of punitive damages.[611] A French company had sold clothing to English merchants but after delivery the buyers failed to pay the agreed price. The seller brought its payment claim before the Commercial

605 *Folliott v. Ogden* [1790] 3 Term Rep 726; *Huntington v Attrill* [1893] AC 150.

606 J. Fawcett & J.M. Carruthers, *Cheshire, North & Fawcett: Private International Law*, Oxford, Oxford University Press, 14th edition, 2008, 126.

607 M. Polonsky, "Particular Issues Affecting the Recognition and Enforcement of U.S. Judgments", 19 *International Law Practicum* 2006, 156.

608 *Raulin v. Fisher* [1911] 2 KB 93.

609 J. Fawcett & J.M. Carruthers, *Cheshire, North & Fawcett: Private International Law*, Oxford, Oxford University Press, 14th edition, 2008, 561; R. Merkin, "Enforceability of Awards of Punitive Damages in the United Kingdom", *International Journal of Insurance Law* 1994, 21.

610 *S.A Consortium General Textiles v. Sun and Sand Agencies Ltd.* [1978] Q.B. 279.

611 Although the damages for "*résistance abusive*" were not qualified as punitive by the Court of Appeal.

Court of Lille. In addition, it sought a further 10.000 francs on the basis of "*résistance abusive*"[612], a head of damages awardable in France where a defendant has unjustifiably opposed the plaintiff's claim. The Lille court gave judgment in default of appearance for the plaintiffs for the amount claimed, interest and costs. Enforcement of the judgment in England was governed by the 1933 Foreign Judgments Act which regulates enforcement for judgments originating in countries with which the UK has a mutual recognition treaty. The defendants resisted enforcement of the 10.000 francs (awarded as a result of the unreasonable refusal by the defendants to pay a plain claim) in England on the ground that the French judgment imposed a penalty. Under section 1(2)(b) of the Act, sums payable in respect of a penalty are excluded from enforcement. The defendants further relied on section 4(1)(a)(v) which states that enforcement should be denied when it would violate public policy of the requested state.[613]

276. As to the characterisation of the sum for the "*résistance abusive*", all three judges in the Court of Appeal agreed that the amount for the unreasonable withholding of sums under a valid claim was compensatory, not penal and, therefore, enforceable.[614] Lord DENNING believed it to be compensation for losses not covered by an award of interest, such as loss of business caused by want of cash flow, or for costs of the proceedings not covered by the court's order for costs. He however expanded *obiter dictum* upon the issue and summarised the defendants' argument as sustaining that the 10.000 francs were punitive or exemplary damages which amounted to a penalty and were, therefore, unenforceable under section 1(2)(b) of the 1933 Act.[615] He repeated the conventional idea that a fine or other penalty only refers to sums payable to the state by way of punishment and that a sum payable to a private individual is not a fine or penalty.[616]

277. Although given in *dicta*, Lord DENNING's statements relating to punitive damages are interesting given the hybrid nature of punitive damages. They are awarded not to compensate (at least not always and not primarily) but to punish the wrongdoer for reprehensible conduct. However, they are not payable to the state. Lord DENNING's remark seems to explicitly support the view that, despite their inherent criminal nature, for enforcement purposes in England punitive damages avoid the penal label because they are awarded to a private

612 Article 1153 of the French Civil Code.

613 This public policy exception is similar to the one at common law.

614 N. Edwards & R.G. Lee, "Recognition and enforcement in English law of money judgments from outside the UK", *International Banking and Financial Law* 1994, 2.

615 The other judges in the case, Lord Justice GOFF and Lord Justice SHAW, did not refer to the notion "punitive damages".

616 *S.A Consortium General Textiles v. Sun and Sand Agencies Ltd.* [1978] Q.B. 299–300.

person instead of to the state.[617, 618] Lord DENNING further ruled that English public policy does not oppose the enforcement of a claim for exemplary damages because these are *"still considered to be in conformity with the public policy in the United States and many of the great countries of the Commonwealth"*.[619] He thereby indicated that punitive damages do not pose a problem from a public policy perspective either.[620] However, the *obiter* character of his elaboration should be underlined, leading to the conclusion that, at the very least, the enforceability of (U.S.) punitive damages in the UK has not yet been definitively settled.

278. The idea of accepting punitive damages for enforcement could be called into question. POLONSKY, for instance, argues that a viable argument could be made that an English court should not enforce a foreign award for punitive damages. As punitive damages are awarded to victims acting as private attorneys-general in order to punish the tortfeasor, the English court could take the language used by the foreign court at face value and treat the award of "punitive" damages as a penalty. It could then declare the punitive award a violation of public policy for that reason and subsequently decline enforcement.[621] Moreover, according to POLONSKY, civil litigation should be intended for the recovery of compensation for the plaintiff's loss and English courts should not lend their assistance to the awarding of a profit to the victim.[622] This position is in our view indirectly supported by PTIA's rejection of multiple damages. Although PTIA does not deal with punitive damages other than those arrived at by applying a multiplier, it could be argued that the unenforceability of punitive damages should *a fortiori* follow from the unenforceability of multiple damages. In chapter 5 we, however, defend the position that U.S. punitive damages should be enforceable in the European Union, provided they pass an excessiveness analysis.

279. In our view it is curious how, on the one hand, the enforcement of punitive damages seems to be accepted by Lord DENNING and distinguished scholars such as DICEY and MORRIS. The reasoning behind this acceptance is that punitive

---

617 L. Collins (ed.), *Dicey & Morris on the conflict of laws*, London, Sweet and Maxwell, 13th edition, 2000, 476.

618 As mentioned *supra* in no. 48 in some U.S. states split-recovery systems are in place. Only the part going to the plaintiff would thus be eligible for enforcement in the UK.

619 *S.A Consortium General Textiles v. Sun and Sand Agencies Ltd.* [1978] Q.B. 300.

620 The same conclusion was reached by the Supreme Court of Australia (Full Court) and the British Columbia Court of Appeal: *Benefit Strategies Group Inc v. Prider* [2005] SASC 194 and *Old North State Brewing Co v. Newlands Services Inc* [1999] 4 WWR 573.

621 M. Polonsky, "Particular Issues Affecting the Recognition and Enforcement of U.S. Judgments", 19 *International Law Practicum* 2006, 157.

622 M. Polonsky, "Particular Issues Affecting the Recognition and Enforcement of U.S. Judgments", 19 *International Law Practicum* 2006, 158.

damages cannot be qualified as penal since they are not awarded to the state but to the plaintiff. On the other hand, multiple damages, a subcategory of punitive damages, are not enforceable because they are barred by a statute (PTIA). They are even deemed to be so unacceptable that the compensatory "basic award" (*i.e.* before multiplying) cannot be enforced either. Multiple damages are, however, mostly far more moderate compared to punitive damages which are "*plucked out of the air*".[623]

280. Until the *ratio decidendi* of a judgment deals with the issue of enforcement of foreign punitive damages, Lord DENNING's *obiter dictum* in *S.A Consortium General Textiles v. Sun and Sand Agencies Ltd.* remains the only authority to rely on in support of the enforcement of such damages. The risk of unenforceability in England is, therefore, real.[624] The compensatory damages in a judgment for punitive damages will in any case be enforceable because PTIA does not apply and the punitive damages thus do not "infect" the compensatory damages. The compensatory damages are another head of damages which can be severed from the punitive award. The severing of judgments in order to distinguish enforceable from unenforceable portions was demonstrated in, for example, *Raulin v. Fisher* and *Lewis v. Eliades.*

4.4. FRANCE

4.4.1. CONDITIONS FOR ENFORCEMENT

281. The French rules on the recognition and enforcement of foreign judgments are not codified but have been created by the case law of the *Cour de cassation* (Supreme Court) and the lower courts.[625]

282. Before 1964 the enforcement of the foreign judgment depended on whether the judgment was correct on the merits. The review of the merits of

---

623 R. Merkin, "Enforceability of Awards of Punitive Damages in the United Kingdom", *International Journal of Insurance Law* 1994, 23.

624 M. Polonsky, "Particular Issues Affecting the Recognition and Enforcement of U.S. Judgments", 19 *International Law Practicum* 2006, 158. According to ROUHETTE it is even likely that punitive damages will not be enforced: T. Rouhette, "The availability of punitive damages in Europe: growing trend or nonexistent concept?", 74 *Defense Counsel Journal* 2007, 335.

625 B. Janke & F.-X. Licari, "Enforcing Punitive Damage Awards in France after Fountaine Pajot", 60 *The American Journal of Comparative Law* 2012, 780, footnote 18; N. Meyer Fabre, "Recognition and Enforcement of U.S. Judgments in France – Recent Developments", *The International Dispute Resolution News* spring 2012, 6; N. Meyer Fabre, "Enforcement Of U.S. Punitive Damages Award in France: First Ruling Of The French Court Of Cassation In X. v. Fountaine Pajot December 1, 2010", *Mealey's International Arbitration Report* January 2011, 2.

the case (*révision au fond*) consisted of the French courts verifying whether the foreign judge had made a proper assessment of the facts and had properly applied the law to these facts. In its *Munzer* judgment of 1964 the *Cour de cassation* abolished this doctrine and instead established five requirements for the enforcement of foreign judgments.[626] The judgment shall be enforced if the following conditions are fulfilled: (1) the foreign court must have jurisdiction from a French perspective, *i.e.* the application of the French private international law rules would have led to the jurisdiction of the foreign court; (2) the foreign court must have properly applied its rules and procedure; (3) the foreign court must have applied the law that the French private international law rules would have designated; (4) the foreign judgment must not be contrary to French international public policy; and (5) the foreign judgment must not have been obtained for the sole purpose of avoiding the applicable law (*fraude à la loi*[627]).[628]

283. The third requirement in fact still entailed a form of *révision au fond* because the French courts would apply their own private international law rules to determine the law the foreign court should have applied. The *Cour de cassation*, therefore, softened the rule over the years[629], eventually completely removing the third requirement from the enforcement test in 2007 in *Cornelissen*.[630] In *Bachir* the Supreme Court had already done away with the second condition.[631] The requirement indeed gave French courts the power to revise the foreign judgment in light of the foreign law. Although this type of review is not identical to *révision au fond* (which reviews the judgment from the perspective of the enforcing judge's legal system), it is probably even worse

---

626 G. Cuniberti, "The Liberization of the French Law of Foreign Judgments", 56 *International Law & Competition Law Quarterly* 2007, 932; N. Meyer Fabre, "Recognition and Enforcement of U.S. Judgments in France – Recent Developments", *The International Dispute Resolution News* spring 2012, 6.

627 *Fraude à la loi* means that the plaintiff is not allowed to manipulate jurisdiction, for example by changing his nationality, in order to escape a judgment under French law.

628 Cass. Civ. 1st, 7 January 1964, *Munzer, Bull.*, I, no. 15; B. Janke & F.-X. Licari, "Enforcing Punitive Damage Awards in France after Fountaine Pajot", 60 *The American Journal of Comparative Law* 2012, 785; G. Cuniberti, "The Liberization of the French Law of Foreign Judgments", 56 *International Law & Competition Law Quarterly* 2007, 932.

629 See G. Cuniberti, "The Liberization of the French Law of Foreign Judgments", 56 *International Law & Competition Law Quarterly* 2007, 937.

630 Cass. civ. 2st, 20 February 2007, *Cornelissen, Bull.*, I, no. 68, case no. 05-14.082; P. Bernard & H. Salem, "Further developments for qualification of foreign judgments for recognition and enforcement in France: the test for punitive damage awards", *International Bar Association* 2011, 16; G. Cuniberti, "The Liberization of the French Law of Foreign Judgments", 56 *International Law & Competition Law Quarterly* 2007, 938.

631 Cass. civ. 1st, 4 October 1967, *Bachir, Bull.*, I, no. 277; N. Meyer Fabre, "Enforcement Of U.S. Punitive Damages Award in France: First Ruling Of The French Court Of Cassation In X. v. Fountaine Pajot, December 1, 2010", *Mealey's International Arbitration Report* January 2011, 2; N. Meyer Fabre, "Recognition and Enforcement of U.S. Judgments in France – Recent Developments", *The International Dispute Resolution News* spring 2012, 6.

as it allows the French courts to criticise their foreign counterparts' application of their own law.[632] Instead, the *Cour de cassation* added a procedural prong to the public policy obstacle (the fourth condition), obliging the enforcing courts to assess whether the foreign court had respected the fundamental principles of procedure.[633]

284. The first requirement equally underwent crucial developments in the period after *Munzer*. The Supreme Court first specified that an "actual connection between the dispute and the country of the foreign court" ("*le litige se rattache de manière characterise au pays dont le juge a été saisi*") is enough to meet this condition. In addition to this characterised link between the case and the foreign country, the plaintiff's choice for the foreign forum must not be fraudulent (this corresponds to the fifth prong of the *Munzer* judgment).[634] This clarification gave the French courts the possibility to recognise and enforce foreign judgments from courts retaining jurisdiction on grounds unknown to French jurisdiction rules as long as these grounds are serious and not exorbitant.[635]

285. However, the *Cour de cassation* carved out an important exception. The enforcement of the foreign judgment could be refused if there existed a ground for exclusive jurisdiction in France. Two important bases of exclusive jurisdiction for the French courts existed at the time. Article 14 of the French Civil Code provided exclusive jurisdiction over French plaintiffs and article 15 of the Code established exclusive jurisdiction over French defendants.[636] In the beginning of the 19th century, the *Cour de cassation* had already extended the scope of these articles of jurisdiction to the law of enforcement of foreign judgments.[637] In reality, the exception overshadowed the general principle in favour of enforcement as most foreign judgments offered for enforcement in

632 G. Cuniberti, "The Liberization of the French Law of Foreign Judgments", 56 *International Law & Competition Law Quarterly* 2007, 932–933.

633 Cass. civ. 1st, 4 October 1967, *Bachir*, *Bull.*, I, no. 277; N. Meyer Fabre, "Enforcement Of U.S. Punitive Damages Award in France: First Ruling Of The French Court Of Cassation In X. v. Fountaine Pajot, December 1, 2010", *Mealey's International Arbitration Report* January 2011, 2; N. Meyer Fabre, "Recognition and Enforcement of U.S. Judgments in France – Recent Developments", *The International Dispute Resolution News* spring 2012, 6.

634 Cass. civ. 1st, 6 February 1985, *Simitch*, *Bull.*, I, no. 55, case no. 83-11241; N. Meyer Fabre, "Enforcement Of U.S. Punitive Damages Award in France: First Ruling Of The French Court Of Cassation In X. v. Fountaine Pajot, December 1, 2010", *Mealey's International Arbitration Report* January 2011, 2; N. Meyer Fabre, "Recognition and Enforcement of U.S. Judgments in France – Recent Developments", *The International Dispute Resolution News* spring 2012, 6.

635 G. Cuniberti, "The Liberization of the French Law of Foreign Judgments", 56 *International Law & Competition Law Quarterly* 2007, 933.

636 Cass. civ. 1st, 6 February 1985, *Simitch*, *Bull.*, I, no. 55, case no. 83-11241; N. Meyer Fabre, "Recognition and Enforcement of U.S. Judgments in France – Recent Developments", *The International Dispute Resolution News* spring 2012, 6.

637 G. Cuniberti, "The Liberization of the French Law of Foreign Judgments", 56 *International Law & Competition Law Quarterly* 2007, 934.

France involve at least one French party. French litigants were thus in effect shielded from enforcement.[638]

286. As to the fourth requirement, it is important to yet again emphasise the nature of the public policy defence. In private international law cases the relevant yardstick to be used is international public policy (*ordre public international*) and not internal or domestic public policy (*ordre public interne*). In our view French case law and doctrine make this distinction more clearly, in comparison with the other nations looked at in this book. French international public policy contains those fundamental rules which the French legal system requires to be respected, even in international cases.[639] Only international public policy can form an obstacle for the application of a foreign law or the enforcement of a foreign judgment. The scope of the international public policy is much narrower than its domestic counterpart's scope.[640] The distinction derives from the idea that the French forum should be more tolerant in an (inherently culturally more diverse) international context than in purely domestic affairs.[641] The corrective mechanism of international public policy should only intervene in truly extraordinary cases.[642] Moreover, it is not the foreign law or the foreign judgment itself that must be analysed but the outcome that its application or enforcement produces in the forum. Therefore, the enforcement of a foreign judgment can only be rejected if the result of the exequatur would be "manifestly repugnant" to international public policy.[643]

4.4.2. CASE LAW ON THE ENFORCEMENT OF PUNITIVE DAMAGES

a. *Court of Appeal Paris*

287. Janke and Licari make note of a decision of 2004 on the enforcement of punitive damages. To our knowledge, this was the first confrontation the French

---

638 B. Janke & F.-X. Licari, "Enforcing Punitive Damage Awards in France after Fountaine Pajot", 60 *The American Journal of Comparative Law* 2012, 787.

639 A.S. Sibon, "Enforcing Punitive Damages Awards in France: Facing Proportionality within International Public Policy", available at <http://ssrn.com/abstract=2382817>.

640 P. Mayer & V. Heuzé, *Droit international privé*, Paris, Montchrestien, 2004, 149, no. 205; P. Bernard & H. Salem, "Further developments for qualification of foreign judgments for recognition and enforcement in France: the test for punitive damage awards", *International Bar Association* 2011, 18.

641 B. Janke & F.-X. Licari, "Enforcing Punitive Damage Awards in France after Fountaine Pajot", 60 *The American Journal of Comparative Law* 2012, 792.

642 B. Janke & F.-X. Licari, "Enforcing Punitive Damage Awards in France after Fountaine Pajot", 60 *The American Journal of Comparative Law* 2012, 792.

643 B. Janke & F.-X. Licari, "Enforcing Punitive Damage Awards in France after Fountaine Pajot", 60 *The American Journal of Comparative Law* 2012, 792.

legal system had with (U.S.) punitive damages. The Court of First Instance of Paris refused exequatur of a California judgment awarding punitive damages because punishment belongs to the monopoly of the state and punitive damages are, moreover, contrary to the principle of full compensation (*compensation intégrale*).[644] The Civil as well as the Criminal Chamber of the *Cour de cassation* had indeed held in previous cases that a victim may not suffer a loss nor gain a profit from the compensation granted to him.[645] The Court of Appeal of Paris upheld the judgment of the Court of First Instance of Paris.[646]

288. There were, however, signs that the Supreme Court might decide differently on the matter. First, French courts did enforce penal elements in civil cases, such as penalty clauses in private contracts and foreign sanctions based on contempt of court. Second, the French doctrine seemed to agree that punitive damages are not contrary to public policy if the sum awarded is not disproportionate or excessive.[647] A Supreme Court judgment was, therefore, needed to settle the issue.

b. *Fountaine Pajot case of the Cour de cassation*

i. California Superior Court

289. The much anticipated ruling came in 2010 in the case *Schlenzka & Langhorne v. Fountaine Pajot*.[648] In 1999 a California couple, Peter Schlenzka and Julie Langhorne, purchased a 56-foot Marquises catamaran from Rod Gibbons' Cruising Cats USA, an authorised dealer and agent for the French manufacturer, Fountaine Pajot S.A. The sale price amounted to USD 826.009. It was agreed between the parties that Fountaine Pajot would first exhibit the catamaran in a Miami boat show before delivering it to the buyers in Miami in a like-new condition.

However, in December 1999, a few months before the show, the vessel suffered extensive damage in a notorious storm while moored in the port

---

644 Tribunal de Grande Instance Paris, 15 July 2004, 1st chambre, no. 03/09481, *Consorts Chapgier v. Taitbout Prévoyance & B. Mesqui*, 8; B. Janke & F.-X. Licari, "Enforcing Punitive Damage Awards in France after Fountaine Pajot", 60 *The American Journal of Comparative Law* 2012, 778.

645 Cass. civ. 2nd, 23 January 2003, *Bull. Civ.* II, no. 20; Criminal Chamber, 19 May 2009, no. 08–82.666.

646 Cour d'appel Paris, 1st Chamber, 6th Section, 9 November 2006, RG no. 04/22000; D. Motte-Suraniti, "Punitive damages and exequatur under French law", 20 December 2010, 3, available at <www.motte-suraniti-avocat.com/doc/Punitive_damages_and_exequatur_under_French_law.pdf>.

647 B. Janke & F.-X. Licari, "Enforcing Punitive Damage Awards in France after Fountaine Pajot", 60 *The American Journal of Comparative Law* 2012, 778 and the references contained therein.

648 Cass. Civ. 1st, 1 December 2010, *Schlenzka & Langhorne v. Fountaine Pajot S.A*, no. 09–13303, *Recueil Dalloz* 2011, 423.

of La Rochelle, where it was manufactured. The severe winds caused the boat to break loose and collide with other vessels. Fountaine Pajot withheld this information from the purchasers and also did not disclose the fact that repair works had been performed. At delivery, the couple thus believed the catamaran to be in excellent condition. The seller's superficial repairs, however, had not resolved the structural problems and the buyers soon experienced issues with the catamaran.[649]

290. Based on the jurisdiction clause in the contract, the couple brought suit in the California Superior Court (Alameda County). Fountaine Pajot first resisted the jurisdiction of the U.S. court by invoking article 15 of the French Civil Code which reads: "*Un Français pourra être traduit devant un tribunal de France, pour des obligations par lui contractées en pays étranger, même avec un étranger*" ("A French national can be brought before a French court, for contractual obligations he entered into abroad, even with a foreigner").[650] At the time article 15 was interpreted against its literal meaning as giving exclusive jurisdiction to French courts over contractual cases involving a French defendant.[651] The defendant's argument, however, failed and the American court decided the dispute on the merits.

291. Fountaine Pajot first tried to defend against the plaintiffs' discovery requests but later completely withdrew from the trial. On 26 February 2003 the California court found in favour of the plaintiffs and awarded USD 1.391.650,12 in actual damages. It further ruled that Fountaine Pajot's behaviour in relation to the sale amounted to fraud under article 3294 of the California Civil Code. This article enumerates types of conduct for which punitive damages are available. The court perceived the defendant's absence from the trial as part of a plan to escape accountability and conceal its financial worth. It determined that USD 1.460.000, *i.e.* 20 percent of the defendant's net worth (which it estimated to be around USD 7.3 million), in punitive damages would be sufficient to punish and deter the French company without causing financial ruin. Lastly, the court decided to allow an exception to the American rule on attorneys' fees which states that each party shall bear their own costs, even if they prevail in the law suit. On the basis of the federal Magnuson-Moss Warranty Act[652] a victorious consumer may recover reasonable legal costs. The

649 The facts of the case are to be found in the judgment of the French district court of Rochefort: Tribunal de Grande Instance Rochefort, *Peter Schlenzka & Julie Langhorne v. S.A. Fountaine Pajot*, 12 November 2004, no. 03/01276, *unpublished decision.*

650 Translation by the author.

651 B. Janke & F.-X. Licari, "Enforcing Punitive Damage Awards in France after Fountaine Pajot", 60 *The American Journal of Comparative Law* 2012, 781.

652 15 USC 2310(d)(2).

plaintiffs were awarded USD 402.084,33 in attorneys' fees, bringing the total amount to USD 3.253.734,45.[653]

ii. Rochefort District Court and Poitiers Court of Appeal

292. The American couple then had to enforce the judgment against the defendant's assets in France. They requested the *Tribunal de Grande Instance*[654] of Rochefort to grant enforcement of the California judgment. The court, however, refused to allow enforcement of the foreign decision by relying on article 15 of the French Civil Code. The exorbitant interpretation of article 15 meant that French nationals and companies could always avoid the enforcement of a foreign judgment in France. This was possible on the condition that they had not waived the exclusive jurisdiction by contractually agreeing to the jurisdiction of another court or by voluntarily appearing before a court without challenging that court's jurisdiction.[655] In the eyes of the Rochefort court Fountaine Pajot – as a French defendant – enjoyed the right only to be sued before the French courts. The Rochefort court found that the defendant had not renounced this privilege but had instead contested the California Superior Court's jurisdiction by referring to article 15 of the French Civil Code. The court further did not deny the existence of a jurisdiction clause in favour of the courts of California but pointed out that there were two separate contracts. A first contract existed between the plaintiffs and the agent Rod Gibbons' Cruising Cats and another one between the agent and Fountaine Pajot. The jurisdiction agreement in the first contract was not binding on Fountaine Pajot because it was not a party to that contract. The Rochefort court saw insufficient evidence to sustain that the agent was acting on behalf of the French company. The delivery contract between Rod Gibbons' Cruising Cats and Fountaine Pajot, on the other hand, did not contain a choice for the California courts but instead designated the Commercial Court of La Rochelle as the venue to settle any disputes arising from the contract. This reasoning led the court to conclude that exequatur of the American judgment should be refused.[656] The *Cour d'appel* of Poitiers confirmed this decision on 28 June 2005.[657]

---

[653] California Superior Court 26 February 2003, *Schlenzka v. Pajot*, case no. 837722-1; B. Janke & F.-X. Licari, "Enforcing Punitive Damage Awards in France after Fountaine Pajot", 60 *The American Journal of Comparative Law* 2012, 782.

[654] The Tribunal de Grande Instance is the first instance court in civil cases.

[655] N. Meyer Fabre, "Recognition and Enforcement of U.S. Judgments in France – Recent Developments", *The International Dispute Resolution News* spring 2012, 6–7.

[656] Tribunal de Grande Instance Rochefort, *Peter Schlenzka & Julie Langhorne v. S.A. Fountaine Pajot*, 12 November 2004, no. 03/01276, *unpublished opinion*; B. Janke & F.-X. Licari, "Enforcing Punitive Damage Awards in France after Fountaine Pajot", 60 *The American Journal of Comparative Law* 2012, 783.

[657] Unpublished decision.

293. In 2006 the French Supreme Court reversed its view on the interpretation of article 15 of the Civil Code. It held in *Prieur* that article 15 does not contain a ground of exclusive jurisdiction but rather merely provides an option.[658] One year later article 14 was equally characterised as non-exclusive in nature.[659] French parties thus lost their protection against the execution of foreign decisions in France.[660]

294. This shift in the *Cour de cassation*'s case law came as a godsend for Schlenzka and Langhorne. They petitioned the French Supreme Court for a reversal of the *Cour d'appel*'s ruling. Their demand was successful as the *Cour d'appel* referred to the modified jurisdictional prong of the *Munzer* test.[661] The case was remanded to the Poitiers Court of Appeal for determination whether the revised jurisdictional criterion and the two other requirements (no violation of French international public policy and no *fraude à la loi*) for enforcement were fulfilled.

295. In its decision of 26 February 2009 the Poitiers *Cour d'appel* held that there was a sufficient connection between the defendant Fountaine Pajot and California and no indication of any fraudulent forum shopping.[662] The request for exequatur, however, was rejected yet again by the Court. It found punitive damages to be contrary to French international public policy.[663] The *Cornelissen* case had dealt with treble damages but the *Cour de cassation* did not address the issue of punitive damages as the decision to enforce the U.S. judgment completely turned on the jurisdictional prong of the enforcement requirements.[664]

296. The Court of Appeal identified several arguments why the U.S. punitive damages violated French international public policy. First, civil liability aims

---

658 Cass. civ. 1st, 23 May 2006, *Prieur*, *Bull.* 2006, I, No. 254, No. 04-12777; P. Bernard & H. Salem, "Further developments for qualification of foreign judgments for recognition and enforcement in France: the test for punitive damage awards", *International Bar Association* 2011, 16, footnote 7.

659 Cass. civ. 1st, 22 May 2007, *Fercometal*, *Bull.* 2007, I, No. 195, No. 04-14716.

660 N. Meyer Fabre, "Enforcement Of U.S. Punitive Damages Award in France: First Ruling Of The French Court Of Cassation In X. v. Fountaine Pajot, December 1, 2010", *Mealey's International Arbitration Report* January 2011, 2.

661 Cass. civ. 1st, 22 May 2007, no. 05-20473, *Bull.* 2007, I, no. 196.

662 Cour d'Appel de Poitiers, 26 February 2009, *Schlenzka v. S.A. Fountaine Pajot*, no. 07/02404, 137 *JDI* 2010, 1230; N. Meyer Fabre, "Enforcement Of U.S. Punitive Damages Award in France: First Ruling Of The French Court Of Cassation In X. v. Fountaine Pajot, December 1, 2010", *Mealey's International Arbitration Report* January 2011, 3.

663 Cour d'Appel Poitiers, 26 February 2009, *Schlenzka v. S.A. Fountaine Pajot*, no. 07/02404, 137 *JDI* 2010, 1230.

664 P. Bernard & H. Salem, "Further developments for qualification of foreign judgments for recognition and enforcement in France: the test for punitive damage awards", *International Bar Association* 2011, 18; B. Janke & F.-X. Licari, "Enforcing Punitive Damage Awards in France after Fountaine Pajot", 60 *The American Journal of Comparative Law* 2012, 790.

to put the victim of a tort in the position he or she would have been in had the harmful act not occurred. The system focuses exclusively on the victim's damage to determine the appropriate amount of compensation.[665] The extent of the fault or the tortfeasor's financial situation – which are factors taken into consideration when awarding punitive damages – are therefore completely irrelevant.[666] Second, the Court ruled that punitive damages constitute a windfall for the plaintiff, resulting in unjust enrichment.[667] Third, the punitive damages awarded (USD 1.460.000) to the California couple were manifestly disproportionate as they largely exceeded the sale price (USD 826.009) and the compensatory damages (USD 1.391.650,12).[668] The Court noted that such disproportionate punitive damages violate article 8 of the 1789 *Déclaration des droits de l'Homme et du Citoyen* (Declaration of Human Rights of Man and of the Citizen) which requires penalties to be proportionate. These considerations led the Court to refuse enforcement of not just the punitive damages but of the entire award.[669]

iii. Doctrinal criticism of the Court of Appeal's judgment

297. The Court of Appeal's ruling received scholarly disapproval for various reasons. First, it has been argued that the Court incorrectly classified the principle of full compensation as a rule of international public policy. According to Janke and Licari the principle instead belongs to the wider realm of domestic public policy.[670] As mentioned before, foreign judgments can only be rejected under the more restricted international public policy test.[671] For almost

665 S. Lootgieter, "Punitive damages and French courts", 2, originally retrieved from <http://lacba.org/Files/Main Folder/Sections/International Law/Files/120313-PUNITIVE DAMAGES AND FRENCH COURTS.pdf>.

666 C. Di Meglio & K. Ponczek, "Order to pay punitive damages not contrary to public policy", International Law Office – Legal Newsletter, 14 April 2011, no page numbers, available at <www.internationallawoffice.com>.

667 B. Grange, "Case comment: French Supreme Court and punitive damages: one step forward?", *International Arbitration Law Review* 2011, no. 2; N. Meyer Fabre, "Enforcement Of U.S. Punitive Damages Award in France: First Ruling Of The French Court Of Cassation In X. v. Fountaine Pajot, December 1, 2010", *Mealey's International Arbitration Report* January 2011, 3.

668 Y. Guillotte, "Recognition and enforcement of a U.S. judgment awarding punitive damages: the position of the French Supreme Court", 3, originally retrieved from <www.soulier-avocats.com/upload/documents/Soulier_YG_exequatur_punitive_damages_january_2011.pdf>; C. Di Meglio & K. Ponczek, "The French Supreme Court holds that an order to pay punitive damages is not, in itself, contrary to French international public policy", *Paris International Litigation Bulletin* July 2011, 6.

669 Cour d'Appel Poitiers, 26 February 2009, *Schlenzka v. S.A. Fountaine Pajot*, no. 07/02404, 137 *JDI* 2010, 1230.

670 B. Janke & F.-X. Licari, "Enforcing Punitive Damage Awards in France after Fountaine Pajot", 60 *The American Journal of Comparative Law* 2012, 791 and 793.

671 See *supra* no. 208.

fifty years the *Cour de cassation* has consistently held that the principle of full compensation cannot be regarded as part of *ordre public internationale*.[672] The early decisions dealt with cases in which injured parties were awarded less compensation than the total amount of harm sustained. The French Supreme Court did not find this to be in contradiction with international public policy. The commentators derived from the general way in which these judgments were formulated that the same reasoning applied to awards going beyond what is needed to compensate the plaintiff.[673] Later, the *Cour de cassation expressis verbis* confirmed that a deviation from the principle of full compensation is in conformity with French international public policy.[674]

298. Second, it is noted that the awarding of punitive damages not always leads to a windfall and sometimes not even to full compensation of the damage suffered. There are in reality factual or legal obstacles which might hinder the recovery of the full amount of damage. The American rule on attorneys' fees probably forms the most significant impediment to making the victim whole. Punitive damages can, therefore, bridge the gap and help achieve full compensation.[675] Although this reasoning may be correct in some instances, it does not hold water in the case at hand because the California Superior Court provided a separate amount of damages as compensation for the legal costs incurred. The punitive damages awarded to the California plaintiffs, therefore, did in fact constitute a windfall. However, one could argue that the enrichment is not unjust because its origin lies in a judgment.[676] Besides, punitive damages could be viewed as rather preventing the unjust enrichment of the tortfeasor who has committed a "*faute lucrative*", *i.e.* an

---

672 F.-X. Licari, "Prendre les punitive damages au sérieux: propos critiques sur un refus d'accorder l'exequatur à une décision californienne ayant alloué des dommages intérêts punitifs", *Journal du droit international (Clunet)* October/November/December 2010/4, 1245.

673 Cass. Civ. 1st, 30 May 1967, *Bull.*, I, no. 189, *Kieger*, D. 1967, comment P. Malaurie; Cass. civ. 1st, 15 December 1969, *Bull.*, I, no. 393; O. Cachard, "Observations", case note under Cass. 1 December 2010, *Droit Maritime Français* April 2011, 337; G. Cavalier, "Punitive Damages and French International Public Policy", in R. Stürner and M. Kawono (eds.), *Comparative Studies on Business Tort Litigation*, Tübingen, Mohr Siebeck, 2011, 222 and footnote 16 and the references contained therein.

674 Cass. Crim., 16 June 1993, *Bull.* crim., no. 214, no. 92–83871; Cass. Civ., 1 September 2003, no. 00–22294: JurisData no. 2003–020395; *Bull. Civ.* I, no. 39; F.-X. Licari, "Prendre les punitive damages au sérieux: propos critiques sur un refus d'accorder l'exequatur à une décision californienne ayant alloué des dommages intérêts punitifs", *Journal du droit international (Clunet)* October/November/December 2010/4, 1245.

675 B. Janke & F.-X. Licari, "Enforcing Punitive Damage Awards in France after Fountaine Pajot", 60 *The American Journal of Comparative Law* 2012, 790, footnote 57.

676 B. Janke & F.-X. Licari, "Enforcing Punitive Damage Awards in France after Fountaine Pajot", 60 *The American Journal of Comparative Law* 2012, 791, footnote 58.

offence whose benefits for the wrongdoer are not neutralised by merely paying damages.[677, 678]

299. A last criticism on the judgment relates to the Court's application of the United Nations Convention on Contracts for the International Sale of Goods (CISG). Article 74 CISG implicitly excludes punitive damages: "*Damages for breach of contract by one party consist of a sum equal to the loss, including loss of profit, suffered by the other party as a consequence of the breach. Such damages may not exceed the loss which the party in breach foresaw or ought to have foreseen at the time of the conclusion of the contract, in the light of the facts and matters of which he then knew or ought to have known, as a possible consequence of the breach of contract*". However, it is clear that the CISG is not applicable in this case as vessels are excluded from its scope of application (article 2 (e)). Moreover, the California couple acted in the capacity of consumers as they bought the vessel to sail around the world with their children. Such sales contracts for goods for personal or family use are equally outside the ambit of the Convention (article 2 (a)).[679] Given these criticisms, it was interesting to see whether the *Cour de cassation* would express disagreement with the decision.

iv. French Supreme Court

1. Acceptance of punitive damages

300. The American litigants appealed the judgment before the *Cour de cassation*. This required the French Supreme Court for the first time in its history to take a stance on the enforcement of punitive damages. On 1 December 2010 it ruled: "*[...] le principe d'une condemnation à des dommages intérêts punitifs, n'est pas, en soi, contraire à l'ordre public, il en est autrement lorsque le montant alloué est disproportionné au regard du préjudice subi et des manquements aux obligations contractuelles du débiteur [...]*" ("[...] the principle of awarding punitive damages is not, in itself, contrary to public policy; this is not the case when the amount awarded is disproportional to the loss suffered and to the contractual breach of the debtor [...]").[680]

---

677 M. Requejo Isidro, "Punitive Damages From a Private International Law Perspective" in H. Koziol & V. Wilcox (eds.), *Punitive Damages: Common Law and Civil Law Perspectives*, Vienna, Springer, 2009, 249, footnote 49.

678 F.-X. Licari, "Prendre les punitive damages au sérieux: propos critiques sur un refus d'accorder l'exequatur à une décision californienne ayant alloué des dommages intérêts punitifs", *Journal du droit international (Clunet)* October/November/December 2010/4, 1256.

679 B. Janke & F.-X. Licari, "Enforcing Punitive Damage Awards in France after Fountaine Pajot", 60 *The American Journal of Comparative Law* 2012, 793–794.

680 Cass. Civ. 1st, 1 December 2010, *Schlenzka & Langhorne v. Fountaine Pajot S.A*, no. 09-13303, *Recueil Dalloz* 2011, 423.

301. According to the Supreme Court punitive damages are in themselves not contrary to (international) public policy. U.S. punitive damages can, therefore, in principle be enforced in France. In light of the fact that penal sanctions are not enforceable in France[681], this statement implicitly confirms the civil nature of a punitive damages award.[682] The Court's ruling makes it clear that objections against the enforcement of punitive damages based on the idea that they violate the divide between criminal and private law, like the *Tribunal de Grande Instance of Paris* had raised in 2004[683], should be dismissed.[684] This liberal, welcoming attitude of France's Supreme Court appears at first sight to be very progressive. It is, however, nothing more than an accurate reflection of the legal status quo. As we will demonstrate in detail in chapter 5, the concept of punitive damages can no longer be held to contravene international public policy. French civil law contains enough punitive traces to support the position that it would be hypocritical to condemn foreign punitive damages by principle.[685]

2. Limits on the acceptance of punitive damages

302. Moreover, the acceptance of punitive damages is by no means absolute. The Court attaches an important caveat to the general rule. Punitive damages do violate international public policy when their amount is "*disproportional to the damage suffered and the breach of the contractual obligations of the debtor*".[686] In other words: although the concept of punitive damages conforms to international public policy, the proportionality of the award is still a rule of international public policy.[687] Unlike the Court of Appeal of Poitiers[688], the *Cour de cassation* does not seem to require that this disproportionality is manifest.[689]

---

681 F.-X. Licari, "Prendre les punitive damages au sérieux: propos critiques sur un refus d'accorder l'exequatur à une décision californienne ayant alloué des dommages intérêts punitifs", *Journal du droit international (Clunet)* October/November/December 2010/4, 1240.

682 F.-X. Licari, "La compatibilité de principe des punitive damages avec l'ordre public international: une décision en trompe-l'œil de la Cour de cassation?", *Recueil Dalloz* 10 February 2011, 425.

683 See *supra* no. 287.

684 F.-X. Licari, "La compatibilité de principe des punitive damages avec l'ordre public international: une décision en trompe-l'œil de la Cour de cassation?", *Recueil Dalloz* 10 February 2011, 425.

685 C.I. Nagy, "Recognition and enforcement of US judgments involving punitive damages in continental Europe", *Nederlands Internationaal Privaatrecht* 2012, 9 and 11.

686 Cass. civ. 1st, 1 December 2010, *Schlenzka & Langhorne v. Fountaine Pajot S.A*, no. 09-13303, Recueil Dalloz 2011, 423.

687 A.S. Sibon, "Enforcing Punitive Damages Awards in France: Facing Proportionality within International Public Policy", available at <http://ssrn.com/abstract=2382817>.

688 See *supra* no. 296.

689 P. Bernard & H. Salem, "Further developments for qualification of foreign judgments for recognition and enforcement in France: the test for punitive damage awards", *International Bar Association* 2011, 19. In the final part of the ruling the Court nevertheless mentions that the Court of Appeal was not incorrect in finding the punitive award to be manifest disproportionate. In our opinion this reference should be understood as confirming the

The centre of the public policy analysis shifts from the incompatibility of the concept of punitive damages itself to an investigation of their amount.[690] The real obstacle for punitive damages under the public policy test is no longer the compensation dogma but rather the distinct issue of excessiveness.

303. Although proportionality is regarded as a public law concept[691], almost two years before the Court's ruling in *Fountaine Pajot* the *Cour de cassation* already applied the proportionality standard in a private international law context.

304. In *Blech* the *Cour de cassation* was faced with the question whether a pecuniary penalty sanctioning non-compliance with a U.S. court order could be granted enforcement in France.[692] American citizen Richard Blech had committed fraud as CEO of Credit Bancorp. In order to trace the proceeds of the Ponzi scheme that had been set up, the U.S. District Court of the Southern District of New York appointed Loewenson as receiver. Loewenson obtained an injunction ordering Blech to cooperate in his investigation. As Blech failed to do so, Loewenson subsequently filed for an order compelling Blech to pay USD 100 per day of non-compliance with the initial injunction. This amount was to be doubled for every additional day of non-cooperation in the liquidation process and the tracing of diverted assets. Blech continued to refuse to assist the receiver and was found in contempt of court. Due to Blech's prolonged inactivity, the penalty had reached USD 13 million. The receiver then attempted to enforce the order in France because Blech was a French resident who owned property there.

305. Both the *Tribunal de Grande Instance* of Thonon-les-Bains and the *Cour d'appel* of Chambéry allowed enforcement of the order. The *Cour de cassation* first determined that the foreign order was similar to an "*astreinte*", *i.e.* "*a court order that threatens to compel a debtor who has an outstanding obligation to pay her creditor a sum of money unless she performs the obligation*".[693] According to the Supreme Court the sanction had a civil character[694] and was, therefore,

---

Court of Appeal's decision by reiterating its own words and not as a holding of a more general scope.

690 B. Janke & F.-X. Licari, "Enforcing Punitive Damage Awards in France after Fountaine Pajot", 60 *The American Journal of Comparative Law* 2012, 794–795; P. Bernard & H. Salem, "Further developments for qualification of foreign judgments for recognition and enforcement in France: the test for punitive damage awards", *International Bar Association* 2011, 18.

691 See for instance: J. Cianciardo, "The principle of Proportionality: The Challenges of Human Rights", 3 *Journal of Civil Law Studies* 2010, 177–186.

692 Cass. civ. 1st, 28 January 2009, no. 07–11.729, Blech, *Bull.*, I, no.15.

693 M.P. Michell, "Imperium by the Back Door: The Astreinte and the Enforcement of Contractual Obligations in France", 51 *University of Toronto Faculty of Law Review* 1993, 252.

694 The Court's ruling in Fountaine Pajot that punitive damages are a civil remedy is consistent with this finding: F.-X. Licari, "La compatibilité de principe des punitive damages avec l'ordre

eligible for enforcement in France. The Court then examined whether the foreign sanction was proportionate. It compared the amount of the penalty (over USD 13 million) with the fault committed by the defendant (the underlying fraud). The total sum defrauded amounted to USD 200 million. The sanction was, therefore, found to fulfil the proportionality requirement.[695] By making a comparison between the degree of misconduct and the amount of the penalty the Court essentially employed a criminal law mechanism in civil liability.[696]

306. The Supreme Court's judgment in *Fountaine Pajot* did not contain specific criteria on how to determine the excessiveness of a foreign punitive award. It merely stated that punitive damages should not be disproportionate in relation to the injury suffered and the breach of the contractual obligations of the debtor.[697] There was no reference to the wealth of the wrongdoer, although the defendant's financial condition was an important consideration in the California judgment and is so in most states of the U.S.[698] The lack of practical guidance leaves lower judges wondering at which point punitive damages become disproportional.[699]

307. As the determination of the proportional nature of the award lies in the discretion of the lower courts, the absence of a bright-line standard creates uncertainty.[700] On the one hand, one could argue that the French Supreme Court required a comparison between the amount of punitive damages and the amount of compensatory damages awarded (or in the words of the Court: the injury suffered). This criterion reminds us of the second *BMW* guidepost.[701] It was the approach taken by the Poitiers Court of Appeal.[702] Like the Court of

---

public international: une décision en trompe-l'œil de la Cour de cassation?", *Recueil Dalloz* 10 February 2011, 425.

695 Cass. civ. 1st, 28 January 2009, no. 07–11.729, Blech, *Bull.*, I, no.15.

696 B. Janke & F.-X. Licari, "Enforcing Punitive Damage Awards in France after Fountaine Pajot", 60 *The American Journal of Comparative Law* 2012, 798–800.

697 Cass. civ. 1st, 1 December 2010, *Schlenzka & Langhorne v. Fountaine Pajot S.A*, no. 09–13303, Recueil Dalloz 2011, 423.

698 O. Cachard, "Observations", case note under Cass. 1 December 2010, *Droit Maritime Français* April 2011, 339; N. Meyer Fabre, "Enforcement Of U.S. Punitive Damages Award in France: First Ruling Of The French Court Of Cassation In X. v. Fountaine Pajot, December 1, 2010", *Mealey's International Arbitration Report* January 2011, 3. See *supra* no. 56.

699 P. Bernard & H. Salem, "Further developments for qualification of foreign judgments for recognition and enforcement in France: the test for punitive damage awards", *International Bar Association* 2011, 19; J. Juvenal, "Dommages-intérêts punitifs: comment apprécier la conformité à l'ordre public international?", *La Semaine Juridique Edition Générale* no. 6, 7 February 2011, 257–259.

700 A.S. Sibon, "Enforcing Punitive Damages Awards in France: Facing Proportionality within International Public Policy", available at <http://ssrn.com/abstract=2382817>.

701 See *supra* no. 80.

702 See *supra* no. 296; P. Bernard & H. Salem, "Further developments for qualification of foreign judgments for recognition and enforcement in France: the test for punitive damage awards", *International Bar Association* 2011, 19.

Appeal, the *Cour de cassation* concluded in that regard that the punitive damages largely exceeded the compensatory damages (the difference between both being USD 70.000).[703, 704] This could be interpreted as establishing a 1:1 maximum ratio between punitive and compensatory damages.[705] Such a 1:1 boundary stands in sharp contrast with the single digit rule (*i.e.* a maximum ratio of 9:1) established by the U.S. Supreme Court.[706] Although the California Superior Court complied with the U.S. Supreme Court's delineations, exceeding the 1:1 limit by only a handful of percentage points proved fatal for the punitive award's chances of enforcement in France.[707]

308. On the other hand, one cannot simply ignore the Supreme Court's reference in *Fountaine Pajot* to the defendant's breach of contract ("*des manquements aux obligations contractuelles du débiteur*").[708] The Court presumably meant the seriousness of the defendant's breach of contract.[709] It is of course the contractual nature of the dispute between the U.S. litigants and Fountaine Pajot that inspired the language of the Supreme Court. The *Cour de cassation* is in principle bound by the description of the facts laid out by the Court of Appeal. However, most punitive damages in the U.S. originate in tort cases. Punitive damages in contract cases are possible if the behaviour constituting the breach of contract is also a tort for which punitive damages are available.[710] Expanding upon the terminology of the Court in an attempt to formulate a general rule applicable to punitive damages, the notion could perhaps be read as the seriousness of the debtor's wrongful behaviour, the degree

---

703 Cass. civ. 1st, 1 December 2010, *Schlenzka & Langhorne v. Fountaine Pajot S.A*, no. 09-13303, *Recueil Dalloz* 2011, 423; N. Meyer Fabre, "Recognition and Enforcement of U.S. Judgments in France – Recent Developments", *The International Dispute Resolution News* spring 2012, 9.

704 There is an argument for adding the amount awarded for attorneys' fees (*in casu* USD 402.084,33) to the compensatory damages when calculating the ratio. Legal costs are in essence also a form of loss caused by the defendant. Of course, this scenario is quite exceptional because U.S. litigants almost always bear their own costs, even if they win the case. In chapter 6 in no. 520 we argue that legal fees should remain separate from the compensatory damages, following the example of the *Cour de cassation*.

705 S. Lootgieter, "Punitive damages and French courts", 3, originally retrieved from <http://lacba.org/Files/Main Folder/Sections/International Law/Files/120313-PUNITIVE DAMAGES AND FRENCH COURTS.pdf>; N. Meyer Fabre, "Enforcement Of U.S. Punitive Damages Award in France: First Ruling Of The French Court Of Cassation In X. v. Fountaine Pajot, December 1, 2010", *Mealey's International Arbitration Report* January 2011, 4.

706 See *supra* no. 86–87.

707 B. Janke & F.-X. Licari, "Enforcing Punitive Damage Awards in France after Fountaine Pajot", 60 *The American Journal of Comparative Law* 2012, 801 and footnote 113.

708 P. Bernard & H. Salem, "Further developments for qualification of foreign judgments for recognition and enforcement in France: the test for punitive damage awards", *International Bar Association* 2011, 19; C.I. Nagy, "Recognition and enforcement of US judgments involving punitive damages in continental Europe", *Nederlands Internationaal Privaatrecht* 2012, 9.

709 B. Janke & F.-X. Licari, "Enforcing Punitive Damage Awards in France after Fountaine Pajot", 60 *The American Journal of Comparative Law* 2012, 776.

710 See *supra* no. 47.

of culpability or the blameworthiness of the fault.[711] This corresponds to the first *BMW* guidepost.[712] The Court could have used the suggested language, notwithstanding the contractual origin of the litigation, because the punitive damages were probably more connected to Fountaine Pajot's fraudulent and deceitful conduct surrounding the breach of contract than to the actual breach (the non-conformity of the vessel).[713]

309. Under this second view, in addition to the amount of compensatory damages given to the victim, the defendant's conduct should thus be taken into account when assessing whether the punitive portion of a foreign judgment is excessive.[714] In our view this could mean that the enforcement judge can modulate the 1:1 maximum ratio according to the reprehensibility of the defendant's conduct. This approach however encounters a fundamental problem: it seems to allow a revival of *révision au fond* which was abolished in 1964 in *Munzer.*[715]

310. Despite suggesting the breach of contract as one of the two factors to measure the proportionality of the punitive damages, the *Cour de cassation* did not take the defendant's conduct into account (at least not explicitly).[716] It merely stated that the Court of Appeal could have rightfully concluded that the punitive award was manifestly disproportionate because the punitive damages largely exceeded the purchase price and the cost of the repairs.[717] The *Cour de cassation*

711 N. Meyer Fabre, "Enforcement Of U.S. Punitive Damages Award in France: First Ruling Of The French Court Of Cassation In X. v. Fountaine Pajot, December 1, 2010", *Mealey's International Arbitration Report* January 2011, 4; C.I. Nagy, "Recognition and enforcement of US judgments involving punitive damages in continental Europe", *Nederlands Internationaal Privaatrecht* 2012, 9.

712 See *supra* no. 80.

713 See *supra* no. 291; N. Meyer Fabre, "Recognition and Enforcement of U.S. Judgments in France - Recent Developments", *The International Dispute Resolution News* spring 2012, 9, footnote 25.

714 C.I. Nagy, "Recognition and enforcement of US judgments involving punitive damages in continental Europe", *Nederlands Internationaal Privaatrecht* 2012, 9.

715 Numerous authors note that the proportionality test reintroduces a *révision au fond*: F.-X. Licari, "La compatibilité de principe des punitive damages avec l'ordre public international: une décision en trompe-l'œil de la Cour de cassation?", *Recueil Dalloz* 10 February 2011, 426–427; P. Bernard & H. Salem, "Further developments for qualification of foreign judgments for recognition and enforcement in France: the test for punitive damage awards", *International Bar Association* 2011, 19; J. Juvenal, "Dommages-intérêts punitifs: comment apprécier la conformité à l'ordre public international?", *La Semaine Juridique Edition Générale* no. 6, 7 February 2011, 257–259; B. Janke & F.-X. Licari, "Enforcing Punitive Damage Awards in France after Fountaine Pajot", 60 *The American Journal of Comparative Law* 2012, 801–802.

716 N. Meyer Fabre, "Enforcement Of U.S. Punitive Damages Award in France: First Ruling Of The French Court Of Cassation In X. v. Fountaine Pajot December 1, 2010", *Mealey's International Arbitration Report* January 2011, 4; F.-X. Licari, "La compatibilité de principe des punitive damages avec l'ordre public international: une décision en trompe-l'œil de la Cour de cassation?", *Recueil Dalloz* 10 February 2011, 426.

717 Cass. civ. 1st, 1 December 2010, *Schlenzka & Langhorne v. Fountaine Pajot S.A*, no. 09-13303, *Recueil Dalloz* 2011, 423.

could not allow partial enforcement but instead had to reject the U.S. judgment in its entirety because the plaintiffs had not requested enforcement of only the compensatory damages in case the punitive damages were deemed unacceptable. The prohibition on *ultra petita* rulings thus left the U.S. plaintiffs empty-handed.

v. The enforcement of punitive damages after *Fountaine Pajot*

311. However, the plaintiffs' strategic choice[718] in *Fountaine Pajot*, resulting in the total rejection of the U.S. judgment, does not affect the fate of other U.S. judgments containing punitive damages. If requested, enforcement of only the compensatory damages can be granted.[719] It is vital for partial enforcement that the U.S. judgment clearly identifies and singles out the punitive damages because the prohibition on *révision au fond* (a prohibition to review the foreign judgment on its merits) forbids a French court to reduce the global amount of damages a foreign court has awarded.[720]

312. Although the *Cour de cassation* opened the door to punitive damages by accepting the concept itself under international public policy, scholars have argued that the proportionality test is a clear reminder of the French distrust and hostility towards this foreign institute.[721] GUILLOTTE fears that French judges will employ their sovereign appraisal to determine the punitive damages to be disproportionate, thereby further blocking their enforcement in France.[722] In any case, it seems that, given the Supreme Court's 1:1 maximum ratio between punitive and compensatory damages, only a limited number of U.S. punitive damages will be granted enforcement in France.[723] Only litigants having been

---

718 Informal contact with the lawyers handling the case revealed that the lack of request for partial enforcement was the result of a tactical choice. They opted not to submit subsidiary requests in order not to weaken the main request of enforcement of the entire American judgment.

719 O. Cachard, "Le contrôle juridictionnel des jugements étrangers ordonnant des Punitive Damages", *Revue Lamy Droit des Affaires* 2013, 140; A.S. Sibon, "Enforcing Punitive Damages Awards in France: Facing Proportionality within International Public Policy", available at <http://ssrn.com/abstract=2382817>.

720 N. Meyer Fabre, "Recognition and Enforcement of U.S. Judgments in France – Recent Developments", *The International Dispute Resolution News* spring 2012, 9; N. Meyer Fabre, "Enforcement Of U.S. Punitive Damages Award in France: First Ruling Of The French Court Of Cassation In X. v. Fountaine Pajot December 1, 2010", *Mealey's International Arbitration Report* January 2011, 4.

721 B. Janke & F.-X. Licari, "Enforcing Punitive Damage Awards in France after Fountaine Pajot", 60 *The American Journal of Comparative Law* 2012, 795.

722 Y. Guillotte, "Recognition and enforcement of a U.S. judgment awarding punitive damages: the position of the French Supreme Court", 3, originally retrieved from <www.soulier-avocats.com/upload/documents/Soulier_YG_exequatur_punitive_damages_january_2011.pdf>.

723 F.-X. Licari, "La compatibilité de principe des punitive damages avec l'ordre public international: une décision en trompe-l'œil de la Cour de cassation?", *Recueil Dalloz*

awarded punitive damages equal to or less than the amount of the compensatory damages are likely to be successful in executing the punitive award against the defendant's assets in France.[724] For this reason multiple damages will not be granted exequatur in France.[725] However, the *Cour de cassation*'s mentioning of a second factor, the defendant's behaviour, next to the loss suffered, complicates matters even further. If the acceptable level of punitive damages depends on the French judge's assessment of the blameworthiness of the defendant's behaviour, it is very difficult to predict whether the U.S. judgment will be enforced in France.

313. Plaintiffs in the U.S. seeking punitive damages which they want to execute in France, therefore, need to be aware of the risk attached to presenting French courts a punitive damages award for them to enforce. They have to anticipate the possibility that the punitive portion of their award cannot be realised in France, especially when the ratio between punitive and compensatory damages exceeds 1:1.[726] If the plaintiff decides to attempt to obtain enforcement of the whole judgment, he or she is advised to request partial enforcement (*i.e.* enforcement of only the compensatory damages) in subsidiary order. This method gives the requested court a fall-back option in case enforcement of the whole award is rejected.

314. Janke and Licari suggest that plaintiffs can avoid problems with punitive damages by trying to inflate the compensatory damages. The latter pose no enforcement issues. In the U.S. non-economic damages appear to contain both a compensatory and a punitive element.[727] In order to obtain such "punitive compensatory damages"[728] the plaintiff's lawyer could try to convince the jury to include a vindictive element in moral damages, damages for pain and

10 February 2011, 426; B. Janke & F.-X. Licari, "Enforcing Punitive Damage Awards in France after Fountaine Pajot", 60 *The American Journal of Comparative Law* 2012, 802.

724 S. Lootgieter, "Punitive damages and French courts", 4, originally retrieved from <http://lacba.org/Files/Main Folder/Sections/International Law/Files/120313-PUNITIVE DAMAGES AND FRENCH COURTS.pdf>.

725 P. Bernard & H. Salem, "Further developments for qualification of foreign judgments for recognition and enforcement in France: the test for punitive damage awards", *International Bar Association* 2011, 20.

726 S. Lootgieter, "Punitive damages and French courts", 4, originally retrieved from <http://lacba.org/Files/Main Folder/Sections/International Law/Files/120313-PUNITIVE DAMAGES AND FRENCH COURTS.pdf>.

727 See Second Restatement of Torts, §908, comment (c) (1997): "*In many cases in which compensatory damages include an amount for emotional distress, such as humiliation or indignation aroused by the defendant's act, there is no clear line of demarcation between punishment and compensation and a verdict for a specified amount frequently includes elements of both.*"

728 C.M. Sharkey, "Crossing the Punitive-Compensatory Divide" in B.H. Bornstein et al. (eds.), *Civil Juries and Civil Justice: Psychological and Legal Perspectives*, New York, Springer, 2008, 79.

suffering and other non-economic damages awards.[729] Every dollar that can be transferred from the punitive damages heading to the compensatory damages section of the judgment can more easily penetrate the French borders.

315. Two judgments rendered shortly after the *Fountaine Pajot* ruling deal with the exequatur of U.S. punitive damages in France. On 4 March 2011 the Court of Appeal of Poitiers decided in a case between plaintiff Charles Edward S. and defendants Mary Helen N. and Philippe D. Following a breach of a building contract by S., a Texas court had on 30 June 2006 awarded N. and D. around USD 759.000 to compensate for the economic loss, around USD 170.000 in interests and USD 1.500.000 in "supplementary" damages. On 13 February 2009 the *Tribunal de Grande Instance* of Saintes granted enforcement of the U.S. judgment. The Court of Appeal reversed this decision. It repeated the principle of the *Fountaine Pajot* ruling and observed that the amount of punitive damages largely exceeded the amount awarded to compensate for the damages suffered by N. and D. For that reason, the judgment violated international public policy and could not be enforced in France.[730]

316. This decision seems to be consistent with the interpretation of the *Fountaine Pajot* judgment as introducing a 1:1 maximum ratio between compensatory and punitive damages.[731] The Poitiers Court seems to have noticed that the ratio did not meet the 1:1 maximum and, therefore, did not satisfy the proportionality standard. Identical to the *Cour de cassation* in *Fountaine Pajot*, the Court of Appeal did not refer to the conduct of the defendant, the second prong of the proportionality test the *Cour de cassation* established in *Fountaine Pajot*, when applying the proportionality requirement to the facts of the case. The Court of Appeal ignored the request for enforcement of all damages except the "supplementary" ones, in case the Court would find the latter to be in violation of international public policy. Subsequently, the whole judgment was denied enforcement.

317. In a case before the Court of Appeal of Paris, the appellant Georgia Lee as representative ("receiver") of Sierra National Insurance Holdings sought to enforce three California judgments. The first two are particularly relevant. In the first judgment of 1 December 2005 the California Court awarded USD 10.846.246 on the basis of unjust enrichment. The second decision of 21 December 2005 awarded the same amount in punitive damages. After the *Tribunal de Grande Instance* of Paris rejected the request for exequatur on 2 December 2009, the Court of Appeal of Paris sided with the appellant. In its

[729] B. Janke & F.-X. Licari, "Enforcing Punitive Damage Awards in France after Fountaine Pajot", 60 *The American Journal of Comparative Law* 2012, 802.

[730] Court of Appeal Poitiers 4 March 2011, case no. 09/02077.

[731] See *supra* no. 307.

decision of 30 June 2011 it ruled that the defendant did not demonstrate that the judgments violate international public policy.[732] The *Cour de cassation* annulled this judgment on 7 November 2012 because the Court of Appeal had *inter alia* failed to address the defendant's argument that the California judgments were disproportional in relation to the damage suffered.[733] The case was referred to the Court of Appeal of Versailles which did not touch upon the proportionality of the punitive award but rejected the enforcement of the California judgment of 21 December 2005 for reasons of procedural international public policy.[734]

318. In our opinion the 1:1 maximum ratio rule was complied with in this case because the compensatory damages equal the punitive damages. Perhaps the Court of Appeal of Paris noticed this and, therefore, granted enforcement. However, it should have inserted this reasoning in the judgment in order to comply with its obligation to motivate its judgments. Remarkably, the *Cour de cassation* did not mention the conduct of the defendant as one of the factors in the proportionality test. The Supreme Court only referred to the damage sustained.

4.5. SPAIN

4.5.1. CONDITIONS FOR ENFORCEMENT

319. The enforcement of foreign judgments from non-EU countries that do not have a relevant convention with Spain is governed by articles 951–958 of the Code of Civil Procedure of 1881.[735] The jurisdiction to decide on the enforcement of foreign judgments lies since 1 January 2004 with the courts of first instance.[736]

4.5.2. THE SUPREME COURT'S CASE OF *MILLER IMPORT CORP. V. ALABASTRES ALFREDO, S.L.*

a. *Federal District Court Houston*

320. In the case of *Miller Import Corp. v. Alabastres Alfredo, S.L.* of 13 November 2001 the Spanish Supreme Court (*Tribunal Supremo*) dealt with

732 Court of Appeal Paris 30 June 2011, case no. 10/00293.

733 Cass. civ. 1st, 7 November 2012, case no. 11–23871, *Petites Affiches* 10 January 2013, 9.

734 Court of Appeal Versailles, 19 September 2013, no. 13/02154.

735 Ley de Enjuiciamiento Civil 1881, available at <http://noticias.juridicas.com/base_datos/Privado/lec.html>.

736 Article 955 Ley de Enjuiciamiento Civil 1881, available at <http://noticias.juridicas.com/base_datos/Privado/lec.html>; F. Ramos Romeu, "Litigation Under the Shadow of an Exequatur: The Spanish Recognition of U.S. Judgments", *International Lawyer* 2004, 951.

a request for enforcement of a U.S. judgment containing punitive damages.[737] At the time, the civil division of the Spanish Supreme Court had exclusive jurisdiction over a request for enforcement of judgments coming from abroad.[738] Litigation between the plaintiffs Miller Import Corp. (domiciled in the U.S.) and Florence S.R.L. (domiciled in Italy) and defendant Alabastres Alfredo, S.L. (domiciled in Spain) arose before the Federal District Court for the Southern District of Texas (Houston Hall) in Houston. The plaintiffs alleged that the Spanish defendant had infringed intellectual property rights by manufacturing falsified labels of a registered trademark in Spain. In a judgment of 21 August 1998 the American court followed the plaintiffs' arguments and awarded treble damages.[739] Before the Supreme Court the defendant argued, among other things, that enforcement should be refused on public policy grounds.

b. *Spanish Supreme Court*

i. Public policy analysis

321. The section of the Supreme Court's judgment addressing the punitive damages is at times very confusing and incoherent. It offers very little structure and leaves the reader to find his own way through the vague sentences in an attempt to retrieve the Court's reasoning. After noting that punitive damages are not acknowledged in Spanish law, the Supreme Court first emphasised that its intent was not to usurp legislative competence in the matter but rather to assess the foreign judgment under substantive public policy as identified by Spanish courts.[740]

322. It noted that the Texas money award contained some damages that did not serve a compensatory objective but were more punitive, sanction-like and preventive in nature. The Court classified compensation for injuries as part of (Spanish) international public policy. However, it added that coercive, sanctioning mechanisms are not uncommon in the areas of (Spanish) substantive law, specifically contract law, and procedure. According to the Court the presence of such punitive mechanisms in private law to compensate the shortcomings of

---

737 Spanish Supreme Court 13 November 2001, Exequatur no. 2039/1999, *Aedipr* 2003, 914.

738 F. Ramos Romeu, "Litigation Under the Shadow of an Exequatur: The Spanish Recognition of U.S. Judgments", *International Lawyer* 2004, 951; M. Requejo Isidro, "Punitive Damages – Europe Strikes Back?", presentation delivered at the British Institute of International and Comparative Law, 2 November 2011, London, text on file with the author.

739 Federal District Court for the Southern District of Texas (Houston Hall) 21 August 1998, *unpublished and archived*. The exact amount of the treble damages is unknown as it is not mentioned in the judgment of the Spanish Supreme Court.

740 S.R. Jablonski, "Translation and comment: enforcing U.S. punitive damages awards in foreign courts – a recent case in the Supreme Court of Spain", 24 *Journal of Law and Commerce* 2004–2005, 229.

criminal law is consistent with the doctrine of minimum intervention in penal law. This doctrine is embedded in the Spanish legal system and requires the legislature to first counter unwanted conduct by employing less invasive remedial intervention, such as civil penalties. Criminal penalties should only be used as *ultimum remedium*.[741] Furthermore, it is often difficult to differentiate concepts of compensation. The example of moral damages to which the Court refers makes this point clear. Moral damages fulfil a compensatory role (the reparation of moral damage) as well as a sanctioning function and it is not easy to distinguish between the two.[742] In Spanish law a minimal overlap between civil law (compensation) and criminal law (punishment) is thus not completely unknown.[743, 744] In making their public policy analysis, the Court finally added, courts should not lose sight of the connection between the matter and the (Spanish) forum. This is of course a reference to the theory of *Inlandsbeziehung*, which regulates the strength of the public policy exception according to the case's proximity to the forum.[745] All these reasons led the Court to the conclusion that punitive damages as a concept do not oppose public policy.[746]

ii. Proportionality

323. This finding however did not end the public policy test. The principle of proportionality was the second and final yardstick the award needed to overcome before enforcement could be allowed. The Court considered two

741 F. Quarta, "Class Actions, Extra-Compensatory Damages, and Judicial Recognition in Europe", Conference paper – "Extraterritoriality and Collective Redress", London 15 November 2010, Draft 19 November 2010, 10.

742 C.I. Nagy, Recognition and enforcement of US judgments involving punitive damages in continental Europe, *Nederlands Internationaal Privaatrecht* 2012, 9.

743 S.R. Jablonski, "Translation and comment: enforcing U.S. punitive damages awards in foreign courts – a recent case in the Supreme Court of Spain", 24 *Journal of Law and Commerce* 2004–2005, 229; C.I. Nagy, Recognition and enforcement of US judgments involving punitive damages in continental Europe, *Nederlands Internationaal Privaatrecht* 2012, 9.

744 Compare with the *Fimez* judgment of the Italian Supreme Court which completely ruled out such an overlap: see *supra* no. 226.

745 M. Requejo Isidro, "Punitive Damages: How Do They Look Like When Seen From Abroad?" in L. Meurkens & E. Nordin (eds.), *The Power of Punitive Damages – Is Europe Missing Out?*, Cambridge – Antwerp – Portland, Intersentia, 2012, 326–327; M. Requejo Isidro, "Punitive Damages From a Private International Law Perspective" in H. Koziol & V. Wilcox (eds.), *Punitive Damages: Common Law and Civil Law Perspectives*, Vienna, Springer, 2009, 247.

746 Spanish Supreme Court 13 November 2001, Exequatur no. 2039/1999, *Aedipr* 2003, 914.; M. Otero Crespo, "Punitive Damages Under Spanish Law: A Subtle Recognition?" in L. Meurkens & E. Nordin (eds.), *The Power of Punitive Damages – Is Europe Missing Out?*, Cambridge – Antwerp – Portland, Intersentia, 2012, 289; M. Requejo Isidro, "Punitive Damages From a Private International Law Perspective" in H. Koziol & V. Wilcox (eds.), *Punitive Damages: Common Law and Civil Law Perspectives*, Vienna, Springer, 2009, 247–248; M. Requejo Isidro, "Punitive Damages: How Do They Look Like When Seen From Abroad?" in L. Meurkens & E. Nordin (eds.), *The Power of Punitive Damages – Is Europe Missing Out?*, Cambridge – Antwerp – Portland, Intersentia, 2012, 326.

elements to be relevant when assessing the (potentially) excessive nature of the treble damages: (1) the predictability of the award and (2) the nature of the interests protected.[747]

324. The Court first referred to the fact that the treble damages arose *ex lege*. The legal provisions sanctioning infringements of the intellectual property rights at hand took the intentional character and the gravity of the defendant's behaviour into account and foresaw a tripling of the amount of compensatory damages. This reliance on the statutory origin of the punitive damages begs the question whether punitive damages developed by case law would be predictable enough for the Spanish Supreme Court.[748] In our opinion the absence of a written provision would not automatically rule out the enforcement of the judgment.[749] One wonders what would happen to punitive awards coming from states where punitive damages legislation does not provide for caps.[750] In those states the only restraint on the amount of punitive damages comes from the American courts, most notably from the U.S. Supreme Court's case law regarding due process. The Spanish Supreme Court confirmed that the U.S. courts are prudent in policing the proportionality of damages awarded.[751] Moreover, legality leads to foreseeability but it does not guarantee proportionality. The legislature's intervention to fix the amount of the punitive damages (whether by establishing a maximum, a minimum or an appropriate range) does not make the award proportional in all cases. Furthermore, the foreign country's idea of proportionality may vary from the Spanish legislature's estimation.[752]

325. As to the second aspect of the proportionality criterion the Court argued that in a market economy the safeguarding of intellectual property rights is

747 M. Requejo Isidro, "Punitive Damages: How Do They Look Like When Seen From Abroad?" in L. Meurkens & E. Nordin (eds.), *The Power of Punitive Damages – Is Europe Missing Out?*, Cambridge – Antwerp – Portland, Intersentia, 2012, 327–328.

748 M. Requejo Isidro, "Punitive Damages: How Do They Look Like When Seen From Abroad?" in L. Meurkens & E. Nordin (eds.), *The Power of Punitive Damages – Is Europe Missing Out?*, Cambridge – Antwerp – Portland, Intersentia, 2012, 328.

749 M. Requejo Isidro, "Punitive Damages – Europe Strikes Back?", presentation delivered at the British Institute of International and Comparative Law, 2 November 2011, London, text on file with the author.

750 M. Requejo Isidro, "Punitive Damages – Europe Strikes Back?", presentation delivered at the British Institute of International and Comparative Law, 2 November 2011, London, text on file with the author.

751 Spanish Supreme Court 13 November 2001, Exequatur no. 2039/1999, *Aedipr* 2003, 914; S.R. Jablonski, "Translation and comment: enforcing U.S. punitive damages awards in foreign courts – a recent case in the Supreme Court of Spain", 24 *Journal of Law and Commerce* 2004–2005, 229.

752 M. Requejo Isidro, "Punitive Damages – Europe Strikes Back?", presentation delivered at the British Institute of International and Comparative Law, 2 November 2011, London, text on file with the author.

important. Moreover, this interest in offering protection to such rights is not strictly local but is shared universally by countries that harbour similar judicial, social and economic values.[753] The common desire to protect the interests at stake justified the awarding of an amount of twice the compensatory damages on top of the compensation granted.[754] The importance of the underlying *ratio legis* will thus determine the outcome of the proportionality analysis.[755] REQUEJO ISIDRO has suggested other rights of high importance outside the field of intellectual property: environmental protection, protection of human rights, freedom, legal certainty and dignity.[756]

326. Commentators seem to agree that the Court's willingness to enforce the treble damages in this case does not mean that every punitive award will easily pass the public policy exception.[757] According to JABLONSKI the judgment should be interpreted narrowly. It should be seen as inspired by the specific facts of the case (and, therefore, not as laying down a general rule[758]).[759] REQUEJO ISIDRO even doubts whether punitive damages awards will be enforced in future cases. She underlines the fact that there is only a single decision. Under article 1.6 of the Spanish Civil Code case law constitutes a source of law if the doctrine set is *repeatedly* upheld by the Supreme Court, which requires at least two judgments. She further argues that national jurisdictional rules at the time coincidentally allowed the Supreme Court to rule on the case, without any prior litigation on the lower levels.[760] In France, on the other hand, the *Fountaine Pajot* case

---

753 Spanish Supreme Court 13 November 2001, Exequatur no. 2039/1999, *Aedipr* 2003, 914.

754 S.R. Jablonski, "Translation and comment: enforcing U.S. punitive damages awards in foreign courts – a recent case in the Supreme Court of Spain", 24 *Journal of Law and Commerce* 2004–2005, 230.

755 M. Requejo Isidro, "Punitive Damages: How Do They Look Like When Seen From Abroad?" in L. Meurkens & E. Nordin (eds.), *The Power of Punitive Damages – Is Europe Missing Out?*, Cambridge – Antwerp – Portland, Intersentia, 2012, 328.

756 M. Requejo Isidro, "Punitive Damages – Europe Strikes Back?", presentation delivered at the British Institute of International and Comparative Law, 2 November 2011, London, text on file with the author.

757 S.R. Jablonski, "Translation and comment: enforcing U.S. punitive damages awards in foreign courts – a recent case in the Supreme Court of Spain", 24 *Journal of Law and Commerce* 2004–2005, 227 and 230; M. Requejo Isidro, "Punitive Damages – Europe Strikes Back?", presentation delivered at the British Institute of International and Comparative Law, 2 November 2011, London, text on file with the author; F. Ramos Romeu, "Litigation Under the Shadow of an Exequatur: The Spanish Recognition of U.S. Judgments", *International Lawyer* 2004, 968.

758 To the extent that the creation of rules is even possible for courts in Civil Law countries, given the absence of precedent.

759 S.R. Jablonski, "Translation and comment: enforcing U.S. punitive damages awards in foreign courts – a recent case in the Supreme Court of Spain", 24 *Journal of Law and Commerce* 2004–2005, 230.

760 M. Requejo Isidro, "Punitive Damages – Europe Strikes Back?", presentation delivered at the British Institute of International and Comparative Law, 2 November 2011, London, text on file with the author.

travelled through the pyramidal court system to reach the Supreme Court.[761] In our opinion it does not matter how the Supreme Court came to rule on the case. Besides, the verdict of the *Cour de cassation* deviated from the two lower French courts. Whatever the case may be, the enforcement of the *compensatory* damages of a foreign judgment containing punitive damages should never be obstructed by the international public policy exception.[762]

4.6. CONCLUSION

327. This chapter discussed the various approaches towards the enforcement of punitive damages taken by the Member States Italy, Germany, England, France and Spain. It became clear that every country has construed the international public policy exception differently.

328. The Supreme Courts in Italy and Germany have rejected punitive damages because they argued that the concept itself violates international public policy. In 2007 in *Glebosky v. Fimez* the Italian *Corte di Cassazione* refused to accept that Italian private law holds any punitive considerations. It found that penalty clauses and moral damages are not comparable to punitive damages. Five years later it reiterated this position by stating that the Italian civil liability rules only pursue compensatory, and not punitive, aims.

Already in 1992, in the case of *John Doe v. Eckhard Schmitz*, the *Bundesgerichtshof* ruled that U.S. punitive damages awards cannot be enforced in the German territory. The German Supreme Court referred to various arguments underlying this decision. It underlined the compensatory function of German private law and noted that enrichment of the plaintiff is prohibited. The Supreme Court further held that punishment and deterrence are objectives that belong in the realm of criminal law. Punitive damages interfere with the state's monopoly on penalisation because a private person acts as public prosecutor. The defendant cannot rely on the fundamental guarantees that are available to him in criminal law proceedings. The *Bundesgerichtshof* also rejected the parallel between penalty clauses and punitive damages.

329. The likelihood of recovering U.S. punitive damages in Italy or Germany is, therefore, virtually nil. In Germany, however, the compensatory part of the punitive damages award will be declared enforceable provided this part is

---

761 M. Requejo Isidro, "Punitive Damages – Europe Strikes Back?", presentation delivered at the British Institute of International and Comparative Law, 2 November 2011, London, text on file with the author.

762 F. Ramos Romeu, "Litigation Under the Shadow of an Exequatur: The Spanish Recognition of U.S. Judgments", *International Lawyer* 2004, 968.

clearly indicated in the American judgment. In Italy the Supreme Court did not contemplate this option.

330. France and Spain, on the other hand, have accepted the compatibility of punitive damages with international public policy. The Spanish *Tribunal Supremo* was the first one to accept the enforceability of punitive damages in the case of *Miller v. Alabastres* in 2001. It acknowledged the existence of punitive elements in Spanish private law. The presence of these punitive mechanisms demonstrates that Spanish civil law sometimes concerns itself with punishment in addition to compensation. Punitive damages could thus not be viewed as a violation of international public policy. Around a decade later the French Supreme Court in *Schlenka & Langhorne v. Fountaine Pajot* reached the same conclusion.

331. Both the Spanish and the French Supreme Court subsequently focused on an investigation of the amount granted by the foreign court. *Excessive* punitive damages are problematic in light of the international public policy exception. In France the *Cour de cassation* seems to have limited its tolerance of punitive damages to an amount equal to the compensatory damages granted, although it is unclear to what extent the blameworthiness of the defendant's conduct can be taken into account. In Spain the level of acceptance is much higher as the *Tribunal Supremo* allowed the enforcement of the American treble damages judgment. It put forward two criteria to assess the excessiveness of the award: (1) the predictability of the award and (2) the nature of the interests protected.

332. England offers a mixed outlook on the enforcement of third state punitive damages. Multiple damages, a subcategory of punitive damages, are statutorily barred by PTIA. The presence of a multiple element taints the whole multiple award, rendering the compensatory part unenforceable as well. Other heads of damages are not in jeopardy. Whether other forms of punitive damages can survive the English courts' scrutiny is uncertain. Foreign fines or penalties are not enforceable in England. Lord Denning's *obiter dictum* in *S.A. Consortium General Textiles v Sun and Sand Agencies Ltd.* explained that punitive damages cannot be equated to a fine or a penalty because they are not awarded to the state. Furthermore, according to Lord Denning, English public policy does not oppose punitive damages awards. Further case law is, nevertheless, needed to confirm this welcoming attitude.

333. In our view the progressive stance adopted by the French and Spanish Supreme Court is the correct one. Outside the five European countries we studied in this chapter we find further support for this contention. In Greece the

Supreme Court (*Areopag*) had to rule on the enforceability of a Texas judgment awarding punitive damages. The *Areopag* accepted that punitive damages are not as such a violation of (international) public policy. Instead, it investigated the possible excessiveness of the punitive damages. It found that the punitive award was disproportionate to the compensatory part as the amount of the punitive damages was more than the damage sustained.[763]

Chapter 5 explains that the traditional defence of holding the concept of punitive damages itself to be a violation of international public policy cannot be supported given the presence of punitive traces within private law. Chapter 6 then attempts to set out how the excessiveness test (as the second prong of the international public policy obstacle) should operate.

---

763 Greek Supreme Court, decision no. 17/1999, *Nomiko Bina i Miniaion Nomikon Periodikon* 2000, 461–464; C.D. Triadafillidis, "Anerkennung und Vollstreckung von punitive damages – Urteilen nach kontinentalem und insbesondere nach griechischem Recht", *Praxis des Internationalen Privat- und Verfahrensrechts* 2002, 236–238; M. Requejo Isidro, "Punitive Damages: How Do They Look Like When Seen From Abroad?" in L. Meurkens & E. Nordin (eds.), *The Power of Punitive Damages – Is Europe Missing Out?*, Cambridge – Antwerp – Portland, Intersentia, 2012, 326; M. Requejo Isidro, "Punitive Damages From a Private International Law Perspective" in H. Koziol & V. Wilcox (eds.), *Punitive Damages: Common Law and Civil Law Perspectives*, Vienna, Springer, 2009, 247; C.I. Nagy, "Recognition and enforcement of US judgments involving punitive damages in continental Europe", *Nederlands Internationaal Privaatrecht* 2012, 9.

CHAPTER 5

TRACES OF PUNITIVE DAMAGES IN THE EU MEMBER STATES

334. Chapter 4 made clear that the international public policy exception is the yardstick used by the courts in the five Member States examined to decide on the enforceability of American punitive damages judgments. Like any type of private law judgment, a foreign punitive damages judgment should not violate international public policy if it wants to stand a chance at the enforcement stage. Similarly, chapter 3 made clear that the penetration of U.S. punitive damages through the field of applicable law is only possible if the international public policy of the forum is not offended by this type of damages.[764]

335. In this chapter we explore the concept of international public policy. Rather than preoccupying ourselves with further defining the notion, we focus on what it contains, or better, what it should contain. We briefly categorise and expand upon the arguments employed by the Member States courts under the international public policy exception to deny the enforcement of U.S. punitive damages awards. Where possible, we attempt to refute them. Finally, we express and elaborate on the opinion that Member States' courts should not refuse the enforcement of American punitive damages because their own legal systems contain private law instruments akin to punitive damages or pursuing identical or similar goals. This opinion forms the main contention of this chapter.

336. The relevant issue is not whether these 'punitive traces' are completely identical to punitive damages or form an alternative to them. The question is rather whether their existence in the legal systems of the Member States as well as in European Union law supports our contention that European continental systems sometimes pursue penal and/or deterrent goals in private law. In this chapter we answer this question in the affirmative.

---

764 As stated, the escape mechanism of article 13.1 of the Hague Service Convention bears some resemblance to an international public policy standard. However, the exception in that provision should be construed differently than the international public policy yardstick of applicable law and enforcement. The standard of review in the area of service of process was discussed in chapter 2 and will not be dealt with in this chapter.

337. We argue that courts should not treat U.S. punitive damages as, in themselves, contrary to international public policy.[765] American punitive damages should only be analysed under the excessiveness prong of the international public policy test.[766] Although this chapter focuses on the enforcement of judgments, it should be noted that the inferences drawn also apply to the private international law area of applicable law. U.S. punitive damages as such should not be disallowed under international public policy when they are part of the applicable law. They should only be barred to the extent that they are of an excessive nature. In chapter 6 we then formulate guidelines as to how courts should assess the possible excessiveness of a punitive damages rule (applicable law) or award (enforcement of judgments).

5.1. THE FLUIDITY OF (INTERNATIONAL) PUBLIC POLICY

338. The notion of public policy has already been discussed in chapters 3 and 4.[767] The difference between domestic public policy and international public policy was explained. In private international law cases the more narrow notion of international public policy comes into play because in those types of cases more deference towards foreign nations, its laws and its judgments needs to be shown.[768]

339. The concept of public policy, whether it is the national or the international version, is a fluid and elusive notion.[769] It is subject to gradual changes through

765 G. Nater-Bass, "U.S.-Style Punitive Damages Awards and their Recognition and Enforcement in Switzerland and Other Civil-Law Countries", 28 *Deutsch-Amerikanische Juristen-Vereinigung Newsletter* 2003, 160.

766 F.-X. Licari, "Prendre les punitive damages au sérieux: propos critiques sur un refus d'accorder l'exequatur à une décision californienne ayant alloué des dommages intérêts punitifs", *Journal du droit international (Clunet)* October/November/December 2010/4, 1262.

767 See *supra* no. 177–180 and 208.

768 P. Mayer & V. Heuzé, *Droit international privé*, Paris, Montchrestien, 2004, 149, no. 205; A. Mills, *The Confluence of Public and Private International Law – Justice, Pluralism and Subsidiarity in the International Constitutional Ordering of Private Law*, Cambridge, Cambridge University Press, 2009, 275–277; A. Mills, "The Dimensions of Public Policy in Private International Law", *Journal of Private International Law* 2008, 213; P. Bernard & H. Salem, "Further developments for qualification of foreign judgments for recognition and enforcement in France: the test for punitive damage awards", *International Bar Association* 2011, 18; B. Janke & F.-X. Licari, "Enforcing Punitive Damage Awards in France after Fountaine Pajot", 60 *The American Journal of Comparative Law* 2012, 792.

769 V. Behr, "Punitive Damages in American and German Law – Tendencies Towards Approximation of Apparently Irreconcilable Concepts", 78 *Chicago-Kent Law Review* 2003, 153.

time.[770] It is exactly the evolutionary nature of international public policy that we want to highlight in this chapter. As Mr. Justice BURROWS stated in 1824 on the topic of public policy: "*It is a very unruly horse, and when once you get astride it you never know where it will carry you. It may lead you from sound law*".[771] Using the same analogy, we believe that with regard to punitive damages some European courts have ridden the horse but have directed it in such a way as to arrive at the wrong destination.

340. We indeed argue that the traditional interpretation of international public policy, as rejecting the concept of punitive damages, no longer holds true. It cannot be sustained that the outright rejection of punitive damages as a concept is that fundamental as to merit international public policy protection. The private law systems of the five Member States examined in chapter 4 contain punitive-like measures which put the public-private law divide into question. In such a context it is unacceptable to employ the international public policy exception to reject foreign punitive damages in private international law cases. Instead, Member States should undertake an excessiveness check to determine whether the punitive amount awarded is acceptable in light of international public policy. This proportionality analysis could be viewed as a second phase of the international public policy test.

5.2. ARGUMENTS AGAINST THE ENFORCEMENT OF U.S. PUNITIVE DAMAGES

341. In chapter 4 we set out how the courts of five relevant Member States have reacted to requests for enforcement of American punitive damages judgments. Both the Italian and the German Supreme Court have taken a very hostile stance towards foreign punitive damages, holding the concept itself to be contrary to international public policy (the first prong of the international public policy exception). In England the attitude towards the enforcement of punitive damages is mixed. The English legislator has explicitly forbidden enforcement for one form of punitive damages, namely multiple damages. Other forms of punitive damages arguably can be enforced, although further case law is required to confirm this. In Spain and France, on the other hand, the Supreme Court has moved away from this argument and has ruled that punitive damages can only be rejected if their amount is excessive/disproportional (excessiveness prong of

[770] H. Auf'mkolk, "U.S. punitive damages awards before German courts – Time for a new approach", *Freiburg Law Students Journal* 2007, 4; A.J. Belohlavek, "Public Policy and Public Interest in International Law and EU Law", *Czech Yearbook of International Law* 2012, 142.

[771] *Richardson v. Mellish* [1824] 2 Bing 229, 252.

the international public policy exception). As stated, the latter approach has our approval.

342. Case law has formulated a number of objections against punitive damages (*i.e.* the first prong of the public policy test). These can be divided in different categories. It should however be borne in mind that courts mostly relied on a combination of several objections and that there exists a certain amount of overlap between these different objections. The categorisation of objections is, therefore, to some extent artificial but is used for educational purposes. For that reason, we will not attempt to illustrate each objection with a reference to all the courts that might have employed that argument.

343. We should also emphasise that these objections have been raised in enforcement proceedings (*i.e.* in a private international law setting). However, we tend to think that some of these objections appear to be more appropriate in a discussion about the introduction of punitive damages in substantive law. We should not forget that what we are dealing with is the question whether or not these damages can penetrate our legal order through a foreign judgment (or through foreign law in the case of the area of applicable law). We do not discuss the controversial and more far-reaching question as to whether EU Member States should introduce such a remedy in their legal systems.[772] This is an important nuance.

5.2.1. VIOLATION OF THE (STRICT) COMPENSATORY FUNCTION OF PRIVATE LAW

344. The principle of full or strict compensation has been used as an argument to refuse the enforcement of foreign judgments containing punitive damages. The courts attached such importance to the adherence of this principle that they held it to be part of international public policy.

345. In the EU Member States which are the subject of this book the principle of full compensation is the fundamental rule underlying the civil liability system. The principle of full compensation implies that the victim of an unlawful act causing damage should receive what is necessary to compensate for all, but nothing more than, the harm he or she suffered.[773] The civil liability system

---

772 On this topic: R.C. Meurkens, *Punitive Damages – The Civil Remedy in American Law. Lessons and Caveats for Continental Europe*, Deventer, Kluwer, 2014.

773 Whether they receive it in practice is a totally different matter. See, for instance, Lewis and Morris who argue that victims in personal injury cases in the United Kingdom do not obtain the full amount they need because the calculation does not take sufficient account of the effects of inflation and the increase in life expectancy: R. Lewis & A. Morris, "Tort

intends to put the injured party in the position he or she would have been in had the damaging event not occurred (known as *restitution in integrum*).[774] Compensation forms the only objective of the damages awarded to the injured party. Damages should, therefore, be limited to compensate for the loss suffered (*damnum emergens*) and for any lost profits (*lucrum cessans*). This is sometimes referred to as strict compensation.[775]

346. When seeking the appropriate amount of compensation it is said that the emphasis lies on the extent of the harm caused and that, consequently, the focus is completely on the victim. The seriousness of the wrongful conduct or the person of the wrongdoer are irrelevant. This retrospective and victim-oriented approach stands in sharp contrast with U.S. punitive damages which are tortfeasor-orientated and to a large extent prospective in that they pursue deterrence of the wrongdoer and the general public. Punitive damages are, nevertheless, also retrospective to some degree as punishment looks back at the unwanted behaviour in order to correct it.[776]

347. Below we will identify several 'punitive traces' in (EU, continental European and English) private law.[777] The existence of extra-compensatory elements demonstrates that private law sometimes deviates from the strict compensation principle. The dogma of strict compensation is in fact nothing but a myth.[778] The granting of international public policy protection to this principle, as some courts have done[779], should, therefore, be denounced.[780] Whether the principle of full compensation belongs to the broader realm of domestic public policy need not be answered here.[781] What is crucial for the

---

Law Culture in the United Kingdom: Image and Reality in Personal Injury Compensation", 17 May 2012, 21–22, available at <http://papers.ssrn.com/sol3/papers.cfm?abstract_id=2061618>.

774 D.G. Owen, *Philosophical Foundations of Tort Law*, New York, Oxford University Press, 1997, 21; W. Van Gerven, J. Lever & P. Larouche, *Tort Law*, Oxford, Hart Publishing, 2000, 770.

775 T. Rouhette, "The availability of punitive damages in Europe: growing trend or nonexistent concept?", 74 *Defense Counsel Journal* 2007, 321–322.

776 V. Behr, "Punitive Damages in American and German Law – Tendencies Towards Approximation of Apparently Irreconcilable Concepts", 78 *Chicago-Kent Law Review* 2003, 113.

777 See *infra* no. 363 *et seq.*

778 P. Jestaz, "Les dommages et interest en quête d'un fondement", *Revue Lamy Droit des Affaires* 2013, 109–110.

779 See, for instance, the decision of the Court of Appeal of Poitiers in the case of *Fountaine Pajot*: Cour d'Appel Poitiers, 26 February 2009, *Schlenzka v. S.A. Fountaine Pajot*, no. 07/02404, 137 *JDI* 2010, 1230.

780 F.-X. Licari, "Prendre les punitive damages au sérieux: propos critiques sur un refus d'accorder l'exequatur à une décision californienne ayant alloué des dommages intérêts punitifs", *Journal du droit international (Clunet)* October/November/December 2010/4, 1248.

781 Janke and Licari have answered this question in the affirmative: B. Janke & F.-X. Licari, "Enforcing Punitive Damage Awards in France after Fountaine Pajot", 60 *The American Journal of Comparative Law* 2012, 791 and 793.

purposes of private international law is that the principle should not be included under international public policy.

5.2.2. WINDFALL FOR THE PLAINTIFF: UNJUST ENRICHMENT

348. According to the principle of full compensation, damages are meant to compensate the victim for the loss suffered but they may under no circumstance result in his enrichment.[782] One of the arguments against allowing the enforcement of punitive damages, therefore, goes that such damages enrich the plaintiff. The victim obtains a profit through the punishing – which is done for the public interest – of the wrongdoer. The victim is placed in a better position than he was in before the wrong was committed.[783] In criminal law the punishment of the culprit does not lead to a windfall for the victim.

349. As rightly argued by MAGNUS, this argument is disputable as it does not explain why deeply unwanted conduct should not be discouraged by specific private law sanctions.[784] Moreover, it is the plaintiff who has taken the initiative, trouble and risk of seeking punitive damages.[785] It could be argued that the plaintiff is most fit to receive the punitive damages, as he is the one upholding the common interest.[786] Once the objectives of deterrence and punishment have been achieved, it becomes irrelevant where the punitive damages end up.[787] Furthermore, Civil Law tradition dictates that the commission of a wrong cannot make the tortfeasor better off (reflected in the adage "*Nemo ex suo delicto meliorem suam condicionem facere potest*").[788] Punitive damages eliminate the enrichment of the wrongdoer who has committed a tort of which the benefits outweigh the damages due. It could be argued that the cancellation of the tortfeasor's windfall is so important that the enrichment of the victim should be

---

782 C.I. Nagy, "Recognition and enforcement of US judgments involving punitive damages in continental Europe", *Nederlands Internationaal Privaatrecht* 2012, 5.

783 A. Reed, "Exemplary Damages: A Persuasive Argument for their Retention as a Mechanism of Retributive Justice", 15 *Civil Justice Quarterly* 1996, 131.

784 U. Magnus, "Punitive Damages and German Law" in L. Meurkens & E. Nordin (eds.), *The Power of Punitive Damages – Is Europe Missing Out?*, Cambridge – Antwerp – Portland, Intersentia, 2012, 250.

785 Y. Adar, "Touring the Punitive Damages Forest: A Proposed Roadmap", *Osservatorio del diritto civile e commerciale* 2012, 346.

786 Y. Adar, "Touring the Punitive Damages Forest: A Proposed Roadmap", *Osservatorio del diritto civile e commerciale* 2012, 345.

787 The Irish Law Reform Commission, Report on Aggravated, Exemplary and Restitutionary Damages, LRC 60–2000, 2000, no. 1.15 and 2.046, available at <www.lawreform.ie/_fileupload/Reports/rAggravatedDamages.htm>.

788 C.I. Nagy, "Recognition and enforcement of US judgments involving punitive damages in continental Europe", *Nederlands Internationaal Privaatrecht* 2012, 10.

tolerated as a necessary evil.[789] It could also be said that punitive damages, as an instrument of private retribution, symbolise the private victory of the plaintiff over the defendant. A logical consequence of that argument is that the plaintiff should be awarded these damages.[790] Lastly, legislators in some U.S. states have endeavoured to reduce the extent of the windfall by enacting split-recovery statutes, directing part of the punitive damages to the treasury or to a public fund.[791]

5.2.3. VIOLATION OF THE PRIVATE – PUBLIC LAW DIVIDE

350. Courts have also invoked the division between private and public law (criminal law) as an international public policy objection against the enforcement of U.S. punitive damages. They raised concerns about accepting a penal remedy into private law. They argued that punishment belongs to the realm of public law and does not have a place in private law which has a compensatory purpose. A crime is a public wrong, a wrong committed to the whole of society, whereas a tort is a private wrong, a wrong to an individual member of society.[792] The former, therefore, needs punishment and deterrence, the latter only requires compensation of the victim.[793]

351. Although we accept compensation as the primary function of private law[794], it is in reality not the only function of tort law.[795] Compensatory damages have additional side-effects, besides the primary objective of

---

789 F.-X. Licari, "Prendre les punitive damages au sérieux: propos critiques sur un refus d'accorder l'exequatur à une décision californienne ayant alloué des dommages intérêts punitifs", *Journal du droit international (Clunet)* October/November/December 2010/4, 1256.

790 Y. Adar, "Touring the Punitive Damages Forest: A Proposed Roadmap", *Osservatorio del diritto civile e commerciale* 2012, 345–346.

791 V. Wilcox, "Punitive Damages in England" in H. Koziol & V. Wilcox (eds.), *Punitive Damages: Common Law and Civil Law Perspectives*, Vienna, Springer, 2009, 37.

792 R. Zimmermann, *The Law of Obligations, Roman Foundations of the Civilian Tradition*, Deventer, Kluwer, 1992, 902.

793 L. Meurkens, "The Punitive Damages Debate in Continental Europe: Food for Thought" in L. Meurkens & E. Nordin (eds.), *The Power of Punitive Damages – Is Europe Missing Out?*, Cambridge – Antwerp – Portland, Intersentia, 2012, 17.

794 S.F. Deakin, A. Johnston & B.S. Markesinis, *Markesinis and Deakin's Tort Law*, Oxford, Clarendon Press, 2008, 52; L. Meurkens, "The Punitive Damages Debate in Continental Europe: Food for Thought" in L. Meurkens & E. Nordin (eds.), *The Power of Punitive Damages – Is Europe Missing Out?*, Cambridge – Antwerp – Portland, Intersentia, 2012, 17; R. De Ángel Yagüez, *Algunas previsiones sobre el futuro de la responsabilidad civil (con especial atención a la reparación del daño)*, Madrid, Cuadernos Civitas, 1995, 229–233; M. Otero Crespo, "Punitive Damages Under Spanish Law: A Subtle Recognition?" in L. Meurkens & E. Nordin (eds.), *The Power of Punitive Damages – Is Europe Missing Out?*, Cambridge – Antwerp – Portland, Intersentia, 2012, 287.

795 W.V.H. Rogers, *Winfield and Jolowicz on Tort*, London, Sweet & Maxwell, 2006, 2–3.

restoring the victim.[796] Punishment and deterrence are such by-products of compensatory damages. Compensatory damages indeed offer some, albeit limited, amount of punishment and deterrence.[797] The prospect of having to pay an award of damages, in itself, discourages wrongful behaviour.[798] An award of compensatory damages also serves as a (minimal) form of punishment in that it produces an unfavourable legal consequence for the wrongdoer.[799]

352. The inherent punitive effect of compensatory damages is exemplified in *Rookes v. Barnard*, the leading case on punitive damages in England. Lord Devlin stated that punitive damages should only be awarded "*if, but only if*" the sum fixed for compensation is insufficient to punish the defendant.[800] This prerequisite for punitive damages is construed on the premise that compensatory damages have a basic penal ramification.[801]

353. Moreover, as will be extensively demonstrated below, in the studied private law systems extra-compensatory measures with punitive and/or deterrent considerations can be found. The existence of the latter within private law is in principle inconsistent with the separation between private and public law. The dogmatic distinction between the private and public domain is, thus, blurred, or even overturned, by the legal reality. In our opinion the divide cannot prevent that private law to some extent supports the objectives of criminal law.[802]

---

796 C.I. Nagy, "Recognition and enforcement of US judgments involving punitive damages in continental Europe", *Nederlands Internationaal Privaatrecht* 2012, 5; U. Magnus, "Comparative Report on the Law of Damages" in U. Magnus (ed.), *Unification of Tort Law: Damages*, The Hague, Kluwer Law International, 2001, 185; M. Otero Crespo, "Punitive Damages Under Spanish Law: A Subtle Recognition?" in L. Meurkens & E. Nordin (eds.), *The Power of Punitive Damages – Is Europe Missing Out?*, Cambridge – Antwerp – Portland, Intersentia, 2012, 285; V. Wester-Ouisse & T. Thiede, "Punitive Damages in France: A New Deal? – A commentary on Cour de cassation (France), 1st civil chamber, 1 December 2010, case no 1090", *Journal of European Tort Law* 2012, 122.

797 M. Otero Crespo, "Punitive Damages Under Spanish Law: A Subtle Recognition?" in L. Meurkens & E. Nordin (eds.), *The Power of Punitive Damages – Is Europe Missing Out?*, Cambridge – Antwerp – Portland, Intersentia, 2012, 287 and 300; F. Pantaleón, "Principles of European Tort Law: Basis of Liability and Defences. A critical view 'from outside'", *InDret* 2005, 6.

798 M. Otero Crespo, "Punitive Damages Under Spanish Law: A Subtle Recognition?" in L. Meurkens & E. Nordin (eds.), *The Power of Punitive Damages – Is Europe Missing Out?*, Cambridge – Antwerp – Portland, Intersentia, 2012, 286.

799 J.M. Pena Lopez, "Función, naturaleza y sistema de la responsabilidad civil aquiliana en el ordenamiento jurídico español", *Revista de derecho privado* 2004, 180.

800 *Rookes v. Barnard* (1964) U.K.H.L, 38 (H.L.).

801 V. Wilcox, "Punitive Damages in England" in H. Koziol & V. Wilcox (eds.), *Punitive Damages: Common Law and Civil Law Perspectives*, Vienna, Springer, 2009, 26–27 and 33.

802 U. Magnus, "Punitive Damages and German Law" in L. Meurkens & E. Nordin (eds.), *The Power of Punitive Damages – Is Europe Missing Out?*, Cambridge – Antwerp – Portland, Intersentia, 2012, 248.

354. It should also be borne in mind that the strict public-private distinction within EU Member States stems from historical choices and is only the fruit of the modern age.[803] Roman law, for instance, did not uphold such a strict boundary.[804] The divide is, therefore, not necessarily permanent. Societal opinion is not rigid but subject to change and could require a reconsideration of the distinction.[805]

355. In England the argument is far less important because common law countries tend to place less emphasis on the public-private law division.[806] This is clearly evidenced by the acceptance of punitive damages as a remedy in England.[807]

5.2.4. AN INTRUSION ON THE PENAL MONOPOLY OF THE STATE

356. Closely linked with the private-public law border argument is the objection that punitive damages constitute an infringement of the state's monopoly to prosecute wrongful behaviour.[808] It has been argued that punishment, an objective of criminal law, is a public matter and should remain under the control of the state authorities. The exercise of this public power should not be transferred to private persons through the instrument of punitive damages. Private individuals only represent their own interest and lack the objectivity and accountability to fulfil this public task.[809]

357. Nagy successfully dismisses this concern by raising three different points. First, both criminal sanctions and punitive damages are imposed by courts. It is

---

803 G. Wagner, *Neue Perspektiven im Schadensersatzrecht – Kommerzialisierung, Strafschadensersatz, Kollektivschaden, Gutachten A zum 66. Deutschen Juristentag*, Munich, Beck, 2006, 73; H. Koziol, "Punitive Damages: Admission into the Seventh Legal Heaven or Eternal Damnation? Comparative Report and Conclusions" in H. Koziol & V. Wilcox (eds.), *Punitive Damages: Common Law and Civil Law Perspectives*, Vienna, Springer, 2009, 293.

804 See *supra* no. 33.

805 C. Cauffman, "Naar een punitief Europees verbintenissenrecht? Een rechtsvergelijkende studie naar de draagwijdte, de grondwettelijkheid en de wenselijkheid van het bestraffend karakter van het verbintenissenrecht", *Tijdschrift voor Privaatrecht* 2007, 852–853.

806 L. Meurkens, "The Punitive Damages Debate in Continental Europe: Food for Thought" in L. Meurkens & E. Nordin (eds.), *The Power of Punitive Damages – Is Europe Missing Out?*, Cambridge – Antwerp – Portland, Intersentia, 2012, 16.

807 See *infra* no. 372 *et seq.*

808 J. Mörsdorf-Schulte, *Funktion und Dogmatik US-amerikanischer punitive damages. Zugleich ein Beitrag zur Diskussion um die Zustellung und Anerkennung in Deutschland*, Tübingen, Mohr Siebeck, 1999, 298.

809 L. Meurkens, "The Punitive Damages Debate in Continental Europe: Food for Thought" in L. Meurkens & E. Nordin (eds.), *The Power of Punitive Damages – Is Europe Missing Out?*, Cambridge – Antwerp – Portland, Intersentia, 2012, 17–18.

therefore difficult to see any real difference between the two. Punitive damages are referred to as 'private sanctions' because a private plaintiff is involved but at the end of the day punitive damages are awarded by a court, just like criminal sanctions.

Second, when one looks just outside the EU Member States examined, one notices in Austria an action referred to as '*Subsidiaranklage*' ('subsidiary private prosecution'). The Austrian legal system allows the victim to bring an action instead of the public prosecutor if the latter has declined to open an investigation or has dropped the charges (article 72 of the Code of Criminal Procedure). This is not seen as problematic in Austrian law and negates the absolute monopoly of the state.

Third, in Civil Law countries there are even some crimes ('private prosecution offenses') which can be brought to trial by the harmed party without the involvement of the public prosecutor. In Germany, for instance, article 374 (1) of the German Code of Criminal Procedure lists a number of offences for which the victim may bring a private prosecution without needing to have recourse to the public prosecution office first. These include *inter alia* defamation, trespass and most forms of stalking. In France, private prosecution ('*citation directe*') is possible for '*délits*' (misdemeanours) and '*contraventions*' (petty offenses) but not for '*crimes*' (felonies).[810] The state's monopoly on penalisation is thus not as absolute as opponents of punitive damages make it out to be.[811]

5.2.5. LACK OF CRIMINAL LAW SAFEGUARDS

358. A further concern attached to punitive damages is the fact that they impose a penal sanction but are awarded in a private law procedure. The defendant cannot rely on the fundamental criminal law safeguards which are guaranteed to him in a criminal procedure.[812]

---

810 The procedure is to be found in articles 389 to 392-1 of the *Code de procédure pénale* (Code of Criminal Procedure).

811 C.I. Nagy, "Recognition and enforcement of US judgments involving punitive damages in continental Europe", *Nederlands Internationaal Privaatrecht* 2012, 5.

812 H. Koziol, "Punitive Damages: Admission into the Seventh Legal Heaven or Eternal Damnation? Comparative Report and Conclusions" in H. Koziol & V. Wilcox (eds.), *Punitive Damages: Common Law and Civil Law Perspectives*, Vienna, Springer, 2009, 302; L. Meurkens, "The Punitive Damages Debate in Continental Europe: Food for Thought" in L. Meurkens & E. Nordin (eds.), *The Power of Punitive Damages – Is Europe Missing Out?*, Cambridge – Antwerp – Portland, Intersentia, 2012, 18; Law Commission for England and Wales, Aggravated, Exemplary and Restitutionary Damages, LC No. 247, 1997, 1.21, available at <http://lawcommission.justice.gov.uk/docs/lc247_aggravated_exemplary_and_restitutionary_damages.pdf>.

359. Two important principles form the cornerstones of criminal law. The principle of legality requires both the crime and the penalty to be laid down in law prior to the occurrence of the conduct (*nullum crimen sine previa lege/ nulla poena sine previa lege*). Legal provisions allowing for punitive damages are said to be too vague and too broadly-phrased to offer clarity as to which conduct is impermissible. Legal subjects encounter difficulties understanding the legislator's reference to "malicious" or "grossly negligent" when defining behaviour giving rise to punitive damages.[813] In addition to the principle of legality, the prohibition of double adjudication (*ne bis in idem*) protects a person from being prosecuted or punished twice for the same allegation. The awarding of punitive damages alongside a criminal sanction is believed to be problematic in light of the *ne bis in idem* principle.[814]

360. Criminal law defendants can also rely on an array of evidential safeguards. Article 6 of the European Convention on Human Rights plays a pivotal role in this regard. A person accused of a crime is presumed innocent until proven guilty. The prosecutor will need to present evidence in order to show guilt beyond a reasonable doubt, a standard which is higher than in private law proceedings. In the latter the plaintiff will need to prove his claims. There are, however, circumstances in which the burden of proof is reversed. Furthermore, throughout the criminal process the suspect/accused enjoys the right to be silent. In private law proceedings these guarantees do not exist.[815] Whether these differences are so insurmountable as to rule out private law partly supporting the functions of criminal law remains to be seen.[816]

---

813 L. Meurkens, "The Punitive Damages Debate in Continental Europe: Food for Thought" in L. Meurkens & E. Nordin (eds.), *The Power of Punitive Damages – Is Europe Missing Out?*, Cambridge – Antwerp – Portland, Intersentia, 2012, 19.

814 N. Jansen & L. Rademacher, "Punitive Damages in Germany" in H. Koziol & Venessa Wilcox (eds.), *Punitive Damages: Common Law and Civil Law Perspectives*, Vienna, Springer, 2009, 76; U. Magnus, "Punitive Damages and German Law" in L. Meurkens & E. Nordin (eds.), *The Power of Punitive Damages – Is Europe Missing Out?*, Cambridge – Antwerp – Portland, Intersentia, 2012, 249; Law Commission for England and Wales, Aggravated, Exemplary and Restitutionary Damages, LC No. 247, 1997, 1.21, available at <http://lawcommission.justice.gov.uk/docs/lc247_aggravated_exemplary_and_restitutionary_damages.pdf>; Y. Adar, "Touring the Punitive Damages Forest: A Proposed Roadmap", *Osservatorio del diritto civile e commerciale* 2012, 318–319.

815 L. Meurkens, "The Punitive Damages Debate in Continental Europe: Food for Thought" in L. Meurkens & E. Nordin (eds.), *The Power of Punitive Damages – Is Europe Missing Out?*, Cambridge – Antwerp – Portland, Intersentia, 2012, 19–20; U. Magnus, "Punitive Damages and German Law" in L. Meurkens & E. Nordin (eds.), *The Power of Punitive Damages – Is Europe Missing Out?*, Cambridge – Antwerp – Portland, Intersentia, 2012, 248.

816 U. Magnus, "Punitive Damages and German Law" in L. Meurkens & E. Nordin (eds.), *The Power of Punitive Damages – Is Europe Missing Out?*, Cambridge – Antwerp – Portland, Intersentia, 2012, 249.

5.2.6. INEQUALITY BETWEEN CREDITORS

361. A final critique on the mechanism of punitive damages relates to the imbalance it supposedly creates between foreign creditors and domestic creditors. The German Supreme Court in *John Doe v. Eckhard Schmitz*[817], for instance, asserted that foreign creditors have an advantage over domestic creditors. If the enforcement of foreign punitive awards would be allowed in Europe, the beneficiary of such an award would be able to recover more money in comparison with a domestic creditor of the same debtor. The local creditor cannot recover more than the compensatory damages as the remedy of punitive damages is not available in Europe.

362. This reasoning is unfounded.[818] Some countries have more generous rules than others. In today's world some level of harmonisation does exist in certain regions (for instance the European Union) but a complete global harmonisation of laws is unattainable. The existence of divergent laws across nations is in our view thus an invariable aspect of the legal reality. The invocation of the imbalance-argument in order to deny the plaintiff what is owed to him after the resolution of a foreign dispute amounts to protectionism and should be frowned upon. In our opinion the argument is not a consideration to be taken into account when enforcing foreign judgments and it certainly does not deserve to receive international public policy status.

5.3. PUNITIVE ELEMENTS IN EUROPEAN PRIVATE LAW

363. In addition to refuting each argument individually, we assert that it is possible to dismiss the objections against the enforceability of punitive damages in a more global way. If it can be demonstrated that the legal systems of France, Spain, Italy, England and Germany contain private law instruments which resemble punitive damages or which pursue the same goals, internal legal coherence would demand the acceptance of U.S. punitive damages at the enforcement stage. When a legal system itself contains punitive-like remedies in private law, it cannot declare punitive damages unenforceable by using the international public policy shield.[819] Member States would be guilty of legal

---

817 BGH 4 June 1992, *Neue Juristische Wochenschrift* 1992, 3104.

818 A number of reasons were already set out: see *supra* no. 244.

819 V. Behr, "Punitive Damages in American and German Law – Tendencies Towards Approximation of Apparently Irreconcilable Concepts", 78 *Chicago-Kent Law Review* 2003, 153; M. Tolani, "U.S. Punitive Damages Before German Courts: A Comparative Analysis with Respect to the Ordre Public", 17 *Annual Survey of International & Comparative Law* 2011, 207; F. Quarta, "Foreign Punitive Damages Decisions and Class Actions in Italy", in

hypocrisy if they were to reject U.S. punitive damages as violating international public policy while at the same time acknowledging or condoning similar instruments in their substantive law.[820]

364. This section of the book therefore suggests that the objections enumerated above[821] do not hold water because the liability systems of France, Germany, Spain, Italy and England contain punitive and/or deterrent legal instruments in their private law. The presence of these punitive and/or preventive elements is not explicitly recognised (except in England) but becomes apparent when subjecting the private law of these countries to careful scrutiny. In addition to these five Member States, European Union law will also form the subject of our investigation as the existence of punitive-like damages can be detected therein as well.

365. First, we need to set the parameters for these 'punitive traces'. How do we define what instruments qualify as 'punitive traces' and what instruments do not? Put differently, how can we define whether a legal institution, a tendency in the case law, a statutory provision etc. amounts to punitive-like damages? There are different criteria but it is important to note from the outset that not every legal institution that we discuss fulfils all of the criteria. In fact, except England that accepts exemplary damages, none of the countries we analyse openly accepts punitive damages. The legal provisions or the tendencies in case law thus meet the criteria in different degrees. Some instruments have more resemblance(s) to punitive damages than others. The more criteria are fulfilled, the closer the instrument comes to full-blown punitive damages.

366. An important criterion is the extra-compensatory nature of the legal instrument. Admittedly, not every extra-compensatory remedy has a punitive objective (*e.g.* the English concept of unjust enrichment[822]). It could even be argued that whether or not such a punitive objective underlies a certain extra-compensatory mechanism is of secondary importance because as soon as a measure goes beyond compensation of the victim, its mere existence erodes the principle of full or strict compensation. The fact that the victim in a private law proceeding can recover more than the loss suffered is, in itself, thus very relevant. The existence of extra-compensatory measures in private law debunks

D. Fairgrieve and E. Lein (eds.), *Extraterritoriality and Collective Redress*, Oxford, Oxford University Press, 2012, 275–276.

820 J. Berch, "The Need for Enforcement of U.S. Punitive Damages Awards by the European Union", 19 *Minnesota Journal of International Law* 2010, 77; C.I. Nagy, "Recognition and enforcement of US judgments involving punitive damages in continental Europe", *Nederlands Internationaal Privaatrecht* 2012, 11.

821 See *supra* no. 344 *et seq.*

822 See *infra* no. 438.

the widely-accepted dogma of strict compensation. The existence of such legal instruments, by itself, thus already offers a strong indication that strict compensation is not a matter of international public policy.

367. Additionally, the objectives pursued by the private law instrument play an important role. When the private law remedy pursues punishment and/or deterrence, it fulfils some of the functions of criminal law. This is an essential characteristic of U.S. punitive damages. We do not express any opinion on whether this overlap of functions is wanted or needed. We merely register the existence of this overlap and, subsequently, derive from it an effect on the content of international public policy. It should be underlined that the punishment and deterrence we look for are different from and go beyond the (minimal) amounts of punishment and deterrence which are generated as side-effects or by-products of compensatory damages.[823]

368. A last indication in order to recognise an instrument akin to punitive damages is the recipient. Punitive damages are awarded to a private party. However, although this criterion is helpful, it is not decisive. Some of the remedies described below (*e.g.* *Zwangsgeld* and *Ordnungsgeld*) are attributed to the treasury. In our view this does not detract from the punitive-like status of these measures.

369. We do not take the amount of the punitive damages into account as a factor, as opposed to some scholars.[824] It does not matter how small or large the extra-compensatory portion of an award is. In our opinion the extra-compensatory nature in itself, combined with the punitive and/or deterrent intentions and possibly a private party as recipient are the key elements.

370. The identification of such measures is not a clear-cut process. It is very difficult to discern between measures satisfying enough criteria to qualify as a 'punitive trace' and others that do not. The fact that, except for exemplary damages in England, none of the instruments described below are actually branded punitive damages, adds to the difficulty to create black and white categories.

371. It is, in any case, not our intention to provide an exhaustive list of punitive traces. There is no official marker to measure whether the content of the international public policy of a nation has changed. We, therefore, do not know how many punitive instruments in private law are needed to remove the

---

823 See *supra* no. 351.

824 See *e.g.* J.-S. Borghetti, "Punitive Damages in France" in H. Koziol & V. Wilcox (eds.), *Punitive Damages: Common Law and Civil Law Perspectives*, Vienna, Springer, 2009, 60.

international public policy objection against punitive damages. The tendency to use punitive elements in our private law systems, however, provides a strong indication of the change in the international public policy outlook on U.S. punitive damages.

5.3.1. EXEMPLARY DAMAGES IN ENGLAND

372. The most obvious presence of punitive damages in the five Member States investigated is to be found in England. As explained above[825], punitive damages find their origin in the English system. England has acknowledged the remedy since the cases of *Huckle v. Money*[826] and *Wilkes v. Wood*[827] in the eighteenth century.[828, 829] It was, however, not until 1964 in the case of *Rookes v. Barnard* that this type of damages was specifically identified as "punitive" or "exemplary".[830] It should be noted that the term "aggravated damages" is not a synonym for punitive damages in England. This is in clear contrast to the United States where the term is sometimes used to refer to punitive damages. Aggravated damages are a form of compensatory damages in the English legal system.[831]

373. In *Rookes v. Barnard* the House of Lords laid down three categories under which punitive damages are available.[832] Lord DEVLIN first suggested that it may well be thought that exemplary damages confuse the civil and criminal functions of the law.[833] He, however, explained that: "[...] *there are certain categories of cases in which an award of exemplary damages can serve a useful purpose in vindicating the strength of the law and thus affording a practical justification for admitting into the civil law a principle which ought logically to belong to the criminal*".[834]

374. The House of Lords as per Lord DEVLIN opined that oppressive, arbitrary or unconstitutional action by the servants of the government could

---

825 See *supra* no. 34.

826 *Huckle v. Money*, 95 English Reports, King's Bench (Eng. Rep.) 768 (K.B. 1763).

827 *Wilkes v. Wood*, 98 Eng. Rep. 498–499 (C.P. 1763).

828 D.D. Ellis, "Fairness and Efficiency in the Law of Punitive Damages", 56 *Southern California Law Review 1982*, 12.

829 Before that time multiple damages existed in various statutes.

830 V. Wilcox, "Punitive Damages in England" in H. Koziol & V. Wilcox (eds.), *Punitive Damages: Common Law and Civil Law Perspectives*, Vienna, Springer, 2009, 7.

831 A.J. Sebok & V. Wilcox, "Aggravated Damages" in H. Koziol & V. Wilcox (eds.), *Punitive Damages: Common Law and Civil Law Perspectives*, Vienna, Springer, 2009, 257.

832 *Rookes v. Barnard* (1964) U.K.H.L, 37–38 (H.L.).

833 *Rookes v. Barnard* (1964) U.K.H.L, 34 (H.L.).

834 *Rookes v. Barnard* (1964) U.K.H.L, 37 (H.L.).

warrant punitive damages. It was held that: "[...] *the servants of the government are also the servants of the people and the use of their power must always be subordinate to their duty of service*". This first category of course relates to some of the earliest cases such as *Huckle v. Money*[835] and *Wilkes v. Wood*[836] in which additional damages were awarded for oppressive conduct by public officers.[837] Lord DEVLIN clarified that oppressive conduct by private persons or entities does not fall into this category.[838] Most cases under this category involve misconduct by police officers.[839]

375. The second category contains cases in which the defendant calculated his behaviour in order to make a profit which may exceed the compensation payable to the victim. Lord DEVLIN explained that the law should show that it cannot be broken with impunity, whenever a defendant calculates that the money generated from the wrongdoing will probably be of a larger amount than the damages at risk. In essence, punitive damages under this category teach the wrongdoer that tort does not pay.[840] The most notable examples under this category are cases in which a landlord unlawfully evicts a tenant. Defamation cases form the second important group of cases which could lead to punitive damages under this heading.[841]

376. In addition to the two common law categories, Lord DEVLIN construed a third category in which he placed punitive damages expressly provided for by statute.[842] Parliament, for instance, wanted to protect persons who serve in the armed forces by disallowing the enforcement of certain civil judgments against them. To that end, it enacted the Reserve and Auxiliary Forces (Protection of Civil Interests) Act 1951. Enforcement can only take place if leave of an appropriate court has been obtained. Section 13(2) of the Act authorises the court to award exemplary damages for failure of compliance with this restriction if it thinks fit to do so. In considering this question the court may take account of the defendant's conduct. This statute seemed to be – until

835 *Huckle v. Money*, 95 English Reports, King's Bench (Eng. Rep.) 768 (K.B. 1763).

836 *Wilkes v. Wood*, 98 Eng. Rep. 498–499 (C.P. 1763).

837 See *supra* no. 34; V. Wilcox, "Punitive Damages in England" in H. Koziol & V. Wilcox (eds.), *Punitive Damages: Common Law and Civil Law Perspectives*, Vienna, Springer, 2009, 9.

838 *Rookes v. Barnard* (1964) U.K.H.L, 37 (H.L.).

839 V. Wilcox, "Punitive Damages in England" in H. Koziol & V. Wilcox (eds.), *Punitive Damages: Common Law and Civil Law Perspectives*, Vienna, Springer, 2009, 11.

840 *Rookes v. Barnard* (1964) U.K.H.L, 37–38 (H.L.).

841 V. Wilcox, "Punitive Damages in England" in H. Koziol & V. Wilcox (eds.), *Punitive Damages: Common Law and Civil Law Perspectives*, Vienna, Springer, 2009, 12; T. Ingman, *The English Legal Process*, Oxford, Oxford University Press, 13th edition, 2010, 326.

842 *Rookes v. Barnard* (1964) U.K.H.L, 38 (H.L.).

recently – the only one providing for exemplary damages.[843] In 2013, however, Parliament introduced the Crime and Courts Act. It makes exemplary damages available for the tortious publication of news-related material (section 34(1)(c)). The court may award exemplary damages if it is satisfied that the defendant's conduct has shown a deliberate or reckless disregard of an outrageous nature for the claimant's rights, the conduct is such that the court should punish the defendant for it, and other remedies would not be adequate to punish that conduct (section 34(6)). The Act shields publishers who were members of an approved regulator at the material time (section 34(2)) but this protection is not absolute (section 34(3)).

377. In *AB v. South West Water Services Ltd.* the Court of Appeal laid down that exemplary damages are only available for causes of action for which there had been an award of exemplary damages prior to *Rookes v. Barnard.*[844] For torts created after 1964, therefore, no exemplary damages could be granted. The House of Lords in *Kuddus v. Chief Constable of Leicester Constabulary* overruled that decision less than a decade later. It rejected the requirement that the plaintiff must demonstrate that his claim is one in respect of which exemplary damages had been awarded before the decision in *Rookes v. Barnard.*[845] Exemplary damages are thus awardable for any cause of action that satisfies one of Lord DEVLIN's categories, irrespective of whether that cause of action had given rise to exemplary damages prior to *Rookes v. Barnard.*

378. It is, however, not sufficient that the claim of the plaintiff falls within one of the three categories set out. Lord DEVLIN expressed three considerations which he thought should always be borne in mind when considering an award for exemplary damages, regardless of the category under which they are granted. First, the plaintiff cannot recover such damages unless he is the victim of the punishable behaviour. Second, he noted that the "weapon" of exemplary damages should be employed with restraint. Exemplary damages should be awarded with respect to the principle of moderation and should not exceed the amount necessary to meet the objectives of punishment and deterrence. Lord DEVLIN anticipated that it might become necessary to place some arbitrary limit on the award of exemplary damages.[846] Third, the means of the parties are essential in the assessment of exemplary damages. In practice evidence of the plaintiff's

843 T. Ingman, *The English Legal Process*, Oxford, Oxford University Press, 13th edition, 2010, 325.

844 *AB v. South West Water Services Ltd.* [1993] QB 507.

845 *Kuddus v. Chief Constable of Leicester Constabulary* [2001] 2 WLR 1789.

846 For an overview of the guidelines that have been formulated in this regard: V. Wilcox, "Punitive Damages in England" in H. Koziol & V. Wilcox (eds.), *Punitive Damages: Common Law and Civil Law Perspectives*, Vienna, Springer, 2009, 39–43.

means is seldom adduced.[847] Furthermore, Lord DEVLIN stated that everything which aggravates or mitigates the defendant's conduct is relevant.[848, 849]

379. Lord DEVLIN then introduced the "*if, but only if*"-test. The jury should only award exemplary damages "*if, but only if*", the compensatory damages they intend to award are inadequate to punish and deter the defendant and to mark their disapproval of the conduct in question.[850]

380. In *Rookes v. Barnard* the House of Lords thus limited the applicability of punitive damages to a much greater extent than the U.S. courts did. Yet, England is the only country of the five countries examined in this book, where such damages are generally accepted and explicitly classified as punitive damages. Although the scope of punitive damages is far more restricted than in the United States, the possibility to obtain punitive damages in England firmly adds to the idea that private law in the European Union is also concerned with punishment and deterrence (going above the inherent penal and deterrent effect of tort law).

5.3.2. MULTIPLE DAMAGES

a. *Regulation 1768/95 implementing the agricultural exemption*

381. In European law there are provisions which allow for punitive damages. One could, for instance, point to article 18 of Regulation 1768/95 as proof of the existence of punitive awards within European law.[851] This Regulation contains rules which implement the agricultural exemption as provided for in article 14 paragraph 3 of Regulation 2100/94 on Community plant variety rights.[852] The exemption allows farmers to use, for purposes of safeguarding agricultural production, propagating material which is covered by a Community plant

---

847 Law Commission for England and Wales, Aggravated, Exemplary and Restitutionary Damages, LC No. 247, 1997, 1.153, available at <http://lawcommission.justice.gov.uk/docs/lc247_aggravated_exemplary_and_restitutionary_damages.pdf>.

848 *Rookes v. Barnard* (1964) U.K.H.L, 38 (H.L.); V. Wilcox, "Punitive Damages in England" in H. Koziol & V. Wilcox (eds.), *Punitive Damages: Common Law and Civil Law Perspectives*, Vienna, Springer, 2009, 25.

849 For additional factors which courts have considered to be relevant for the assessment of exemplary damages: V. Wilcox, "Punitive Damages in England" in H. Koziol & V. Wilcox (eds.), *Punitive Damages: Common Law and Civil Law Perspectives*, Vienna, Springer, 2009, 28–32.

850 *Rookes v. Barnard* (1964) U.K.H.L, 38 (H.L.).

851 Regulation No. 1768/95 of 24 July 1995 implementing rules on the agricultural exemption provided for in Article 14 (3) of Council Regulation No. 2100/94 on Community plant variety rights, *OJ* L 173 of 25 July 1995, 14–21.

852 Council Regulation No. 2100/94 of 27 July 1994 on Community plant variety rights, *OJ* L 227 of 1 September 1994, 1–30.

variety right. Article 18 of Regulation 1768/95 deals with special civil law claims and reads (emphasis added):

1. *A person referred to in Article 17 may be sued by the holder to fulfil his obligations pursuant to Article 14 (3) of the basic Regulation as specified in this Regulation.*
2. *If such person has repeatedly and intentionally not complied with his obligation pursuant to Article 14 (3) 4th indent of the basic Regulation, in respect of one or more varieties of the same holder, the liability to compensate the holder for any further damage pursuant to Article 94 (2) of the basic Regulation shall cover at least* a lump sum calculated on the basis of the quadruple average amount charged for the licensed production *of a corresponding quantity of propagating material of protected varieties of the plant species concerned in the same area, without prejudice to the compensation of any higher damage.*

382. Under this provision of Regulation 1768/95 the right holder is thus awarded a multiple of the actual loss incurred. This overcompensation of the victim could be understood as punitive in nature. Admittedly, the scope of this Regulation is quite limited and restricted to the particular field of plant breeders' rights within intellectual property.[853] However, article 18.2 demonstrates a willingness to derogate from purely compensatory considerations in private law.

b. French Mining Law 1810

383. In France there is a 19th century Mining Law which provides for double damages.[854] Article 43 of the Act lays down the obligation for the owner of a mine to pay an indemnity to the owner of the land where the mine is situated. Article 43 creates a special rule in case of temporary mining. If one year after the mining has ended the land cannot be cultivated like before the mining, the mine owner will have to pay an increased indemnity. This indemnity is arrived at by doubling what the damaged land would have produced. It is clear that awarding a sum equal to twice the loss suffered amounts to punitive-like damages.

5.3.3. DOUBLE LICENSE FEE FOR GEMA

384. Among the measures which are not purely compensatory in nature one could also include the double license fee for the *Gesellschaft für musikalische Aufführungs- und mechanische Vervielfältigungsrechte* (GEMA).[855] GEMA is a

---

853 B.A. Koch, "Punitive Damages in European Law" in H. Koziol & V. Wilcox (eds.), *Punitive Damages: Common Law and Civil Law Perspectives*, Vienna, Springer, 2009, 208–209.

854 Loi no. 5401 du 21 avril 1810 concernant les Mines, les Minières et les Carrières, *Bull. des lois* 1810, no. 285, 355.

855 P. Müller, *Punitive Damages und deutsches Schadensersatzrecht*, Berlin, de Gruyter, 2000, 126–132; Report of the Monopolskommission, Das allgemeine Wettbewerbsrecht in der Siebten GWB-Novelle, March 2004, 42, no. 79, available at <www.monopolkommission.

collecting society and a performance rights organisation. It protects the rights of lyricists, composers and music publishers in Germany. If GEMA discovers an infringement of the intellectual property rights held by one of its members, it charges a double license fee to the infringing party. The idea behind this 100% addition to the ordinary license fee is that these supplementary damages compensate for the organisational costs GEMA incurs and the expensive monitoring activities it performs.[856] This practice has been accepted by the *Bundesgerichtshof* whose case law could be interpreted as highlighting that, absent this sanctioning mechanism, there would be no incentive for infringers to follow the rules.[857] Interestingly, GEMA is the only association allowed to adopt this remedy as its usage for other copyright violations has been refused.[858]

385. There is an argument for attaching a punitive and/or deterrent dimension to this double fee. The additional damages could be explained as compensation for the financial and other efforts that were made to protect the right holder against the violation of the infringer. However, it should be remarked that it is not normal practice to compensate for detection costs.[859] Moreover, there will be instances where the double license fee will result in the infringer having to bear a proportion of the (general) expenses incurred by GEMA that goes beyond the costs made in his individual case. When making the tortfeasor liable for damage he has not caused, it could be said that sanctioning considerations are laid bare.

5.3.4. SURCHARGE OF BENEFITS IN SPANISH SOCIAL SECURITY LAW

386. In Spanish law article 123 of the *Ley General de la Seguridad Social*[860] (General Act on Social Security) provides a clear example of a punitive provision

de/sg_41/text_s41.pdf>; *contra* U. Magnus, "Punitive Damages and German Law" in L. Meurkens & E. Nordin (eds.), *The Power of Punitive Damages – Is Europe Missing Out?*, Cambridge – Antwerp – Portland, Intersentia, 2012, 254; *contra* N. Jansen & L. Rademacher, "Punitive Damages in Germany" in H. Koziol & V. Wilcox (eds.), *Punitive Damages: Common Law and Civil Law Perspectives*, Vienna, Springer, 2009, 83.

856 N. Jansen & L. Rademacher, "Punitive Damages in Germany" in H. Koziol & V. Wilcox (eds.), *Punitive Damages: Common Law and Civil Law Perspectives*, Vienna, Springer, 2009, 82–83.

857 BGH 24 June 1955, *BGHZ* 17, 376; BGH 10 March 1972, *BGHZ* 59, 286; BGH 15 November 1994, *Neue Juristische Wochenschrift* 1995, 861; G. Wagner, "The Protection of Personality Rights against Invasions by Mass Media in Germany" in H. Koziol & A. Warzilek (eds.), *Persönlichkeitsschutz gegenüber Massenmedien – The Protection of Personality Rights against Invasions by Mass Media*, Vienna, Springer, 2005, 174, no. 104.

858 BGH 9 March 1966, *GRUR* 1966, 570; BGH 22 January 1986, *BGHZ* 97, 37.

859 U. Magnus, "Punitive Damages and German Law" in L. Meurkens & E. Nordin (eds.), *The Power of Punitive Damages – Is Europe Missing Out?*, Cambridge – Antwerp – Portland, Intersentia, 2012, 254.

860 Real Decreto Legislativo 1/1994, de 20 de junio, por el que se aprueba el Texto Refundido de la Ley General de la Seguridad Social, *BOE* no. 154, 29 June 1994, 20658–20708, available at <www.boe.es/diario_boe/txt.php?id=BOE-A-1994-14960>.

within private law.[861] The article of the Act deals with the legal consequences of a labour accident or an occupational disease caused by the employer's fault. When the harm to the worker was caused by faulty equipment, in a workplace without obligatory safety devices or where safety and hygiene measures were not observed, the benefits paid out (by the state) to the employee will be increased by 30 to 50% depending on the seriousness of the employer's wrongdoing.[862] The provision further lays down that under these circumstances the employer is liable for the surcharge and cannot insure himself against this liability.[863] Lastly, the liability for the additional amount is independent from and compatible with any criminal (or other) liability.[864]

387. The victim of a labour accident or an occupational disease is thus entitled to receive increased financial benefits in case his condition can be attributed to the employer. This financial burden is imposed by the Spanish Department of Employment and has to be borne by the employer. The exact percentage (between 30 and 50) depends on the assessment of the gravity of the employer's wrong. This criterion reflects the tortfeasor-oriented approach of punitive damages and contradicts the idea of (compensatory) damages which are strictly related to the victim's loss. Furthermore, the instrument of the surcharge appears to have a punitive as well as a deterrent objective. It aims at punishing the employer for allowing the damaging event to take place and contributes to the prevention of such accidents by seeking the employer's compliance with his duties in the future.[865] The punitive and deterrent nature of the administrative sanction has been explicitly confirmed by the Spanish Supreme Court in a decision of 23 April 2009.[866]

388. A number of other characteristics of the employer's surcharge are also reminiscent of punitive damages. First, like punitive damages in the U.S., the amount is payable to the victim and not to the state.[867] Second, the liability under article 123 of the *Ley General de la Seguridad Social* does not exclude any criminal (or other) liability the employer might incur. The same goes for

861 T. Fausten & R. Hammesfahr, "Punitive damages in Europe: Concern, threat or non-issue?", Armonk, Swiss Re, 2012, 8; M. Luque Parra, C. Gómez Ligüerre & J.A. Ruiz García, "Workplace Injuries and Tort Liability", *InDret* 02/2002, 10, available at <www.indret.com/pdf/021_en.pdf>; M. Otero Crespo, "Punitive Damages Under Spanish Law: A Subtle Recognition?" in L. Meurkens & E. Nordin (eds.), *The Power of Punitive Damages – Is Europe Missing Out?*, Cambridge – Antwerp – Portland, Intersentia, 2012, 294–295.

862 Article 123.1. General Act on Social Security.

863 Article 123.2. General Act on Social Security.

864 Article 123.3. General Act on Social Security.

865 M. Otero Crespo, "Punitive Damages Under Spanish Law: A Subtle Recognition?" in L. Meurkens & E. Nordin (eds.), *The Power of Punitive Damages – Is Europe Missing Out?*, Cambridge – Antwerp – Portland, Intersentia, 2012, 294.

866 Spanish Supreme Court (Civil Chamber, Plenary Section) 23 April 2009, *RJ* 2009, 4140.

867 Split recovery schemes are of course an exception to this general principle.

U.S. punitive damages. A wrongdoer can face criminal prosecution and still be ordered to pay punitive damages with regard to the same conduct. Following the case law of the U.S. Supreme Court the civil court should take the possible criminal sanctions into account in order to avoid excessive punitive awards.[868]

5.3.5. PENALTY CLAUSE

389. The contractual penalty is another form of punishment within private law. Various legal systems in the European Union allow parties to insert a penalty clause into their contract. In Germany, for instance, article 339 of the BGB confirms the validity of such a clause. A penalty clause leads to the party failing to perform his obligation or failing to do it properly having to pay an amount of money as penalty to the other party. The clause is intended to encourage performance or, in other words, to deter the party from breaching the contract.[869] The party requesting payment of the penalty does not have to prove the existence of any real damage. The (indirect) penal effect of the clause is thus obvious.[870]

390. The German Civil Code does leave an opening for the penalty to be reduced. If the payable penalty is disproportionally high, it may be reduced by the judge to a reasonable amount (article 343 BGB). Even in that case, however, there is still a real possibility that the reduced amount will exceed the actual damage suffered. As such, the other party will receive more than the amount of the damages incurred.[871] Moreover, between merchants article 348 of the German Commercial Code applies. This provision excludes the possibility of reduction of the penalty clause.

391. In France penalty clauses (*clauses pénales*) also exist in private law (article 1226 Civil Code). The judge also has the power to reduce the amount agreed upon if he finds the sum to be manifestly excessive (article 1152, paragraph 2 Civil Code). Courts are, however, not allowed to award the other

---

868 *BMW of North America, Inc. v. Gore*, 517 U.S. 574–575, (1995).

869 T. Rouhette, "The availability of punitive damages in Europe: growing trend or nonexistent concept?", 74 *Defense Counsel Journal* 2007, 324.

870 M. Tolani, "U.S. Punitive Damages Before German Courts: A Comparative Analysis with Respect to the Ordre Public", 17 *Annual Survey of International & Comparative Law* 2011, 199; U. Magnus, "Punitive Damages and German Law" in L. Meurkens & E. Nordin (eds.), *The Power of Punitive Damages – Is Europe Missing Out?*, Cambridge – Antwerp – Portland, Intersentia, 2012, 253; N. Meyer Fabre, "Enforcement Of U.S. Punitive Damages Award in France: First Ruling Of The French Court Of Cassation In X. v. Fountaine Pajot December 1, 2010", *Mealey's International Arbitration Report* January 2011, 3.

871 J.-S. Borghetti, "Punitive Damages in France" in H. Koziol & V. Wilcox (eds.), *Punitive Damages: Common Law and Civil Law Perspectives*, Vienna, Springer, 2009, 57.

party less than the damages actually suffered.[872] This means that the judge could moderate the penalty clause to a level above the damages incurred. The lower limit of the amount of actual damages thus opens the possibility for extra-compensatory damages to be awarded.

392. The Court of Appeal of Venice argued in *Fimez* that penalty clauses are not comparable to punitive damages because they are not awarded by a court but are set in advance by the parties in their contract.[873] The Italian Supreme Court confirmed the Court of Appeal's ruling on this point.[874] The *Bundesgerichtshof* in *John Doe v. Eckhard Schmitz* also declined to accept an equivalence between penalty clauses and punitive damages because contractual penalties arise from the parties' agreement.[875] In the doctrine this argument has also been suggested.[876] In our opinion this reasoning cannot be followed. It is irrelevant that the penal mechanism of the penalty clause originates from the will of the parties. What matters is that Italian private law (along with other private law systems of the Civil Law countries investigated[877]) facilitates the punishment of the contractual party who is in breach. This finding supports our claim that European legal systems to a certain extent make room for penal considerations in private law relationships.

5.3.6. *L' ASTREINTE*

393. The use of penalties in private law can also be demonstrated by referring to the French concept of *l'astreinte*.[878, 879] It is not easy to translate the French word '*astreinte*' into English. It is essentially a periodic penalty imposed by a court on a debtor who fails to perform what is required of him. The penalty payment results from an act (*e.g.* the debtor enters the land of another person

872 Cass. 24 July 1978, *Bull. civ.* I, no. 280, *RTD civ.* 1979, 150, note G. Cornu.

873 Court of Appeal Venice 15 October 2001, *Rep Foro it* 2003, *Delibazione* no. 29; *Giur. It.* II 2002, 1021. See *supra* no. 219.

874 Cass. civ. 19 January 2007, no. 1183, *Rep Foro it* 2007 *v Delibazione* no. 13 and *v Danni Civili* no. 316; *Corr. Giur.*, 2007, 4, 497. See *supra* no. 224.

875 BGH 4 June 1992, *Neue Juristische Wochenschrift* 1992, 3103. See *supra* no. 241.

876 J.-S. Borghetti, "Punitive Damages in France" in H. Koziol & V. Wilcox (eds.), *Punitive Damages: Common Law and Civil Law Perspectives*, Vienna, Springer, 2009, 57.

877 The only country not yet mentioned is Spain. Spanish law recognises the contractual penalty in article 1154 of the Civil Code. There is no provision regarding the reduction of excessive penalty clauses.

878 Articles 33–37 of Loi no. 91–650 du 9 juillet 1991 portant réforme des procédures civiles d'exécution, *JFOR* no. 163 of 14 July 1991, 9228.

879 P. Malaurie, L. Aynès & P. Stoffel-Muck, *Droit Civil, Les obligations*, Paris, Defrénois, 2005, 619, no. 1135; S. Carval, *La responsabilité civile dans sa fonction de peine privée*, Paris, L.G.D.J., 1995, 39, no. 36; N. Meyer Fabre, "Enforcement Of U.S. Punitive Damages Award in France: First Ruling Of The French Court Of Cassation In X. v. Fountaine Pajot December 1, 2010", *Mealey's International Arbitration Report* January 2011, 3.

despite being ordered by a court not to do so) or an omission (*e.g.* he fails to break down an illegally built wall or he does not perform his obligation to pay a certain sum of money) of the debtor. The penalty can be calculated per day of non-compliance but also per infringement.

394. It should be underlined that *l'astreinte*, like punitive damages, is to be paid to the other party in the litigation. The penalty payment, however, does not intend to compensate that party for damages that result from the non-compliance. The sums are due in addition to the compensatory damages. The creditor thus receives more than the harm he suffered.[880] The existence of *l'astreinte* thus contributes to the idea that penal mechanisms are present in private law.

395. We find a similar mechanism in intellectual property law as well. Article 44 of the Spanish Trademark Act, for instance, contains a coercive measure to protect the trademark owner from further infringements.[881] When a court has established that the trademark has been infringed, it will order the cessation of the infringing acts and will award an amount of up to EUR 600 to the trademark owner for each day of delay in the cessation. Article 44 indicates that this measure is a coercive compensation. Legal scholars, however, have asserted that the provision amounts to a coercive fine, with a clear intention to punish.[882] We tend to agree with this view, especially when the amount awarded under article 44 (*i.e.* EUR 600 or less) exceeds the actual harm incurred by the extra day of delay in the cessation.

396. In the context of *l'astreinte* it is useful to mention the German concepts of *Zwangsgeld* and *Ordnungsgeld*. Article 888, (1) ZPO (Code of Civil Procedure) provides that a debtor can be urged by a court to take the action it was ordered to take by levying a penalty payment. The difference with *l'astreinte* lies in the fact that *Zwangsgeld* is paid to the state and not to the creditor. *Ordnungsgeld* is another punitive instrument within German private law.[883] Pursuant to article 890, (1) ZPO the court can condemn a debtor to a coercive fine for each count of the violation of his obligation to cease and desist from actions or for his failure to tolerate actions to be taken. Both *Zwangsgeld* and *Ordnungsgeld* are

---

880 J.-S. Borghetti, "Punitive Damages in France" in H. Koziol & V. Wilcox (eds.), *Punitive Damages: Common Law and Civil Law Perspectives*, Vienna, Springer, 2009, 57–58.

881 Ley 17/2001 de 7 de diciembre, de Marcas, *BOE* 8 December 2001, no. 294.

882 M. Otero Crespo, "Punitive Damages Under Spanish Law: A Subtle Recognition?" in L. Meurkens & E. Nordin (eds.), *The Power of Punitive Damages – Is Europe Missing Out?*, Cambridge – Antwerp – Portland, Intersentia, 2012, 300; P. del Olmo, "Punitive Damages in Spain" in H. Koziol & V. Wilcox (eds.), *Punitive Damages: Common Law and Civil Law Perspectives*, Vienna, Springer, 2009, 148.

883 The German Constitutional Court has confirmed that article 890 ZPO contains penal elements: Bundesverfassungsgericht 14 July 1981, *BVerfGE* 58, 159.

ordered upon application of the creditor but paid to the state. The existence of these two instruments, nevertheless, supports the idea that German private law is also concerned with the regulation of behaviour by the use of punishment. It rebuts the statement that only (German) criminal law contains mechanisms aimed at punishment and deterrence.[884]

5.3.7. INSURANCE LAW

397. The field of insurance forms another area of law where punitive damages can be detected. The legal phenomenon of damages of an extra-compensatory nature in insurance law is found in at least three of the Civil Law jurisdictions which are looked at in this book.

398. In France as well as in Spain these punitive-like damages are provided for by statute. The French *Code des assurances* (Insurance Code) deals with claims liquidation in motor liability insurance. The insurers of motor vehicles have the obligation to offer the victim of an accident compensation within certain deadlines. If liability is uncontested and the damage is quantified, the insurance company has three months to make such an offer for compensation to the injured. This time period starts from the date of the victim's claim.[885] When the offer has not been made within the time limit, the amount of the compensation offered by the insurer or awarded by the court to the victim shall bear interest *ipso jure* at *double* the legal interest rate as from the expiry of the time limit and until the date of the offer or the final judgment.[886] This clearly constitutes a sanction for non-performance by the insurer. This reasoning finds confirmation in the final sentence of article L 211–13 which states: "*Cette pénalité peut être réduite par le juge en raison de circonstances non imputables à l'assureur*" ("This penalty can be reduced by the court for circumstances not attributable to the insurer"). The legislature itself thus views the doubling of the interest due as a penal instrument ("*pénalité*").

399. With regard to compulsory construction insurance, the French Insurance Code provides for the same sanction. When the insurer fails to communicate a compensation offer within the statutory time limits or proposes a compensation offer that is clearly inadequate, the insured may, after he has notified the insurer, incur the expenses necessary to repair the damage. In such event, an interest

884 M. Tolani, "U.S. Punitive Damages Before German Courts: A Comparative Analysis with Respect to the Ordre Public", 17 *Annual Survey of International & Comparative Law* 2011, 204–205.

885 Article L211–9, para. 1.

886 Article L211–13.

double the legal interest rate shall be applied *ipso jure* to the compensation to be paid by the insurer.[887]

400. In the Spanish *Ley de Contrato de Seguro* (Insurance Contract Act) we find a similar rule.[888] Article 18 of the Act provides that the insurer is obliged to pay the compensation at the end of the necessary investigations. He is also under the obligation to pay the minimum amount that he may owe within forty days after the declaration of the accident. If the insurer does not pay the compensation or the minimum amount within the applicable time limits, he has to pay additional interest. The first two years half the legal interest rate is added. After two years the rate of interest cannot be lower than 20%.[889] Again, the amounts due go beyond what is necessary to compensate for loss suffered by the insured.

401. We believe it is irrelevant that the amounts to be paid on top of the normal compensation are minimal compared to the amounts awarded as punitive damages in the United States.[890] What matters in the context of international public policy is that the French and Spanish legislator decided to deviate from the principle of compensation in private law in order to prevent the occurrence of non-compliance by the insurer.

402. In Germany one can find courts that award increased damages in cases of insurance bad faith. The egregious behaviour of the insurance company could, for instance, be the delay of the proceedings or the undue influence of the victim. A case before the *Oberlandesgericht* (Court of Appeal) Frankfurt offers an example of extra-compensatory damages being awarded for the deliberate withholding of payment by an insurer. A doctor had overlooked that his patient had two fractured vertebrae. The woman had to endure severe pain for several months, until a second doctor found the cause of her discomfort. Despite the manifest error of the first doctor, the insurance company declined to pay compensation to the victim.

403. At first instance the woman received EUR 5.000 for pain and suffering. On appeal, however, the *Oberlandesgericht* heavily criticised the behaviour of the insurer. It found that the insurance company had abused its dominant position. It noted that such arrogant behaviour could frequently be observed. Some insurers tend to treat people who are clearly entitled to payment as annoying claimants.

---

887 Article L242–1, para. 5.

888 Ley 50/1980, de 8 de octubre 1980, de Contrato de Seguro, *BOE* 17 October 1980, 23126.

889 Article 20, para. 4.

890 *Contra* J.-S. Borghetti, "Punitive Damages in France" in H. Koziol & V. Wilcox (eds.), *Punitive Damages: Common Law and Civil Law Perspectives*, Vienna, Springer, 2009, 60.

The insurance companies then attempt to drag settlement proceedings for as long as possible for their own economic advantage. The *Oberlandesgericht* could not accept such conduct and subsequently ordered double the amount of damages for pain and suffering solely on the basis of that conduct.[891]

404. In another German judgment we also find this reasoning. In this case before the *Oberlandesgericht* Karlsruhe the victim of a car accident suffered serious injuries and also developed psychological problems.[892] The insurance company of the defendant delayed the payments to the victim. The *Oberlandesgericht* Karlsruhe raised the amount of damages for pain and suffering due to this delay. The court emphasised that the insurer had a public task. When it is clear that the victim is entitled to compensation, the insurance company should pay the claimant who is in an inferior position. The court held that case law should aim to deter the insurance companies from acting in such an abusive manner.[893] The increase in the award for pain and suffering had a clear function of prevention in this case.[894, 895] The *Leitmotiv* in both cases is clear: the principle of compensation in private law is set aside to pursue objectives that normally belong to the realm of criminal law.

405. In the United States punitive damages are available in insurance bad faith cases. In most American states an insurer owes a duty of good faith and fair dealing to their insured. If the insurer violates this "implied covenant of good faith and fair dealing", this contractual breach may constitute a tort for which punitive damages may be awarded.[896] We thus see a similar reaction to the societal problem of bad faith handling of insurance claims on both continents. The only difference between the European Union countries of Germany, France and Spain, on the one hand, and the United States, on the other hand, is the terminology used to describe the legal armoury deployed to combat this type of unwanted behaviour. Whereas the United States call the measure punitive damages, the Member States examined do not use this term. The legal reality, however, shows that both approaches to the issue are closely related, if not identical.

---

891 Oberlandesgericht Frankfurt 7 January 1999, *Neue Juristische Wochenschrift* 1999, 2447.

892 Oberlandesgericht Karlsruhe 2 November 1972, *Neue Juristische Wochenschrift* 1973, 851.

893 Oberlandesgericht Karlsruhe 2 November 1972, *Neue Juristische Wochenschrift* 1973, 853.

894 J. Rosengarten, "Der Präventionsgedanke im deutschen Zivilrecht – Höheres Schmerzensgeld, aber keine Anerkennung und Vollstreckung US-amerikanischer punitive damages?", *Neue Juristische Wochenschrift* 1996, 1935.

895 M. Tolani, "U.S. Punitive Damages Before German Courts: A Comparative Analysis with Respect to the Ordre Public", 17 *Annual Survey of International & Comparative Law* 2011, 197.

896 See *supra* no. 47.

5.3.8. DEFAULT RATE OF INTEREST

406. As discussed, the increase of interest rates in insurance law indicates the existence of punitive considerations in insurance bad faith cases.[897] Also outside insurance law we can observe interest rates going beyond what is needed to compensate the creditor. The European Union issued Directive 2011/7 which deals with late payment in commercial transactions.[898] The Directive seeks to combat delays in payment between commercial parties, thereby fostering the functioning of the internal market.[899] It lays down the obligation for Member States to ensure that a creditor is entitled to interest for late payment without the necessity of a reminder. "Interest for late payment" is defined as interest at a rate which is equal to the sum of the reference rate and at least eight percentage points.[900] The "reference rate" is the interest rate applied by the European Central Bank to its most recent refinancing operations.[901] The idea behind the rule is clear: it should not be more favourable for a debtor to owe money to the creditor than to obtain credit from a bank.

407. We should assess the interest rate from the point of view of the creditor who cannot dispose of the sum owed to him. The loss suffered in such a case can be calculated by looking at the cost for the creditor to acquire a bank loan for the amount owed. The compensatory nature of private law is adhered to as long as the rate stays under the average rate banks charge when issuing a loan. However, to the extent that the interest rate exceeds this bank average it amounts to punitive damages.[902] In the period of January to September 2012, for example, the average interest rate for loans up to EUR 1 million granted to businesses in Germany was 3.4%.[903] The reference rate of the European Central Bank during that period was first 1% and then 0.75%.[904] Germany implemented the Directive by adding the minimum of eight percentage points to the reference rate.[905] Commercial parties were, therefore, on the basis of the German legislation entitled to 9% and 8.75% interest respectively. The biggest gap between the actual interest rate employed and the average market rate for loans was, therefore, at

[897] See *supra* no. 397 *et seq.*

[898] Directive 2011/7 of the European Parliament and of the Council of 16 February 2011 on combating late payment in commercial transactions, *OJ* L 48 of 23 February 2011, 1–10. This Directive replaced Directive 2000/35.

[899] Article 1.1.

[900] Article 2(5) & 2(6).

[901] Article 2(7),(a), (i).

[902] N. Jansen & L. Rademacher, "Punitive Damages in Germany" in H. Koziol & V. Wilcox (eds.), *Punitive Damages: Common Law and Civil Law Perspectives*, Vienna, Springer, 2009, 84.

[903] See: <http://ec.europa.eu/enterprise/policies/finance/data/enterprise-finance-index/access-to-finance-indicators/loans/index_en.htm>.

[904] See the website of the European Central Bank: <www.ecb.europa.eu/stats/monetary/rates/html/index.en.html>.

[905] §288, (2) BGB.

one point 5.6% (*i.e.* 9% minus 3.4%). Equally, it seems that 9% is presumably a much higher return than the creditor could have expected had the money owed been available to him. The sanction provided for by Directive 2011/7 can at times thus be severe and could be viewed as punishment.[906] To put it more broadly, any legal interest higher than the average market interest for loans (and, *a fortiori*, higher than the lowest interest rate available) is extra-compensatory to the extent of the difference. The amount of the excess could be understood as pursuing a punitive aim.

5.3.9. CIVIL FINES

408. French law contains the concept of the *amende civile* (civil fine). A civil fine is essentially a penalty provided for by private law instead of criminal law. The French legislator decided to resort in certain circumstances to penal measures in private law to punish the wrongdoer for his or her unwanted behaviour and to deter the future occurrence of such conduct. Civil fines are administered by civil courts and find their origin in private law statutes.[907] They are independent from the normal compensatory damages awarded to the prevailing party.

409. An example of an *amende civile* can be found in article 50 of the Civil Code. The article provides that a fine of EUR 3 to 30 can be issued against a state official who does not comply with his obligations under articles 34–49 relating to records of civil status. The Civil Code also lays down civil fines in the context of guardianship. The judge of the *tribunal d'instance* in whose territorial jurisdiction the minor has his domicile can sentence those who did not comply with his injunctions to a civil fine (article 388–3 code civil). Pursuant to article 1216 of the *Nouveau Code de Procedure Civil* (Code of Civil Procedure) this fine cannot exceed EUR 3.000. Parties who litigate in a dilatory or abusive fashion can on the basis of article 32–1 of the Code of Civil Procedure be ordered to pay a civil fine not exceeding EUR 3.000.[908] Article 32–1 reminds us of the damages for frivolous law suits in article 96 of the Italian Code of Civil Procedure. Both provisions have the same aim but the latter damages are awarded to the other party instead of to the state.[909] A famous example of a civil fine can be found in article L 442–6 of the *Code de commerce* (Commercial Code). This article enumerates a number of prohibited anti-competitive practices and

906 C. Cauffman, "Naar een punitief Europees Verbintenissenrecht?", *Tijdschrift voor Privaatrecht* 2007, 806.
907 M. Behar-Touchais, "L'amende civile est-elle un substitut satisfaisant à l'absence de dommages et intérêts punitifs?", *Les Petites Affiches* 2002, no. 10.
908 For abusive or dilatory appeal article 559 provides the same civil fine.
909 See *infra* no. 415 *et seq.*

allows competitors to recover damages. On top of these damages the defendant can be sentenced to pay a civil fine of up to EUR 2 million (article 442-6, III, paragraph 2). Finally, reference can be made to article L 651-2 of the *Code de la construction et de l'habitation* (Construction and Housing Code). The article provides that those who change the function of buildings from housing to commercial premises without prior authorisation can be punished with a fine of up to EUR 25.000.

410. It should again be underlined that the relevant question for this book is not whether these civil fines are completely identical to punitive damages or form an alternative to them. The question is rather whether their existence in French law supports our contention that European continental systems sometimes pursue penal goals in private law. We believe this is the case.

411. In our opinion French civil fines bear several similarities to U.S. punitive damages. They are both awarded/issued in addition to the compensatory damages and they both pursue punitive and deterrent objectives within the realm of private law.[910] Both institutions are situated halfway between civil and criminal law.[911] Their penal impact on the 'condemned' party without that party benefitting from the criminal law safeguards stirs controversy both in France[912] and in the U.S.[913]

412. The only difference with punitive damages lies in the fact that the penalty is not paid to the other party in the private litigation but to the state.[914] The victim consequently does not receive more than the amount of the damage he suffered. Civil fines thus do not cause a deviation from the strict compensation principle.[915] In our view, however, the fact that the sum due is destined for the treasury does not prevent the comparison between *amendes civiles* and punitive damages.

---

910 M. Behar-Touchais, "L'amende civile est-elle un substitut satisfaisant à l'absence de dommages et intérêts punitifs?", *Les Petites Affiches* 2002, no. 16.

911 J.-S. Borghetti, "Punitive Damages in France" in H. Koziol & V. Wilcox (eds.), *Punitive Damages: Common Law and Civil Law Perspectives*, Vienna, Springer, 2009, 61–62. See also *supra* no. 29.

912 M. Behar-Touchais, "L'amende civile est-elle un substitut satisfaisant à l'absence de dommages et intérêts punitifs?", *Les Petites Affiches* 2002, no. 25–28.

913 See *supra* no. 30.

914 J.-S. Borghetti, "Punitive Damages in France" in H. Koziol & V. Wilcox (eds.), *Punitive Damages: Common Law and Civil Law Perspectives*, Vienna, Springer, 2009, 61; M. Behar-Touchais, "L'amende civile est-elle un substitut satisfaisant à l'absence de dommages et intérêts punitifs?", *Les Petites Affiches* 2002, no. 22; G. Nater-Bass, "U.S.-Style Punitive Damages Awards and their Recognition and Enforcement in Switzerland and Other Civil-Law Countries", 28 *Deutsch-Amerikanische Juristen-Vereinigung Newsletter* 2003, 156, footnote 29.

915 M. Behar-Touchais, "L'amende civile est-elle un substitut satisfaisant à l'absence de dommages et intérêts punitifs?", *Les Petites Affiches* 2002, no. 19.

413. Two observations support this view. First, in the U.S. split-recovery schemes exist under which part of the punitive damages awarded flows to an entity other than the counterparty of the party ordered to pay punitive damages. That part of the punitive damages still bears the label of punitive damages. Second and most importantly, the fact that the damages are attributed to the state does not weaken the finding that criminal law objectives are to be found in French private law. As indicated above, the purpose of this chapter is to provide evidence that the private law of continental European law systems contains legal concepts which pursue criminal aims.[916] This proof is required to dismantle the idea that U.S. punitive damages are *in se* contrary to international public policy. The legal mechanisms we point out in this chapter do not need to be exact copies of U.S. punitive damages. What is crucial is that they pursue similar (penal and deterrent) aims within the context of private law. Civil fines do indeed attempt to achieve such criminal law objectives.

414. Some scholars assert that civil fines cannot be compared to punitive damages because the amount of a civil fine is in most cases very low.[917] Again, it should be reminded that we do not argue that civil fines are completely the same as punitive damages. For the sake of argument, however, some thoughts on this issue. In our opinion, the suggested difference between 'high' and 'low' civil fines is arbitrary. The penal nature of a sum payable to the state does not disappear simply because the sum is said to be 'low'. Besides, what is 'high' or 'low' also depends on the financial situation of the party who has to pay the fine. For a wealthy party a 'high' fine might be nothing whereas the same amount might bankrupt another party. We, therefore, reject the idea that a fine would derive its penal nature from the (high level of the) amount levied. Moreover, civil fines can sometimes reach 'high' numbers. In the above-mentioned articles on anti-competitive behaviour (article 442–6 of the Commercial Code) and on the changing of the use of buildings (article L 651–2 of the Construction and Housing Code), for instance, the sums due are of a substantial amount.[918]

5.3.10. FRIVOLOUS LITIGATION IN ITALY

415. In Italy a court can order the losing party in a civil procedure to pay damages for abuse of process (*responsabilità processuale aggravata*) to the prevailing party. Article 96, first paragraph of the Code of Civil Procedure

---

916 See *supra* no. 364.

917 J.-S. Borghetti, "Punitive Damages in France" in H. Koziol & V. Wilcox (eds.), *Punitive Damages: Common Law and Civil Law Perspectives*, Vienna, Springer, 2009, 61; M. Behar-Touchais, "L'amende civile est-elle un substitut satisfaisant à l'absence de dommages et intérêts punitifs?", *Les Petites Affiches* 2002, nos. 12 and 34.

918 See *supra* no. 409.

(*Codice di Procedura Civile*) provides that the judge can do so upon request of the prevailing party. In order for such damages to be available the losing party must have brought or defended the case with bad faith or with gross negligence.

416. The legal nature of article 96, first paragraph seems to be disputed in Italy. According to CORONGIU the provision has a punitive function.[919] She supports this opinion by noting the existence of similarities between the remedy under article 96, first paragraph and U.S. punitive damages. First, the conduct required (bad faith or gross negligence) comes quite close to the requirement of "reprehensible conduct" for punitive damages in the United States.[920] Second, she sees a similarity between article 96 and Rule 11 of the Federal Rules of Civil Procedure, which in her view provides for punitive damages in case of frivolous law suits.[921] Rule 11, (b) reads:

> *(b) Representations to the Court. By presenting to the court a pleading, written motion, or other paper – whether by signing, filing, submitting, or later advocating it – an attorney or unrepresented party certifies that to the best of the person's knowledge, information, and belief, formed after an inquiry reasonable under the circumstances:*
>
> *(1) it is not being presented for any improper purpose, such as to harass, cause unnecessary delay, or needlessly increase the cost of litigation;*
> *(2) the claims, defenses, and other legal contentions are warranted by existing law or by a nonfrivolous argument for extending, modifying, or reversing existing law or for establishing new law;*
> *(3) the factual contentions have evidentiary support or, if specifically so identified, will likely have evidentiary support after a reasonable opportunity for further investigation or discovery; and*
> *(4) the denials of factual contentions are warranted on the evidence or, if specifically so identified, are reasonably based on belief or a lack of information.*

417. The sanction for breach of this provision can be found in Rule 11, (c), (1): "*[...] the court may impose an appropriate sanction on any attorney, law firm, or party that violated the rule or is responsible for the violation.*" Rule 11, (c), (4) addresses the nature of this sanction and specifies that the sanction: "*[...] must be limited to what suffices to deter repetition of the conduct or comparable conduct by others similarly situated*". Rule 11 does not literally refer to punitive damages but CORONGIU asserts that the remedy for violation of Rule 11 amounts to punitive

919 S.A.L. Corongiu, *Punitive Damages Awards in the US Judicial Experience and Their Recognition in Italy*, Universita degli studi di Urbino, unpublished PhD thesis, 2004–2005, 65, footnote 81.

920 S.A.L. Corongiu, *Punitive Damages Awards in the US Judicial Experience and Their Recognition in Italy*, Universita degli studi di Urbino, unpublished PhD thesis, 2004–2005, 50.

921 S.A.L. Corongiu, *Punitive Damages Awards in the US Judicial Experience and Their Recognition in Italy*, Universita degli studi di Urbino, unpublished PhD thesis, 2004–2005, 66.

damages. This reasoning leads her to the conclusion that article 96 does not have a compensatory function.[922]

418. It is not our aim to enter into a discussion on the nature of the sanction of Rule 11, (c), (1) but one brief remark needs to be made. Rule 11, (c), (4) enumerates three examples of possible sanctions. Two of those cannot be equated to punitive damages: non-monetary directives and an order to pay a penalty into court (punitive damages are paid to the other party, not the state, although this criterion is not decisive[923]). The third, the payment of part or all of the reasonable attorney's fees and other expenses directly resulting from the violation to the winning party, could perhaps be interpreted as a punitive mechanism in light of the American Rule on costs. Indeed, the attorney's fees normally have to be borne by each party, even if prevailing. The argument that the shifting of any part of the fees is a form of punitive damages is thus not completely without merit.

419. There is some case law interpreting article 96, first paragraph as a punitive provision. Two decisions of the Court of Torre Annunziata, for instance, explicitly awarded "*danni punitivi*" *ex* article 96 in cases dealing with dilatory behaviour of insurance companies. The Court ordered the payment of these damages to the plaintiffs because the insurance companies had refused to negotiate a settlement of the claim, forcing the injured parties to go to court and waste time and money.[924, 925]

420. Other scholars, however, have (implicitly) dismissed the punitive character of the first paragraph of article 96 of the Code of Civil Procedure. They emphasise that the winning party must have suffered damage from the conduct of the losing party and must prove this damage.[926] Italian courts do not often employ this sanction because it is not easy for the prevailing party to prove that it suffered additional damages due to the claim it had to initiate or defend

922 S.A.L. Corongiu, *Punitive Damages Awards in the US Judicial Experience and Their Recognition in Italy*, Universita degli studi di Urbino, unpublished PhD thesis, 2004–2005, 66.

923 Of course, some states established split-recovery schemes. However, even then at least a portion of the award goes to the plaintiff.

924 Court of Torre Annunziata 24 February 2000, *Izzo v. Assitalia and other parties* and 14 March 2000, *Guerra and other parties v. SAI*, note A.M. Musy, "Punitive damages e resistenza temeraria in giudizio: regole definizioni e modelli istituzionali a confront", *Danno e Responsabilità* 11/2000, 1121–1127; M. Requejo Isidro, "Punitive Damages From a Private International Law Perspective" in H. Koziol & V. Wilcox (eds.), *Punitive Damages: Common Law and Civil Law Perspectives*, Vienna, Springer, 2009, 248.

925 The behaviour of the defendants amounted to insurance bad faith and in that regard these cases also fit under the section on punitive damages in insurance law: see *infra* no. 397 *et seq.*

926 S. Grossi & M.C. Pagni, *Commentary on the Italian Code of Civil Procedure*, New York, Oxford University Press, 2010, 148 and 149; M.A. Lupoi, "Recent developments in Italian Civil Procedure Law", *Civil Procedure Review* 2012, 31.

against.[927] In our view, the strict dependence between the damage suffered and the amount awarded is an important indicator of the compensatory intention of article 96, first paragraph. We therefore tend to lean towards a traditional, compensatory explanation of the provision.

421. In 2009, however, the Italian legislator inserted a third paragraph into article 96.[928] Pursuant to this new paragraph, an Italian court may, even of its own motion, order the losing party to pay to the other party an amount of money determined *ex aequo et bono*. This paragraph seems to have introduced punitive damages for abuse of process. A number of arguments support this assertion. First, there is no need to prove any injury as the sanction can be ordered in the absence of any evidence of actual harm. Second, the provision sets no limits on the amount the judge may award but instead leaves absolute discretion to the court when sanctioning the abusive behaviour.[929] Moreover, the paragraph protects the public interest of having an efficient judicial system by deterring abuse of process. The *ratio* of the rule is to punish the vexatory conduct of the losing party.[930] The damages awarded, however, flow to the defendant and not to the state. In our opinion, when we put all these characteristics together, a mechanism closely resembling punitive damages emerges.[931]

5.3.11. PROTECTION OF PERSONALITY RIGHTS

422. The field of personality rights offers an example of deterrence objectives going beyond the normal preventive side-effect of damages. In Germany personality rights received increased attention after the Second World War. Several reasons explain this development. First, the fundamental disregard for human rights and personal freedom during the era of National Socialism made the effective safeguarding of personality rights a stringent matter. Second, technological progress allowed for easier intrusion into the private

---

927 A. De Luca, "Cost and Fee Allocation in Italian Civil Procedure", 5, available at <www-personal.umich.edu/~purzel/national_reports/Italy.pdf>; M.A. Lupoi, "Recent developments in Italian Civil Procedure Law", *Civil Procedure Review* 2012, 31.

928 Article 45, paragraph 12 of Law no. 69 of 18 June 2009.

929 A. De Luca, "Cost and Fee Allocation in Italian Civil Procedure", 5, available at <www-personal.umich.edu/~purzel/national_reports/Italy.pdf>; M.A. Lupoi, "Recent developments in Italian Civil Procedure Law", *Civil Procedure Review* 2012, 31–32; E. Baldoni, *Punitive damages: a comparative analysis*, Universita degli studi di Macerata, unpublished Ph.D thesis, 2012, 135.

930 E. Baldoni, *Punitive damages: a comparative analysis*, Universita degli studi di Macerata, unpublished Ph.D thesis, 2012, 135.

931 See case law supporting this interpretation: Court of Varese, 23 January 2010 and Court of Piacenza, 7 December 2010, both available at <www.ilcaso.it>.

life of people through the use of various methods of surveillance. Lastly, the development of mass media augmented the likelihood of privacy violations.[932]

a. *The creation of a right of personality*

423. The *Bundesgerichtshof* recognised a general right of personality for the first time in 1954. The *Reichsgericht* (Imperial Court of Justice), the supreme criminal and civil court of the German empire from 1879 to 1945, had always declined to do so. In the so-called *Schachtbrief* case a lawyer wrote a letter to a newspaper on behalf of his client, minister Hjalmar Schacht. In it he requested the correction of certain false political statements. The newspaper published the letter under its "Letters from Readers" section. The reproduction did not make it clear that the lawyer was acting on behalf of his client. The publication thus shed a negative light on the lawyer as it gave the impression he was voicing his own political views instead of performing his professional duty. The *Bundesgerichtshof* referred to article 1 (Human Dignity) and article 2 (Personal Freedoms) of the 1949 Constitution and established a general personality right. On the basis of that right it ordered a corrective statement to be issued by the defendant.[933]

424. Four years later in the *Herrenreiter* judgment the *Bundesgerichtshof* awarded damages for infringement of personality rights to a brewery owner whose image was used in advertisement for potency pills. On the picture he was seen riding a horse at a show-jumping competition. The brewery owner sued for damages for injury to his feelings and reputation. The Supreme Court upheld the DM 10.000 granted to the plaintiff by the *Oberlandesgericht* Köln. It noted that article 847 BGB only allows for damages for pain and suffering in case of violations of body, health or freedom. The Court, however, adopted a *contra legem* interpretation of the provision and drew an analogy between infringements of freedom and serious violations of personality rights. Without such an approach no remedy would have been available.[934] It should be noted that only *serious* violations of personality rights could fall under article 847 BGB. This restriction resembles the tortfeasor-oriented approach of punitive damages. The latter can only be awarded for conduct meeting a certain level of

---

932 T.U. Amelung, "Damages Awards for Infringement of Privacy – The German Approach", 14 *Tulane European and Civil Law Forum* 1999, 19; M. Tolani, "U.S. Punitive Damages Before German Courts: A Comparative Analysis with Respect to the Ordre Public", 17 *Annual Survey of International & Comparative Law* 2011, 194.

933 BGH 25 May 1954, *BGHZ* 13, 334.

934 BGH 14 February 1958, *BHGZ* 26, 349; U. Magnus, "Punitive Damages and German Law" in L. Meurkens & E. Nordin (eds.), *The Power of Punitive Damages – Is Europe Missing Out?*, Cambridge – Antwerp – Portland, Intersentia, 2012, 253; H. Beverley-Smith, A. Ohly & A. Lucas-Schloetter, *Privacy, Property and Personality – Civil Law Perspectives on Commercial Appropriation*, New York, Cambridge University Press, 2005, 101.

reprehensibility.[935] Compensatory damages on the other hand are exclusively linked to the damage suffered.[936]

425. In *Ginseng*[937] the plaintiff was a law professor who had brought a ginseng root with him from a stay in Korea. He placed the root at the disposal of his friend, a professor in pharmacology, for research. The latter mentioned in a scientific article on ginseng roots that he had come into possession of genuine Korean ginseng roots "through the kind assistance" of the plaintiff. This led to the plaintiff being described in a popular scientific article as one of the best-known ginseng researchers of Europe. In an advertisement for its tonic containing ginseng the defendant company described the plaintiff as an important scientist who expressed an opinion on its value. Furthermore, in an editorial note, printed in immediate connection with an advertisement in another journal, allusion was made to the use of the product as an aphrodisiac. Both the advertisement and the journal were very widely distributed.

The plaintiff asserted that he had suffered an unauthorised attack on his personality right. In his opinion the advertisement gave rise to the impression that he had been paid to issue an opinion on a controversial topic outside his field of knowledge. Moreover, it seemed he had unprofessionally lent his name to the advertising of a doubtful product. He had suffered damage to his reputation as a learned man and been made an object of ridicule to the public and above all to his students. In relying on *Herrenreiter* he claimed damages for the harm done to him.

The *Bundesgerichtshof* confirmed the first instance decision by the *Landgericht* Düsseldorf which had awarded DM 8000. It emphasised the blameworthiness of the defendant's conduct. The Court again ruled that compensation for immaterial damage can only be awarded when the wrongdoer committed a serious fault. For the first time Germany's Supreme Court also alluded to a preventive consideration in cases of infringement of personality rights.[938, 939]

426. Over a decade later, in *Soraya*, the German Constitutional Court (*Bundesverfassungsgericht*) determined the steps taken by the *Bundesgerichtshof* to be in accordance with the Constitution. The ex-wife of the shah of Iran, Princess Soraya, had brought an action against a German illustrated weekly paper. The latter had brought a front-page story purporting to be the transcript

---

935 See *supra* no. 52.

936 H.Auf'mkolk, "U.S. punitive damages awards before German courts – Time for a new approach", *Freiburg Law Students Journal* 2007, 7.

937 BGH 19 September 1961, *BGHZ* 35, 363.

938 M. Tolani, "U.S. Punitive Damages Before German Courts: A Comparative Analysis with Respect to the Ordre Public", 17 *Annual Survey of International & Comparative Law* 2011, 194.

939 BGH 19 September 1961, *BGHZ* 35, 363.

of an interview with the plaintiff. The interview appeared to reveal much of the plaintiff's private and very private life but was wholly fictitious as it was invented by a freelance journalist. The defendant published the story without investigating whether the interview had actually taken place. A couple of months later the defendant's paper carried another story dealing with Princess Soraya. That time the defendant published a brief statement by the Princess to the effect that the alleged April interview had not taken place.

At first instance, on appeal as well as before the *Bundesgerichtshof* the plaintiff prevailed, receiving DM 15.000 in damages. The defendant then brought the case before the Constitutional Court. In its reasoning the *Bundesverfassungsgericht* made clear that the judiciary has the power to give concrete effect to the existence of legal rules found outside the written law created by the legislature. The Supreme Court had noticed a lacuna in the law and had decided to give expression to certain legal values which were implicitly accepted by the constitutional order (in particular articles 1 and 2 of the Constitution). Given the failure of legislative attempts to protect the right of personality, the courts were entitled to ensure this protection through case law.[940]

b. Caroline von Monaco I: deterrence in private law

427. An important further development took place in *Caroline von Monaco I*. The *Bundesgerichtshof* emphasised the preventive purpose of damages for breach of personality rights.[941] The facts of the case were quite similar to those in the *Soraya* judgment. Two widely distributed German magazines contained a fictitious interview with Princess Caroline. In addition, an article mentioned a number of untrue statements about her. Pictures of her taken by paparazzi also appeared on the cover. The Princess brought a claim for retraction and clarification as well as for monetary compensation for infringement of her personality right. Both at first instance as well as before the Court of Appeal of Hamburg the Princess was granted the right of correction as well as DM 30.000 in damages.[942]

428. The *Bundesgerichtshof* repeated that victims of a breach of the general right of personality are entitled to compensation if the violation is grave. The gravity of the violation depends *inter alia* on the defendant's motive and degree of culpability. The Court found such a grave intrusion on the facts of the case. The defendant knew that Princess Caroline did not want to be interviewed and

---

940 Bundesverfassungsgericht 14 February 1973, *Neue Juristische Wochenschrift* 1973, 1221.

941 U. Magnus, "Punitive Damages and German Law" in L. Meurkens & E. Nordin (eds.), *The Power of Punitive Damages – Is Europe Missing Out?*, Cambridge – Antwerp – Portland, Intersentia, 2012, 253; M. Tolani, "U.S. Punitive Damages Before German Courts: A Comparative Analysis with Respect to the Ordre Public", 17 *Annual Survey of International & Comparative Law* 2011, 195.

942 BGH 15 November 1994, *BGHZ* 128, 1.

instead created a fake interview about the problems in her private life. In order to boost its sales figures it deliberately exposed the plaintiff's private sphere to hundred thousands of readers.

429. The Court further ruled that the compensation of DM 30.000 was not sufficient. It no longer relied on article 847 BGB (damages for pain and suffering) as the basis for the monetary claim. Instead, the redress was held to flow from articles 1 and 2 of the German Constitution. Importantly, this form of redress is meant to serve a preventive purpose as well. Monetary compensation can only properly serve this aim of prevention if the amount due correlates to the fact that the infringement took place for commercial gain. This does not mean that the forced commercialisation of the Princess' personality right should lead to a complete absorption of profits (*i.e.* a restitutionary remedy[943]) but the profits made should be included as a factor in the calculation of the compensation. Where a famous personality is commercially exploited, the amount awarded must act as a real deterrent.[944]

430. When the Court of Appeal of Hamburg reconsidered the case, it followed the *Bundesgerichtshof*'s findings and awarded DM 180.000 in damages. This amount was the highest sum ever awarded in Germany for violation of personality rights as damages in similar cases were up to that point always limited to DM 10.000.[945]

431. Two points of the judgment require further elaboration. First, the Court took the publisher's motive and his degree of culpability in account when determining whether the violation of Caroline of Monaco's right was grave. This seems inconsistent with the victim-focused method of private law. Second, when setting the level of compensation for the breach of privacy, the German Supreme Court held that courts should consider the profits made by the tortfeasor in order to *deter* the defendant and other tabloids. By introducing the purpose of deterrence in violation of privacy cases the *Bundesgerichtshof* arguably crossed the line between compensation and punishment. Indeed, prevention is traditionally associated with objectives of criminal law. By explicitly making deterrence a factor in a private law dispute, the Court blurred the distinction between civil law and criminal law.[946] If the words of presiding judge Erich Steffen are anything to go by, this dogmatic landslide was intentionally caused.

943 T.U. Amelung, "Damages Awards for Infringement of Privacy – The German Approach", 14 *Tulane European and Civil Law Forum* 1999, 21.

944 BGH 15 November 1994, *BGHZ* 128, 1.

945 T.U. Amelung, "Damages Awards for Infringement of Privacy – The German Approach", 14 *Tulane European and Civil Law Forum* 1999, 22; V. Behr, "Myth and Reality of Punitive Damages in Germany", 24 *Journal of Law and Commerce* 2004–2005, 210.

946 T.U. Amelung, "Damages Awards for Infringement of Privacy – The German Approach", 14 *Tulane European and Civil Law Forum* 1999, 23.

He pointed out in an interview after the case that the damages should be painful for the publisher.[947]

432. In our opinion it could, therefore, be argued that the approach taken by the *Bundesgerichtshof* in *Caroline I* does not fit within the traditional framework of compensation but rather corresponds to the ideas behind punitive damages. By focusing on the wrongdoer('s act) and the need to prevent repetition by him or commission by others for the first time, the case breaks away from the orthodox position of loss-restoring and victim-orientated compensation.[948] The use of clear punitive[949] elements in *Caroline I* can thus be seen as breaking down the theoretical walls between private law and public law and demonstrates the existence of mechanisms close to – or at the very least pursuing the same aims as – punitive damages in German private law.

c. *Spanish Act 1/1982*

433. In the context of the protection of personality rights reference should also be made to article 9.3 of the Spanish *Ley Organica* 1/1982 *de proteccion civil del derecho al honor, a la intimidad personal y familiar y a la propia imagen*[950] (Act 1/1982 for the Civil Protection of Honour, Personal and Family Privacy and Image). The Act protects the right to honour, to privacy and to one's own image. Article 9.2 deals with remedies and lists compensation among the available measures to counter illegitimate invasions of the rights protected by the Act.[951] In article 9.3 it is stated that compensation will extend to non-pecuniary losses. These losses will be assessed by having regard to the circumstances of the case and the gravity of the actual damage caused. In addition to the remedy of compensation, article 9.2 grants the victim a claim for appropriation of the profits gained by the wrongdoer as a result of the violation.[952]

---

947 X., "ZRP-Rechtsgespräch mit Vorsitzendem Richter am BGH a. D. Dr. Erich Steffen", *Zeitschrift für Rechtspolitik* 1996, 366.

948 V. Behr, "Myth and Reality of Punitive Damages in Germany", 24 *Journal of Law and Commerce* 2004–2005, 211.

949 V. Behr, "Punitive Damages in American and German Law – Tendencies Towards Approximation of Apparently Irreconcilable Concepts", 78 *Chicago-Kent Law Review* 2003, 136; V. Behr, "Myth and Reality of Punitive Damages in Germany", 24 *Journal of Law and Commerce* 2004–2005, 210.; *contra* N. Jansen & L. Rademacher, "Punitive Damages in Germany" in H. Koziol & V. Wilcox (eds.), *Punitive Damages: Common Law and Civil Law Perspectives*, Vienna, Springer, 2009, 80 and 81; *contra* U. Magnus, "Punitive Damages and German Law" in L. Meurkens & E. Nordin (eds.), *The Power of Punitive Damages – Is Europe Missing Out?*, Cambridge – Antwerp – Portland, Intersentia, 2012, 253.

950 Ley Organica 1/1982, de 5 de mayo, de proteccion civil del derecho al honor, a la intimidad personal y familiar y a la propia imagen, *BOE* no. 115, 14 May 1982, 12546–12548, available at <www.boe.es/buscar/act.php?id=BOE-A-1982-11196>.

951 Article 9.2 c).

952 Article 9.2 d).

434. The argument that the claim for non-pecuniary damages represents a punitive function should in our opinion be rejected. The criterion of the gravity of the damage confirms the compensatory nature of the claim for damages.[953] It is inherent to compensatory damages that they are modulated according to the extent or the seriousness of the damage. Compensatory damages are focused on repairing the harm done to the victim and are completely based on that loss. One could only have acknowledged a punitive undertone in the provision if the Act had referred to the gravity of the conduct (*i.e.* a tortfeasor-oriented perspective).[954]

d. *Gain-based damages – Restitution of unjust enrichment*

435. A second aspect that merits attention is the possibility for the victim to obtain the profits gained by the defendant. Before the amendment to Act 1/1982 in 2010 the profits obtained through the injury of the victim were a factor to be considered in the assessment of damages (and, therefore, mentioned in article 9.3). In this regard reference can be made to the *Bundesgerichtshof* in *Caroline I* which stated that the profits gained by the tortfeasor should be considered when determining the appropriate *quantum* of damages.[955] Article 9.3 now no longer mentions this factor. Instead, article 9.2 of Act 1/1982 provides for the action for appropriation of unlawfully obtained profit as an independent claim which can be brought next to the claim for damages. The question here boils down to determining whether the disgorgement of the wrongdoer's profits obtained as a result of his unlawful act has a punitive slant.

436. We find the same question in intellectual property law as well. In the Member States investigated we identify provisions allowing victims of intellectual property violations to bring disgorgement claims. These originate from article 13 of Directive 2004/48 on the enforcement of intellectual property rights.[956] This article addresses the issue of damages for intellectual property infringements and enables the seizure of profits. In France, for instance, article L.

---

953 M. Martin-Casals & J. Solé Feliu, "The Protection of Personality Rights against Invasions by Mass Media in Spain" in H. Koziol & A. Warzilek (eds.), *Persönlichkeitsschutz gegenüber Massenmedien – The Protection of Personality Rights against Invasions by Mass Media*, Vienna, Springer, 2005, 331, no. 126; T. Vidal Martin, *El derecho al honor y su proteccion desde la constitucion Espanola*, Madrid, Boletin Oficial del Estado y Centro de Estudios Politicos y Constitucionales, 2000, 224; P. del Olmo, "Punitive Damages in Spain" in H. Koziol & V. Wilcox (eds.), *Punitive Damages: Common Law and Civil Law Perspectives*, Vienna, Springer, 2009, 142.

954 Note the opinion of Martin-Casals and Solé Feliu who argue that even the use of the gravity of the conduct could fit within a compensatory framework: M. Martin-Casals & J. Solé Feliu, "The Protection of Personality Rights against Invasions by Mass Media in Spain" in H. Koziol & A. Warzilek (eds.), *Persönlichkeitsschutz gegenüber Massenmedien – The Protection of Personality Rights against Invasions by Mass Media*, Vienna, Springer, 2005, 331–332, no. 128.

955 See *supra* no. 429.

956 Directive 2004/48/EC of the European Parliament and of the Council of 29 April 2004 on the enforcement of intellectual property rights, *OJ* L 157 of 30 April 2004, 45.

331-1-4 of the *Code de la propriété intellectuelle* (Code of Intellectual Property) allows a court to take the profit obtained from the counterfeiting act away from the defendant and award it to the plaintiff.

437. The discussion reminds us of English law and, in particular, the field of restitution (unjust enrichment) and gain-based damages (disgorgement damages or restitutionary damages).[957] When a court strips the defendant of the profits he obtained through his behaviour, it imposes a monetary remedy measured according to the defendant's gain rather than the plaintiff's loss. English law acknowledges the existence of gain-based or disgorgement damages. In the English legal system this non-compensatory remedy is situated somewhere in the no man's land between compensatory damages and punitive damages.[958]

438. In English law the claim for disgorgement of profits runs parallel with punitive damages only in the sense that by compelling the tortfeasor to transfer (a part of) the profits resulting from the unlawful conduct the victim could end up receiving more than the loss he suffered. The profits generated by the defendant could exceed the losses suffered by the claimant. In that sense the remedy of disgorgement of profits thus deviates from traditional tort law. In continental Europe, however, the claimant cannot end up with more than the amount of the damages incurred.[959] On the basis of a claim for unjust enrichment the victim cannot recover above the amount of his damages, even if the enrichment was larger.

439. Although the appropriation of profits in article 9.3 of the Spanish Act 1/1982 and article L. 331-1-4 bears some resemblances to claims for unjust enrichment, it needs to be distinguished from them. The plaintiff can in fact obtain more than his loss.[960] The next step is then to determine whether these damages have a punitive or deterrent agenda. In the context of Act 1-1982 scholars have argued that refunding the profit to the victim does not entail a private sanction.[961] Indeed, assuming for the sake of argument that the

---

957 For a comparative outlook on disgorgement of profits see: E. Hondius & A. Janssen, *Disgorgement of Profits: Gain-Based Remedies throughout the World*, Cham, Springer, 2015.

958 See V. Wilcox, "Punitive Damages in England" in H. Koziol & V. Wilcox (eds.), *Punitive Damages: Common Law and Civil Law Perspectives*, Vienna, Springer, 2009, 51-53.

959 J.-S. Borghetti, "Punitive Damages in France" in H. Koziol & V. Wilcox (eds.), *Punitive Damages: Common Law and Civil Law Perspectives*, Vienna, Springer, 2009, 59, footnote 14.

960 N. Jansen & L. Rademacher, "Punitive Damages in Germany" in H. Koziol & V. Wilcox (eds.), *Punitive Damages: Common Law and Civil Law Perspectives*, Vienna, Springer, 2009, 82; J.-S. Borghetti, "Punitive Damages in France" in H. Koziol & V. Wilcox (eds.), *Punitive Damages: Common Law and Civil Law Perspectives*, Vienna, Springer, 2009, 58.

961 M. Martin-Casals & J. Solé Feliu, "The Protection of Personality Rights against Invasions by Mass Media in Spain" in H. Koziol & A. Warzilek (eds.), *Persönlichkeitsschutz gegenüber Massenmedien - The Protection of Personality Rights against Invasions by Mass Media*,

provision enabling appropriation of damages does intend to pursue punitive or deterrent effects, one would have to admit that the provision is unable to reach this objective. Intentional and highly reprehensible behaviour can result in a lower amount of damages than mere negligent conduct because the damages are dependent on the amount of profits and not on the gravity of the wrongdoer's conduct.[962] In that view articles 9.2 and 9.3 of Act 1/1982 do not contain punitive intentions.[963] The same discussion exists with regard to the seizure of profits in intellectual property law.[964] Unjust enrichment should not be confused with punitive damages.[965]

Vienna, Springer, 2005, 336, no. 138; M. Otero Crespo, "Punitive Damages Under Spanish Law: A Subtle Recognition?" in L. Meurkens & E. Nordin (eds.), *The Power of Punitive Damages – Is Europe Missing Out?*, Cambridge – Antwerp – Portland, Intersentia, 2012, 299.

962 P. del Olmo, "Punitive Damages in Spain" in H. Koziol & V. Wilcox (eds.), *Punitive Damages: Common Law and Civil Law Perspectives*, Vienna, Springer, 2009, 143.

963 M. Otero Crespo, "Punitive Damages Under Spanish Law: A Subtle Recognition?" in L. Meurkens & E. Nordin (eds.), *The Power of Punitive Damages – Is Europe Missing Out?*, Cambridge – Antwerp – Portland, Intersentia, 2012, 298–299; P. del Olmo, "Punitive Damages in Spain" in H. Koziol & V. Wilcox (eds.), *Punitive Damages: Common Law and Civil Law Perspectives*, Vienna, Springer, 2009, 142–143.

964 In favour of a punitive interpretation: P. Scarso, "Punitive Damages in Italy" in H. Koziol & Venessa Wilcox (eds.), *Punitive Damages: Common Law and Civil Law Perspectives*, Vienna, Springer, 2009, 113; V. Behr, "Punitive Damages in American and German Law – Tendencies Towards Approximation of Apparently Irreconcilable Concepts", 78 *Chicago-Kent Law Review* 2003, 146; J.-S. Borghetti, "Punitive Damages in France" in H. Koziol & V. Wilcox (eds.), *Punitive Damages: Common Law and Civil Law Perspectives*, Vienna, Springer, 2009, 58–59. Rejecting such an interpretation: N. Jansen & L. Rademacher, "Punitive Damages in Germany" in H. Koziol & V. Wilcox (eds.), *Punitive Damages: Common Law and Civil Law Perspectives*, Vienna, Springer, 2009, 82; U. Magnus, "Punitive Damages and German Law" in L. Meurkens & E. Nordin (eds.), *The Power of Punitive Damages – Is Europe Missing Out?*, Cambridge – Antwerp – Portland, Intersentia, 2012, 256; T. Fausten & R. Hammesfahr, "Punitive damages in Europe: Concern, threat or non-issue?", Armonk, Swiss Re, 2012, 3; P. del Olmo, "Punitive Damages in Spain" in H. Koziol & V. Wilcox (eds.), *Punitive Damages: Common Law and Civil Law Perspectives*, Vienna, Springer, 2009, 144–145; M. Otero Crespo, "Punitive Damages Under Spanish Law: A Subtle Recognition?" in L. Meurkens & E. Nordin (eds.), *The Power of Punitive Damages – Is Europe Missing Out?*, Cambridge – Antwerp – Portland, Intersentia, 2012, 291 and 300; see also Recital 26 of Directive 2004/48 which explicitly rejects punitive damages: "*The aim is not to introduce an obligation to provide for punitive damages* [...]": C. Vanleenhove, "Punitive Damages and European Law: Quo Vademus?" in L. Meurkens & E. Nordin (eds.), *The Power of Punitive Damages – Is Europe Missing Out?*, Cambridge – Antwerp – Portland, Intersentia, 2012, 341, footnote 30. There is currently a request for a preliminary ruling pending before the European Court of Justice which might shed more light on the relationship between article 13 and Recital 26. In that case the Supreme Court of Poland seeks clarification as to whether a award, made at the request of a party, of damages as a pre-determined lump sum corresponding to twice or three times the amount of the appropriate fee pursuant to article 13 of the directive is permissible in light of recital 26 of the preamble (case C-367/15, *OJ* C 7/8 of 11 January 2016).

965 M. Otero Crespo, "Punitive Damages Under Spanish Law: A Subtle Recognition?" in L. Meurkens & E. Nordin (eds.), *The Power of Punitive Damages – Is Europe Missing Out?*, Cambridge – Antwerp – Portland, Intersentia, 2012, 300.

440. Whatever may be the correct view, the following inferences can be drawn. If and to the extent that the stripping of profits leads to an award of an amount of damages that exceeds the damages suffered, our contention that tort law sometimes steps away from the principle of strict compensation is strengthened. It would then be hypocritical to assert that the principle of strict compensation is one that merits international public policy protection.

441. Furthermore, gain-stripping, at the very least, holds some penal and/or deterrent consideration(s).[966] By disgorging the illegal profits of the defendant, courts try to communicate to the wrongdoer and the public that tort does not pay. That is actually one of the purposes of U.S. punitive damages.[967] It is also the underlying rationale of the second category established by Lord DEVLIN in *Rookes v. Barnard*.[968] It should be added, however, that punitive damages may be awarded under that second category, even if the defendant did not generate any profit.[969]

5.3.12. DETERRENCE OBJECTIVES IN COMBATING DISCRIMINATION IN LABOUR LAW

442. The presence of deterrent considerations in tort law can further be noticed in the area of labour law. EU legislation prohibits discrimination vis-à-vis employees and the European Court of Justice has ruled that sanctions for breach of this prohibition should have a deterrent effect. The issue will be looked at from a German perspective as the cases before the European Court of Justice were referred by German courts. The European Court of Justice's case law in this field evidently equally affects the other Member States.

443. In Directive 76/207 of 10 April 1984 ('Equal Treatment Directive')[970] the European Union laid down the principle of equal treatment for men and women with regard to access to employment and working conditions. The Directive required all Member States to abolish any domestic legislation contravening this fundamental principle (article 5.2(a)). It imposed on Member States the obligation to introduce into their national legal systems such measures as are

[966] T. Fausten & R. Hammesfahr, "Punitive damages in Europe: Concern, threat or non-issue?", Armonk, Swiss Re, 2012, 3.

[967] H. Auf'mkolk, "U.S. punitive damages awards before German courts – Time for a new approach", *Freiburg Law Students Journal* 2007, 8.

[968] See *supra* no. 375.

[969] V. Wilcox, "Punitive Damages in England" in H. Koziol & V. Wilcox (eds.), *Punitive Damages: Common Law and Civil Law Perspectives*, Vienna, Springer, 2009, 52.

[970] Council Directive 76/207 of 9 February 1976 on the implementation of the principle of equal treatment for men and women as regards access to employment, vocational training and promotion, and working conditions, *OJ* L 39 of 14 February 1976, 40.

necessary to enable all persons who consider themselves wronged by a failure to apply to them the principle of equal treatment to pursue their claims by judicial process (article 6).

444. Germany had transformed the Directive into German law in the form of article 611a BGB, introducing a prohibition on gender discrimination in employment. Article 611a (1) of the German Civil Code offered broad protection for workers in the course of their employment relationship as well as during the establishment thereof. Article 611a (2) specified that the employer was liable for damages when the employment relationship had not been established because of its breach of the prohibition of discrimination. It added that these damages were restricted to the loss incurred by the worker as a result of his reliance on the expectation that the establishment of the employment relationship would not be precluded by such a breach. This type of damages is called *Vertrauensschaden* and includes, for instance, losses from expenses made because the candidate believed that a contract was concluded and losses suffered when he refrained from contracting with a third party in the belief that he was already bound by the first contract.[971] There was thus no right for the candidate to be appointed to the position he applied for. In practice labour courts awarded only very small amounts of damages as it was believed that an applicant who had been the victim of discrimination suffered only minimal actual losses, such as frustrated costs of application (*i.e.* expenses for postage).[972]

a. Von Colson

445. In the case of *Sabine von Colson and Elisabeth Kamann v. Land Nordrhein-Westfalen* ('*Von Colson*')[973] the European Court of Justice examined the German implementation of Equal Treatment Directive 76/207. Two women applied for two positions at the all-male Werl prison in North Rhine Westphalia (Germany). Due to the problems and risks attached to female employees working in a prison populated by men, the recruitment officials decided to engage two less well-qualified men to fill the vacancies. The applicants felt they were unlawfully denied employment on grounds of their sex and sought compensation before the German courts. The Hamm Labour Court (*Arbeitsgericht*) referred several questions to the European Court of Justice for a preliminary ruling.

---

971 V. Behr, "Myth and Reality of Punitive Damages in Germany", 24 *Journal of Law and Commerce* 2004–2005, 214, footnote 91.

972 V. Behr, "Myth and Reality of Punitive Damages in Germany", 24 *Journal of Law and Commerce* 2004–2005, 215.

973 ECJ 10 April 1984, Sabine von Colson and Elisabeth Kamann v. Land Nordrhein-Westfalen, C-14/83, *ECR* 1984, 1891. There is also a corresponding case of the same day: ECJ 10 April 1984, Dorit Harz v. Deutsche Tradax GmbH, C-79/83, *ECR* 1984, p. 1921.

446. The European Court of Justice found the transformation of the Directive in article 611a to be inadequate in light of article 6 of the Directive. It held that:

> "*The principle of the effective transposition of the directive requires that the sanctions must be of such nature as to constitute appropriate compensation for the candidate discriminated against and for the employer a means of pressure which it would be unwise to disregard and which would prompt him to respect the principle of equal treatment. A national measure which provides for compensation only for losses actually incurred through reliance on an expectation ("Vertrauensschaden") is not sufficient to ensure compliance with that principle.*"[974]

447. The European Court of Justice acknowledged that Member States are left free to choose appropriate measures to remedy violations of the principle of equal treatment. It ruled, however, that the sanction for unlawful discrimination must be such as "*to guarantee real and effective judicial protection*" as well as having "*a real deterrent effect on the employer*".[975] The European Court of Justice called for higher damages than the costs of postage and other application expenses to be awarded in addition to requiring liability to go beyond mere symbolic payment:[976]

> "*If a Member State chooses to penalize breaches (...) by the award of compensation, then in order to ensure that it is effective and that it has a deterrent effect, that compensation must in any event be adequate in relation to the damage sustained and must therefore amount to more than purely nominal compensation such as, for example, the reimbursement only of the expenses incurred in connection with the application.*"[977]

448. Although the European Court of Justice muddied the waters in this case by using confusing and contradicting language referring to the sanction as compensatory ("*compensation*", "*in relation to the damage sustained*") and non-compensatory ("*deterrent effect*", "*penalize*")[978], it could be argued that these damages for discrimination cannot be explained within the traditional compensatory framework but conversely fit into the concept of punitive

[974] ECJ 10 April 1984, Sabine von Colson and Elisabeth Kamann v. Land Nordrhein-Westfalen, C-14/83, *ECR* 1984, 1891, par. 14.

[975] ECJ 10 April 1984, Sabine von Colson and Elisabeth Kamann v. Land Nordrhein-Westfalen, C-14/83, *ECR* 1984, 1891, par. 23.

[976] N. Jansen & L. Rademacher, "Punitive Damages in Germany" in H. Koziol & V. Wilcox (eds.), *Punitive Damages: Common Law and Civil Law Perspectives*, Vienna, Springer, 2009, 85.

[977] ECJ 10 April 1984, Sabine von Colson and Elisabeth Kamann v. Land Nordrhein-Westfalen, C-14/83, *ECR* 1984, 1891, par. 28.

[978] B.A. Koch, "Punitive Damages in European Law" in H. Koziol & V. Wilcox (eds.), *Punitive Damages: Common Law and Civil Law Perspectives*, Vienna, Springer, 2009, 204.

damages.[979] In its judgment the European Court of Justice arguably ordered the penetration of the objective of deterrence into the realm of private law. In our view this in turn has an impact on the content of the public policy exception in private international law matters.

b. Post-Von Colson case law

449. In order to comply with the requirements of the Directive, as clarified by the European Court of Justice, the German legislator intervened and revised article 611a BGB. The amended version of article 611a (2) provided that the applicant discriminated against could claim appropriate financial compensation not exceeding three months' wages. However, the amendment of the provision did not satisfy the European Court of Justice.

450. In the case of *Nils Draehmpaehl v. Urania Immobilienservice OHG* (*'Draehmpaehl'*)[980] the European Court of Justice had to deal with a case of discriminatory selection for employment. Mr. Draehmpaehl responded to a job advertisement in a Hamburg newspaper stating that defendant Urania was looking for "an experienced female assistant". He did not get a reply and sued Urania in the Hamburg Labour Court (*Arbeitsgericht*) claiming that he was the best qualified applicant and that he had suffered from sex discrimination. He asked for compensation for three and a half months' wages based on article 611a BGB. It should be noted that the plaintiff thus ignored the legislative cap of three months, presumably to allow for judicial testing of the reach of the German legislation by the European Court of Justice.[981]

451. For the second time the European Court of Justice concluded that the German transposition did not comply with the Directive. The European Court of Justice ruled that Member States are not precluded from imposing a ceiling on the compensation payable where the applicant would not have obtained the position due to another candidate's superior profile. Such upper ceiling is not allowed where the applicant would have gotten the job if the discrimination had

---

979 V. Behr, "Myth and Reality of Punitive Damages in Germany", 24 *Journal of Law and Commerce* 2004–2005, 215; N. Jansen & L. Rademacher, "Punitive Damages in Germany" in H. Koziol & V. Wilcox (eds.), *Punitive Damages: Common Law and Civil Law Perspectives*, Vienna, Springer, 2009, 84–85; *contra* B.A. Koch, "Punitive Damages in European Law" in H. Koziol & V. Wilcox (eds.), *Punitive Damages: Common Law and Civil Law Perspectives*, Vienna, Springer, 2009, 204.

980 ECJ 22 April 1997, Nils Draehmpaehl v. Urania Immobilienservice OHG, C-180/95, *ECR* 1997, 2195.

981 V. Behr, "Myth and Reality of Punitive Damages in Germany", 24 *Journal of Law and Commerce* 2004–2005, 213.

not occurred.[982] The European Court of Justice did, however, deviate from its decision in *Marshall II* as it seemed to depart from the need of full compensation in favour of the standard of adequate compensation for the employee.

452. *M. Helen Marshall v. Southampton and South-West Hampshire Area Health Authority* ('*Marshall II*')[983] concerned a discriminatory dismissal. Miss Marshall felt she had been the victim of unlawful discrimination on grounds of sex as she had been dismissed because she had attained the qualifying age for a State pension, that age being different under national legislation for women than for men. Her claim was upheld by the Court of Appeal which remitted the question of compensation to the Industrial Tribunal. The English Sex Discrimination Act, however, provided for an *ex ante* cap on the damages an Industrial Tribunal could award.

In his Opinion, Advocate-General VAN GERVEN took the view that compensation must be adequate in relation to the damage sustained but does not have to be equal thereto.[984] He did not find the imposition of an upper limit on the compensation payable an automatic failure to implement the Directive.[985] The European Court of Justice, however, declined to follow the Advocate General's reasoning and reaffirmed the principle of full compensation.[986] England's system use of an upper limit was, therefore, found to be in violation of the Directive.[987]

453. The lesson to be drawn from both *Marshall II* and *Draehmpaehl* is that limits on damages are not acceptable in light of the Directive since they may discourage injured parties from bringing their case to court and they may, therefore, have no dissuasive effect on the employer. More importantly, the caps are criticised because they prevent victims from receiving compensation adequate to the losses sustained.[988]

As opposed to its *Marshall II* decision, the European Court of Justice in *Draehmpaehl* did not mention the need for "full" compensation but accepts

---

982 ECJ 22 April 1997, Nils Draehmpaehl v. Urania Immobilienservice OHG, C-180/95, *ECR* 1997, 2195, par. 37.

983 ECJ 2 August 1993, M. Helen Marshall v. Southampton and South-West Hampshire Area Health Authority, C-271-91, *ECR* 1993, 4367.

984 Opinion of Mr. Advocate General Van Gerven delivered on 26 January 1993, *ECR* 1993, 4367, par. 17.

985 Opinion of Mr. Advocate General Van Gerven delivered on 26 January 1993, *ECR* 1993, 4367, par. 29.

986 ECJ 2 August 1993, M. Helen Marshall v. Southampton and South-West Hampshire Area Health Authority, C-271-91, *ECR* 1993, 4367, par. 26.

987 ECJ 2 August 1993, M. Helen Marshall v. Southampton and South-West Hampshire Area Health Authority, C-271-91, *ECR* 1993, 4367, par. 32.

988 B.A. Koch, "Punitive Damages in European Law" in H. Koziol & V. Wilcox (eds.), *Punitive Damages: Common Law and Civil Law Perspectives*, Vienna, Springer, 2009, 205.

"adequate" compensation as effective judicial protection.[989] In our view the European Court of Justice thus allowed for a deviation from the principle of full compensation. Admittedly, the scope of this deviation is limited to the remedies against discrimination in the work-related arena but it constitutes a deviation nonetheless. Such a movement could suffice to alter the international public policy label attached to the principle of full compensation in private law, especially when taking the European Court of Justice's call for deterrent mechanisms in *Von Colson* and *Draehmpaehl* into account.

c. *Directive 2002/73*

454. The deterrence objective of the damages for breach of employment discrimination, as pronounced by the European Court of Justice, found its way into an amendment of the Equal Treatment Directive. This amendment to the original Equal Treatment Directive came into effect in 2002.[990] Under paragraph 2 of new article 6 Member States have to "*introduce into their national legal systems such measures as are necessary to ensure real and effective compensation or reparation as the Member States so determine for the loss and damage sustained by a person injured as a result of discrimination, in a way which is dissuasive and proportionate to the damage suffered; such compensation or reparation may not be restricted by the fixing of a prior upper limit* (...)". Article 8d further requires Member States to "*lay down the rules on sanctions applicable to infringements of the national provisions adopted pursuant to this Directive, and [to] take all measures necessary to ensure that they are applied. The sanctions, which may comprise the payment of compensation to the victim, must be* effective, proportionate and dissuasive" (emphasis added).

455. This last phrase is nothing novel; it finds its origin in the *Commission v. Hellenic Republic* (*'Greek Maize'*) judgment of the European Court of Justice.[991] In that case the Court pointed out that, according to article 5 of the EEC Treaty, Member States have to take all measures necessary to guarantee the application and effectiveness of Community law.[992] As was already said in *Von Colson*, the Member States are free to choose the penalties necessary to achieve this. They

---

989 K. Oliphant, "The Nature and Assessment of Damages" in H. Koziol & R. Schulze (eds.), *Tort Law of the European Community*, Vienna, Springer, 2008, 253.

990 Directive 2002/73 of the European Parliament and of the Council of 23 September 2002 amending Council Directive 76/207 on the implementation of the principle of equal treatment for men and women as regards access to employment, vocational training and promotion, and working conditions, *OJ* L 269 of 5 October 2002, 15.

991 ECJ 21 September 1989, Commission of the European Communities v. Hellenic Republic, C-387/97, *ECR* 1989, 2965.

992 ECJ 21 September 1989, Commission of the European Communities v. Hellenic Republic, C-387/97, *ECR* 1989, 2965, par. 23.

do, however, have to ensure that infringements of Community law are penalised under conditions, both procedural and substantial, which are analogous to those applicable to infringements of national law of a similar nature and importance and which, in any event, make the penalty "*effective, proportionate and dissuasive*".[993] Despite its 'boiler-plate' character, this formula has ever since been pervasive throughout the various pieces of European legislation and EU case law.[994] Most of the occurrences of this mantra[995] use the word "penalties" which seems to imply that they do not wish to touch upon private law remedies, whereas others speak of "sanctions" with some specifying that this is "without prejudice to Member States' civil liability regimes".[996] This would mean they wish to draw a distinction between private law remedies and administrative or other "sanctions".[997]

456. The German *Allgemeines Gleichbehandlungsgesetz* (AGG) (Equal Treatment Act) of 2006 now provides for the prohibition on discrimination previously found in article 611a BGB. The Act is the incorporation of four EU Directives (including Directive 2002/73 amending Directive 76/207) into German law.[998] Article 15 reflects the deterrence function recognised by the European Court of Justice. The ceiling (of 3 monthly salaries) on the available damages now only applies if the employee would not have been recruited if the selection had been made without unequal treatment. In Germany, therefore, candidates who never had a ghost of a chance of employment, can obtain substantial amounts of damages if they were discriminated against in the process. One could see a regulatory function in this sanction as it punishes the employer for unwanted and socially reprehensible conduct.[999] Although Jansen

---

993 ECJ 21 September 1989, Commission of the European Communities v. Hellenic Republic, C-387/97, *ECR* 1989, 2965, par. 24.

994 B.A. Koch, "Punitive Damages in European Law" in H. Koziol & V. Wilcox (eds.), *Punitive Damages: Common Law and Civil Law Perspectives*, Vienna, Springer, 2009, 200.

995 C. Vanleenhove, "Punitive Damages and European Law: Quo Vademus?" in L. Meurkens & E. Nordin (eds.), *The Power of Punitive Damages - Is Europe Missing Out?*, Cambridge - Antwerp - Portland, Intersentia, 2012, 345.

996 For an extensive list of each category see: B.A. Koch, "Punitive Damages in European Law" in H. Koziol & V. Wilcox (eds.), *Punitive Damages: Common Law and Civil Law Perspectives*, Vienna, Springer, 2009, 200–201, footnotes 15–17.

997 B.A. Koch, "Punitive Damages in European Law" in H. Koziol & V. Wilcox (eds.), *Punitive Damages: Common Law and Civil Law Perspectives*, Vienna, Springer, 2009, 200–201.

998 The other three are: Council Directive 2000/43 implementing the principle of equal treatment between persons irrespective of racial or ethnic origin, Council Directive 2000/78 establishing a general framework for equal treatment in employment and occupation and Council Directive 2004/113 implementing the principle of equal treatment between men and women in the access to and supply of goods and services.

999 N. Jansen & L. Rademacher, "Punitive Damages in Germany" in H. Koziol & Vanessa Wilcox (eds.), *Punitive Damages: Common Law and Civil Law Perspectives*, Vienna, Springer, 2009, 85.

and RADEMACHER view this rule as an "*insignificant exception*"[1000] to the basic principle of compensation, it is our contention that it is relevant in changing the international public policy nature of the full compensation rule. Even if not sufficient on its own to have such an impact, combined with the other traces of punitive mechanisms discussed in this chapter, it forms an element in the process of refuting the idea of incorporating the full compensation rule into international public policy.

5.3.13. COVERT 'PUNITIVE DAMAGES' AWARDED UNDER THE GUISE OF MORAL DAMAGES

457. In our opinion moral damages offer a breeding ground for punitive damages. An inherent characteristic of these extra-patrimonial damages is that they cannot be quantified monetarily in an objective manner. It is, for example, very difficult to place a monetary value on pain and suffering. Judges, therefore, inevitably enjoy freedom when assessing these types of damages. This enables them to consider multiple aspects rather than solely the extent of the harm suffered by the victim. If this theory is correct, then parts of moral damages are in fact covert punitive damages.

458. In France JOURDAIN expresses this idea as well. He notes that some French lawyers and academics believe that French courts sometimes calculate damages not exclusively using the harm suffered by the plaintiff. These courts take additional factors into account, such as the behaviour of the wrongdoer. If the courts find the conduct to be a deliberate violation of the victim's rights, they punish the tortfeasor by inflating the moral damages.[1001, 1002] The difference between the moral damages actually awarded and what the moral damages would have been if the judge had not deemed expansion of the moral damages necessary, is punitive in nature. These additional damages come close to punitive damages as they are measured by the reprehensibility of the defendant's actions.

459. French courts enjoy a wide discretion to evaluate and set the damages in the cases before them. In that regard they escape the control of the French

---

[1000] N. Jansen & L. Rademacher, "Punitive Damages in Germany" in H. Koziol & V. Wilcox (eds.), *Punitive Damages: Common Law and Civil Law Perspectives*, Vienna, Springer, 2009, 85.

[1001] P. Jourdain, "Rapport introductif", *Les Petites Affiches* 2002, 3, no. 7.

[1002] Similarly, the information report of the First Legislative Chamber Law Commission on the reform of French civil liability, the so-called BÉTEILLE & ANZIANI report, refers to the statements made by CARVAL who identifies the same practice in Italian and German civil courts: A. Anziani & L. Béteille, Rapport d'information fait au nom de la commission des lois constitutionnelles par le groupe de travail relative à la responsabilité civile, 15 July 2009, 84 available at: <www.senat.fr/rap/r08-558/r08-5581.pdf>.

Supreme Court. The *Cour de cassation* can only quash a decision if it finds that the lower court has not adhered to the principle of *réparation intégrale* (full reparation). French judges are, however, under no obligation to explain how they reached the amount of damages they awarded. They can resort to stating that the harm suffered will be compensated by the damages granted, without any further justification or elaboration. Only in the rare cases[1003] where courts do explain how they came to the amount of damages and indicate that they took more factors than only the harm into account, will the *Cour de cassation* be able to intervene.[1004]

460. The *réparation intégrale* rule is also a reason why it is by no means easy, if at all possible, to prove the existence of these hidden punitive damages within moral damages. The full reparation standard demands an assessment *in concreto* of the harm suffered. Courts should always look at the facts of the case and cannot fall back on so-called *barèmes*, *i.e.* pre-determined standardised scales of damages, to set the appropriate level of damages. The official admittance of *barèmes* would have opened an opportunity to confirm the existence and measure the size of punitive damages within moral damages. A simple comparison between the *barème* and the amount of moral damages in the judgment would have uncovered the punitive intentions of the judge.[1005]

461. It is very likely that the judges use the *barèmes* unofficially. However, judges will not admit to this in their decision out of fear of having their judgment reversed. We are, therefore, left in the dark as to which of the *barèmes* the court has used (if it has used any at all) and cannot make any comparisons to the amount actually awarded. The prohibition on the use of these *barèmes* thus forms an important obstacle when attempting to prove the presence of punitive elements in moral damage awards.[1006]

462. There are, however, other methods to show that moral damages are sometimes used by courts as a tool to punish the defendant. A study by the French scholar Bourrié-Quenillet, for instance, looked at a number of French cases in which relatives of a deceased person received moral damages. The results of the analysis revealed a difference in the *quantum* of moral

---

1003 See, for instance, a judgment of the Cour de Cassation in which the Cour de Cassation annulled the lower court's decision because damages were set by taking the defendant's fault into consideration: Cass. 8 May 1996, *Bull. Civ.* II, no. 358.

1004 J.-S. Borghetti, "Punitive Damages in France" in H. Koziol & V. Wilcox (eds.), *Punitive Damages: Common Law and Civil Law Perspectives*, Vienna, Springer, 2009, 62.

1005 J.-S. Borghetti, "Punitive Damages in France" in H. Koziol & V. Wilcox (eds.), *Punitive Damages: Common Law and Civil Law Perspectives*, Vienna, Springer, 2009, 63.

1006 J.-S. Borghetti, "Punitive Damages in France" in H. Koziol & V. Wilcox (eds.), *Punitive Damages: Common Law and Civil Law Perspectives*, Vienna, Springer, 2009, 63.

damages depending on whether the death was caused by the defendant's fault or not. Bourrié-Quenillet found that the average award for moral damages was higher when the defendant was sued on the basis of fault liability than on the basis of strict liability. Admittedly, the study examined only a small sample of decisions, namely 536 judgments from the Court of Appeals of Nîmes, Montpellier, Rennes and Paris. The cases involved 1.765 relatives in total. Despite the relatively limited scale, the work nevertheless seems to indicate the existence of hidden punitive considerations in these types of moral damages.[1007]

5.3.14. RECITAL 32 OF THE ROME II REGULATION

463. The Rome II Regulation provides the rules designating the applicable law to non-contractual obligations. Article 26 operates as a general public policy exception, dismissing those provisions of the applicable law whose application is manifestly incompatible with the forum's (international) public policy. In addition to that, the preamble offers more clarity on the European Union's position towards foreign punitive damages. Recital 32, in its relevant part, reads: "*In particular, the application of a provision of the law designated by this Regulation which would have the effect of causing non-compensatory exemplary or punitive damages of an excessive nature to be awarded may, depending on the circumstances of the case and the legal order of the Member State of the court seized, be regarded as being contrary to the public policy* (ordre public) *of the forum.*"

464. As already indicated in chapter 3[1008], recital 32 of the Rome II Regulation puts forward the idea that punitive damages are, as such, not contrary to international public policy. The application of foreign punitive damages can only be barred if the punitive damages to be awarded are excessive. Despite the recital's lack of binding effect, its message is clear: the European legislator does not oppose the concept of punitive damages in the private international law context of applicable law. It is the (potential) disproportionality of such measures that is frowned upon by the European drafters. Although the Rome II Regulation contains rules addressing the question of applicable law, the approach taken may impact the concept of international public policy in matters of enforcement as well.[1009]

1007 M. Bourrié-Quenillet, *L'indemnisation des proches d'une victime décédée accidentellement. Étude d'informatique judiciaire*, Ph.D thesis University of Montpellier 1, 1983, 97–100.

1008 See *supra* no. 195.

1009 C.I. Nagy, "Recognition and enforcement of US judgments involving punitive damages in continental Europe", *Nederlands Internationaal Privaatrecht* 2012, 10.

5.3.15. PUNITIVE DAMAGES THROUGH THE BACKDOOR: THE PRINCIPLE OF EQUIVALENCE IN EU LAW

465. National courts are in certain instances required to award punitive damages for breaches of EU law. According to the EU principle of equivalence remedies made available for the protection of EU rights by national law must not be less favourable than those available for similar domestic rights. In *Brasserie du Pêcheur SA v. Federal Republic of Germany and Reg. v. Secretary of State for Transport, Ex parte Factortame Ltd. (no. 4)* ('*Brasserie du Pêcheur and Factortame*') it was, therefore, established that:

> "(...) *it must be possible to award specific damages, such as the exemplary damages provided for by English law, pursuant to claims or actions founded on Community law, if such damages may be awarded pursuant to similar claims or actions founded on domestic law.*"[1010]

466. Similarly, in *Manfredi v. Lloyd Adriatico Assicurazioni SpA* ('*Manfredi*') the Court held that national courts can award punitive damages for violations of Community law (in this case: an infringement of article 81 EC, now article 101 TFEU) if their national legal system awards such damages for domestic claims.[1011] Following its ruling in *Brasserie du Pêcheur and Factortame* the European Court of Justice affirmed that: "(...) *first, in accordance with the principle of equivalence, if it is possible to award specific damages, such as exemplary or punitive damages, in domestic actions similar to actions founded on the Community competition rules, it must also be possible to award such damages in actions founded on Community rules*".[1012] It is important to understand that in both cases the non-compensatory part of the award is not founded in EU law but is treated as a purely national peculiarity respected at the European level.[1013]

1010 Joined cases ECJ 5 March 1996, Brasserie du Pêcheur SA v. Bundesrepublik Deutschland and The Queen v. Secretary of State for Transport, ex parte: Factortame Ltd and others, *ECR* 1996, 1029, par. 90.

1011 Joined cases ECJ 13 July 2006, Vincenzo Manfredi v. Lloyd Adriatico Assicurazioni SpA, Antonio Cannito v. Fondiaria Sai SpA and Nicolò Tricarico and Pasqualina Murgolo v. Assitalia SpA, *ECR* 2006, 6619; B.A. Koch, "Punitive Damages in European Law" in H. Koziol & V. Wilcox (eds.), *Punitive Damages: Common Law and Civil Law Perspectives*, Vienna, Springer, 2009, 206.

1012 Joined cases ECJ 13 July 2006, Vincenzo Manfredi v. Lloyd Adriatico Assicurazioni SpA, Antonio Cannito v. Fondiaria Sai SpA and Nicolò Tricarico and Pasqualina Murgolo v. Assitalia SpA, *ECR* 2006, 6619, par. 99.

1013 B.A. Koch, "Punitive Damages in European Law" in H. Koziol & V. Wilcox (eds.), *Punitive Damages: Common Law and Civil Law Perspectives*, Vienna, Springer, 2009, 206.

467. The equivalence principle raises issues relevant to private international law. Under section 14(5) of the Irish Competition Act, for instance, exemplary damages are available in actions for breach of national competition law. An Irish judge is thus bound to award punitive damages for violations of EU antitrust rules. When the enforcement of this decision is sought in another Member State, Community law becomes contradictory. On the one hand, it obliges the granting of punitive damages (pursuant to the equivalence principle) but it, on the other hand, does not prevent the requested court from invoking (international) public policy to decline enforcement of the judgment (on the basis of article 46 *iuncto* article 45, 1, a) of the Brussels I*bis* Regulation).[1014] However, this issue will presumably not arise in practice as it seems unlikely that a punitive award originating in one Member State will be denied enforcement in another Member State. Thus far no reported case law has dealt with this situation. The compatibility of punitive damages with international public policy, the core message of this chapter, also applies in the intra-European context. Member States' courts should not decline the enforcement of punitive damages granted by a court of another Member State. The restrictive wording of the public policy exception in article 45, 1, a) Brussels I*bis* Regulation (a *manifest* contrariety with public policy is required to justify refusal) and the principle of mutual trust between Member States add further weight to this contention.[1015]

5.3.16. LEGISLATIVE PROPOSALS INTRODUCING PUNITIVE DAMAGES

468. In addition to the various instruments elaborated on in this chapter, we should also refer to a number of legislative initiatives to introduce punitive damages. These proposals did not reach their goal in the end but they are, nevertheless, indications of a growing willingness to accept punitive damages as a remedy. The proponents must have felt that punitive damages could fit into the legal system. *A fortiori*, the advocates, therefore, must have believed that punitive damages do not cause any public policy concerns (in a private international law sense).

1014 G. Cavalier & J.-S. Queguiner, "Punitive Damages and French Public Policy", Lyon, Lyon Symposium, 4–5 October, 2007, 9, available at: <http://papers.ssrn.com/sol3/papers.cfm?abstract_id=1174363>; C. Vanleenhove, "Punitive Damages and European Law: Quo Vademus?" in L. Meurkens & E. Nordin (eds.), *The Power of Punitive Damages – Is Europe Missing Out?*, Cambridge – Antwerp – Portland, Intersentia, 2012, 347.

1015 M. Requejo Isidro, "Punitive Damages: How Do They Look Like When Seen From Abroad?" in L. Meurkens & E. Nordin (eds.), *The Power of Punitive Damages – Is Europe Missing Out?*, Cambridge – Antwerp – Portland, Intersentia, 2012, 326–327.

a. *Reform drafts of the French Civil Code*

469. In the last decade three different drafts for reform of the French Civil Code have seen the light. In all of them we find a provision introducing punitive damages into the French legal system. The insertion of such a provision indicates the drafters' agreement on the admissibility of the concept in France.[1016] The drafts display divergent opinions as to the requirements (type of damaging conduct, calculation basis, upper limit, beneficiaries...) for an award of punitive damages.[1017] The aim of this chapter of the book is to identify penal and/or deterrent mechanism in private law in order to draw conclusions for the possible admission of such damages via private international law. The objective of this chapter and of the book as a whole is not to reflect on the desirability and feasibility of full-blown punitive damages in continental EU Member States. We will, therefore, not elaborate too extensively on the content of the three drafts, nor will we compare them in detail.[1018]

470. The first draft was the work of a group of academics and judges who took the initiative to propose a revision of the law of obligations (and the law of prescription).[1019] They had found inspiration in the success of a similar project in Germany. The draft is better known as the "Catala Draft", called after Professor Pierre Catala who was one of the leading forces behind the group. It was presented to the French Minister of Justice in 2005. Article 1371 of the Catala Draft authorises judges to award punitive damages for manifestly deliberate wrongs, in particular "lucrative" wrongs. "Lucrative" wrongs are voluntary infringements of legal rules or duties of which the authors know that they will lead to less liability than the profit they will generate. These lucrative wrongs form the second category of conduct for which exemplary damages are available in England.[1020] In the absence of other sanctions (such as criminal

1016 J.-S. Borghetti, "Punitive Damages in France" in H. Koziol & V. Wilcox (eds.), *Punitive Damages: Common Law and Civil Law Perspectives*, Vienna, Springer, 2009, 70; C. Mahé, "Punitive damages in the competing reform drafts of the French Civil Code" in L. Meurkens & E. Nordin (eds.), *The Power of Punitive Damages – Is Europe Missing Out?*, Cambridge – Antwerp – Portland, Intersentia, 2012, 261.

1017 C. Mahé, "Punitive damages in the competing reform drafts of the French Civil Code" in L. Meurkens & E. Nordin (eds.), *The Power of Punitive Damages – Is Europe Missing Out?*, Cambridge – Antwerp – Portland, Intersentia, 2012, 262.

1018 For an in-depth comparison of the three drafts: C. Mahé, "Punitive damages in the competing reform drafts of the French Civil Code" in L. Meurkens & E. Nordin (eds.), *The Power of Punitive Damages – Is Europe Missing Out?*, Cambridge – Antwerp – Portland, Intersentia, 2012, 264–277.

1019 Avant-projet de réforme du droit des obligations (Articles 1101 à 1386 du Code civil) et du droit de la prescription (Articles 2234 à 2281 du Code civil), Rapport à Monsieur Pascal Clément, Garde des Sceaux, Ministre de la Justice, September 2005, supervised by Professors P. Catala and G. Viney, available at <www.justice.gouv.fr/art_pix/RAPPORTCATALASEPTEMBRE2005.pdf>.

1020 See *supra* no. 375.

punishment), the wrongdoers will not be deterred as they stand to gain more than the possible compensation they will have to pay.[1021] The judge may direct part of the punitive damages award to the treasury. Article 1371 of the CATALA Draft further provides that the judge must provide specific reasons for ordering such punitive damages and that he must clearly distinguish their amount from that of other damages awarded to the victim. Lastly, punitive damages may not be the subject of a contract of insurance.[1022] In the later draft of the Ministry of Justice, however, punitive damages were not mentioned.[1023]

471. The call for the creation of a remedy for punitive damages, however, resurfaced in a Senate Information Report of 2009[1024] and, more importantly, in the subsequent legislative proposal of 2010.[1025] The latter document is mostly referred to as the "BÉTEILLE Proposal", after the First Chamber Member Laurent BÉTEILLE who initiated it. Proposed article 1386-25 introduces punitive damages into French law. It provides that a judge can award punitive damages if the law expressly provides so and the damage results from a deliberate wrong or a deliberate breach of contract. It is required that the damage has led to an enrichment of the wrongdoer which compensatory damages cannot eliminate. The judge has to motivate his decision and the amount of the punitive damages may not exceed double the amount of the compensatory damages. The judge decides which share of the award will be paid to the victim. The remaining part will be directed to a fund intended to compensate harm similar to that suffered by the victim. If such a fund does not exist, that portion of the award will instead end up in the treasury.[1026] The Proposal, however, expired on 18 October 2011 and punitive damages thus remain – at least officially – outside French law.

1021 J.-S. Borghetti, "Punitive Damages in France" in H. Koziol & V. Wilcox (eds.), *Punitive Damages: Common Law and Civil Law Perspectives*, Vienna, Springer, 2009, 68.

1022 For translations of article 1371: A. Levasseur & D. Gruning, available at <www.henricapitant.org/sites/default/files/Traduction_definitive_Alain_Levasseur.pdf>; C. Mahé, "Punitive damages in the competing reform drafts of the French Civil Code" in L. Meurkens & E. Nordin (eds.), *The Power of Punitive Damages – Is Europe Missing Out?*, Cambridge – Antwerp – Portland, Intersentia, 2012, 263, footnote 10.

1023 B. Janke & F.-X. Licari, "Enforcing Punitive Damage Awards in France after Fountaine Pajot", 60 *The American Journal of Comparative Law* 2012, 796.

1024 A. Anziani & L. Béteille, Rapport d' information no. 558 fait au nom de la commission des lois constitutionnelles par le groupe de travail relative à la responsabilité civile, July 2009, 79 *et seq.*, available at <www.senat.fr/rap/r08-558/r08-5581.pdf>.

1025 Proposition de loi no. 657 du 9 juillet 2010 portant réforme de la responsabilité civile, presented by senator L. Béteille, sénateur, available at <www.senat.fr/leg/ppl09-657.html>.

1026 Translation of article 1386-25 based on: C. Mahé, "Punitive damages in the competing reform drafts of the French Civil Code" in L. Meurkens & E. Nordin (eds.), *The Power of Punitive Damages – Is Europe Missing Out?*, Cambridge – Antwerp – Portland, Intersentia, 2012, 262–263, footnote 7.

472. The third draft is called the "TERRÉ Tort Draft" and was published in March 2011.[1027] The TERRÉ Group, led by Professor François TERRÉ, also envisaged a punitive damages provision in French liability law. The group consisted of academics and legal practitioners. In article 69 of their draft it is stated that a judge may condemn the wrongdoer to exemplary damages when the harm is caused by an intentional wrong.[1028]

b. Double damages in EU competition law

473. The *Manfredi* judgment mentioned above[1029] has been interpreted by the EU Commission in such a way as to give the impression that punitive damages are part of the *acquis communautaire*.[1030] In an attempt to make private antitrust lawsuits more prominent within the EU, the Commission published a Green Paper on Damages Actions for Breach of the EU antitrust rules in 2005.[1031] This proposal called for the awarding of double damages for horizontal cartel cases and was seen as a means to provide for an incentive for private enforcement of competition law, inspired by the treble damages of U.S. antitrust law.[1032] In 2008 the Commission continued its effort through the adoption of a White Paper. In this proposal, the mechanism of punitive damages in the form of double damages had disappeared. The Paper's primary objective was the improvement of the legal conditions for victims to exercise their right to reparation of all damage suffered as a result of a breach of the EU antitrust rules. It, therefore, took the idea of full compensation as its first and foremost guiding principle.[1033]

474. In the Working Paper accompanying the White Paper the Commission, however, changed its tone and included punitive damages into the *acquis communautaire*. It stated that the European Court of Justice in *Manfredi* did not consider punitive damages to be a violation of European public order but derived from this the idea that the opposite is true.[1034] Moreover,

---

1027 F. Terré (ed.), *Pour une réforme du droit de la responsabilité civile*, Paris, Dalloz, 2011.

1028 Translation based on: C. Mahé, "Punitive damages in the competing reform drafts of the French Civil Code" in L. Meurkens & E. Nordin (eds.), *The Power of Punitive Damages – Is Europe Missing Out?*, Cambridge – Antwerp – Portland, Intersentia, 2012, 263, footnote 11.

1029 See *supra* no. 466.

1030 B.A. Koch, "Punitive Damages in European Law" in H. Koziol & V. Wilcox (eds.), *Punitive Damages: Common Law and Civil Law Perspectives*, Vienna, Springer, 2009, 207.

1031 Green Paper on Damages Actions for Breach of the EC antitrust rules, COM (2005) 672 final, 19 December 2005.

1032 J.Y. Gotanda, "Charting Developments Concerning Punitive Damages: Is the Tide Changing?", 45 *Columbia Journal of Transnational Law* 2007, 520; K. Sein, "Should Estonian Law Provide for an Award of Punitive Damages?", *Juridica International* 2007, 49.

1033 White Paper on damages actions for breach of the EC antitrust rules, COM/2008/0165 final, 3.

1034 Commission Staff Working Paper accompanying the White Paper on damages actions for breach of the EC antitrust rules, SEC/2008/0404 final, 57, no. 190; B.A. Koch, "Punitive

although openly admitting elsewhere[1035] in the Working Paper that the Green Paper's introduction of double damages had triggered a lot of opposition, the Commission claimed that unjust enrichment of the injured party is not legally forbidden under Community law. The European Court of Justice in *Manfredi* had ruled that:

> "(...) *Community law does not prevent national courts from taking steps to ensure that the protection of the rights guaranteed by Community law does not entail the unjust enrichment of those who enjoy them*".[1036]

475. As the Commission officials who wrote the Working Paper construed things, this means that punitive awards can only be reduced if they are deemed to be excessive and thus that such awards are a legitimate form of (unjust) enrichment.[1037] This does not seem to be what the European Court of Justice intended. The Court sought to prevent the (unjust) enrichment of victims, a principle that the Commission itself in the White Paper attaches great importance to.[1038]

476. At the end of legislative process, punitive damages did not make it into the Directive on certain rules governing actions for damages under national law for infringements of the competition law provisions of the Member States and of the European Union.[1039, 1040] The European Commission's efforts to introduce double damages for cartel infringements into substantive law, nevertheless, implicitly indicates a willingness to accept such punitive damages as unproblematic in light of international public policy.[1041]

Damages in European Law" in H. Koziol & V. Wilcox (eds.), *Punitive Damages: Common Law and Civil Law Perspectives*, Vienna, Springer, 2009, 207.

1035 Commission Staff Working Paper accompanying the White Paper on damages actions for breach of the EC antitrust rules, SEC/2008/0404 final, 55, no. 182.

1036 Joined cases ECJ 13 July 2006, Vincenzo Manfredi v. Lloyd Adriatico Assicurazioni SpA, Antonio Cannito v. Fondiaria Sai SpA and Nicolò Tricarico and Pasqualina Murgolo v. Assitalia SpA, *ECR* 2006, p. 6619, par. 99.

1037 Commission Staff Working Paper accompanying the White Paper on damages actions for breach of the EC antitrust rules, SEC/2008/0404 final, 58, no. 192.

1038 B.A. Koch, "Punitive Damages in European Law" in H. Koziol & V. Wilcox (eds.), *Punitive Damages: Common Law and Civil Law Perspectives*, Vienna, Springer, 2009, 207–208.

1039 Directive No. 2014/104 of the European Parliament and of the Council of 26 November 2014 on certain rules governing actions for damages under national law for infringements of the competition law provisions of the Member States and of the European Union, *OJ* L 349 of 5 December 2014, 1. See Recital 13 which prohibits overcompensation, whether by means of punitive, multiple or other damages.

1040 For an extensive discussion of the whole process: A. Ortega Gonzalez, "Punitive damages for cartel infringements: why didn't the Commission grasp the opportunity?" in L. Meurkens & E. Nordin (eds.), *The Power of Punitive Damages – Is Europe Missing Out?*, Cambridge – Antwerp – Portland, Intersentia, 2012, 437–458.

1041 C.I. Nagy, "Recognition and enforcement of US judgments involving punitive damages in continental Europe", *Nederlands Internationaal Privaatrecht* 2012, 6–7.

5.4. CONCLUSION

477. The five Member States looked at in this book all proclaim to provide for a liability system which aims at full compensation of the victim but without enriching the latter. There is said to be a strict divide between private law, which focuses on compensation of the victim, and criminal law, with its aims of punishment and deterrence of the wrongdoer.

478. This chapter sought to demonstrate that EU private law as well as the private law of five EU Member States (Germany, France, Spain, Italy and England) do form a habitat for punitive-like damages, despite punitive damages not having an official existence in Europe (with the exception of England, the birthplace of common law punitive damages[1042]). The European private law systems contain mechanisms jumping the fence between private law and public law (criminal law). This is similar to U.S. punitive damages which can be seen as an institution putting the public-private law divide into question. This finding shakes the traditional dogmatic foundations and has important implications for the private international law arena.

479. At the EU level we referred to, for example, article 18 of Regulation 1768/95 which grants the holders of plant breeders' rights a quadruple of the actual loss suffered in case the farmer does not comply with his requirements under the agricultural exemption. Directive 2011/7 attempts to counteract delays in payment in commercial relationships. It can be argued that the Directive pursues a punitive objective to the extent that the applicable interest rate exceeds the market interest for loans. We also discussed how, under the influence of the European Court of Justice, the Directives on equal treatment are seen to be furthering a deterrence function.

480. Within the Member States various punitive traces can be detected as well. We underlined the punitive aim underlying the institution of penalty clauses, which are accepted in all Civil Law countries we studied. In France we further identified, for instance, the concept of the *amende civile, l'astreinte* as well as the courts' potential punitive agenda when awarding moral damages. In Germany we, for example, pointed to the acceptance of the charging of a double license fee by the collecting society GEMA. Furthermore, in cases of infringements of personality rights the German case law has explicitly mentioned deterrence as a consideration, thereby overriding the strict division between private and public law. In addition, a punitive mechanism for abuse of process could be discerned in article 96 of the Italian Code of Civil Procedure. Spanish law seeks punishment

[1042] J.Y. Gotanda, "Punitive Damages: A Comparative Analysis", 42 *Columbia Journal of Transnational Law* 2004, 398.

in private law as well because it orders an employer to pay an additional amount of benefits to his employee in case the latter's labour accident or disease was caused by the employer. Unsurprisingly, England explicitly provides for punitive damages. Under English law so-called exemplary damages are available in three categories of cases.

481. The presence of these mechanisms in the private law of a number of prominent Member States as well as in European Union law leads to the conclusion that the concept of punitive damages, in itself, can no longer be held to be contrary to international public policy (both in terms of applicable law and in terms of enforcement). The *Cour de cassation* and the Spanish *Tribunal Supremo* already reached this conclusion in their respective decisions on the enforcement of punitive damages (as described in chapter 4). The existence of mechanisms belonging to private law which, nevertheless, pursue punitive and deterrent aims indeed changes the contours of the international public policy exception. The principle of strict compensation, for instance, is not international *ordre public* because the civil liability systems contain legal provisions and judicial decisions departing from it. The rule is not (or perhaps no longer) an absolute principle that merits international public policy protection.

482. Having stripped the objections against the very concept of punitive damages from their international public policy status, the question arises whether this means that (1) Member States' courts should award punitive damages if the applicable U.S. law provides for them and (2) punitive damages should be able to freely penetrate our borders and be enforced in Europe. The answer is that there is still another aspect that acts as a safety valve: the punitive damages award should not be excessive. This proportionality check is the second prong of the international public policy test. In the next chapter we formulate guidelines as to how this excessiveness check should be applied.

CHAPTER 6
PUNITIVE DAMAGES IN APPLICABLE LAW AND ENFORCEMENT OF JUDGMENTS: NORMATIVE CONSIDERATIONS
An Attempt at Formulating Guidelines

483. The aim of this chapter is to list a set of guidelines courts can fall back on when having to apply U.S. law providing for punitive damages or when confronted with a request to enforce an American judgment containing punitive damages.[1043] The concrete guiding principles offered in this chapter are derived from the dominating American rules on punitive damages (chapter 1) as well as the existing case law on the enforcement of punitive damages in the European Union (chapter 4).

6.1. APPLICABLE LAW

484. In chapter 3 it became clear that the public policy (to be understood in its international sense) of the forum regulates the application of foreign rules. At the European level recital 32 of the Rome II Regulation indicates that the public policy clause of article 26 of the Regulation should be interpreted in such a way as to allow the granting of foreign punitive damages, to the extent that they are not excessive. Although devoid of any binding effect, it is to be expected (or hoped) that national courts will construe the public policy mechanism in light of the recital.

485. For those cases still governed by national rules of private international law[1044], the situation is different. In Germany, for instance, the public policy

---

[1043] The service of American punitive damages claims was sufficiently discussed in chapter 2 and does not need any further elaboration nor guidelines.

[1044] For instance torts arising out of the violation of privacy and rights relating to personality (including defamation) as these are excluded from the scope of the Rome II Regulation (article 1.2.g)).

exception for tort cases found in article 40, paragraph 3 EGBGB makes the awarding of U.S. punitive damages impossible.[1045] There is, therefore, a stark contrast between matters falling within the scope of the Rome II Regulation and those outside its ambit.

486. We argue that the national rules should follow the model of the Rome II Regulation. A point-blank refusal to apply U.S. punitive damages when these are appropriate under the foreign law, such as put forward by article 40, paragraph 3 EGBGB, is not in line with the legal status quo. The findings in chapter 5 debunk the argument that punitive damages *in se* violate international public policy. The problem with article 40, paragraph 3 EGBGB lies in the fact that it is a rigid provision which represents and solidifies a hostile view on punitive damages at the time of its introduction. The general public policy exception of article 6 EGBGB, on the other hand, allows for a more flexible interpretation as it orders the court to look at the public policy as it exists at the time the court renders its judgment. However, as article 40, paragraph 3 EGBGB is a more specific provision, it takes precedence over the more general article 6 EGBGB.[1046] Article 40, paragraph 3 EGBGB, therefore, prevents German courts from taking the legal status quo into account.

487. Article 40, paragraph 3 EGBGB actually leads to an internal contradiction within German law. It is possible that U.S. law awards punitive damages in cases in which the German courts also award damages which go beyond normal compensation (personality right infringement cases, for instance[1047]). The refusal (on the basis of article 40, paragraph 3) to apply foreign punitive damages in such circumstances then seems inconsistent.[1048] Moreover, it is also possible that the *lex fori* (*i.e.* German law) replaces the rejected foreign law (*i.e.* U.S. law).[1049] This could lead to the absurd situation where punitive damages are rejected because they have a foreign origin but are replaced by punitive institutions closely resembling punitive damages (as identified in chapter 5) under the domestic law.[1050]

1045 See *supra* no. 203.

1046 V. Behr, "Myth and Reality of Punitive Damages in Germany", 24 *Journal of Law and Commerce* 2004–2005, 201.

1047 See *supra* no. 427–432.

1048 V. Behr, "Myth and Reality of Punitive Damages in Germany", 24 *Journal of Law and Commerce* 2004–2005, 223.

1049 National law should not automatically replace the foreign law. The latter should be modified to remove any concerns. If that is impossible, the *lex fori* may, however, replace the *lex causae*: A. Fuchs, "Article 26" in P. Huber (ed.), *Rome II Regulation – Pocket Commentary*, Munich, Sellier, 2011, 430, no. 19; V. Behr, "Myth and Reality of Punitive Damages in Germany", 24 *Journal of Law and Commerce* 2004–2005, 223.

1050 P. Hay, "Entschädigung und andere Zwecke. Zu Präventionsgedanken im deutschen Schadensersatzrecht, punitive damages und Art. 40 Abs 3 Nr. 2 EGBGB" in G. Hohloch, R. Frank, P. Schlechtriem (eds.), *Festschrift für Hans Stoll zum 75. Geburtstag*, Tübingen, Mohr

488. One proposed solution to such a conflicting position is a flexible interpretation of article 40, paragraph 3 EGBGB. Foreign punitive damages would be allowed to penetrate via the applicable law but only in cases in which German law would also award extra-compensatory damages with punitive and/or deterrent intentions.[1051] This suggestion is, however, very difficult to apply in practice since it is not always clear in which exact cases German courts would award such damages. First, defining these "punitive-like" damages is far from easy as discussed in chapter 5.[1052] Second, as also demonstrated in chapter 5, these damages are not openly labelled as punitive by the German courts.[1053] We hold the opinion that such a rule is not far-reaching enough. Foreign punitive damages should always be applied since the very concept does not offend the forum's international public policy. The only check on their application is a verification of their quantum in order to avoid excessive awards.

489. When assessing foreign punitive damages, judges should in fact only test for excessiveness, and not resort to a principled refusal of such damages. This is the approach taken by the Rome II Regulation's recital 32. The next issue to be dealt with is how a court can determine when this excessiveness threshold has been reached. This chapter will address this question. We will look at the issue mainly from the perspective of the judge faced with a request to enforce U.S. punitive damages. This choice is inspired by two reasons. First, the existence of a handful of cases dealing with the enforcement of U.S. punitive damages (discussed in chapter 4) which prove helpful when attempting to develop guiding principles. In contrast, there is only one known case (discussed in chapter 3) addressing the issue of applying punitive damages under foreign law. Second, the fact that formulating guidance for courts in enforcement cases is more complicated than in matters of applicable law (due to the intervening prohibition of a review of the merits of the case underlying the foreign judgment, also called the prohibition of *révision au fond*[1054]).

490. A court dealing with punitive damages as a result of having to apply U.S. law indeed has an easier task than one dealing with punitive damages as part of a U.S. judgment. The former does not have to take account of the prohibition of *révision au fond*. The court has the discretion to reduce the foreign excessive

---

Siebeck, 2001, 527; M. Requejo Isidro, "Punitive Damages From a Private International Law Perspective" in H. Koziol & V. Wilcox (eds.), *Punitive Damages: Common Law and Civil Law Perspectives*, Vienna, Springer, 2009, 252; P. Klötgen, "L'appréhension des punitive damages par le droit allemande", *Revue Lamy Droit des Affaires* 2013, 128.

1051 M. Requejo Isidro, "Punitive Damages From a Private International Law Perspective" in H. Koziol & V. Wilcox (eds.), *Punitive Damages: Common Law and Civil Law Perspectives*, Vienna, Springer, 2009, 252.

1052 See *supra* no. 370.

1053 See *supra* no. 370.

1054 See *infra* no. 494.

damages provision to an amount which is acceptable under its country's international public policy.[1055] The court can look at the range offered by the U.S. punitive damages provision and locate the point at which the awarding of punitive damages would become excessive. It can then apply the foreign provision up to that number. A European court deciding whether to enforce a U.S. punitive award, on the other hand, has to work with the amount of punitive damages awarded by the U.S. court. The prohibition of *révision au fond* makes it much more controversial to cut the award to an appropriate level.[1056]

491. Apart from the absence of this prohibition, the private international law fields of applicable law and enforcement of judgments bear significant resemblances. The guidelines we suggest in the field of enforcement can thus serve as a model that can be adopted in the area of applicable law as well, with some slight adaptations. The general principles regarding the enforcement of punitive damages judgments set out in the next paragraphs, therefore, apply to a large extent also when a European judge is requested to apply American law providing for punitive damages.

6.2. ENFORCEMENT OF U.S. PUNITIVE DAMAGES JUDGMENTS

492. In what follows we will attempt to put forward a set of guidelines that European judges might find useful when assessing the enforceability of U.S. punitive awards. It has already been stated that courts should not refuse the concept of punitive damages as such but should, on the contrary, resort to an excessiveness review of the punitive damages granted by the American court.

493. First, we will establish guiding principles to determine at which point punitive damages become excessive. These guidelines are derived from the lessons drawn from the U.S. Supreme Court case-law (discussed in chapter 1) as well as from the knowledge acquired through the few cases concerning the enforcement of punitive damages in the European Union (discussed in chapter 4). After that we will discuss what should happen to the punitive award once the acceptable amount has been found. More in particular, we will elaborate whether the prohibition on *révision au fond* imposes an all-or-nothing approach to punitive damages or whether this head of damages can be reduced by the enforcing court to the amount that is acceptable in light of international public policy.

1055 A. Fuchs, "Article 26" in P. Huber (ed.), *Rome II Regulation – Pocket Commentary*, Munich, Sellier, 2011, 430, no. 19.

1056 See *infra* no. 496.

The overall aim is to offer European courts some guidance on how to approach U.S. punitive damages. At the moment, there is no uniformity in the stances taken in the various Member States. This is caused by the fact that the enforcement depends on national law and, more specifically, the national courts' view on international public policy.[1057] It should be noted from the outset that it is extremely difficult, if not impossible, to create absolute rules that apply in every single case. Judicial discretion will always be part of any excessiveness test. The observations we bring forward will hopefully assist courts when making their determination. The guidelines as a whole should create a more receptive and more uniform attitude towards this type of foreign damages.

6.2.1. PROHIBITION OF *RÉVISION AU FOND*

494. Before delving into the various guiding principles, the aforementioned prohibition of *révision au fond* should be discussed. The prohibition of a review on the merits is an overarching issue to consider when dealing with the enforcement of foreign judgments. It forbids requested courts to open a completely new investigation of the case and retry the merits underlying a foreign judgment. Requested jurisdictions should not examine whether the foreign judgment was erroneous in law or in fact. Courts are also not permitted to undertake a review of the private international law analysis performed by the foreign court. The obligation or possibility for the requested court to conduct a *révision au fond* reflects a deep mistrust towards the foreign jurisdiction. The review of the foreign judgment for its legal (substantive or conflicts) correctness is no longer part of the judgment-enforcement practice in most legal systems.[1058] For the enforcement of judgments originating in the European Union, the Brussels I*bis* Regulation also rules out any review of the substance of the judgment.[1059]

495. The international public policy exception does not examine the dispute itself but rather the foreign judgment which adjudicated the dispute. There is a fine line between the appropriate review of a foreign decision for its compliance with the international public policy of the forum and an inappropriate *révision*

1057 See chapter 4.

1058 P. Hay, "On Comity, Reciprocity and Public Policy in U.S. and German Judgments Recognition Practice" in J. Basedow (ed.), *Private Law in the International Arena – Privatrecht in der Internationalen Arena. Liber Amicorum Kurt Siehr*, The Hague, T.M.C. Asser Press, 2000, 243.

1059 Article 52 Regulation no. 1215/2012 of the European Parliament and of the Council of 12 December 2012 on jurisdiction and the recognition and enforcement of judgments in civil and commercial matters, *OJ* L351 of 20 December 2012, 1. Its predecessors contained an almost identical provision: see article 36 of the Brussels I Regulation and article 29 of the EEX Convention.

au fond.[1060] In fact, it could even be said that there is no bright line separating the permissible public policy review from the undesirable *révision au fond.*[1061] In the context of an *ordre public* review there is ultimately always a *révision au fond.* Such review, however, does not examine the substantive legality of the judgment but merely determines whether the (international) public policy has been impaired.[1062]

496. The proscription against *révision au fond* prevents certain possible criteria from being included in the excessiveness test for punitive damages. It is, for instance, one of the reasons why enforcing the American punitive damages to the extent they could have been awarded in the country of the requested court is not the answer to the excessiveness issue.[1063] This method authorises the requested court to reopen the damages determination made by the originating court thereby using principles applicable in the requested forum.[1064] This amounts to a clear *révision au fond.* Moreover, the fact that the requested court through exequatur allows for the awarding of a higher amount than what would have been available under the law of the forum cannot form a valid basis for refusal of enforcement. Of course, there is nothing stopping the court from covertly assimilating the amount of acceptable foreign punitive damages to what it believes the plaintiff would have been able to recover under punitive-like sanctions in the forum. However, this approach cannot have a place as a formal criterion within the excessiveness analysis. Considering that any amount in excess of the result of applying the domestic standards is contrary to international public policy is undesirable.[1065] Similarly, a discovery of the wealth

---

1060 P. Hay, "On Comity, Reciprocity and Public Policy in U.S. and German Judgments Recognition Practice" in J. Basedow (ed.), *Private Law in the International Arena - Privatrecht in der Internationalen Arena. Liber Amicorum Kurt Siehr,* The Hague, T.M.C. Asser Press, 2000, 244; P. Hay, "Contemporary Approaches to Non-Contractual Obligations in Private International Law (Conflict of Laws) and the European Community's "Rome II" Regulation", *The European Legal Forum* 2007, 150.

1061 P. Hay, "On Comity, Reciprocity and Public Policy in U.S. and German Judgments Recognition Practice" in J. Basedow (ed.), *Private Law in the International Arena - Privatrecht in der Internationalen Arena. Liber Amicorum Kurt Siehr,* The Hague, T.M.C. Asser Press, 2000, 245.

1062 R. Stürner, "Anerkennungsrechtlicher und europäischer Ordre Public als Schranke der Vollstreckbarerklärung - der Bundesgerichtshof und die Staatlichkeit in der Europäischen Union" in C.W. Canaris, A. Heldrich, K. Hopt, C. Roxin, K. Schmidt & G. Widmaier (eds.), *50 Jahre Bundesgerichtshof,* Munich, C.H. Beck, 2000, 688–689.

1063 Other objections include: the fact that, apart from in England, punitive damages are not awarded in the European Union and the difficulty to ascertain the amount of punitive-like damages (if any) would have been granted by domestic courts in a particular case.

1064 R. Brand, "Punitive Damages Revisited: Taking the Rationale for Non-Recognition of Foreign Judgments Too Far", 24 *Journal of Law and Commerce* 2005, 194.

1065 M. Requejo Isidro, "Punitive Damages: How Do They Look Like When Seen From Abroad?" in L. Meurkens & E. Nordin (eds.), *The Power of Punitive Damages - Is Europe Missing Out?,* Cambridge - Antwerp - Portland, Intersentia, 2012, 322.

of the defendant[1066] would also run counter of the principle outlawing *révision au fond*.

Keeping the prohibition of *révision au fond* in mind, the following guidelines can be formulated.

6.2.2. ENFORCEMENT IS THE RULE, PUBLIC POLICY OBJECTIONS ARE THE EXCEPTION

497. First and foremost, courts dealing with a request for enforcement of a judgment should remind themselves of the comity of nations. The notion refers to the rules of politeness and courtesy observed by states in their mutual intercourse.[1067] This courtesy between nations entails respecting each other's laws, judgments and institutions. In private international law the doctrine of comity is the legal principle which dictates that a jurisdiction recognise and give effect to judicial decisions rendered in other jurisdictions unless to do so would offend its (international) public policy.[1068] It is more heavily relied on in the United States than in Europe.[1069] Although its status as a legal principle in Europe is uncertain, the idea behind comity, however, is useful to point European courts to the exceptional nature of a refusal to enforce a foreign judgment.

498. The violation of (international) public policy forms a justification for a refusal to recognise and enforce the foreign judgment.[1070] However, this safety valve mechanism should only operate in the most compelling circumstances.[1071] Frequent refusals to grant enforcement on the basis of (international) public policy would contribute to the development of anarchy in international

[1066] M. Bernet & N.C. Ulmer, "Recognition and Enforcement in Switzerland of US Judgments Containing an Award of Punitive Damages", 22 *International Business Lawyer* 1994, 274.

[1067] W.E. Hall, *A Treatise on International Law*, Oxford, Clarendon Press, 7th edition, 1917, 14, no. 1.

[1068] J.K. Bleimaier, "The Doctrine of Comity in Private International Law", 24 *Catholic University Law Review* 1979, 327.

[1069] As to comity Paul noted that "*Comity is a ready explanation for much of what courts do in public and private international law. In the name of comity, U.S. courts often recognize and enforce foreign judgments or limit domestic jurisdiction to hear claims or apply law, even where foreign law is contrary to U.S. law or policy*": J.R. Paul, "Comity in International Law", 32 *Harvard International Law Journal* 1991, 2. For a summary account of the early history of comity: H.E. Yntema, "The Comity Doctrine", 65 *Michigan Law Review* 1966, 9–32. For a recent comprehensive account of international comity in American law: W.S. Dodge, "International Comity in American Law", 115 *Columbia Law Review* 2015, 2071–2142.

[1070] J.K. Bleimaier, "The Doctrine of Comity in Private International Law", 24 *Catholic University Law Review* 1979, 330.

[1071] J.K. Bleimaier, "The Doctrine of Comity in Private International Law", 24 *Catholic University Law Review* 1979, 330–331.

affairs.[1072] The escape clause should be reserved for extreme cases.[1073] When deciding on the enforceability of an American punitive damages award, courts in the European Union should thus lean towards acceptance rather than rejection. The traditional maxim of *in dubio pro recognitione* supports this suggested attitude.[1074]

6.2.3. THE COMPENSATORY DAMAGES AWARDED SHOULD ALWAYS BE GRANTED ENFORCEMENT

499. As to American punitive damages judgments specifically, it should first of all be emphasised that the enforcement of the compensatory damages granted to the prevailing party is unproblematic.[1075] Compensation of the victim forms the foundational objective of civil liability systems in Europe. The compensatory damages awarded are not in jeopardy by the presence of punitive damages in the judgment. This requires, however, that the judgment clearly singles out the compensatory damages because the prohibition of *révision au fond* forbids a court to reduce the global amount of (unspecified) damages a foreign court has awarded.[1076] Even if the compensatory damages are very high in comparison to the compensation standards of the requested forum, they should be accepted for enforcement.[1077] In England section 5 of the Protection of Trading Interests Act 1980 prevents the enforcement of foreign multiple damages. A literal reading of the provision leads to the conclusion that the compensatory element of the multiple damages is unenforceable as

---

1072 J.K. Bleimaier, "The Doctrine of Comity in Private International Law", 24 *Catholic University Law Review* 1979, 331.

1073 See for Germany for instance: J. Zekoll, "The Enforceability of American Money Judgments Abroad: A Landmark Decision by the German Federal Court of Justice", 30 *Columbia Journal of Transnational Law* 1992, 646; V. Behr, "Myth and Reality of Punitive Damages in Germany", 24 *Journal of Law and Commerce* 2004–2005, 204; M. Tolani, "U.S. Punitive Damages Before German Courts: A Comparative Analysis with Respect to the Ordre Public", 17 *Annual Survey of International & Comparative Law* 2011, 201; H. Bungert, "Enforcing U.S. Excessive and Punitive Damages Awards in Germany", 27 *International Lawyer* 1993, 1079.

1074 C.I. Nagy, "Recognition and enforcement of US judgments involving punitive damages in continental Europe", *Nederlands Internationaal Privaatrecht* 2012, 10.

1075 O. Cachard, "Le contrôle juridictionnel des jugements étrangers ordonnant des Punitive Damages", *Revue Lamy Droit des Affaires* 2013, 140.

1076 N. Meyer Fabre, "Recognition and Enforcement of U.S. Judgments in France – Recent Developments", *The International Dispute Resolution News* spring 2012, 9; N. Meyer Fabre, "Enforcement Of U.S. Punitive Damages Award in France: First Ruling Of The French Court Of Cassation In X. v. Fountaine Pajot December 1, 2010", *Mealey's International Arbitration Report* January 2011, 4.

1077 See, for instance, the *Bundesgerichtshof*'s ruling in *John Doe v. Eckhard Schmitz* where it was held that the damages for pain and suffering could be enforced even though their amount was very high to German standards: BGH 4 June 1992, *Neue Juristische Wochenschrift* 1992, 3100–3102.

well.[1078] Provisions such as section 5 of PTIA detract from the 'sanctity' of compensatory damages and should thus be abolished.

500. Plaintiffs should take note of national procedural rules prohibiting *ultra petita* rulings. The latter forbid a court from awarding to a party that what he or she has not claimed. Parties seeking enforcement of an American punitive damages judgment in the European Union should not solely request the enforcement of the entire judgment. They are advised not to put all their eggs in one basket but to also request enforcement of the compensatory damages only. That way the possible unenforceability of the punitive damages does not affect the enforceability of the uncontroversial compensatory damages. If plaintiffs do not provide alternatives to the enforcing court, they might find themselves in the same situation as plaintiffs Schlenka and Langhorne in the French case *Fountaine Pajot.* Their (lawyers') strategic plan[1079] backfired and resulted in a total rejection of the California judgment.

6.2.4. THE COMPENSATORY PORTION OF THE PUNITIVE DAMAGES SHOULD BE ENFORCED

501. A second consideration requested courts in the European Union should keep in mind relates to the compensatory function some punitive awards partly pursue. Compensation can indeed be one of the possible reasons an American court grants punitive damages.[1080] The compensatory objective of punitive damages should not pose any problem under international public policy because compensating the victim forms the cornerstone upon which private laws in the European Union are based.[1081] Opponents of enforcing punitive damages in European legal systems often invoke the argument that such damages violate the solely compensatory intentions of private law.[1082] This argument loses any power it might hold when the punitive damages awarded in the United States are in part meant to compensate the plaintiff. Enforcing that part of an award can, therefore, not be problematic under the public policy test. This additional, compensatory function of punitive damages does not bridge the gap between the European monistic, compensatory system of damages

---

1078 See *supra* no. 260.

1079 Informal contact with the lawyers handling the case revealed that the lack of request for partial enforcement was the result of a tactical choice. They opted not to submit subsidiary requests in order not to weaken the main request of enforcement of the entire American judgment.

1080 See *supra* no. 64–66.

1081 In chapter 5 we demonstrated that there are deviations from this principle. However, despite these deviations compensation remains the basic rule.

1082 See *supra* no. 344 *et seq.*

and the American dualistic system. It could, however, narrow the gap to a degree such that a monistic system at least in part accepts punitive damages awards.[1083]

502. In the case of *John Doe v. Eckhard Schmitz* the German *Bundesgerichtshof* mentioned the possibility of enforcing the compensatory portion of a punitive award.[1084] The California Superior Court had awarded the plaintiff USD 350.260 in compensation and USD 400.000 in punitive damages. It had attributed 40% of the entire award to compensate the young victim's lawyer. Germany's highest civil court decided that it would allow the enforcement of punitive damages if and to the extent that the punitive award serves a compensatory function.[1085] The *Bundesgerichtshof* referred to the lawyer's fees which are in principle not recoverable given the American rule on costs. Awarding legal fees through punitive damages enables the plaintiff to achieve full compensation.[1086] The fact that the American court had indicated its desire to shift these legal fees to the losing party could have made it possible to enforce these fees. However, the *Bundesgerichtshof* required that the foreign court clearly states its intention to charge this cost against the punitive damages. It found that the California Superior Court had not fulfilled this requirement because the American court had granted 40% of the *entire* award to the plaintiff's counsel. The *Bundesgerichtshof* did not find any reliable information in the California judgment or in the transcript to support the finding that the punitive damages were intended to cover the legal costs incurred by the plaintiff. The *Bundesgerichtshof* could not exclude the possibility that the compensatory damages – which the *Bundesgerichtshof* found to be generous – already included an element addressing those costs.[1087, 1088]

503. We agree with the approach taken by the German Supreme Court. A requested court should accept punitive damages to the extent they serve a compensatory function. The foreign judgment should, however, explicitly identify the court's intention to attach a compensatory function to the punitive award.[1089] It should also indicate which numerical part of the punitive damages

---

1083 V. Behr, "Punitive Damages in American and German Law – Tendencies Towards Approximation of Apparently Irreconcilable Concepts", 78 *Chicago – Kent Law Review* 2003, 122.

1084 BGH 4 June 1992, *Neue Juristische Wochenschrift* 1992, 3103.

1085 BGH 4 June 1992, *Neue Juristische Wochenschrift* 1992, 3103.

1086 V. Behr, "Punitive Damages in American and German Law – Tendencies Towards Approximation of Apparently Irreconcilable Concepts", 78 *Chicago – Kent Law Review* 2003, 123.

1087 C.I. Nagy, "Recognition and enforcement of US judgments involving punitive damages in continental Europe", *Nederlands Internationaal Privaatrecht* 2012, 8.

1088 BGH 4 June 1992, *Neue Juristische Wochenschrift* 1992, 3103.

1089 A case could be made for allowing the requested court to use the transcript of the foreign court's proceedings if this document makes it possible to know the foreign court's reasoning.

is to be used for this compensatory objective. This reasoning does not only apply to legal fees but to any form of loss. In addition to the lawyer's fees, the *Bundesgerichtshof* made reference to losses that are difficult to prove and losses that are not covered by other types of damages. It also imagined that damages stripping the defendant of the gains acquired through the wrongful behaviour are recoverable through the head of punitive damages.[1090, 1091] In essence, any 'disadvantage' that the foreign court clearly deems recoverable via the punitive damages award should be enforced in the European Union. In our view legal costs will be the most common and important form of compensation to be recovered via the punitive damages awards.

504. The facts of the *Fimez* case[1092] in Italy provide an example of the need of a clear demarcation (within the punitive damages awarded) between the amount pursuing compensatory aims and the portion seeking real punitive ends. The District Court of Jefferson County in Alabama awarded the American plaintiff USD 1 million dollars without specifying the nature of the award. The Venice Court of Appeal classified the award as punitive. The Alabama wrongful death statute applied to the traffic accident in which the plaintiff's son lost his life. Under that legislation compensatory damages cannot be recovered and only punitive damages can be obtained. The Supreme Court of Alabama clarified, however, that the punitive damages in such wrongful death cases pursue punitive as well as compensatory objectives.[1093] Even if the Venice Court of

1090 See for an example of a (non-EU) case of disgorgement of profits the litigation between S.F. Inc. and T.C.S. AG before the Swiss courts (District Court Basel-Stadt 1 February 1989, upheld by the Basel-Stadt Court of Appeal 1 December 1989, *Basler Juristische Mitteilungen* 1991, 31–38). The California District Court had awarded USD 50.000 in punitive damages under English law for the misappropriation of containers. Both the District Court of Basel and the Basel Court of Appeal enforced the USD 50.000 since its primary purpose was to restitute the unjust profit to the plaintiff, thereby avoiding the unjust enrichment of the defendant. The fact that the amount was a mere estimate of the defendant's unlawful profit was not seen as an obstacle to enforcement: M. Bernet & N.C. Ulmer, "Recognition and Enforcement in Switzerland of US Judgments Containing an Award of Punitive Damages", 22 *International Business Lawyer* 1994, 273; D. Favalli & J.M. Matthews, "Recognition and Enforcement of U.S. class action judgments and settlements in Switzerland", *Schweizerische Zeitschrift für internationales und Europäisches Recht* 2007, 634–635.

1091 W. Wurmnest, "Recognition and Enforcement of U.S. Money Judgments in Germany", 23 *Berkeley Journal of International Law* 2005, 196–197; G. Nater-Bass, "U.S.-Style Punitive Damages Awards and their Recognition and Enforcement in Switzerland and Other Civil-Law Countries", 28 *Deutsch-Amerikanische Juristen-Vereinigung Newsletter* 2003, 156; G. Wegen & J. Sherer, "Recognition and Enforcement of U.S. Punitive Damages in Germany – A Recent Decision of the German Federal Court of Justice", 21 *International Business Lawyer* 1993, 486; A.R. Fiebig, "The Recognition and Enforcement of Punitive Damage Awards in Germany: Recent Developments", 22 *Georgia Journal of International & Comparative Law* 1992, 649.

1092 See *supra* no. 214.

1093 *Savannah & Memphis Railroad v. Shearer*, 58 Ala. (1877), 680; *South & North Alabama Railroad v. Sullivan*, 59 Ala. (1877), 278; *Estes Health Care Ctrs Inc v. Bannerman*, 411 So2d (1982), 113; F. Quarta, "Class Actions, Extra-Compensatory Damages, and Judicial

Appeal would have been aware of the dual intentions of the Alabama wrongful death statute and would have been willing to enforce the compensatory portion of the award, it would have been unable to do so due to the prohibition of *révision au fond*. The enforcing court cannot ascertain the motives behind the award if the foreign court has not provided clear and comprehensible information itself. Although a compensatory element might be hidden in a punitive award, the rendering court's lack of identification ties the hands of the requested court. If the requested court were to examine the punitive award and were to distinguish the individual grounds that make up the overall amount of punitive damages, the prohibition of review of the merits would be violated.[1094]

505. The enforcement of the compensatory part of a punitive damages award is supported by the Hague Choice of Court Convention of 30 June 2005. This convention is aimed at ensuring the effectiveness of choice of court agreements between parties in international contracts. The Convention lays down uniform rules conferring jurisdiction on the court designated by the parties to a cross-border dispute in civil and commercial matters. In addition, it determines the conditions upon which a judgment rendered by the designated court of a Contracting State shall be recognised and enforced in all other Contracting States. The Convention entered into force on 1 October 2015 following the deposition of the instrument of approval on 11 June 2015 by the European Union.[1095] The EU (Denmark excepted) thereby became the second Contracting State after Mexico which triggered the entry into force of the Convention for the EU and Mexico.[1096]

506. Article 11 of the Hague Choice of Court Convention addresses the issue of damages and provides: *(1) Recognition or enforcement of a judgment may be refused if, and to the extent that, the judgment awards damages, including exemplary or punitive damages, that do not compensate a party for actual loss or harm suffered. (2) The court addressed shall take into account whether and to what extent the damages awarded by the court of origin serve to cover costs*

Recognition in Europe", Conference paper – "Extraterritoriality and Collective Redress", London 15 November 2010, Draft 19 November 2010, 6–7; F. Quarta, "Foreign Punitive Damages Decisions and Class Actions in Italy", in D. Fairgrieve and E. Lein (eds.), *Extraterritoriality and Collective Redress*, Oxford, Oxford University Press, 2012, 276.

1094 G. Nater-Bass, "U.S.-Style Punitive Damages Awards and their Recognition and Enforcement in Switzerland and Other Civil-Law Countries", 28 *Deutsch-Amerikanische Juristen-Vereinigung Newsletter* 2003, 160.

1095 For the signing of the Convention by the EU see: Council decision 2009/237/EC of 26 February 2009 on the signing on behalf of the European Community of the Convention on Choice of Court Agreements, *OJ* L 133 of 29 May 2009, 1. For the approval of the Convention by the EU see: Council decision 2014/887/EU of 4 December 2014 on the approval, on behalf of the European Union, of the Hague Convention of 30 June 2005 on Choice of Court Agreements, *OJ* L 353 of 10 December 2014, 5.

1096 Article 31(1) of the Convention.

and expenses relating to the proceedings.[1097] Despite the flexible nature of the provision ("*may be refused*"), article 11(1) demonstrates a mistrust against punitive damages and a fear that a favourable attitude toward them might reduce the number of states accepting the Convention. The provision does not require the courts of a Contracting Party to compare the incoming judgment with their (international) public policy. The punitive portion of the judgment may (but does not have to) be rejected simply because the damages awarded are non-compensatory in nature.[1098]

507. More importantly in the context of this chapter is the fact that article 11(2) supports our contention that the compensatory part of a punitive award should be granted enforcement in the European Union. It orders the requested court to take the legal costs awarded under the heading of punitive damages into account. A court cannot refuse to recognise those parts of the punitive award that are meant to cover legal costs, which in Civil Law jurisdictions would normally be passed on to the losing party.[1099] The Hague Choice of Court Convention thus confirms, at least for legal costs, that punitive damages should be enforced to the extent that they pursue a compensatory objective. The Convention's scope is limited to cases where the court's jurisdiction is based on the parties' agreement.[1100] The rule in article 11(2) could be applied to other civil and commercial cases as well as there seems to be no obvious reason why the application of the public policy exception should vary according to the original court's jurisdiction.[1101]

508. In the case of *John Doe v. Eckhard Schmitz* the *Bundesgerichtshof* could have applied its own rule differently. Instead of outright rejecting the punitive damages completely, it could have enforced part of them. The American court had reserved 40% of the *entire* amount for the plaintiff's lawyer. The *Bundesgerichtshof* could have taken 40% of the unproblematic compensatory damages (*i.e.* USD 140.104) and could have charged that amount against the (unenforceable) punitive damages. This would have guaranteed the enforcement of purely compensatory sums.[1102] However, the position taken

---

[1097] Article 9 of the proposed draft text for a future Hague convention relating to recognition and enforcement of judgments contains an identical provision. See <https://assets.hcch.net/upload/wop/gap2016pd07a_en.pdf>.

[1098] J. Berch, The Need for Enforcement of U.S. Punitive Damages Awards by the European Union, 19 *Minnesota Journal of International Law* 2010, 77 & 94, footnote 190.

[1099] C.I. Nagy, "Recognition and enforcement of US judgments involving punitive damages in continental Europe", *Nederlands Internationaal Privaatrecht* 2012, 10.

[1100] Article 1(1) of the Convention.

[1101] C.I. Nagy, "Recognition and enforcement of US judgments involving punitive damages in continental Europe", *Nederlands Internationaal Privaatrecht* 2012, 10.

[1102] P. Hay, "The Recognition and Enforcement of American Money-Judgments in Germany – The 1992 Decision of the German Supreme Court", 40 *The American Journal of Comparative Law* 1992, 747–748.

by the German Supreme Court is not unreasonable given the language of the judgment. The California Superior Court is to blame for the poor formulation of its own decision. If the American court had clearly set out that the legal fees were awarded under the guise of punitive damages, it would have avoided any interpretational problems on the German side.

6.2.5. U.S. PUNITIVE DAMAGES GOING ABOVE A 9:1 RATIO ARE, IN PRINCIPLE, SUSPECT

509. When contemplating tolerable levels of punitive damages for enforcement purposes, it is of course fruitful to remind ourselves of the limits the U.S. system itself has placed on punitive damages awards. As explained in chapter 1,[1103] the United States Supreme Court in *BMW of North America, Inc. v. Gore* created three guideposts to help determine whether a punitive award is constitutionally excessive: (1) the reprehensibility of the defendant's conduct, (2) the ratio between the punitive and compensatory damages awarded and (3) a comparison of the punitive damages to the criminal penalties that could be imposed for similar misconduct.[1104] The second guidepost brings some form of mathematical certainty into the assessment of excessiveness.

510. In the *dicta* of the *State Farm Mutual Automobile Insurance Co. v. Campbell* judgment the United States Supreme Court expanded upon this guidepost. It effectively laid down a 9:1 maximum ratio between punitive and compensatory damages by stating that "*in practice, few awards exceeding a single-digit ratio between punitive and compensatory damages, to a significant degree, will satisfy due-process*".[1105] The establishment of this upper limit has its ramifications for European courts faced with a request for enforcement of an American punitive damages judgment. If the American legal system itself has identified double-digit ratios between punitive and compensatory awards as constitutionally unacceptable, it seems only logical that European judges should also treat this 9:1 ratio as an outer limit to be conformed with in order to make the judgment enforceable. It would make no sense for a European court to allow the enforcement of judgments that violate the federal Constitution in their country of origin.

511. However, the U.S. Supreme Court – rightfully – did not construe this bright line limit as a rigid one. It had already held previously that an egregious case with small economic damages could warrant an upward deviation from

1103 See *supra* no. 80.
1104 *BMW of North America, Inc. v. Gore*, 517 U.S. 574–575 (1995).
1105 *State Farm Mutual Automobile Insurance Co. v. Campbell et al.*, 538 U.S. 425 (2003).

the maximum ratio.[1106] In the case of *State Farm Mutual Automobile Insurance Co. v. Campbell* the U.S. Supreme Court then ruled that: "*when compensatory damages are substantial, then a lesser ratio perhaps only equal to compensatory damages, can reach the outermost limit of the due process guarantee*".[1107] In that case it considered an award of USD 1 million in compensatory damages to be substantial.[1108] In the double-digit rule's flexibility lies its weakness as a guiding rule for European judges. European courts can use the 9:1 ceiling as an important indication but should remain cautious as the U.S. Supreme Court itself allows (upwards and downwards) exceptions to the rule depending on the circumstances of the case.

6.2.6. A 1:1 RATIO MIGHT BE THE APPROPRIATE LIMIT

512. The 9:1 ratio ceiling is the limit imposed by the American legal system. European courts are, however, under no obligation to accept this relatively high threshold as the maximum level of their tolerance. They are entitled to set a lower ratio as the boundary of excessiveness for private international law purposes. The use of a ratio is prompted by the search for some form of (numerical) guidance for European judges. Linking the punitive damages to the compensatory damages contributes to foreseeability based on economically calculable factors.[1109] By attaching the acceptable amount of punitive damages to the compensatory damages, their effect becomes somehow more compensation-related, thereby narrowing the gap with the American legal system.[1110]

513. Determining a correct number is inevitably a difficult enterprise, filled with a degree of arbitrariness. As we attempt to offer concrete guidelines to European judges, we, nevertheless, suggest a ratio which we believe to be workable. In our opinion a 1:1 ratio could be the starting point in cases where enforcement of an American punitive damages award is requested.

514. The case law analysed in chapter 4 offers support for this choice. In *Fountaine Pajot* the *Cour de cassation* seems to have laid down a maximum ratio

---

1106 *BMW of North America, Inc. v. Gore*, 517 U.S. 582 (1995).

1107 *State Farm Mutual Automobile Insurance Co. v. Campbell et al.*, 538 U.S. 425 (2003).

1108 *State Farm Mutual Automobile Insurance Co. v. Campbell et al.*, 538 U.S. 426 (2003).

1109 V. Behr, "Punitive Damages in American and German Law – Tendencies Towards Approximation of Apparently Irreconcilable Concepts", 78 *Chicago – Kent Law Review* 2003, 150. Behr himself made this statement in the context of the U.S. case law delineating the constitutional boundaries of punitive damages but it can, in our view, be used in the debate around the development of the excessiveness test.

1110 V. Behr, "Punitive Damages in American and German Law – Tendencies Towards Approximation of Apparently Irreconcilable Concepts", 78 *Chicago – Kent Law Review* 2003, 117. The same remark as in the previous footnote applies.

between punitive and compensatory damages of 1:1. It rejected the punitive damages awarded by the California court because the punitive damages exceeded the compensatory damages.[1111] Later French case law also seems to make use of this ratio.[1112]

In *John Doe v. Eckhard Schmitz* the German *Bundesgerichtshof* rejected the punitive damages for contrariety of the concept itself with international public policy. It, nevertheless, hypothetically took its reasoning a step further and subjected the punitive award to an excessiveness analysis. It stated that the punitive damages granted by the American court would fail the proportionality test because they were higher in amount than the sum of all the compensatory damages.[1113] It thus suggested that a 1:1 ratio might be the outer limit of acceptable punitive damages under international public policy.

515. The 1:1 ratio is not completely new. We find it in the case law of the U.S. Supreme Court as well. The U.S. Supreme Court referenced in *State Farm Mutual Automobile Insurance Co. v. Campbell* to "*a lesser ratio perhaps only equal to compensatory damages*" as the "*the outermost limit of the due process guarantee*" when the compensatory damages are substantial.[1114] In *Exxon Shipping Co.* v. *Baker* the U.S. Supreme Court established a strict 1:1 ratio for federal maritime tort cases.[1115] Lastly, looking outside the selected five EU countries, it could perhaps be argued that the Greek Supreme Court applied this ratio when rejecting the punitive damages awarded by an American court.[1116]

516. The chosen ratio might not be perfect in all circumstances. Think, for instance, of the situation where the American court issues punitive damages on top of nominal damages. As explained in chapter 1,[1117] this is entirely possible because punitive damages require a finding of either actual or nominal damage.[1118] In those type of cases the ratio would of course not work.

517. Without any form of guidance, however, courts are basically left to their own devices. Scholars who have called for the introduction of an excessiveness test mostly did not offer concrete suggestions on how to develop such a test. NAGY has, in our view, undertaken the most praiseworthy effort at formulating

1111 Cass. Civ. 1st, 1 December 2010, *Schlenzka & Langhorne v. Fountaine Pajot S.A*, no. 09-13303, *Recueil Dalloz* 2011, 423.

1112 Court of Appeal Poitiers 4 March 2011, case no. 09/02077; Court of Appeal Paris 30 June 2011, case no. 10/00293. See *supra* no. 315–318 for a discussion of these cases.

1113 BGH 4 June 1992, *Neue Juristische Wochenschrift* 1992, 3104.

1114 *State Farm Mutual Automobile Insurance Co. v. Campbell et al.*, 538 U.S. 425 (2003).

1115 *Exxon Shipping Co. v. Baker*, 554 U.S. 471 (2008). See *supra* no. 92–93.

1116 Greek Supreme Court, decision no. 17/1999, *Nomiko Bina i Miniaion Nomikon Periodikon* 2000, 461–464.

1117 See *supra* no. 64.

1118 A.J. Sebok, "Punitive Damages in the United States" in H. Koziol & V. Wilcox (eds.), *Punitive Damages: Common Law and Civil Law Perspectives*, Vienna, Springer, 2009, 171.

guiding rules for the enforcement of foreign punitive awards. However, when arriving at the difficult issue of excessiveness, he also fails to provide adequate guidance. The author introduced the "marginal recovery approach", inspired by the marginal cost concept in economics. In a model of perfect competition, an undertaking produces its goods or services until its marginal cost (the cost related to the production of one additional unit) reaches the market price. Applying this to the enforcement of punitive damages, NAGY advances that a court should enforce the foreign punitive award to the point that it reaches the court's level of intolerance. It should start from what he calls the "in-the-pocket compensation", which refers to the amount of money that would remain in the plaintiff's pocket on the basis of the law of the forum. This, for instance, means taking the allocation of legal costs through the punitive award into account. This seems to coincide with our statement that the compensatory portion of a punitive award should be enforced, provided it is clearly distinguished. From there, the court is advised to ask itself whether the enforcement of each additional dollar would violate (international) public policy.[1119] Although a correct theory, it does nothing concrete to help European judges find the point of intolerance. All it does is use an economics model to instruct the courts to do what they already know is asked of them, *i.e.* determine what amount of punitive damages is unacceptable under international public policy.

518. This book wants to go beyond previous scholarship and offer concrete tools for European courts to separate acceptable punitive damages from the intolerable ones. A ratio calculation might not be the only way to tackle the enforcement of U.S. punitive damages judgments but it can act as a strong first indicator.

519. In our view, the suggested ratio reflects a measure of reasonableness, striking the balance between not allowing enough of the foreign remedy and opening our borders too liberally. Under this proposed ratio the treble part of an American treble damages judgment, for instance, would be deemed unacceptable in light of international public policy. The 1:1 ratio is situated between, on the one hand, the acceptance of the Spanish Supreme Court in *Miller v. Alabastres* of treble damages (*i.e.* a 2:1 ratio) and the BÉTEILLE Proposal for an article 1386–25 in the French Civil Code which allows the imposition of punitive damages to a maximum amount of twice the level of compensatory damages[1120] (*i.e.* also a 2:1 ratio) and, on the other hand, a suggestion by the author STREBEL. Commenting on the situation in Switzerland, this scholar admitted that it is almost impossible

1119 C.I. Nagy, "Recognition and enforcement of US judgments involving punitive damages in continental Europe", *Nederlands Internationaal Privaatrecht* 2012, 11.

1120 Translation of article 1386–25 based on: C. Mahé, "Punitive damages in the competing reform drafts of the French Civil Code" in L. Meurkens & E. Nordin (eds.), *The Power of Punitive Damages – Is Europe Missing Out?*, Cambridge – Antwerp – Portland, Intersentia, 2012, 262–263, footnote 7.

to come up with figures. He, nevertheless, asserted that punitive damages truly designed to punish and deter are outrageous for enforcement purposes if they exceed 50% of the actual damages (*i.e.* a 1:2 ratio).[1121] The 1:1 ratio is slightly lower than LENZ's proposal to enforce U.S. punitive damages in Switzerland in an amount of up to 130% of the actual damages (*i.e.* a 1,3:1 ratio), depending on the intensity of the *Binnenbeziehung*[1122] of the case.[1123] Interestingly, research in the United States has shown that in the vast majority of cases the ratio between punitive and compensatory damages lies between 0.88 and 0.98 to 1.[1124] A European standard of 1:1 thus seems to cover most of the American punitive damages judgments.

520. STREBEL's reference to "truly punitive damages" actually leads us to an important question. Should damages awarded for legal fees be counted when calculating the ratio between punitive and compensatory damages?[1125] It is quite rare for a U.S. court to order the losing party to pay the winning party's legal costs given the American rule on costs. If they do, they usually award compensation for legal fees under a separate heading. That was the case in *Fountaine Pajot* where the California awarded the sum of USD 402.084,33 for legal fees, next to the normal compensatory damages and the punitive damages. The *Cour de Cassation* did not include the legal fees heading into the ratio calculation.[1126] This method seems reasonable and can be followed. This means that legal fees awarded in the form of punitive damages should first be deducted from the punitive award before the court makes the comparison between the punitive and compensatory damages.[1127]

1121 F. Strebel, "The Enforcement of Foreign Judgements and Foreign Public Law", 21 *Loyola of Los Angeles International and Comparative Law Review* 1999, 104–105.

1122 This is the connection of the facts of the case to the requested forum. See *infra* no. 523 *et seq.* for a more detailed discussion of the possible influence of this concept on any suggested ratio.

1123 C. Lenz, *Amerikanische Punitive Damages vor dem Schweizer Richter*, Zürich, Schulthess, 1992, 183–191. The author further asserts that enforcement of the full amount should be granted in cases where there is, apart from the presence of the defendant's assets, no *Binnenbeziehung*.

1124 T. Eisenberg, J. Goerdt, B. Ostrom, D. Rottman & M.T. Wells, "The Predictability of Punitive Damages", 23 *Journal of Legal Studies* 1997, 652; T. Eisenberg, N. LaFountain, B. Ostrom, D. Rottman & M.T. Wells, "Juries, Judges and Punitive Damages: An Emperical Study", 87 *Cornell Law Review* 2002, 754; T. Eisenberg, P.L. Hannaford-Agor, M. Heise, N. LaFountain, G.T. Munsterman, B. Ostrom & M.T. Wells, "Juries, Judges, and Punitive Damages: Empirical Analyses Using the Civil Justice Survey of State Courts 1992, 1996, and 2001 Data", 3 *Journal of Emperical Legal Studies* 2006, 278.

1125 This is an issue American courts are struggling with as well. See the pending case *Nickerson v. Stonebridge Insurance* (no. S213873) before the California Supreme Court as well as the Illinois Appellate Court of Illinois (First District, Third Division) decision of 2 March 2016 in *Crowley v. Watson* (no. 1–14–2847).

1126 Cass. civ. 1st, 1 December 2010, *Schlenzka & Langhorne v. Fountaine Pajot S.A*, no. 09–13303, *Recueil Dalloz* 2011, 423.

1127 Given the fact that legal fees should be enforceable due to their compensatory objective (see part 6.2.4.), it also seems reasonable as a trade-off to not add them to the compensatory damages (thereby preventing inflation of the latter).

521. Our reliance on a ratio is caused by the ambition to bring some measurable certainty into the excessiveness assessment. It has the benefit of not running afoul of the prohibition of review of the merits (*révision au fond*). In contrast, using factors such as the blameworthiness of the conduct would, in our view, amount to forbidden *révision au fond*. The blameworthiness of the behaviour of the defendant corresponds to the first guidepost of *BMW v. Gore* (referred to as the reprehensibility of the conduct in that case).[1128] The U.S. Supreme Court attached utmost importance to the guidepost for determining constitutional reasonableness.[1129] The French Supreme Court in *Fountaine Pajot* also mentioned the seriousness of the defendant's conduct (our interpretation of "*manquements aux obligations contractuelles du débiteur*"[1130]), although it is not clear if it actually incorporated the factor into its proportionality analysis.[1131]

522. In sum, the 1:1 ratio can prove to be a valuable starting point for the European courts' proportionality test. It should, however, not be viewed as an all-embracing or rigid rule. As the excessiveness test invariably requires a case-by-case assessment, there are special circumstances and influencing factors which might call for an adaptation of the ratio. One such intervening factor is the case's degree of connection to the requested forum.

6.2.7. THE WEAKER THE CASE'S CONNECTION TO THE REQUESTED FORUM, THE MORE TOLERANCE SHOULD BE SHOWN

523. According to the German theory of *Inlandsbeziehung* (also referred to as *Inlandsbezug* or *Binnenbeziehung*) the intensity of the international public policy exception depends on the case's proximity to the forum.[1132, 1133] The notion of *Inlandsbeziehung* has been translated as "forum contacts".[1134] It

1128 *BMW of North America, Inc. v. Gore*, 517 U.S. 574–575 (1995).

1129 *BMW of North America, Inc. v. Gore*, 517 U.S. 575, (1995).

1130 Cass. civ. 1st, 1 December 2010, *Schlenzka & Langhorne v. Fountaine Pajot S.A*, no. 09-13303, *Recueil Dalloz* 2011, 423.

1131 See *supra* no. 310.

1132 M. Requejo Isidro, "Punitive Damages From a Private International Law Perspective" in H. Koziol & V. Wilcox (eds.), *Punitive Damages: Common Law and Civil Law Perspectives*, Vienna, Springer, 2009, 247.

1133 For a study of the concept from a German and French perspective: N. Joubert, *La notion de liens suffisants avec l'ordre juridique (Inlandsbeziehung) en droit international privé*, Paris, LexisNexis – Litec, 2007.

1134 P. Hay, "The Recognition and Enforcement of American Money-Judgments in Germany – The 1992 Decision of the German Supreme Court", 40 *The American Journal of Comparative Law* 1992, 740; J. Zekoll, "The Enforceability of American Money Judgments Abroad: A Landmark Decision by the German Federal Court of Justice", 30 *Columbia Journal of Transnational Law* 1992, 652.

reflects the forum state's interest in a close policing of its international public policy.[1135] There must be an interest in preventing the foreign judgment from being enforced.[1136] The closer the case's connection to the requested court's forum, the stronger the international public policy exception will be. The more connected the case (in terms of the facts and the parties) is to the territory of the requested state, the more interest the requested forum has to let the values of its own legal system influence the enforcement decision, and the less deference is given to the foreign court's judgment. The connection between the situation and the forum can be of a personal or a territorial nature. On the contrary, if the link to the forum is weaker, the forum's interest in intervening is less and the level of tolerance toward the foreign judgment is higher. If the level of contacts to the forum being requested to enforce the judgment is low or non-existent, the application of the (international) public policy clause is softened and more tolerance should, therefore, be granted.[1137] In the case of punitive damages, this would mean that the amount deemed acceptable for enforcement should, all other factors being equal, be higher. The European courts' attitude with regard to U.S. punitive damages awards will thus also depend on the case's factual connection to their territory.

524. There is case law explicitly highlighting the closeness of the underlying case to the requested country as a valuable consideration when deciding on the enforceability of a punitive damages judgment. Both the German Supreme Court in *John Doe v. Eckhard Schmitz* and the Spanish Supreme Court in *Miller v. Alabastres* referred to the concept of *Inlandsbeziehung* in their reasoning.[1138, 1139]

1135 S. Baumgartner, "How well do U.S. judgments fare in Europe?", 40 *George Washington International Law Review* 2008–2009, 205, footnote 189.

1136 V. Behr, "Punitive Damages in American and German Law – Tendencies Towards Approximation of Apparently Irreconcilable Concepts", 78 *Chicago – Kent Law Review* 2003, 153.

1137 M. Requejo Isidro, "Punitive Damages From a Private International Law Perspective" in H. Koziol & V. Wilcox (eds.), *Punitive Damages: Common Law and Civil Law Perspectives*, Vienna, Springer, 2009, 246.

1138 Reference can also be made to the aforementioned Swiss case between S.F. Inc. and T.C.S. AG (see *supra* footnote no. 1090), decided three years before the Bundesgerichtshof's judgment in *John Doe v. Eckhard Schmitz*. In the Swiss case the District Court of Basel held that there was, apart from the defendant's domicile, no *Binnenbeziehung*. The District Court pointed to the fact that the defendant offered its services worldwide, to the claim related to a contract regarding the transport of military goods between the U.S. and England and to the parties' choice for English law. These findings called for great restraint in the application of the public policy exception: District Court Basel-Stadt 1 February 1989, upheld by the Basel-Stadt Court of Appeal 1 December 1989, *Basler Juristische Mitteilungen* 1991, 34–35; M. Bernet & N.C. Ulmer, "Recognition and Enforcement in Switzerland of US Judgments Containing an Award of Punitive Damages", 22 *International Business Lawyer* 1994, 273; S. Baumgartner, "How well do U.S. judgments fare in Europe?", 40 *George Washington International Law Review* 2008–2009, 220–221.

1139 In the French case *Fountaine Pajot* the *Cour de cassation* did not analyse the connection between the matter and the forum; it can be assumed that the connection was not at all

525. The *Bundesgerichtshof* first briefly provided insight on the extent of the concept of *Inlandsbeziehung*. It explained that the international public policy exception mechanism in applicable law (to be found in article 6 EGBGB[1140]) requires a sufficiently strong domestic relationship but that this is even more the case for the public policy exception in enforcement matters (to be found in article 328 (1), 4 of the German Code of Civil Procedure). When a judgment is sought to be enforced, forum contacts are of even higher importance as the court is no longer called upon to adjudicate the claim or the amount of compensation.[1141] When dealing with an enforcement request the court only needs to ascertain whether *the result* enforcement would produce would be acceptable in the forum.[1142] The German Supreme Court explained that the proportionality test must take the remoteness of the underlying fact pattern into consideration and that the absence of sufficient contacts to Germany mandates that a greater tolerance be shown toward the foreign decision.[1143]

526. In the case before the *Bundesgerichtshof* the sexual abuse took place in the United States and both the victim and the perpetrator held American citizenship. The matter involved a tort claim filed by one American against another. In the relevant period in which the crime occurred both were California residents.[1144] The defendant only took up residence in Germany after his criminal conviction. The defendant's German nationality was the only other factor connecting the case to Germany.[1145] The connection to the German forum was, therefore, very low. The public policy exception was, nevertheless, employed to block the enforcement of the California judgment. Despite the slight connection to the forum, the German Supreme Court did not tolerate the punitive award.[1146] This

---

negligible: C.I. Nagy, "Recognition and enforcement of US judgments involving punitive damages in continental Europe", *Nederlands Internationaal Privaatrecht* 2012, 9. The damage to the vessel, for instance, occurred in a French port.

1140 At the time of the judgment article 6 EGBGB provided for the public policy clause when determining the applicable law. However, nowadays the specific public policy provision of article 40, paragraph 3, EGBGB takes precedence and rules out punitive damages completely.

1141 P. Hay, "The Recognition and Enforcement of American Money-Judgments in Germany – The 1992 Decision of the German Supreme Court", 40 *The American Journal of Comparative Law* 1992, 740.

1142 BGH 4 June 1992, *BGHZ* 118, 348.

1143 BGH 4 June 1992, *ZIP* 1992, 1270; J. Zekoll, "The Enforceability of American Money Judgments Abroad: A Landmark Decision by the German Federal Court of Justice", 30 *Columbia Journal of Transnational Law* 1992, 653.

1144 C.I. Nagy, "Recognition and enforcement of US judgments involving punitive damages in continental Europe", *Nederlands Internationaal Privaatrecht* 2012, 8.

1145 BGH 4 June 1992, *BGHZ* 118, 348–349. Hay even asserts that it is not a relevant forum contact in the context of the public policy exception in enforcement cases: P. Hay, "The Recognition and Enforcement of American Money-Judgments in Germany – The 1992 Decision of the German Supreme Court", 40 *The American Journal of Comparative Law* 1992, 741, footnote 42.

1146 The low degree of connection did, however, cause the German Supreme Court to accept the award for pain and suffering: BGH 4 June 1992, *ZIP* 1270.

reveals the *Bundesgerichtshof*'s profound dislike for punitive damages at the time.[1147]

527. The Spanish Supreme Court in *Miller v. Alabastres* also attached importance to the case's proximity to the forum. It stated that the court cannot lose sight of the relation the matter presents to the Spanish forum when deciding whether there is a violation of public policy. This can be seen as a clear reference to the *Inlandsbeziehung*.[1148] The Spanish Supreme Court, however, did not go beyond this mere mention and did not apply the concept to the facts of the case (at least not explicitly in the judgment). It could be argued that there was at least a certain degree of *Inlandsbeziehung* in the factual pattern because the manufacture of the trademark infringing labels took place in Spain.

528. ZEKOLL criticises the use of *Inlandsbeziehung* for the public policy analysis of the incoming judgment. Although his observations relate to the German situation, they, nevertheless, could be extended to the other European legal systems as well. He argues that constitutional rights are not implicated to a greater degree when the defendant is more closely associated with the German forum. According to ZEKOLL the Supreme Court's reasoning suggests that a defendant with strong ties to Germany may rely on public policy protection to a larger degree than defendants who lack such contact. The *Bundesgerichtshof*'s judgment would lead to a difference in treatment between, for instance, a German company with no corporate presence in the United States whose products cause harm to American consumers and a German defendant with permanent residence in the United States whose negligent driving injured an American citizen. The former would be able to shield more behind the public policy clause whereas the latter would not be able to invoke the public policy clause to the same extent.[1149]

529. ZEKOLL does see a role for *Inlandsbeziehung* in the applicable law context. In the conflict of laws analysis there is a heightened interest of the German forum because it has to adjudicate the case on the merits. Intervention of German law through the public policy clause is then less likely if the facts are

1147 C.I. Nagy, "Recognition and enforcement of US judgments involving punitive damages in continental Europe", *Nederlands Internationaal Privaatrecht* 2012, 8.

1148 Spanish Supreme Court 13 November 2001, Exequatur no. 2039/1999, *Aedipr* 2003, 914; M. Requejo Isidro, "Punitive Damages: How Do They Look Like When Seen From Abroad?" in L. Meurkens & E. Nordin (eds.), *The Power of Punitive Damages – Is Europe Missing Out?*, Cambridge – Antwerp – Portland, Intersentia, 2012, 326–327; M. Requejo Isidro, "Punitive Damages From a Private International Law Perspective" in in H. Koziol & V. Wilcox (eds.), *Punitive Damages: Common Law and Civil Law Perspectives*, Vienna, Springer, 2009, 247.

1149 J. Zekoll, "The Enforceability of American Money Judgments Abroad: A Landmark Decision by the German Federal Court of Justice", 30 *Columbia Journal of Transnational Law* 1992, 653.

only remotely connected to the German forum.[1150] Conversely, if there is a close relationship with the German territory, the courts are more inclined to pre-empt foreign rules by applying German law. In the field of enforcement of judgments, the interests of the forum are significantly less because the court deals with an incoming final decision which a competent foreign court rendered after full adjudication of the dispute.[1151]

530. Recital 32 of the Rome II Regulation could perhaps harbour a reference to the *Inlandsbeziehung* concept as it reads: "[...] *application of a provision of the law designated by this Regulation which would have the effect of causing non-compensatory exemplary or punitive damages of an excessive nature to be awarded may,* depending on the circumstances of the case and the legal order of the Member State of the court seized, *be regarded as being contrary to the public policy (ordre public) of the forum*" (own emphasis). These two criteria (circumstances of the case and the legal order of the forum) could, with some goodwill, be understood as requiring the forum court to include *Inlandsbeziehung* as a factor in its applicable law analysis. However, this is far from certain as it has already been noted that the introduction of a principle of proximity into European Law is currently being discussed in legal theory[1152] and that its application to the public policy exception as laid down in European regulations has not yet been established.[1153]

6.2.8. THE NATURE OF THE INTERESTS PROTECTED

531. Next to the connection to the forum, the interest at stake is the second parameter to be evaluated before international public policy can be activated. *Inlandsbeziehung* modulates the strength of the public policy according to the closeness of the case to the forum. The stronger the interest protected by international public policy is, the less relevant the link to the forum must be to

---

1150 Again, article 40, paragraph 3, EGBGB did not exist yet and, therefore, the public policy exception of article 6 EGBGB applied.

1151 J. Zekoll, "The Enforceability of American Money Judgments Abroad: A Landmark Decision by the German Federal Court of Justice", 30 *Columbia Journal of Transnational Law* 1992, 654.

1152 For instance in: M. Fallon, "Le principe de proximité dans le droit de l'Union européenne" in M.N. Jobard-Bachellier, P. Mayer & P. Lagarde (eds.), *Mélanges en l'honneur de Paul Lagarde; Le droit international privé: esprit et méthodes*, Paris, Dalloz, 2005, 241.

1153 Directorate-General for Internal Policies, Policy Department Citizens' Rights and Constitutional Affairs, Legal Affairs, The public-policy exception and the Proposal for a Regulation of the European Parliament and of the Council on jurisdiction, applicable law, recognition and enforcement of decisions and authentic instruments in matters of succession and the creation of a European Certificate of Succession, (COM(2009)154), 2010, 18, available at <www.europarl.europa.eu/document/activities/cont/201012/20101210ATT08870/20101210ATT08870EN.pdf>.

activate public policy.[1154] The opposite is also true. The degree of connection to the forum and the importance of the interest thus act as communicating vessels.

532. It is perhaps in this regard that the second criterion of the proportionality analysis in the Spanish case of *Miller v. Alabastres* can be given meaning. In the case a Texas court awarded treble damages against the Spanish defendant for trademark infringement. The Spanish Supreme Court attached particular importance to the nature of the interests protected. It found that not only the Spanish legal system[1155] but nations all over the world highly value the protection of intellectual property rights. Market economies globally set great store by the upholding of these rights.[1156] A common desire to protect the interest at stake might thus lead to more tolerance on the side of the enforcing court. Human rights in particular form an important interest to consider but also the safeguarding of the environment, freedom, dignity and legal certainty could be put forward as such strong interests.[1157] The criterion does not cause any conceptual problems as it does not amount to *révision au fond* because the requested court is not reviewing the merits of the case.

6.2.9. REDUCING THE PUNITIVE AWARD TO THE TOLERABLE LEVEL IS ALLOWED

533. Once the requested court has determined, with the help of the guidelines formulated, that the punitive award is not excessive, the judgment can be granted enforcement. More difficult is the situation in which the punitive damages award does not pass the excessiveness test. Two possible scenarios are imaginable. One, called the "selective partial exequatur"[1158], where the court declares the whole punitive damages heading of the judgment unenforceable and enforces only the compensatory damages (if requested). Two, called the "reductive partial exequatur"[1159], where the court enforces the punitive damages up to the amount it deems to be tolerable in light of public policy.

1154 E. Rodriguez Pineau, "European Union International Ordre Public", *Spanish Yearbook of International Law* 1993–1994, 65.

1155 As discussed in chapter 5, Spanish law even provides for a coercive fine in the field of trademarks: see *supra* no. 395.

1156 Spanish Supreme Court 13 November 2001, Exequatur no. 2039/1999, *Aedipr* 2003, 914.

1157 M. Requejo Isidro, "Punitive Damages – Europe Strikes Back?", presentation delivered at the British Institute of International and Comparative Law, 2 November 2011, London, text on file with the author.

1158 B. Janke & F.-X. Licari, "Enforcing Punitive Damage Awards in France after Fountaine Pajot", 60 *The American Journal of Comparative Law* 2012, 803.

1159 B. Janke & F.-X. Licari, "Enforcing Punitive Damage Awards in France after Fountaine Pajot", 60 *The American Journal of Comparative Law* 2012, 803.

534. The first scenario establishes an all-or-nothing approach: either all the punitive damages are enforced or all of them are rejected. Enforcement or rejection should always relate to the whole punitive award. The second scenario allows the judge to reduce the amount of the punitive damages if he finds the awarded sum excessive, instead of having to opt for either total enforcement or total rejection of the punitive award. He can determine the point at which the punitive damages become disproportionate, throw out the excessive amount and enforce the remaining non-excessive portion of the punitive award.

535. The French *Cour de cassation* opted for the first approach in *Fountaine Pajot*. The French Supreme Court determined that the 1:1 ratio between punitive and compensatory damages had been exceeded by the American judgment. This finding of excessiveness led to the rejection of the whole punitive damages award.[1160] Similarly, the German *Bundesgerichtshof* in *John Doe v. Eckhard Schmitz* spoke out against partitioning the punitive award, by stating that the requested court should not be allowed to cut up the punitive damages awarded based on its own free judgment.[1161]

536. The choice between both options stems from different interpretations of the prohibition of *révision au fond*. The first approach incorporates the idea that the arbitrary splitting of the punitive award would amount to forbidden *révision* au fond. Under this view the judge is not allowed to chop the punitive award according to its own discretion to strike the right balance but can only accept or reject the punitive award as a whole.[1162] The punitive damages heading should be enforced or rejected in its entirety. Under the second approach the judge is allowed to cut the punitive award to a level which is acceptable to the forum. The prohibition to review the merits of an incoming judgment does not prevent the requested court to sever the acceptable amount of punitive damages from the excessive, non-tolerable part of the punitive award. Instead of having to rule on the head of punitive damages as a whole, the court is allowed to modify the amount to a numerical level compatible with the international public policy of the forum.[1163]

1160 Cass. civ. 1st, 1 December 2010, *Schlenzka & Langhorne v. Fountaine Pajot S.A*, no. 09–13303, *Recueil Dalloz* 2011, 423.

1161 BGH 4 June 1992, *Neue Juristische Wochenschrift* 1992, 3104; P.J. Nettesheim & H. Stahl, "Recent Development – Bundesgerichtshof Rejects Enforcement of United States Punitive Damages Award", 28 *Texas International Law Journal* 1993, 423.

1162 C.I. Nagy, "Recognition and enforcement of US judgments involving punitive damages in continental Europe", *Nederlands Internationaal Privaatrecht* 2012, 8.

1163 G.A.L. Droz, "Variations Pordea", *Revue Critique du Droit International Privé* 2000, 194; B. Janke & F.-X. Licari, "Enforcing Punitive Damage Awards in France after Fountaine Pajot", 60 *The American Journal of Comparative Law* 2012, 803; F.-X. Licari, "Prendre les punitive damages au sérieux: propos critiques sur un refus d'accorder l'exequatur à une décision californienne ayant alloué des dommages intérêts punitifs", *Journal du droit international*

537. It is our belief that a European court should be allowed to reduce the amount of the punitive damages to the level it finds acceptable in light of international public policy. The all-or-nothing approach requiring the court to either take or leave the punitive award should not be followed. Cutting down the punitive award (to, for instance, our tentatively suggested 1:1 ratio) does not amount to *révision au fond* because the European court is not giving its opinion about the merits of the foreign case. The requested court is not reforming the foreign court's examination of the facts of the case or second-guessing the foreign court's adjudication of the matter. It is not questioning whether the foreign decision was correct in fact and/or in law. By curtailing the amount of punitive damages, the requested court is merely stating that, for private international law purposes, the forum's tolerance of this particular remedy goes up to a certain mathematical level but not beyond.

538. Even if it is not the intention of the requested court, the curtailing of the punitive award might be held *in effect* to amount to such a forbidden *révision au fond*. Besides, prohibiting the curtailing of compensatory damages while at the same time calling for the reduction of punitive damages would amount to a double standard. However, even if the reduction of the punitive damages is indeed seen as a form of *révision au fond*[1164], this does not change our preference for the technique. Some of the few fellow advocates of the reductive partial exequatur approach call for the exceptional setting aside of the prohibition in order to allow the judge to enforce the punitive award up to the amount that passes the excessiveness scrutiny.[1165] This should not be treated as an absurd proposal because it could be argued that any substantive public policy control already amounts to an explicitly permissible limited *révision au fond*.[1166]

(Clunet) October/November/December 2010/4, 1261; C.I. Nagy, "Recognition and enforcement of US judgments involving punitive damages in continental Europe", *Nederlands Internationaal Privaatrecht* 2012, 11; F. Strebel, "The Enforcement of Foreign Judgements and Foreign Public Law", 21 *Loyola of Los Angeles International and Comparative Law Review* 1999, 104; D. Favalli & J.M. Matthews, "Recognition and Enforcement of U.S. class action judgments and settlements in Switzerland", *Schweizerische Zeitschrift für internationales und Europäisches Recht* 2007, 635.

1164 See, for instance, Gaudemet-Tallon who asserts in the context of the Brussels I Regulation that reducing the amount of a "condamnation" that is considered excessive (*i.e. exequatur partiel réductif*) is not allowed as it is a form of *révision au fond*: H. Gaudemet-Tallon, *Compétence et exécution des jugements en Europe*, Paris, LGDJ, 2010, 489.

1165 G.A.L. Droz, "Variations Pordea", *Revue Critique du Droit International Privé* 2000, 194; B. Janke & F.-X. Licari, "Enforcing Punitive Damage Awards in France after Fountaine Pajot", 60 *The American Journal of Comparative Law* 2012, 803; F.-X. Licari, "Prendre les punitive damages au sérieux: propos critiques sur un refus d'accorder l'exequatur à une décision californienne ayant alloué des dommages intérêts punitifs", *Journal du droit international (Clunet)* October/November/December 2010/4, 1262.

1166 G. Nater-Bass, "U.S.-Style Punitive Damages Awards and their Recognition and Enforcement in Switzerland and Other Civil-Law Countries", 28 *Deutsch-Amerikanische Juristen-Vereinigung Newsletter* 2003, 159.

Allowing the numerical chop would then be included in the realm of permissible public policy review.

539. The approval of the second approach brings a degree of fairness into the excessiveness analysis. Under the all-or-nothing approach one excess dollar could theoretically be the difference between being able to enforce all of the punitive damages or none of them. Withholding a large punitive award based on the presence of a small excessive amount of punitive damages would be a denial of justice and an unjust penalty for the plaintiff.[1167] The possibility of a partial enforcement of the punitive damages leads to fairer results for plaintiffs and defendants who are no longer subjected to a random spin of the wheel. Plaintiffs in American litigation should also not be fearful that the amount of punitive damages they are requesting is going to be deemed excessive for European enforcement standards. They can claim the amount they feel appropriate before the American courts without concern that they will be unable to enforce any of the punitive damages in Europe because the amount of punitive damages received is too high.[1168]

6.3. THE INTENSITY OF THE INTERNATIONAL PUBLIC POLICY EXCEPTION: *ORDRE PUBLIC PLEIN* VERSUS *ORDRE PUBLIC ATTÉNUÉ*

540. Now that has been established that punitive damages as part of the applicable foreign law and punitive damages awarded in a foreign judgment are both subjected to an excessiveness test under the international public policy and guidelines for the application thereof have been suggested, one question remains. It relates to the strength of the international public policy exception in both areas. Is the international public policy mechanism stronger in applicable law than in enforcement of judgments or vice versa?

541. Under one view the involvement of the international public policy exception in enforcement is allowed to be higher than when applying foreign law. In the European Union the principle of *exequatur sur exequatur ne vaut* forbids

[1167] G.A.L. Droz, "Variations Pordea", *Revue Critique du Droit International Privé* 2000, 194; B. Janke & F.-X. Licari, "Enforcing Punitive Damage Awards in France after Fountaine Pajot", 60 *The American Journal of Comparative Law* 2012, 803; F.-X. Licari, "Prendre les punitive damages au sérieux: propos critiques sur un refus d'accorder l'exequatur à une décision californienne ayant alloué des dommages intérêts punitifs", *Journal du droit international (Clunet)* October/November/December 2010/4, 1261.

[1168] Admittedly, the use of punitive damages in the United States as a pressure method towards the defendant will only increase. See in that regard also footnote 163.

the enforcement of a national judgment enforcing a foreign decision.[1169, 1170] If the plaintiff wants to enforce his judgment in multiple Member States, he is required to request enforcement of the original judgment in each of these countries. He cannot rely on one judgment granting exequatur and seek further enforcement of this judgment in other Member States because an exequatur does not travel.[1171] In enforcement of judgments the effect of the public policy intervention is thus limited to the territory of the requested state.[1172]

Conversely, the international public policy exception should be less intrusive in the field of applicable law. The application of this – national – mechanism in choice-of-law *"essentially elevates [the forum's international] public policy to a pan-European level [...], as all other Member States will have to recognise that judgment"*.[1173] The opinion of one Member State would be forced upon all others because the judgment rendered will benefit from virtually unhindered enforcement under the Brussels I*bis* Regulation.

542. We, however, see things differently. In our view public policy has a greater role to play in applicable law than in enforcement.[1174] The field of applicable law calls for a more profound international public policy control. When a European judge applies American punitive damages he is asked to welcome punitive damages as a matter of substantive law. This is far more shocking to the forum than allowing the entrance of punitive damages via the doorway of

1169 The legal basis for this mantra is the idea that the recognition of a third state's judgment is a procedural matter and, therefore, not entitled to recognition under the Brussels I (now Brussels I*bis*) regime: P. Hay, "Recognition of a Recognition Judgment Within the European Union: "Double exequatur" and the Public Policy Barrier" in P. Hay, L. Vékás, Y. Elkana & N. Dimitrijevic (eds.), *Resolving international conflicts: liber amicorum Tibor Várady*, Budapest – New York, Central European University Press, 2009, 147.

1170 This might be different for the Common Law jurisdiction of England where the foreign judgment gets transformed into a local judgment. See *supra* no. 254.

1171 P. Hay, "Recognition of a Recognition Judgment Within the European Union: "Double exequatur" and the Public Policy Barrier" in P. Hay, L. Vékás, Y. Elkana & N. Dimitrijevic (eds.), *Resolving international conflicts: liber amicorum Tibor Várady*, Budapest – New York, Central European University Press, 2009, 144.

1172 A. Rushworth, "Remedies and the Rome II Regulation" in J. Ahern & W. Binchy (eds.), *The Rome II Regulation on the Law Applicable to Non-Contractual Obligations*, Leiden – Boston, Martinus Nijhoff Publishers, 2009, 201.

1173 A. Rushworth, "Remedies and the Rome II Regulation" in J. Ahern & W. Binchy (eds.), *The Rome II Regulation on the Law Applicable to Non-Contractual Obligations*, Leiden – Boston, Martinus Nijhoff Publishers, 2009, 201.

1174 M. Requejo Isidro, "Punitive Damages From a Private International Law Perspective" in H. Koziol & V. Wilcox (eds.), *Punitive Damages: Common Law and Civil Law Perspectives*, Vienna, Springer, 2009, 320; E. de Kezel, "The Protection and Enforcement of Private Interests by (the Recognition of US) Punitive Damages in Belgium" in L. Meurkens & E. Nordin (eds.), *The Power of Punitive Damages – Is Europe Missing Out?*, Cambridge – Antwerp – Portland, Intersentia, 2012, 234; S. Baumgartner, "Understanding the Obstacles to the Recognition and Enforcement of U.S. Judgments Abroad", 45 *New York University Journal of International Law and Politics* 2013, 993–994, footnote 99.

judgment enforcement. In the latter case the situation is fully created abroad, not by the European court itself, therefore causing less interference with the receiving legal system.[1175] Moreover, due to the free circulation of judgments in the European Union, the international public policy mechanism in choice-of-law is the last checkpoint before the institution of punitive damages fully penetrates the whole European fortress. The elevation of one Member State's idea of fundamental values to a pan-European level is a mere consequence of the European Union's principle of mutual trust and, therefore, needs to be accepted as such. The international public policy barrier in enforcement is, in contrast, less significant because the impact is limited to one territory only.[1176] The weakened effect of international public policy in enforcement compared to applicable law is referred to as *ordre public atténué*.[1177] On the other hand, the more intense application of international public policy in the choice-of-law analysis is known as *ordre public plein*.[1178]

6.4. CONCLUSION

543. As to the enforcement of punitive damages, this chapter advanced a number of concrete guiding principles that European judges can work with when confronted with American punitive damages judgments. These rules are not all-encompassing or exhaustive but can help requested courts to make well-informed decisions. The recommendations to the European courts are formulated in such a way as to respect the prohibition of *révision au fond*.

544. The guidelines can be summarised as follows:

- Enforcement is the rule, the international public policy mechanism is the exception: a rejection on public policy grounds is an exceptional measure and should be employed as such.

1175 G. Cavalier, "Punitive Damages and French International Public Policy" in R. Stürner and M. Kawono (eds.), *Comparative Studies on Business Tort Litigation*, Tübingen, Mohr Siebeck, 2011, 222.

1176 E. de Kezel, "The Protection and Enforcement of Private Interests by (the Recognition of US) Punitive Damages in Belgium" in L. Meurkens & E. Nordin (eds.), *The Power of Punitive Damages – Is Europe Missing Out?*, Cambridge – Antwerp – Portland, Intersentia, 2012, 234; M. Requejo Isidro, "Punitive Damages From a Private International Law Perspective" in H. Koziol & V. Wilcox (eds.), *Punitive Damages: Common Law and Civil Law Perspectives*, Vienna, Springer, 2009, 320.

1177 M. Requejo Isidro, "Punitive Damages From a Private International Law Perspective" in H. Koziol & V. Wilcox (eds.), *Punitive Damages: Common Law and Civil Law Perspectives*, Vienna, Springer, 2009, 245–246.

1178 See for instance: Cass. 17 April 1953, *Bull.* 1953, no. 121.

- The compensatory damages awarded should always be granted enforcement: courts are encouraged to enforce separate awards for compensatory damages.
- The compensatory portion of the punitive damages should be enforced: any clearly exposed part of the punitive damages award that fulfils a compensatory role is unproblematic in light of the international public policy exception and should be accepted by the courts of the Member States.
- U.S. punitive damages going above a 9:1 ratio are, in principle, suspect: the U.S. Supreme Court's rejection of double digit ratios between punitive damages and compensatory damages should act as a strong signal to Member States' courts regarding the maximum level of punitive damages the latter should tolerate.
- A 1:1 ratio could be a possible boundary for the enforcement of U.S. punitive damages awards: in individual cases this maximum ratio can then further be modulated according to (1) the degree of connection between the case and the forum and (2) the nature of the interest protected.
- Courts may reduce the head of punitive damages to an acceptable amount: the excessiveness analysis of the American punitive damages should not be construed as an all-or-nothing affair.

545. These recommendations apply *mutatis mutandis* in the context of applicable law as well. The intensity of the international public policy is, however, higher in this field of private international law compared to its attenuated effect when dealing with enforcement of judgments. Not all guidelines are of course transposable to the field of choice-of-law. The suggestion dealing with the compensatory damages awarded as well as the one encouraging awareness of the possible compensatory function of the punitive award are specific to the situation of enforcement of judgments. Finally, as the interdiction of *révision au fond* does not come into play in the private international law arena of applicable law, the court can – within the parameters of the applicable foreign rules – freely set the amount it believes to be permissible under international public policy.

CHAPTER 7
CONCLUSION

546. Punitive damages are an important tool in the United States' societal model which relies on private enforcement through tort litigation as a means to achieve public safety. In that sense they act as a reward to incentivise private plaintiffs to seek redress for their own violated interests, thereby contributing to the common good.[1179] Despite being under constant scrutiny, they have a strong foothold on the other side of the ocean.

547. The extra-compensatory institution of punitive damages has no official existence in the European Union. The state and not private persons are the prime actors in crafting and implementing social welfare policy. The governments of the European Member States attain public interest goals through regulation, state supervision and social security, rather than through the encouragement of private legal action.[1180] The only major exception to the express rejection of punitive damages can be found in England, the nation of their modern birthplace, which provides for an acknowledgment of exemplary damages in limited circumstances.[1181]

548. The expansion of global trade and intercontinental tourism increases the number of cross-border law suits. In such transnational litigation it is inevitable that a jurisdiction is faced with a legal institution that is alien to the substantive law of the forum. Punitive damages are such an institution. Private international law offers an interesting perspective as it forms a country's first line of defence

[1179] J. Mallor & B.S. Roberts, "Punitive Damages: On the Path to a Principled Approach?", 50 *Hastings Law Journal* 1999, 1003; L. Meurkens, "The punitive damages debate in Continental Europe: food for thought" in L. Meurkens & E. Nordin (eds.), *The Power of Punitive Damages – Is Europe Missing Out?*, Cambridge – Antwerp – Portland, Intersentia, 2012, 20–21; U. Magnus, "Punitive Damages and German Law" in L. Meurkens & E. Nordin (eds.), *The Power of Punitive Damages – Is Europe Missing Out?*, Cambridge – Antwerp – Portland, Intersentia, 2012, 251; E. de Kezel, "The Protection and Enforcement of Private Interests by (the Recognition of US) Punitive Damages in Belgium" in L. Meurkens & E. Nordin (eds.), *The Power of Punitive Damages – Is Europe Missing Out?*, Cambridge – Antwerp – Portland, Intersentia, 2012, 225–226.

[1180] L. Meurkens, "The punitive damages debate in Continental Europe: food for thought" in L. Meurkens & E. Nordin (eds.), *The Power of Punitive Damages – Is Europe Missing Out?*, Cambridge – Antwerp – Portland, Intersentia, 2012, 20–21 and 27.

[1181] *Rookes v. Barnard* (1964) U.K.H.L, 37–38 (H.L.).

against a remedy described as "*the Trojan horse of the Americanisation of continental law*".[1182] A nation's private international law attitude indicates the country's level of tolerance towards a foreign concept unknown in its own legal system.

549. In applicable law and enforcement of judgments the openness of Civil Law jurisdictions is measured through the international public policy exception. This derivative from domestic public policy contains only the most fundamental values of the forum and is, therefore, narrower in scope than its internal counterpart. For service of process the Hague Service Convention introduces an autonomous notion ("the sovereignty or security of the state") that is akin to the domestic international public exception. An investigation of the current private international law situation in the European Union reveals that the degree of receptiveness varies greatly depending on the area of private international law.

550. The response to the first sub-question of the research thus requires a clear distinction. In the area of service of process the escape clause foreseen by the Hague Service Convention does not form an impediment to the service of American punitive damages claims. The German experience demonstrates that a refusal to effectuate service can only be justified in the narrow circumstances in which there is "an abuse of process from the outset". It is highly unlikely that a claim for punitive damages, by itself, would meet this high threshold.

551. The case law dealing with the enforcement of U.S. punitive damages tells another story. The traditional approach of the European courts is one of refusal to enforce this type of damages for a variety of reasons. Punitive damages run counter to the strictly compensatory purpose of tort law, creating an unjust enrichment for the victorious plaintiff. The institution is a civil remedy with penal effects putting the boundary between private and public law into question and infringing the state's monopoly on punishment. Moreover, they are awarded without offering the defendant any of the procedural safeguards that a suspect is entitled to in criminal law. These arguments support the courts' decision to stop punitive damages at the European borders.

552. This antipathetic position can be found in the early decision of the German *Bundesgerichtshof* in *John Doe v. Eckhard Schmitz* and in the ruling of

---

1182 Y. Lambert-Faivre & S. Porchy-Simon, *Droit du dommage corporel - Systèmes d'indemnisation*, Paris, Dalloz, 2009, no. 92 and 375; H. Honsell, "Amerikanische Rechtskultur" in P. Forstmoser, H.S. von der Crone, R.H. Weber & D. Zobl (eds.), *Festschrift für Roger Zäch zum 60. Geburtstag. Der Einfluss des europäischen Rechts auf die Schweiz*, Zurich, Schulthess Verlag, 1999, 39; F.-X. Licari, "La compatibilité de principe des punitive damages avec l'ordre public international: une décision en trompe-l'œil de la Cour de cassation?", *Recueil Dalloz* 10 February 2011, 427.

the Italian Supreme Court in *Fimez*. With regard to multiple damages, a specific form of punitive damages, England takes the same hostile stance as PTIA bars the enforcement of such damages completely. This is surprising given the presence of exemplary damages in its own legal system.

553. Since the turn of the century, however, several judgments have displayed a more welcoming attitude. In addition to the Greek Supreme Court, both the Spanish Tribunal *Supremo* in *Miller v. Alabastres* and the French Supreme Court in *Fountaine Pajot* have found that punitive damages as a concept do not violate international public policy. Such awards should in principle be granted enforcement. The punitive damages can only be rejected if they are deemed to be excessive.

554. The European private international law regime regarding the application of foreign law in non-contractual matters arguably corresponds with this progressive trend in the case law on enforcement. Recital 32 of the Rome II Regulation supplements and clarifies the instrument's general international public policy exception. It allows the awarding of punitive damages through the application of foreign law. Only *excessive* punitive damages may be refused by the Member States on the basis of their international public policy exception. On the other side of the spectrum, the German national rules, applicable in cases falling outside the scope of the Regulation, prohibit foreign damages which obviously serve purposes other than an adequate compensation of the injured party. The German courts, therefore, have to reject U.S. punitive damages if their conflict of laws analysis leads them to the law of an American state.

555. As concerns the second sub-question, the conclusion again depends on the field of private international law.[1183] The current attitude towards American punitive damages in service of process is worthy of support. The very restricted interpretation of the refusal ground in the Hague Service Convention contributes to the realisation of the Convention's goal of a simplified and expeditious cross-border exchange of judicial documents. The service stage is not the suitable phase to deal with public policy concerns about the remedy of punitive damages. The outcome of the American law suit is uncertain at the time of service. Any objections should be raised if and when the judgment awarding punitive damages is brought before the European courts for enforcement. Besides, any issues surrounding the possible refusal of cooperation can simply be avoided by opting for domestic service in lieu of service abroad or by strategically waiting to file a claim for punitive damages until the defendant has been served in Europe.

[1183] M. Requejo Isidro, "Punitive Damages: How Do They Look Like When Seen From Abroad?" in L. Meurkens & E. Nordin (eds.), *The Power of Punitive Damages – Is Europe Missing Out?*, Cambridge – Antwerp – Portland, Intersentia, 2012, 329.

556. In contrast to the approval of the state of play in service of process, the conventional judicial approach disallowing the enforcement of punitive damages for fundamental reasons is to be criticised. The same applies to national choice-of-law rules, such as article 40, paragraph 3 of the German EGBGB, which prevent the awarding of punitive damages, irrespective of the amount the judge wishes to grant.

557. A dismissal of punitive damages on principle fails to recognise the legal reality in the Member States and at the EU level. The private law systems of the Member States contain remedies and institutions which deviate from the strictly compensatory agenda of tort law. Their pursuit of deterrence and/or punishment puts pressure on the exclusively compensatory function of the civil liability system. Although this observation might threaten the "dogmatic purity" of the system, it is a reality that cannot be ignored.[1184] The existence of such punitive-like measures might not be enough to declare a revolution in substantive law or even in domestic public policy but arguably does have an impact on the international public policy exception.

558. If European nations award punitive damages themselves (England being the prime example) or deploy concepts and institutions that closely resemble such damages or pursue the same aims (the Civil Law Member States), they cannot reject American punitive damages just because they originate overseas. It would, first of all, violate the coherence of their legal system and, secondly, would testify to an ambiguous attitude. In the words of the American judge Benjamin N. Cardozo: "*We are not so provincial as to say that every solution of a problem is wrong because we deal with it otherwise at home*".[1185]

559. Besides, one must not forget that due to the political and social differences, plaintiffs in the United States might rely on the enforcement of their punitive award to secure their future. The underlying American social and cultural context with its lack of a social net and its relatively inactive government increases the relevance of punitive damages for the American plaintiff's existence.[1186] On the other side of the coin, parties who are active in

---

1184 H. Auf'mkolk, "U.S. punitive damages awards before German courts – Time for a new approach", *Freiburg Law Students Journal* 2007, 10; M. Otero Crespo, "Punitive Damages Under Spanish Law: A Subtle Recognition?" in L. Meurkens & E. Nordin (eds.), *The Power of Punitive Damages – Is Europe Missing Out?*, Cambridge – Antwerp – Portland, Intersentia, 2012, 300.

1185 *Loucks v. Standard Oil Co. of New York*, C 120 N. E., 201 (N.Y. 1918) (Cardozo, J.).

1186 M. Tolani, "U.S. Punitive Damages Before German Courts: A Comparative Analysis with Respect to the Ordre Public", 17 *Annual Survey of International & Comparative Law* 2011, 205; L. Meurkens, "The punitive damages debate in Continental Europe: food for thought" in L. Meurkens & E. Nordin (eds.), *The Power of Punitive Damages – Is Europe Missing Out?*, Cambridge – Antwerp – Portland, Intersentia, 2012, 20.

different jurisdictions must accept that their activities can also lead to liability for punitive damages.[1187] They cannot be immune from these damages simply because of their favourable geographic location.

560. Moreover, a principled acceptance of punitive damages is warranted because the traditionally glaring contrast between both continents is fading. In the United States there has been a trend on multiple echelons to reduce punitive damages, most notably by the U.S. Supreme Court's case law with regard to the Due Process Clause of the Fourteenth Amendment. Conversely, the exertion of punitive-like concepts that do not fit neatly into the compensatory corset in Europe indicates a movement towards the American system. This development seems not yet to have reached its end.[1188] The gap between the two divergent views on punitive damages is thus narrowing.[1189] This does not mean that the reception of American punitive damages in private international law should be blind or unquestioning. The *amount* of the punitive damages can still offend the values underlying the international public policy mechanism, justifying a rejection of the excessive award.

561. The progressive current in the enforcement case law as well as the approach embodied in recital 32 of the Rome II Regulation reflect this proposed change of mentality toward punitive damages. In order to be congruent with the private law systems of the Member States examined, the marginal international public policy control should not focus on the foreign concept itself but rather on the possible excessiveness of the institution. European courts should limit themselves to verifying the amount of the punitive damages (for enforcement) or applying the American law granting punitive damages only to the extent that they are not excessive (for applicable law).

562. This leads us to the answering of the third sub-question. A prohibition of excessiveness is an aspect of the requested nation's desire for reasonableness and seeks individualisation.[1190] The proportionality test, therefore, inherently requires a concrete case-by-case assessment. It is, nevertheless, possible to

---

1187 M. Requejo Isidro, "Punitive Damages: How Do They Look Like When Seen From Abroad?" in L. Meurkens & E. Nordin (eds.), *The Power of Punitive Damages – Is Europe Missing Out?*, Cambridge – Antwerp – Portland, Intersentia, 2012, 329–330.

1188 V. Behr, "Punitive Damages in American and German Law – Tendencies Towards Approximation of Apparently Irreconcilable Concepts", 78 *Chicago-Kent Law Review* 2003, 161.

1189 V. Behr, "Punitive Damages in American and German Law – Tendencies Towards Approximation of Apparently Irreconcilable Concepts", 78 *Chicago-Kent Law Review* 2003, 150.

1190 F.-X. Licari, "Prendre les punitive damages au sérieux: propos critiques sur un refus d'accorder l'exequatur à une décision californienne ayant alloué des dommages intérêts punitifs", *Journal du droit international (Clunet)* October/November/December 2010/4, 1260.

formulate guiding principles that European courts should keep in mind when confronted with requests for enforcement of punitive damages. These guidelines grow from the concern that the excessiveness assessment would completely boil down to an exercise of "*I know it when I see it*", to quote Justice Potter STEWART on his description of the threshold test for obscenity.[1191, 1192] This would have a negative effect on the legal certainty of litigants.

563. Looking at the enforcement of American judgments containing punitive damages, European courts should first ascertain whether the foreign court has awarded separate compensatory damages and accept this head of damages. Likewise, properly identified compensatory punitive damages can also be granted enforcement as they counter imperfect compensation in the United States.

It is further suggested that as a foundation courts should, subsequently, start from a 1:1 ratio between punitive and compensatory damages, a standard far below the 9:1 maximum imposed by the U.S. Supreme Court. This ratio is then subjected to adjustment according to the case's connection to the forum (*Inlandsbeziehung*) and the nature of the interests at issue. Several factors influence the level of *Inlandsbeziehung*. Examples are: the residence of the parties, their nationality, the place of the damage, the agreed place of performance or the applicable law to the dispute. Under this proposed approach mathematical certainty is combined with flexible criteria that guarantee an individualised treatment of each separate case.

In case of doubts, the primacy of comity considerations over the exceptional mechanism of international public policy should prevail. This argument is even stronger in light of the cautious convergence in attitude toward punitive damages on both sides of the Atlantic.

Finally, once the court has settled on an acceptable amount of punitive damages, it is to enforce the punitive award up to that amount. As such, an all-or-nothing approach to the enforcement of a punitive awarded is avoided and digestible portions of this type of damages can find their way into the Civil Law stomach.[1193]

The guidelines should not pose any problems of *révision au fond*. Even if they are found to be a violation, as might be the case for the reduction of the punitive award, this minor deviation to the principle of the prohibition of the review of the merits should be tolerable.

1191 *Jacobellis v. Ohio*, 378 U.S., 197 (1964).

1192 F.-X. Licari, "Prendre les punitive damages au sérieux: propos critiques sur un refus d'accorder l'exequatur à une décision californienne ayant alloué des dommages intérêts punitifs", *Journal du droit international (Clunet)* October/November/December 2010/4, 1258.

1193 C.I. Nagy, "Recognition and enforcement of US judgments involving punitive damages in continental Europe", *Nederlands Internationaal Privaatrecht* 2012, 7.

564. These guidelines apply *mutatis mutandis* to the application of American law in a European court case. The intensity of the international public policy exception is, however, stronger than in the field of the enforcement of judgments (*ordre public plein* versus *ordre public atténué*).

565. In sum, the answer to the overarching main research question in this book is that service of process should be completely open for punitive damages claims. Punitive damages as part of the applicable law or in an American judgment, on the other hand, should be allowed to penetrate the European borders but only in reasonable amounts.

566. This newfound receptiveness in private international law can act as a factor in the debate on the introduction of punitive damages in substantive laws throughout the European Union. Only time will tell whether such legislative changes accommodating for the remedy of punitive damages will see the light of day.

BIBLIOGRAPHY

ARTICLES

Adar, Y., "Touring the Punitive Damages Forest: A Proposed Roadmap", *Osservatorio del diritto civile e commerciale* 2012, 301–348.

Allarousse, V., "A Comparative Approach to the Conflict of Characterisation in Private International Law", 23 *Case Western Reserve Journal of International Law* 1991, 479–516.

Amelung, T.U., "Damages Awards for Infringement of Privacy - The German Approach", 14 *Tulane European and Civil Law Forum* 1999, 15–47.

Auf'mkolk, H., "U.S. punitive damages awards before German courts - Time for a new approach", *Freiburg Law Students Journal* 2007, 1–10.

Barrett, J.M., "Contort: Tortious Breach of the Implied Covenant of Good Faith and Fair Dealing in Noninsurance Commercial Contracts - Its Existence and Desirability", 60 *Notre Dame Law Review* 1985, 510–529.

Baumgartner, S., "How well do U.S. judgments fare in Europe?", 40 *George Washington International Law Review* 2008–2009, 173–231.

Baumgartner, S., "Understanding the Obstacles to the Recognition and Enforcement of U.S. Judgments Abroad", 45 *New York University Journal of International Law and Politics* 2013, 965–1001.

Beaumont, P. & Tang, Z., "Classification of Delictual Damages: *Harding v Wealands* and the Rome II Regulation", *Edinburgh Law Review* 2008, 131–137.

Behar-Touchais, M., "L'amende civile est-elle un substitut satisfaisant à l'absence de dommages et intérêts punitifs?", *Les Petites Affiches* 2002, 36–44.

Behr, V., "Punitive Damages in American and German Law - Tendencies Towards Approximation of Apparently Irreconcilable Concepts", 78 *Chicago - Kent Law Review* 2003, 105–161.

Behr, V., "Myth and Reality of Punitive Damages in Germany", 24 *Journal of Law and Commerce* 2004–2005, 197–224.

Belohlavek, A.J., "Public Policy and Public Interest in International Law and EU Law", *Czech Yearbook of International Law* 2012, 117–148.

Berch, J., "The Need for Enforcement of U.S. Punitive Damages Awards by the European Union", 19 *Minnesota Journal of International Law* 2010, 55–106.

Bernard, P. & Salem, H., "Further developments for qualification of foreign judgments for recognition and enforcement in France: the test for punitive damage awards", *International Bar Association* 2011, 16–20.

Bernet, M. & Ulmer, N.C., "Recognition and Enforcement in Switzerland of US Judgments Containing an Award of Punitive Damages", 22 *International Business Lawyer* 1994, 272–275.

Beucher, K.J. & Sandage, J.B., "United States Punitive Damage Awards in German Courts: The Evolving German position on Service and Enforcement", 23 *Vanderbilt Journal of Transnational Law* 1990–1991, 967–991.

Bleimaier, J.K., "The Doctrine of Comity in Private International Law", 24 *Catholic University Law Review* 1979, 327–332.

Böhmer, C., "Spannungen im deutsch-amerikanischen Rechtsverkehr in Zivilsachen", *Neue Juristische Wochenschrift* 1990, 3049–3054.

Brand, R., "Punitive Damages Revisited: Taking the Rationale for Non-Recognition of Foreign Judgments Too Far", 24 *Journal of Law and Commerce* 2005, 181–196.

Browne, K., "Punitive damages in the U.S.: a primer for insurance buyers and brokers", Armonk, Swiss Re, 2011, 12 p.

Bungert, H., "Enforcing U.S. Excessive and Punitive Damages Awards in Germany", 27 *International Lawyer* 1993, 1075–1090.

Cachard, O., "Observations", case note under Cass. 1 December 2010, *Droit Maritime Français* April 2011, 333–340.

Cachard, O., "Le contrôle juridictionnel des jugements étrangers ordonnant des Punitive Damages", *Revue Lamy Droit des affaires* 2013, 137–140.

Calandrillo, S.P., "Penalizing Punitive Damages: Why the Supreme Court Needs a Lesson in Law and Economics", 78 *George Washington Law Review* 2010, 774–821.

Cauffman, C., "Naar een punitief Europees verbintenissenrecht? Een rechtsvergelijkende studie naar de draagwijdte, de grondwettelijkheid en de wenselijkheid van het bestraffend karakter van het verbintenissenrecht", *Tijdschrift voor Privaatrecht* 2007, 799–871.

Cavalier, G. & Queguiner, J.-S., "Punitive Damages and French Public Policy", Lyon, Lyon Symposium, 4–5 October, 2007, 1–9, available at: <http://papers.ssrn.com/sol3/papers.cfm?abstract_id=1174363>.

Cianciardo, J., "The principle of Proportionality: The Challenges of Human Rights", 3 *Journal of Civil Law Studies* 2010, 177–186.

Clermont, K.M. & Sherwin, E., "A Comparative View of Standards of Proof", 50 *American Journal of Comparative Law* 2002, 243–275.

Colby, T.B., "Beyond the Multiple Punishment Problem: Punitive Damages as Punishment for Individual, Private Wrongs", 87 *Minnesota Law Review* 2003, 583–678.

Cuniberti, G., "The Liberization of the French Law of Foreign Judgments", 56 *International Comparative Law Quarterly* 2007, 931–939.

Curran, V.G., "U.S. Discovery and Foreign Blocking Statutes", *Louisiana Law Review* 2016, forthcoming, available at <http://papers.ssrn.com/sol3/papers.cfm?abstract_id=2732802>.

Del Rossi, A.F. & Kip Viscusi, W., "The Changing Landscape of Blockbuster Punitive Damage Awards", Vanderbilt Law & Economics Research Paper No. 09-33, 2009, 116–161.

De Luca, A., "Cost and Fee Allocation in Italian Civil Procedure", 1–13, available at <www-personal.umich.edu/~purzel/national_reports/Italy.pdf>.

Di Meglio, C. & Ponczek, K., "Order to pay punitive damages not contrary to public policy", 14 April 2011, no page numbers, available at <www.internationallawoffice.com>.

Di Meglio, C. & Ponczek, K., "The French Supreme Court holds that an order to pay punitive damages is not, in itself, contrary to French international public policy", *Paris International Litigation Bulletin* July 2011, 6–7.

Dodge, W.S., "International Comity in American Law", 115 *Columbia Law Review* 2015, 2071–2142.

Dollinger, J., "World Public Policy: Real International Public Policy in the Conflict of Laws", 17 *Texas International Law Journal* 1982, 167–194.

Droz, G.A.L., "Variations Pordea", *Revue Critique du Droit International Privé* 2000, 181–198.

Eisenberg, T., Goerdt, J., Ostrom, B., Rottman, D. & Wells, M.T., "The Predictability of Punitive Damages", 23 *Journal of Legal Studies* 1997, 623–661.

Eisenberg, T., "Engle v. R.J. Reynolds Tobacco Co.: Lessons In State Class Actions, Punitive Damages, and Jury Decision-Making Damage Awards in Perspective: Behind the Headline-Grabbing Awards in Exxon Valdez and Engle", 36 *Wake Forest Law Review* 2001, 1129–1155.

Eisenberg, T., LaFountain, N., Ostrom, B., Rottman, D. & Wells, M.T., "Juries, Judges and Punitive Damages: An Empirical Study", 87 *Cornell Law Review* 2002, 743–782.

Eisenberg, T., Hannaford-Agor P.L., Heise, M., LaFountain, N., Munsterman, G.T., Ostrom, B. & Wells, M.T., "Juries, Judges, and Punitive Damages: Empirical Analyses Using the Civil Justice Survey of State Courts 1992, 1996, and 2001 Data", 3 *Journal of Emperical Legal Studies* 2006, 263–295.

Edwards, N. & Lee, R.G., "Recognition and enforcement in English law of money judgments from outside the UK", *International Banking and Financial Law* 1994, 1–8.

Ellis, D.D., "Fairness and Efficiency in the Law of Punitive Damages", 56 *Southern California Law Review* 1982, 1–77.

Fausten, T. & Hammesfahr, R., "Punitive damages in Europe: Concern, threat or non-issue?", Armonk, Swiss Re, 2012, 14 p.

Favalli, D. & Matthews, J.M., "Recognition and Enforcement of U.S. class action judgments and settlements in Switzerland", *Schweizerische Zeitschrift für internationales und Europäisches Recht* 2007, 611–636.

Fiebig, A.R., "The Recognition and Enforcement of Punitive Damage Awards in Germany: Recent Developments", 22 *Georgia Journal of International & Comparative Law* 1992, 635–657.

Fowler, R., "Why Punitive Damages Should Be a Jury's Decision in Kansas: A Historical Perspective", 52 *Kansas Law Review* 2004, 631–666.

Friedrich, B., "Federal Constitutional Court Grants Interim Legal Protection Against Service of a Writ of Punitive Damages Suit", *German Law Journal* 2003, 1233–1240.

Galanter, M., "Shadow Play: The Fabled Menace of Punitive Damages", *Wisconsin Law Review* 1998, 1–14.

Gotanda, J.Y., "Punitive Damages: A Comparative Analysis", 42 *Columbia Journal of Transnational Law* 2004, 391–444.

Gotanda, J.Y, "Charting Developments Concerning Punitive Damages: Is the Tide Changing?", 45 *Columbia Journal of Transnational Law* 2007, 507–528.

Grange, B., "Case comment: French Supreme Court and punitive damages: one step forward?", *International Arbitration Law Review* 2011, no. 2–3.

Guillotte, Y., "Recognition and enforcement of a U.S. judgment awarding punitive damages: the position of the French Supreme Court", 1–4, originally retrieved from <www.soulier- avocats.com/upload/documents/Soulier_YG_exequatur_punitive_damages_january_2011.pdf>.

Harris, A.P., "Rereading Punitive Damages: Beyond the Public/Private Distinction", 40 *Alabama Law Review* 1989, 1079–1116.

Hay, P., "The Recognition and Enforcement of American Money-Judgments in Germany – The 1992 Decision of the German Supreme Court", 40 *The American Journal of Comparative Law* 1992, 729–750.

Hay, P., "Contemporary Approaches to Non-Contractual Obligations in Private International Law (Conflict of Laws) and the European Community's "Rome II" Regulation", *The European Legal Forum* 2007, 137–152.

Hay, P. & Walker, R., "The Proposed U.S.-UK Recognition-of-Judgments Convention: Another Perspective", 18 *Virginia Journal of International Law* 1978, 753–770.

Hollmann, H.H., "Auslandszustellung in U.S.-amerikanischen Zivil- und Verwaltungssachen", *Recht der internationalen Wirtschaft* 1982, 784–798.

Jablonski, S.R., "Translation and comment: enforcing U.S. punitive damages awards in foreign courts – a recent case in the Supreme Court of Spain", 24 *Journal of Law and Commerce* 2004–2005, 225–243.

Janke, B. & Licari, F.-X., "Enforcing Punitive Damage Awards in France after Fountaine Pajot", 60 *The American Journal of Comparative Law* 2012, 775–804.

Jestaz, P., "Les dommages et interest en quête d'un fondement", *Revue Lamy Droit des Affaires* 2013, 109–111.

Jourdain, P., "Rapport introductif", *Les Petites Affiches* 2002, 3–7.

Juvenal, J., "Dommages-intérêts punitifs: comment apprécier la conformité à l'ordre public international?", *La Semaine Juridique Edition Générale* no. 6, 7 February 2011, 257–259.

Kahn, T.J., "The Protection of Trading Interests Act of 1980: Britain's Response to U.S. Extraterritorial Antitrust Enforcement", 2 *Northwestern Journal of International Law & Business* 1980, 476–516.

Kellman, E., "Enforcement of Judgments and Blocking Statutes: Lewis v Eliades", 53 *International & Comparative Law Quarterly* 2004, 1025–1030.

Klötgen, P., "L'appréhension des punitive damages par le droit allemande", *Revue Lamy Droit des Affaires* 2013, 124–128.

Koch, H., "Zur Praxis der Rechtshilfe im amerikanisch-deutschen Prozessrecht – Ergebnisse einer Umfrage zu den Haager Zustellungs- und Beweisübereinkommen", *Praxis des Internationalen Privat- und Verfahrensrechts* 1985, 245–249.

Kühn, W., "Rico Claims in International Arbitration and their Recognition in Germany", 11 *Journal of International Arbitration* 1994, 37–49.

Lenhardt, L.L., "Service of U.S. Punitive Damages Complaint Passes Constitutional Muster in Germany", 29 *Vanderbilt Journal of Transnational Law* 1996, 291–302.

Levine, H.R., "Demonstrating and Preserving the Deterrent Effect of Punitive Damages in Insurance Bad Faith Actions", 13 *University of San Francisco Law Review* 1979, 613–638.

Lewis, R. & Morris, A., "Tort Law Culture in the United Kingdom: Image and Reality in Personal Injury Compensation", 17 May 2012, 1–42, available at <http://papers.ssrn.com/sol3/papers.cfm?abstract_id=2061618>.

Licari, F.-X., "Prendre les punitive damages au sérieux: propos critiques sur un refus d'accorder l'exequatur à une décision californienne ayant alloué des dommages intérêts punitifs", *Journal du droit international (Clunet)* October/November/December 2010/4, 1230–1263.

Licari, F.-X., "La compatibilité de principe des punitive damages avec l'ordre public international: une décision en trompe-l'œil de la Cour de cassation?", *Recueil Dalloz* 10 February 2011, 423–427.

Lootgieter, S., "Punitive damages and French courts", 1–4, originally retrieved from <http://lacba.org/Files/MainFolder/Sections/InternationalLaw/Files/120313-PUNITIVE DAMAGES AND FRENCH COURTS.pdf>.

LS Lexjus Sinacta, "Italian Supreme Court Confirms Stance On Punitive Damages", International Law Office – Legal Newsletter, 21 December 2012, no page numbers, available at <www.intemationallawoffice.com>.

Lupoi, M.A., "Recent developments in Italian Civil Procedure Law", *Civil Procedure Review* 2012, 25–51.

Luque Parra, M., Gómez Ligüerre, C. & Ruiz García, J.A., "Workplace Injuries and Tort Liability", *InDret* 02/2002, 1–16, available at <www.indret.com/pdf/021_en.pdf>.

Malcolm, E., "Winning the fight for the enforcement of US damages", 15 *Entertainment Law Review* 2004, 133–134.

Mallor, J. & Roberts, B.S., "Punitive Damages: On the Path to a Principled Approach?", 50 *Hastings Law Journal* 1999, 1001–1014.

Martiny, D., "Recognition and Enforcement of Foreign Money Judgments in the Federal Republic of Germany", 35 *American Journal of Comparative Law* 1987, 721–759.

Merkin, R., "Enforceability of Awards of Punitive Damages in the United Kingdom", *International Journal of Insurance Law* 1994, 18–27.

Meyer Fabre, N., "Enforcement Of U.S. Punitive Damages Award in France: First Ruling Of The French Court Of Cassation In X. v. Fountaine Pajot December 1, 2010", *Mealey's International Arbitration Report* January 2011, 1–7.

Meyer Fabre, N., "Recognition and Enforcement of U.S. Judgments in France – Recent Developments", *The International Dispute Resolution News* spring 2012, 6–10.

Michell, M.P., "Imperium by the Back Door: The Astreinte and the Enforcement of Contractual Obligations in France", 51 *University of Toronto Faculty of Law Review* 1993, 250–276.

Mills, A., "The Dimensions of Public Policy in Private International Law", *Journal of Private International Law* 2008, 201–236.

Morris, C., "Punitive Damages in Tort Cases", 44 *Harvard Law Review* 1931, 1173–1194.

Morisse, H., "Die Zustellung U.S.-amerikanischer Punitive-damages-Klagen in Deutschland", *Recht der Internationalen Wirtschaft* 1995, 370–373.

Motte-Suraniti, D., "Punitive damages and exequatur under French law", 20 December 2010, 1–6, available at <www.motte-suraniti-avocat.com/doc/Punitive_damages_and_exequatur_under_French_law.pdf>.

Musy, A.M., "Punitive damages e resistenza temeraria in giudizio: regole definizioni e modelli istituzionali a confront", *Danno e Responsabilità* 11/2000, 1121–1127.

Nagy, C.I., "Recognition and enforcement of US judgments involving punitive damages in continental Europe", *Nederlands Internationaal Privaatrecht* 2012, 4–11.

Nater-Bass, G., "U.S.-Style Punitive Damages Awards and their Recognition and Enforcement in Switzerland and Other Civil-Law Countries", 28 *Deutsch-Amerikanische Juristen-Vereinigung Newsletter* 2003, 154–160.

Nettesheim, P.J. & Stahl, H., "Bundesgerichtshof Rejects Enforcement of United States Punitive Damages Award", 28 *Texas International Law Journal* 1993, 415–425.

Nichols, A.G., Jr., "Comment, Punitive Damages in Mississippi – A Brief Survey", 37 *Mississippi Law Journal* 1965, 131–156.

Ostoni, L., "Italian Rejection of Punitive Damages in a U.S. Judgment", 24 *Journal of Law and Commerce* 2004–2005, 245–262.

Owen, D.G., "Punitive Damages Overview Functions, Problems and Reform", 39 *Villanova Law Review* 1994, 363–413.

Pantaleón, F., "Principles of European Tort Law: Basis of Liability and Defences. A critical view 'from outside'", *InDret* 2005, 1–8.

Paul, J.R., "Comity in International Law", 32 *Harvard International Law Journal* 1991, 1–79.

Pena Lopez, J.M., "Función, naturaleza y sistema de la responsabilidad civil aquiliana en el ordenamiento jurídico español", *Revista de derecho privado* 2004, 174–208.

Perczek, J., "On Efficiency, Deterrence, and Fairness: A Survey of Punitive Damages Law and a Proposed Jury Instruction", 27 *Suffolk University Law Review* 1993, 825–904.

Piekenbrock, A., "Zur Zustellung kartellrechtlicher treble damages-Klagen in Deutschland", *Praxis des Internationalen Privat- und Verfahrensrechts* 2006, 4–10.

Polonsky, M., "Particular Issues Affecting the Recognition and Enforcement of U.S. Judgments", 19 *International Law Practicum* 2006, 156–159.

Posner, R.A., "The Concept of Corrective Justice in Recent Theories of Tort Law", 10 *Journal of Legal Studies* 1981, 187–206.

Priest, G.L., "Punitive Damages Reform: The Case of Alabama", 56 *Louisiana Law Review* 1996, 825–840.

Quarta, F., "Recognition and Enforcement of U.S. Punitive Damages Awards in Continental Europe: The Italian Supreme Court's Veto", 31 *Hastings International & Comparative Law Review* 2008, 753–782.

Quarta, F., "Class Actions, Extra-Compensatory Damages, and Judicial Recognition in Europe", Conference paper – "Extraterritoriality and Collective Redress", London 15 November 2010, Draft 19 November 2010, 1–12.

Ramos Romeu, F., "Litigation Under the Shadow of an Exequatur: The Spanish Recognition of U.S. Judgments", *International Lawyer* 2004, 945–972.

Reed, A., "Exemplary Damages: A Persuasive Argument for their Retention as a Mechanism of Retributive Justice", 15 *Civil Justice Quarterly* 1996, 130–140.

Redish, M.H. & Mathews, A.L., "Why Punitive Damages are Unconstitutional", 53 *Emory Law Journal* 2004, 1–54.

Requejo Isidro, M., "Punitive Damages – Europe Strikes Back?", presentation delivered at the British Institute of International and Comparative Law, 2 November 2011, London, text on file with the author.

Robbennolt, J.K., "Determining Punitive Damages: Empirical Insights and Implications for Reform", 50 *Buffalo Law Review* 2002, 103–203.

Rodriguez Pineau, E., "European Union International Ordre Public", *Spanish Yearbook of International Law* 1993–1994, 43–85.

Rosengarten, J., "Der Präventionsgedanke im deutschen Zivilrecht – Höheres Schmerzensgeld, aber keine Anerkennung und Vollstreckung US-amerikanischer punitive damages?", *Neue Juristische Wochenschrift* 1996, 1935–1938.

Rouhette, T., "The availability of punitive damages in Europe: growing trend or nonexistent concept?", 74 *Defense Counsel Journal* 2007, 320–342.

Ryan, P.S., "Revisiting the United States application of punitive damages: separating myth from reality", 10 *ILSA Journal of International & Comparative Law* 2003, 69–93.

Sales, J.B. & Cole, K.B., Jr., "Punitive Damages, A Relic That Has Outlived Its Origins", 37 *Vanderbilt Law Review* 1984, 1117–1172.

Schubert, W., "Simplifying Punitive Damages: Due Process and the Pursuit of Manageable Awards and Procedures in U.S. Courts", *European Journal of Consumer Law* 2011, 829–861.

Schwartz, V.E., Behrens, M.A. & Mastrosimone, J.P., "Reining in Punitive Damages "Run Wild": Proposals for Reform by Courts and Legislatures", 65 *Brooklyn Law Review* 1999, 1003–1036.

Sebok, A.J., "Why the Latest Chapter in the Napster Saga Raises Issues About U.S./European Judicial Cooperation", 2003, no page numbers, available at <http://writ.news.findlaw.com/sebok/20031117.html>.

Sebok, A.J., "Punitive Damages: From Myth to Theory", 92 *Iowa Law Review* 2007, 957–1036.

Sein, K., "Should Estonian Law Provide for an Award of Punitive Damages?", *Juridica International* 2007, 46–54.

Sibon, A.S., "Enforcing Punitive Damages Awards in France: Facing Proportionality within International Public Policy", no page numbers, available at <http://ssrn.com/abstract=2382817>.

Smit, H., "The Proposed United States-United Kingdom Convention on Recognition and Enforcement of Judgments: A Prototype for the Future?", 17 *Virginia Journal of International Law* 1977, 443–468.

Stiefel, E.C., Stürner, R. & Stadler, A., "The Enforceability Of Excessive U.S. Punitive Damage Awards In Germany", 39 *American Journal of Comparative Law* 1991, 779–802.

Strebel, F., "The Enforcement of Foreign Judgements and Foreign Public Law", 21 *Loyola of Los Angeles International and Comparative Law Review* 1999, 55–129.

Tolani, M., "U.S. Punitive Damages Before German Courts: A Comparative Analysis with Respect to the Ordre Public", 17 *Annual Survey of International & Comparative Law* 2011, 185–207.

Traverso & Associati, "Foreign Punitive Damages Awards Conflict With Italian Public Order", International Law Office – Legal Newsletter, 27 May 2003, no page numbers, available at <www.intemationallawoffice.com>.

Triadafillidis, C.D., "Anerkennung und Vollstreckung von punitive damages – Urteilen nach kontinentalem und insbesondere nach griechischem Recht", *Praxis des Internationalen Privat- und Verfahrensrechts* 2002, 236–238.

Wegen, G. & Sherer, J., "Recognition and Enforcement of US Punitive Damages Judgments in Germany – A Recent Decision of the German Federal Court of Justice", 21 *International Business Lawyer* 1993, 485–488.

Wegen, G. & Sherer, J., "Germany: Federal Court of Justice decision concerning the recognition and enforcement of U.S. judgments awarding punitive damages", 32 *International Legal Materials* 1993, 1320–1346.
Wester-Ouisse, V. & Thiede, T., "Punitive Damages in France: A New Deal? – A commentary on Cour de cassation (France), 1st civil chamber, 1 December 2010, case no 1090", *Journal of European Tort Law* 2012, 115–122.
Wölki, C., "Das Haager Zustellungsabkommen und die U.S.A.", *Recht der internationalen Wirtschaft* 1985, 530–535.
Wurmnest, W., "Recognition and Enforcement of U.S. Money Judgments in Germany", 23 *Berkeley Journal of International Law* 2005, 175–200.
X., "Enjoining the Application of the British Protection of Trading Interests Act in Private American Antitrust Litigation", 79 *Michigan Law Review* 1981, 1574–1606.
X, "Italian Supreme Court Affirms Position Against Punitive Damage Awards", 31 January 2013, no page numbers, available at <www.goldbergsegalla.com/resources/news-and-updates/italian-supreme-court-affirms-position-against-punitive-damage-awards>.
X., "ZRP-Rechtsgespräch mit Vorsitzendem Richter am BGH a. D. Dr. Erich Steffen", *Zeitschrift für Rechtspolitik* 1996, 366–367.
Yelenick, M.Y. & M. Pulaski-Kelly, M., "Court Discusses Guidelines for Review of Punitive Damages", 18 January 2001, no page numbers, available at <www.internationallawoffice.com>.
Yntema, H.E., "The Comity Doctrine", 65 *Michigan Law Review* 1966, 9–32.
Zekoll, J., "The Enforceability of American Money Judgments Abroad: A Landmark Decision by the German Federal Court of Justice", 30 *Columbia Journal of Transnational Law* 1992, 641–659.
Zipursky, B.C., "A Theory of Punitive Damages", 84 *Texas Law Review* 2005, 105–171.

BOOKS

Baldoni, E., *Punitive damages: a comparative analysis*, Universita degli studi di Macerata, unpublished Ph.D thesis, 2012, 184 p.
Beverley-Smith, H., Ohly, A. & Lucas-Schloetter, A., *Privacy, Property and Personality – Civil Law Perspectives on Commercial Appropriation*, New York, Cambridge University Press, 2005, 245 p.
Blatt, R.L., Hammesfahr, R.W. & Nugent, L.S., *Punitive Damages: A State-by-State Guide to Law and Practice*, Eagan, Minnesota, Thomson Reuters/West, 2008, 863 p.
Born, G., *International Civil Litigation in United States Courts: Commentary and Materials*, The Hague, Kluwer Law International, 1996, 1145 p.
Bourrié-Quenillet, M., *L'indemnisation des proches d'une victime décédée accidentellement. Étude d'informatique judiciaire*, Ph.D thesis University of Montpellier 1, 1983, 255 p.
Buckland, W.W., *A Text-Book of Roman Law from Augustus to Justinian*, Cambridge, Cambridge University Press, 3rd edition (revised by D. Stein), 1963, 764 p.
Burnham, W., *Introduction to the law and Legal system of the United States*, St. Paul – Minnesota, Thomson/West, 4th edition, 2006, 716 p.

Carval, S., *La responsabilité civile dans sa fonction de peine privée*, Paris, L.G.D.J., 1995, 418 p.

Centner, T.J., *America's Blame Culture. Pointing Fingers and Shunning Restitution*, Durham, North Carolina, Carolina Academic Press, 2008, 266 p.

Collins, L. (ed.), *Dicey & Morris on the conflict of laws*, London, Sweet and Maxwell, 13th edition, 2000, 1622 p.

Corongiu, S.A.L., *Punitive Damages Awards in the US Judicial Experience and Their Recognition in Italy*, Universita degli studi di Urbino, unpublished PhD thesis, 2004–2005, 120 p.

Damrosch, L.F. et al., *International Law*, St. Paul, Minnesota, West Group, 2001, 1678 p.

Deakin, S.F., Johnston, A. & Markesinis, B.S., *Markesinis and Deakin's Tort Law*, Oxford, Clarendon Press, 2008, 1056 p.

De Ángel Yagüez, R., *Algunas previsiones sobre el futuro de la responsabilidad civil (con especial atención a la reparación del daño)*, Madrid, Cuadernos Civitas, 1995, 242 p.

Dickinson, A., *The Rome II Regulation – The Law Applicable to Non-Contractual Obligations*, Oxford-New York, Oxford University Press, 2008, 797 p.

Dobbs, D., Hayden, P. & Bublick, E., *The Law of Torts, Practitioner Treatise Series*, Minneapolis, West, 2011, 912 p.

Fawcett, J. & Carruthers, J.M., *Cheshire, North & Fawcett: Private International Law*, Oxford, Oxford University Press, Fourteenth Edition, 2008, 1390 p.

Garner, B.A. (ed.), *Black's Law Dictionary*, St. Paul, West, 3rd pocket edition, 2006, 840 p.

Gaudemet-Tallon, H., *Compétence et exécution des jugements en Europe*, Paris, LGDJ, 2010, 750 p.

Grossi, S. & Pagni, M.C., *Commentary on the Italian Code of Civil Procedure*, New York, Oxford University Press, 2010, 556 p.

Hall, W.E., *A Treatise on International Law*, Oxford, Clarendon Press, 7th edition, 1917, 864 p.

Hondius, E. & Janssen, A., *Disgorgement of Profits: Gain-Based Remedies throughout the World*, Cham, Springer, 2015.

Ingman, T., *The English Legal Process*, Oxford, Oxford University Press, 13th edition, 2010, 504 p.

Joubert, N., *La notion de liens suffisants avec l'ordre juridique (Inlandsbeziehung) en droit international privé*, Paris, LexisNexis – Litec, 2007, 612 p.

Kircher, J.J. & Wiseman, C.M., *Punitive Damages Law and Practice*, part 1, Eagan, Minnesota, Thomson/West, 2000, loose-leaf.

Lambert-Faivre, Y. & Porchy-Simon, S., *Droit du dommage corporel – Systèmes d'indemnisation*, Paris, Dalloz, 2009, 1056 p.

Lenz, C., *Amerikanische Punitive Damages vor dem Schweizer Richter*, Zürich, Schulthess, 1992, 191 p.

Malaurie, P., Aynès, L. & Stoffel-Muck, P., *Droit Civil, Les obligations*, Paris, Defrénois, 2005, 846 p.

Mayer, P. & Heuzé, V., *Droit international privé*, Paris, Montchrestien, 2004, 784 p.

McLuhan, M., *The Gutenberg Galaxy: The Making of Typographic Man*, Toronto, Toronto University Press, 1962, 293 p.

Meurkens, R.C., *Punitive Damages – The Civil Remedy in American Law. Lessons and Caveats for Continental Europe*, Deventer, Kluwer, 2014, 455 p.

Mills, A., *The Confluence of Public and Private International Law - Justice, Pluralism and Subsidiarity in the International Constitutional Ordering of Private Law*, Cambridge, Cambridge University Press, 2009, 420 p.
Mörsdorf-Schulte, J., *Funktion und Dogmatik US-amerikanischer punitive damages. Zugleich ein Beitrag zur Diskussion um die Zustellung und Anerkennung in Deutschland*, Tübingen, Mohr Siebeck, 1999, 325 p.
Müller, P., *Punitive Damages und deutsches Schadensersatzrecht*, Berlin, de Gruyter, 2000, 432 p.
Ndikum, P.F. & Ndikum, S.-D., *Encyclopaedia of International Aviation Law: Liability Rules Developed by European Union, Australian, United Kingdom and United States of America Courts According to European Community Treaty - Warsaw 1929 - Montreal 1999*, Volume 3, 2013, 1194 p.
Nicholas, B., *An Introduction to Roman Law*, Oxford, Oxford University Press, 1969, 281 p.
Owen, D.G., *Products Liability Law*, St. Paul, Minnesota, Thomson/West, 2005, 1385 p.
Owen, D.G., *Philosophical Foundations of Tort Law*, New York, Oxford University Press, 1997, 528 p.
Plender, R. & Wilderspin, M., *The European Private International Law of Obligations*, London, Sweet & Maxwell, 2009, 1053 p.
Rogers, W.V.H., *Winfield and Jolowicz on Tort*, London, Sweet & Maxwell, 2006, 1143 p.
Schlosser, P., *Der Justizkonflikt zwischen USA und Europa*, Berlin, de Gruyter, 1985, 47 p.
Schlosser, P., *EU-Zivilprozessrecht*, Munich, Beck, 2003, 672 p.
Schlueter, L.L., *Punitive Damages - Volume I*, Newark, New Jersey, LexisNexis, 2005.
Sedgwick, T., *A Treatise on the Measure of Damages vol. 1*, revised by A.G. Sedgwick & J.H. Beale, New York, Baker, Voorhis & Co. Law Publishers, 9th edition, 1913.
Shapo, M.S., *Principles of tort law*, St. Paul, Minnesota, Thomson/West, 2010, 595 p.
Terré, F., (ed.), *Pour une réforme du droit de la responsabilité civile*, Paris, Dalloz, 2011, 224 p.
Van Dam, C., *European Tort Law*, Oxford, Oxford University Press, 2006, 538 p.
Van Gerven, W., Lever, J. & Larouche, P., *Tort Law*, Oxford, Hart Publishing, 2000, 969 p.
Vidal Martin, T., *El derecho al honor y su proteccion desde la constitucion Espanola*, Madrid, Boletin Oficial del Estado y Centro de Estudios Politicos y Constitucionales, 2000, 389 p.
Wagner, G., *Neue Perspektiven im Schadensersatzrecht - Kommerzialisierung, Strafschadensersatz, Kollektivschaden, Gutachten A zum 66. Deutschen Juristentag*, Munich, Beck, 2006, 135 p.
Yeazell, S.C., *Civil Procedure*, New York, Aspen Law & Business, 2008, 912 p.
Zimmermann, R., *The Law of Obligations, Roman Foundations of the Civilian Tradition*, Deventer, Kluwer, 1992, 1241 p.

CONTRIBUTIONS IN BOOKS

Borghetti, J.-S., "Punitive Damages in France" in H. Koziol & V. Wilcox, *Punitive Damages: Common Law and Civil Law Perspectives*, Vienna, Springer, 2009, 55–73.

Boskovic, O., "Le domaine de la loi applicable" in S. Corneloup & N. Joubert (eds.), *Le Règlement Communautaire Rome II sur la loi applicable aux obligations non contractuelles*, Paris, Litec, 2008, 183–195.

Brooke, H., "A Brief Introduction: The Origins of Punitive Damages" in H. Koziol & V. Wilcox (eds.), *Punitive Damages: Common Law and Civil Law Perspectives*, Vienna, Springer, 2009, 1–3.

Cavalier, G., "Punitive Damages and French International Public Policy", in R. Stürner and M. Kawono (eds.), *Comparative Studies on Business Tort Litigation*, Tübingen, Mohr Siebeck, 2011, 219–232.

de Kezel, E., "The Protection and Enforcement of Private Interests by (the Recognition of US) Punitive Damages in Belgium" in L. Meurkens & E. Nordin (eds.), *The Power of Punitive Damages – Is Europe Missing Out?*, Cambridge – Antwerp – Portland, Intersentia, 2012, 213–244.

del Olmo, P., "Punitive Damages in Spain" in H. Koziol & V. Wilcox (eds.), *Punitive Damages: Common Law and Civil Law Perspectives*, Vienna, Springer, 2009, 137–154.

Fallon, M., "Le principe de proximité dans le droit de l'Union européenne" in M.N. Jobard-Bachellier, P. Mayer & P. Lagarde (eds.), *Mélanges en l'honneur de Paul Lagarde; Le droit international privé: esprit et méthodes*, Paris, Dalloz, 2005, 241–262.

Fuchs, A., "Article 26" in P. Huber (ed.), *Rome II Regulation – Pocket Commentary*, Munich, Sellier, 2011.

Gash, J., "Understanding and Solving the Multiple Punishments Problem" in L. Meurkens & E. Nordin (eds.), *The Power of Punitive Damages – Is Europe Missing Out?*, Cambridge – Antwerp – Portland, Intersentia, 2012, 65–105.

Hay, P., "On Comity, Reciprocity and Public Policy in U.S. and German Judgments Recognition Practice" in J. Basedow (ed.), *Private Law in the International Arena – Privatrecht in der Internationalen Arena. Liber Amicorum Kurt Siehr*, The Hague, T.M.C. Asser Press, 2000, 237–249.

Hay, P., "Entschädigung und andere Zwecke. Zu Präventionsgedanken im deutschen Schadensersatzrecht, punitive damages und Art. 40 Abs 3 Nr. 2 EGBGB" in G. Hohloch, R. Frank, P. Schlechtriem (eds.), *Festschrift für Hans Stoll zum 75. Geburtstag*, Tübingen, Mohr Siebeck, 2001, 521–532.

Hay, P., "Recognition of a Recognition Judgment Within the European Union: "Double exequatur" and the Public Policy Barrier" in P. Hay, L. Vékás, Y. Elkana & N. Dimitrijevic (eds.), *Resolving international conflicts: liber amicorum Tibor Várady*, Budapest – New York, Central European University Press, 2009, 143–164.

Honsell, H., "Amerikanische Rechtskultur" in P. Forstmoser, H.S. von der Crone, R.H. Weber & D. Zobl (eds.), *Festschrift für Roger Zäch zum 60. Geburtstag. Der Einfluss des europäischen Rechts auf die Schweiz*, Zurich, Schulthess Verlag, 1999, 39–56.

Geistfeld, M.A., "Due Process and the Deterrence Rationale for Punitive Damages" in L. Meurkens & E. Nordin (eds.), *The Power of Punitive Damages – Is Europe Missing Out?*, Cambridge – Antwerp – Portland, Intersentia, 2012, 107–118.

Huber, P., "Playing the same old song – German courts, the "Napster"-case and the international law of service of process" in H.P. Mansel, T. Pfeiffer, H. Kronke, C. Kohler & R. Hausmann (eds.), *Festschrift für Erik Jayme*, Munich, Sellier European Law Publishers, 2004, 361–370.

Jansen, N. & Rademacher, L., "Punitive Damages in Germany" in H. Koziol & V. Wilcox (eds.), *Punitive Damages: Common Law and Civil Law Perspectives*, Vienna, Springer, 2009, 75–86.

Koch, B.A., "Punitive Damages in European Law" in H. Koziol & V. Wilcox (eds.), *Punitive Damages: Common Law and Civil Law Perspectives*, Vienna, Springer, 2009, 197–209.

Koziol, H., "Punitive Damages: Admission into the Seventh Legal Heaven or Eternal Damnation? Comparative Report and Conclusions" in H. Koziol & V. Wilcox, *Punitive Damages: Common Law and Civil Law Perspectives*, Vienna, Springer, 2009, 275–308.

Magnus, U., "Comparative Report on the Law of Damages" in U. Magnus (ed.), *Unification of Tort Law: Damages*, The Hague, Kluwer Law International, 2001, 185–217.

Magnus, U., "Punitive Damages and German Law" in L. Meurkens & E. Nordin (eds.), *The Power of Punitive Damages - Is Europe Missing Out?*, Cambridge - Antwerp - Portland, Intersentia, 2012, 245–260.

Mahé, C., "Punitive damages in the competing reform drafts of the French Civil Code" in L. Meurkens & E. Nordin (eds.), *The Power of Punitive Damages - Is Europe Missing Out?*, Cambridge - Antwerp - Portland, Intersentia, 2012, 261–281.

Martin-Casals, M. & Solé Feliu, J., "The Protection of Personality Rights against Invasions by Mass Media in Spain" in H. Koziol & A. Warzilek (eds.), *Persönlichkeitsschutz gegenüber Massenmedien - The Protection of Personality Rights against Invasions by Mass Media*, Vienna, Springer, 2005, 287–339.

Meurkens, L., "The punitive damages debate in Continental Europe: food for thought" in L. Meurkens & E. Nordin (eds.), *The Power of Punitive Damages - Is Europe Missing Out?*, Cambridge - Antwerp - Portland, Intersentia, 2012, 3–62.

Morse, R., "Substance and Procedure: Aspects of Damages in Torts in the Conflict of Laws" in The Permanent Bureau of the Hague Conference, *A Commitment to Private International Law. Essays in honour of Hans van Loon*, Cambridge-Antwerp-Portland, Intersentia, 2013, 389–396.

Oliphant, K., "The Nature and Assessment of Damages" in H. Koziol & R. Schulze (eds.), *Tort Law of the European Community*, Vienna, Springer, 2008, 241–271.

Ortega Gonzalez, A., "Punitive damages for cartel infringements: why didn't the Commission grasp the opportunity?" in L. Meurkens & E. Nordin (eds.), *The Power of Punitive Damages - Is Europe Missing Out?*, Cambridge - Antwerp - Portland, Intersentia, 2012, 437–458.

Otero Crespo, M., "Punitive Damages Under Spanish Law: A Subtle Recognition?" in L. Meurkens & E. Nordin (eds.), *The Power of Punitive Damages - Is Europe Missing Out?*, Cambridge - Antwerp - Portland, Intersentia, 2012, 283–310.

Quarta, F., "Foreign Punitive Damages Decisions and Class Actions in Italy" in D. Fairgrieve and E. Lein (eds.), *Extraterritoriality and Collective Redress*, Oxford, Oxford University Press, 2012, 269–284.

Rasmussen-Bonne, H.E., "The Pendulum Swings Back: The Cooperative Approach of German Courts to International Service of Process" in P. Hay, L. Vekas, Y. Elkana & N. Dimitrijevic (eds.), *Resolving International Conflicts - Liber Amicorum Tibor Varady*, Budapest - New York, Central European University Press, 2009, 231–253.

Requejo Isidro, M., "Punitive Damages From a Private International Law Perspective" in H. Koziol & V. Wilcox (eds.), *Punitive Damages: Common Law and Civil Law Perspectives*, Vienna, Springer, 2009, 237–256.

Requejo Isidro, M., "Punitive Damages: How Do They Look Like When Seen From Abroad?" in L. Meurkens & E. Nordin (eds.), *The Power of Punitive Damages – Is Europe Missing Out?*, Cambridge – Antwerp – Portland, Intersentia, 2012, 311–335.

Rushworth, A., "Remedies and the Rome II Regulation" in J. Ahern & W. Binchy (eds.), *The Rome II Regulation on the Law Applicable to Non-Contractual Obligations*, Leiden – Boston, Martinus Nijhoff Publishers, 2009, 199–218.

Sebok, A.J. & Wilcox, V., "Aggravated Damages" in H. Koziol & V. Wilcox, *Punitive Damages: Common Law and Civil Law Perspectives*, Vienna, Springer, 2009, 257–274.

Sebok, A.J., "Punitive Damages in the United States" in H. Koziol & V. Wilcox (eds.), *Punitive Damages: Common Law and Civil Law Perspectives*, Vienna, Springer, 2009, 155–196.

Sebok, A.J., "The U.S. Supreme Court's Theory of Common Law Punitive Damages" in L. Meurkens & E. Nordin (eds.), *The Power of Punitive Damages – Is Europe Missing Out?*, Cambridge – Antwerp – Portland, Intersentia, 2012, 133–146.

Sharkey, C.M., "Crossing the Punitive-Compensatory Divide" in B.H. Bornstein et al. (eds.), *Civil Juries and Civil Justice: Psychological and Legal Perspectives*, New York, Springer, 2008, 79–104.

Stürner, R., "Der Justizkonflikt zwischen USA und Europa" in W.J. Habscheid (ed.), *Der Justizkonflikt mit den Vereinigten Staaten von Amerika*, Bielefeld, Gieseking, 1986, 3–63.

Stürner, R., "Anerkennungsrechtlicher und europäischer Ordre Public als Schranke der Vollstreckbarerklärung – der Bundesgerichtshof und die Staatlichkeit in der Europäischen Union" in C.W. Canaris, A. Heldrich, K. Hopt, C. Roxin, K. Schmidt & G. Widmaier (eds.), *50 Jahre Bundesgerichtshof*, Munich, C.H. Beck, 2000, 677–697.

Tebbens, H.D., "Punitive damages: towards a rule of reason for U.S. awards and their recognition elsewhere" in G. Venturini & S. Bariatti (eds.), *Liber Fausto Pocar, Volume II – Nuovi strumenti del diritto internazionale private*, Milan, Giuffre, 2009, 273–290.

Vanleenhove, C., "Punitive Damages and European Law: Quo Vademus?" in L. Meurkens & E. Nordin (eds.), *The Power of Punitive Damages – Is Europe Missing Out?*, Cambridge – Antwerp – Portland, Intersentia, 2012, 337–353.

von Hein, J., "Recent German Jurisprudence on Cooperation with the United States" in E. Gottschalk, R. Michaels, G. Rühl & J. von Hein (eds.), *Conflict of Laws in a Globalized World*, Cambridge, Cambridge University Press, 2007, 101–125.

Wagner, G., "The Protection of Personality Rights against Invasions by Mass Media in Germany" in H. Koziol & A. Warzilek (eds.), *Persönlichkeitsschutz gegenüber Massenmedien – The Protection of Personality Rights against Invasions by Mass Media*, Springer, Vienna, 2005, 137–179.

Wilcox, V., "Punitive Damages in England" in H. Koziol & V. Wilcox, *Punitive Damages: Common Law and Civil Law Perspectives*, Vienna, Springer, 2009, 7–53.

INTERNET SITES

<http://europa.eu/about-eu/countries/member-countries/index_en.htm>
<www.imf.org/external/pubs/ft/weo/2013/02/weodata/index.aspx>
<http://abnormaluse.com/?s=liebeck>
<www.hcch.net/index_en.php?act=conventions.status&cid=17>
<www.hcch.net/upload/auth14_de.pdf>
<http://europa.eu/about-eu/countries/member-countries/index_en.htm>
<www.imf.org/external/pubs/ft/weo/2013/02/weodata/index.aspx>
<http://ec.europa.eu/enterprise/policies/finance/data/enterprise-finance-index/access-to-finance-indicators/loans/index_en.htm>
<www.ecb.europa.eu/stats/monetary/rates/html/index.en.html>

MISCELLANEOUS

Amended proposal for a European Parliament and Council Regulation on the law applicable to non-contractual obligations ("Rome II"), 21 February 2006, COD/2003/0168.

Cohen, T.H., Punitive Damages Awards in Large Counties, 2001, U.S. Department of Justice, Doc. No. NCJ-208445.

Cohen, T.H. & Langton, L., Civil Bench and Jury Trials in State Courts, 2005, Bureau of Justice Statistics, 28 October 2008.

Commission Staff Working Paper accompanying the White Paper on damages actions for breach of the EC antitrust rules, SEC/2008/0404 final.

Common Position adopted by the Council on 25 September 2006 with a view to the adoption of a Regulation of the European Parliament and of the Council on the law applicable to non-contractual obligations ("Rome II") No. 22/2006, *OJ* C 289/3, 68–83.

DeFrances, C.J. et al., Civil Jury Cases and Verdicts in Large Counties, 1992, U.S. Department of Justice, Doc. No. NCJ-154346.

Directorate-General for Internal Policies, Policy Department Citizens' Rights and Constitutional Affairs, Legal Affairs, The public-policy exception and the Proposal for a Regulation of the European Parliament and of the Council on jurisdiction, applicable law, recognition and enforcement of decisions and authentic instruments in matters of succession and the creation of a European Certificate of Succession, (COM(2009)154), 2010, available at <www.europarl.europa.eu/document/activities/cont/201012/20101210ATT08870/20101210ATT08870EN.pdf>.

Draft Report on the proposal for a regulation of the European Parliament and of the Council on the law applicable to non-contractual obligations ("Rome II"), COD/2003/0168.

European Commission, Directorate-General for Trade, European Union, Trade in Goods with USA, 16 April 2014, available at <http://trade.ec.europa.eu/doclib/docs/2006/september/tradoc_113465.pdf>.

European Union Committee of the House of Lords, The Rome II Regulation, 8th Report of Session 2003–2004.

Explanatory Memorandum to the Proposal for a Regulation of the European Parliament and the Council on the law applicable to non-contractual obligations ("Rome II"), COM/2003/0427 final.

Green Paper on Damages Actions for Breach of the EC antitrust rules, COM (2005) 672 final, 19 December 2005.

Law Commission for England and Wales, Aggravated, Exemplary and Restitutionary Damages, LC No. 247, 1997, available at <http://lawcommission.justice.gov.uk/docs/lc247_aggravated_exemplary_and_restitutionary_damages.pdf>.

Position of the Bundesrechtsanwaltskammer (The German Federal Bar) on the Preliminary Draft Proposal for a Council Regulation on the Law Applicable to Non-Contractual Obligations, available at <http://ec.europa.eu/justice/news/consulting_public/rome_ii/contributions/bundesrechtsanwaltskammer_en.pdf>.

Report of the Monopolskommission, Das allgemeine Wettbewerbsrecht in der Siebten GWB-Novelle, March 2004, available at <www.monopolkommission.de/sg_41/text_s41.pdf>.

Special Commission Report on the Operation of the Hague Service Convention and the Hague Evidence Convention, 17–20 April 1989, *International Legal Materials* 1989, 1556–1569.

The Irish Law Reform Commission, Report on Aggravated, Exemplary and Restitutionary Damages, LRC 60–2000, 2000, available at <www.lawreform.ie/_fileupload/Reports/rAggravatedDamages.htm>.

White Paper on damages actions for breach of the EC antitrust rules, COM/2008/0165 final.

www.ingramcontent.com/pod-product-compliance
Ingram Content Group UK Ltd.
Pitfield, Milton Keynes, MK11 3LW, UK
UKHW051921100926
8556IPUK00021B/1309